THE CONSTANT LIBERAL

The Life and Work of Phyllis Bottome

BY THE SAME AUTHOR

Barbara Leigh Smith Bodichon: Feminist, Artist and Rebel

Practical Visionaries: Women, Education and Social Progress 1790–1930 (co-edited with Mary Hilton)

Teacher Training at Cambridge: The Initiatives of Oscar Browning and Elizabeth Hughes (co-authored with Mark McBeth)

June 2010

THE CONSTANT LIBERAL

The Life and Work of Phyllis Bottome

PAM HIRSCH

To Harry,
with thanks for everything!
and to Ros, too!
Lots of love, Pam
xx

QUARTET

First published in 2010 by
Quartet Books Limited
A member of the Namara Group
27 Goodge Street, London W1T 2LD

A catalogue record for this book
is available from the British Library

ISBN 978 0 7043 7160 6

Typeset by Antony Gray
Printed and bound in Great Britain by
T J International Ltd, Padstow, Cornwall

In memory of my
mother and father

JOYCE AND CLIFFORD
BLAKEMORE

who shared the ideals of Phyllis Bottome

Contents

Illustration List

Acknowledgements

At Quartet, Arabella Fenyves has been my book's constant champion, for which I owe her a huge debt of gratitude. And to Naim Attallah and David Elliott, too, I proffer my heartfelt thanks for their brave decision to publish a literary biography about a writer of whom not many people have heard. For Quartet, one of the last of the independent publishers, this is inevitably a risky financial venture. I salute you.

My first and most heartfelt acknowledgements must go to two American scholars: Marilyn Hoder-Salmon's biographical essay gave me my first foothold on Phyllis Bottome's literary career, and Phyllis Lassner's substantive scholarship has served always as an inducement to think deeply about my subject. I thank them both, not only for helping me to start the project, but also for their encouragement along the way.

For their personal recollections of Phyllis Bottome and/or Ernan Forbes Dennis, my grateful thanks go to Beatrice Dennis, Allen Freer, Frederica Freer, Sebastian Halliday, Sheila Lanyon and John Pearson. For expert information on various aspects of the book, I thank Harry Baker, Sarah Jane Checkland, Wendy Pollard, Colin Sell, Frances Spalding and Roz Ridley. I am also grateful to Deborah Moggach for her invitation to visit Phyllis Bottome's last home. And special thanks go to Elizabeth Crawford, book finder *extraordinaire*.

My beloved colleagues Steve Watts and David Whitley have been endlessly tolerant of my obsession with Phyllis Bottome. I thank them for taking on various sections of my teaching while I took sabbatical leave to work on this book. Thanks too for similar support goes to Chris Brown, Rose Hepworth, Georgie Horrell, Louise Joy and Bobbie Wells. I thank the Faculty of Education at the University of Cambridge for paid sabbatical leave and Newnham College for allowing me equivalent time off from my job as graduate tutor to match my faculty sabbatical leave. Without discrete blocks of time in which to think and to walk in someone else's footsteps, it is almost impossible to write someone's life. Both institutions have also made personal grants that have helped offset the cost of the long research process.

Archivists are invaluable and I have had help from many. If I have inadvertently missed anyone out, I apologise. Thanks go to Verity Andrews at the University of Reading, Ann Birch at the Records and Historical Department, Foreign and Commonwealth Office, Becky Cape at the Lilly Library at Indiana University, Ned Comstock at USC Cinematic Arts Library, Jim Fisher at Beinecke Rare Books and Manuscript Library, Katherine Godfrey at Kings College London, Frances Harris at the British Library, Hilary James at the National Archives, Dr Robin Darwall-Smith at Magdalen College, Oxford, Kevin McLaughlin at the San Francisco Conservatory of Music, David Pilling at Tate Millbank, Anne Thomson at Newnham College, Cambridge, and Julia Walworth at Merton College, Oxford. Special thanks, too, go to Les Goodey and Mark Scudder, willing helpmates at the Imaging Services of Cambridge University Library.

Others who are an important part of my support network include Sarah Loveday, Dawn McCloughlin, Richard Nunn, Delia Pluckrose and Ann Waterman. They help me in all sorts of ways.

Most of all, I thank my family for putting up with me: a book written is an endless series of meals not made and attention drifting to another time and another place. I love them immensely. Desmond – always the first friend of my projects – and Stephanie and Sophie have all helped during the course of this project, from chauffeuring me on research trips, to typing up transcripts, to making a timeline, to sorting out computer snafus and making the meals that I didn't get round to. I hope that you like the book that you have helped to bring into being. And to Mark McBeth – pretty much another member of the family – I raise several glasses, as we always seem to like more than one when we get together.

* * *

Quotations from both the published writing and unpublished letters of Phyllis Bottome are reproduced with kind permission of David Higham

Associates, who act on behalf of the copyright holders. I thank the copyright holders for their generosity.

I acknowledge, too, permission to quote from the Max Beerbohm Collection, courtesy of the Warden and Fellows of Merton College, Oxford.

Quotations from the Ezra Pound Papers at Beinecke Rare Book and Manuscript Library, Yale University, and from previously unpublished material, copyright 2009 by Mary Rachenwitz and Omar S. Pound, are reprinted by permission of New Directions Publishing Corporation.

Letters from Phyllis Bottome to Ezra Pound and Upton Sinclair are quoted courtesy of the Lilly Library, Indiana University, Bloomington, Indiana.

Letters from Phyllis Bottome to Basil Liddell Hart are quoted with kind permission of the Trustees of the Liddell Hart Centre for Military Archives.

For quotations of less than 200 words from any publication the author has assumed 'fair usage', while making strenuous efforts to contact all copyright holders.

Introduction

The great question of the freedom of the human will must largely depend on whether the human being is free to will.

PHYLLIS BOTTOME

Phyllis Bottome is a literary insider's tip, a gem waiting to be discovered by chance or through recommendation. I found her by chance. After the death of my parents, looking through their books, I found one or two by Phyllis Bottome. I remembered that my parents admired her politics in some way, although I knew very little about her. I had a vague sense that there was some connection between them reading Phyllis Bottome and my father's abrupt and indignant refusal in the 1950s to join a golf club because he had been 'assured' that they did not accept Jews as members. Then, by a stroke of good fortune, I met the American critic, Phyllis Lassner, at a literary conference and she told me that the British Library had recently bought a substantial cache of Phyllis Bottome's papers. Living in Cambridge, I suddenly had, temptingly near, the possibility of finding out exactly who this woman was. There are three things that call out to the biographer in me: I am drawn to women who have been lost from sight, who were creative – writers, painters or dancers – and who were politically engaged on the liberal left. Phyllis Bottome fitted the bill on all counts, and she also took on the aura of a last gift from my parents.

So who was Phyllis Bottome and why am I making claims for her as a significant writer? First, she was a chronicler of her times, publishing prolifically on politics, social issues, psychology and education. It is not surprising that she has been hard to pin down, in that she cannot be securely fixed with one particular literary movement, or one particular epoch. Born in the late nineteenth century, her first novel was published when she was only twenty and she was writing and publishing up until her death aged eighty-one. She therefore published her first work under Victoria and went on to become an Edwardian, a Georgian and finally an Elizabethan writer.[1] Her career covers the years before the First World War, the inter-war years, and during and after the Second World War. Still writing at the beginning of the 1960s, she had an exceptionally long writing life, a period of sixty years.

She is unusual, too, because she cannot be tied down to one particular location. Brought up in both England and America, she lived for substantial periods in mainland Europe – in Switzerland, Austria, France, Germany and Italy – so she was exceptionally well informed about European affairs as well as being international in outlook. Although she travelled a great deal, she was nevertheless an engaged inhabitant wherever she lived. To some degree I have organised chapters to reflect key places of residence, even though this means a slight degree of chronological overlap. The select timeline on pages 423–9 is intended as a useful point of reference.

She is a skilful writer in a wide variety of genres: she wrote thirty-three novels, twelve collections of short stories and novellas, biography, autobiography and essays on a wide variety of topics. Since she wrote her first novel at seventeen, inevitably, in the early novels, Phyllis Bottome employed some standard Edwardian tropes: the country house and meditations on metropolitan and rural values. Virginia Woolf was inclined to sneer at Edwardian writers' preoccupation with material and social forces, the fabric of things.[2] However, a significant literary development of this period is the so-called New Women fiction, with an accompanying influx of women writers. They wrote novels in which the central characters were women who, while living in flats and boarding houses separate from their families, were attempting to find an independent way of life.[3] Phyllis Bottome was charting this territory in her early work, and was already advocating, right at the beginning of the twentieth century, what was to become the mantra of 1960s' feminism – that the personal is *always* the political. She could never have transformed herself into a modernist, because, as Phyllis Lassner points out, 'at the same time that Bottome was self-consciously polemical and propagandist, modernist writers were questioning the possibility of constructing a coherent political statement'.[4]

However, on most university courses it is modernism that has been reified as the official literary culture of the first part of the twentieth century and this has had the unfortunate side-effect of downgrading a score of significant writers, especially women writers, whose polemical and political agendas required other narrative forms. Recently, feminist critics in particular have started to challenge this casual valuing of one literary category over another – modernism over realism – primarily because it has meant the neglect of many significant writers. At last, there is an emerging canon of twentieth-century women writers whose work, like that of Phyllis Bottome, had been assigned to a space outside literary modernism.[5] In the rescue operation, an umbrella term of 'middlebrow writers' has been utilised, a knowing ironic strategy, for this was a term of abuse employed by Virginia Woolf to describe non-Bloomsbury writers.[6] I regard this biography as part of this important salvage work.[7]

Nicola Beauman's pioneering book, *A Very Great Profession: The Woman's Novel 1914–1939*, has led the way in this project of the re-examination and re-evaluation of early-twentieth-century writers. Her imprint, Persephone Books, has rediscovered dozens of half-forgotten authors, and their popularity shows that many of these writers are as readable today as they were when they were first writing.[8] When I give a lecture on 'Women Writers Between the Wars' in Cambridge, students are surprised that they have not heard of the writers I cite, including Phyllis Bottome. I point out that much radical fiction by women gets dismissed as romance, especially when its protagonist is a woman, and these writers are often condemned as 'cosy', which is undoubtedly a category error for many of them.[9]

Phyllis Bottome's writing became more urgent as her future was challenged by significant political events. She had a most extraordinary life, affording her a wealth of unusual experience. As a young woman her survival was threatened by tuberculosis, although, ironically, the necessity of living in the mountains helped her to escape from a stifling family situation. The threat of the 'white death' paradoxically saved her creative life and it was at St Moritz that she met her future husband. During the trauma of the First World War she took on relief work helping Belgian refugees and also assumed a writing post under John

Buchan at the Ministry of Information. Both of these activities, simultaneously organising personal aid and using her writing skills, would become hallmarks of Bottome's lifelong commitment to social and political causes. Her novels of this era, *Secretly Armed* (1916), *A Certain Star* (1917) and *A Servant of Reality* (1919), are about the homecoming of wounded soldiers and former prisoners of war and the separate role of women in responding to war's havoc.

In 1920 Bottome went to war-ravaged Vienna with her husband, who, after being badly injured in the trenches, took up a job in the diplomatic service, having been trained in military intelligence. From this vantage point, as well as joining Viennese activists in organising food and medical supplies in the starving city, she was able to watch the developing political situation. Her long experience of living in Europe led her to create plots that predicted the fate of European civilisation, with special attention to the representation of the plight of the Jews. Her 1924 novel *Old Wine*, for example, charts the consequences of the fall of the Austro-Hungarian Empire at the end of World War I.

Vienna was the birthplace of psychoanalysis, and its variants. In the 1930s, Bottome became drawn to the Individual Psychology (the name derived from the Latin *individuus* meaning indivisibility) of Alfred Adler . His understanding that a fully developed individual would find happiness through love, work and an integrated role in their community chimed with her liberal values. She studied with him, became a close friend and later wrote his biography. All of her novels are psychologically engaged; in three of them a psychologist is the central figure (*Private Worlds*, *Danger Signal* and *Within the Cup*).

Her most famous work of fiction, *The Mortal Storm* (published in 1937 in the UK and 1938 in the USA), was a seering and psychologically convincing novel showing what fascism means, first to a German family, then to Jews and ultimately to freedom itself. MGM bought the rights to turn it into a film and it was MGM's first openly anti-Nazi film to be screened in isolationist America. Starring James Stewart, *The Mortal Storm* premièred in 1940 at the exact moment when Hitler entered triumphantly into Paris. Not surprisingly it was a blockbuster at the time, and is included in Steve Schneider's selection of *1001 Movies You Must See Before You Die*. Again, when I discuss *The*

Mortal Storm with film students at Cambridge University I find them fascinated by the covert and overt propagandist work of Phyllis Bottome and the Hollywood studios before America entered the war.[10] So, on two separate courses I find that Phyllis Bottome's work engages with discourses of popular culture, including its political impact.

After 1930, Bottome's political, as well as her psychological, analysis was Adlerian. She became convinced that people's political behaviour – not only their personal behaviour – was shaped by their particular historical and social circumstances. Distraught when her father-figure and mentor died suddenly of a heart attack in 1937, she rushed back to Austria to talk to everyone who knew Adler in order to write his biography. She remained in Vienna until three days before Hitler's troops entered on 11 March 1938.

On her return to Britain, she campaigned tirelessly for Jewish refugees, refusing to accept arguments that cast Jewish refugees as an economic threat and a potential fifth column, and she excoriated government policies of severely limiting Jewish immigration as xenophobic. However, *Formidable to Tyrants* (1941) attested to the quiet fortitude of the English people and especially the courage of women, such as those who served in the naval service and ambulance corps; and her novel *London Pride* (1941) depicts a working-class family's valour as the symbol of solidarity and survival under siege.

She also lectured and wrote about international relations and public responsibility. Later in her life, after two experiences of living in Jamaica, she turned her political and literary attention to anti-colonial struggles. Her 1950 novel *Under the Skin* plots racial tensions in Jamaica just after the end of World War II. Her deep commitment to social justice made her aware that the battle against racial persecutions was not over but had to be fought as a global struggle against the remnants of imperial domination.

This hugely long-lasting and varied writing career militates against pigeonholing her as belonging to any one epoch or with any one intellectual group or even one social class. As she said of herself:

> Perhaps it is a mistake for a writer not to live in the forefront of his time with those who are developing through the same events and

> moving in the same direction. Yet I cannot but think myself fortunate never to have become a stereotyped British intellectual. I should have lost my main advantage as a writer: that, throughout a constant change of countries and milieus, I have kept in touch with every profession other than my own and so have never lacked differences of subject and surroundings. I have lived in seven different countries and often shared their immense upheavals and disasters. Classes have no special significance for me; nor have I found that my best friends needed to be intellectuals.[11]

I think this is key to understanding Phyllis Bottome's stance as a writer. Unlike Virginia Woolf, who wanted to commune only with others she defined as intellectuals, and who disapproved of popular music and dancing, Phyllis was just as interested in the life of a peasant farmer in Austria, and the songs he sang, as she was, for example, in Ezra Pound's poetry.

Until fairly recently there has existed in academic ideology a notion of artistic impersonality, which holds that a writer's life and work are entirely separate things. This is one of the tenets of modernism. Like much dogma, this is true up to a point, but in the case of Phyllis Bottome, I would suggest that, *au contraire*, her best novels, *Old Wine* and *The Mortal Storm*, are the ones closest to her experiences of time and place and their power arises from a sense of passionate urgency. Her mind was peculiarly calibrated to pick up the exact word and the exact feeling that indicated not only the personal, but also a whole social and political world. For Phyllis Bottome fiction is the soul of history; in a crunch, ethics rather than aesthetics would prevail. She saw speaking and writing on behalf of the powerless, a moral and political duty.

Phyllis did not have a private income that might have allowed her to write a handful of perfect novels. As a working writer, wholly reliant on her own income, she wrote prolifically, and sometimes her sheer inventiveness, fluidity and excess of imagination prevented her work from achieving formal perfection. The rapidity and urgency of her responses made her quick to react to others' pain, be it of an individual close to her, the plight of the Jews in the thirties or the dilemma of those affected by outdated imperialism and by prejudice against people of colour. Phyllis's empathy is what marks her writing, a capacity to identify with the Other. As one leading Afro-American scholar has expressed it: 'A politics of identification starts not with the possession of identity, but with the capacity to identify with. It asks what we have in common with others, while acknowledging the diversity among ourselves. It is about the promise of a shared humanity.'[12]

In some ways Phyllis seemed to be missing an outer skin, or lacking that splinter of ice which writers are reputed to need in order to discipline their works of art. But precisely because she responded so avidly to everything around her – the personal, the social and the political – her work gives us an insight into the fabric of society in the first half of the twentieth century that perhaps a more aesthetically 'perfect' writer's might not. Her neighbour in St Ives, the Shakespearian scholar Frank Halliday, expressed this best in her obituary:

> ... it is not for sustained passages of fine writing that her work is remarkable. Fine writing, however, was for her only a secondary matter, a by-product: passionately interested in human relationships and the perplexities and predicaments of life, her object was to record her thoughts as they came teeming from her brain, and what she sacrificed in fastidious prose she made up for by spontaneity, freshness, flashes of rare insight and dazzling phrases. And running throughout were wit, humour, pity and indignation: pity for the unfortunate and indignation at any form of inhumanity![13]

As the BBC Radio News commented in 1963, announcing her death to the nation on the 8 a.m. news, Phyllis Bottome was 'the champion of the underprivileged and the misunderstood'.[14]

Several of her books were best-sellers. According to Frank Swinnerton's definition, 'A best-seller is a book written by a sincere author whose talent is greater than the common talent but whose tastes are similar to the popular tastes.'[15] Although Bottome was unabashedly intellectual in her own tastes, and readers referred often to the intellectual appeal of her writing, she seemed always to tune into the *zeitgeist*; four of her novels were made into films in her lifetime, which tends to confirm this. Her contemporary, Vera Brittain, surprised when one of her own books became a best-seller, reflected: 'More significant, perhaps, than common taste is common experience; the experience of a generation, a class, a people, a nation.'[16] And this gets close to an explanation of why Phyllis's books were always popular. Her sense of herself as a European, rather than merely a British writer, is born out by the fact that her books were popular not only in Britain and America, but were also translated into French, Danish, Dutch, Finnish, German, Italian, Portuguese, Spanish and Swedish. Perhaps only Storm Jameson and Rebecca West can be compared with Phyllis Bottome in the sense of their alertness to European politics, but neither of them lived for such long periods in Europe as she did. She is unique.

Her short stories are perhaps especially indicative of her extraordinary versatility and dramatic power. Her lucid style makes reading her work a pleasure. Although sometimes her writing seems simple, this is deceptive. In her best work her ideas have been refined into their essence, like a piece of sculpture by her friend Barbara Hepworth, and, similarly, images linger long in the mind.

Phyllis Bottome's work and life taken together offer a lens though which to understand a significant part of the twentieth century – in peacetime and in war – the writer always scrutinising the political and social mores of the various countries and communities in which she lived. She is a unique observer of the long twentieth century, having lived in mainland Europe for over thirty years, and having watched the developing political situations as an insider rather than an outsider. I hope this biography will serve as a bridge to the writer, her work and the turbulent times in which she lived.

CHAPTER 1

Childhood of a Writer

I think I may truthfully say that I became a successful novelist at the age of four or five.

PHYLLIS BOTTOME, *Search for a Soul*

As Tolstoy famously remarked, 'All happy families resemble one another, but each unhappy family is unhappy in its own way.'[1] From early childhood, Phyllis Bottome was psychologically torn between a free-spirited American family on her father's side and stifling English snobbery on her mother's. This split was played out disastrously within her parents' marriage, and had long-lasting effects on her own development.

Phyllis was a 'gypsy', brought up in a family that seemed incapable of putting down strong roots in any one place. Of necessity, perhaps, she modelled her own character on that of her American paternal grandmother, Margaret Macdonald Bottome. It seems as though a significant gene had skipped a generation. Phyllis's grandmother was a remarkable woman, originally from the Scottish Isles, who married a Methodist preacher, Francis Bottome, 'a gentle, delicate, rather didactic poet-minister'.[2] Aged twenty-four he had left Derbyshire because the Anglican vicar there would not let him hold meetings in the same village. He went first to Canada as a peripatetic preacher in the Wesleyan Church, where his ministry included the Blackfoot Indians. He was then sent to Brooklyn to help the pastor of the Sands Street Church, and there met and married Margaret McDonald. Life was not easy for the wife of a Methodist pastor as they were sent every two years to a new pastorate, sometimes rural, sometimes urban, and never had a permanent home. However, in each place she lived, Margaret made her mark. Phyllis's own life echoes that of her grandmother in this combination of wandering and notable commitment to community, as though it was a kind of genetic inheritance.

Looking after her husband and four sons, Margaret Bottome might have lived an entirely domestic life had not a financial catastrophe occurred. While they were stationed in Tarrytown, New York, Francis Bottome naïvely acted as financial guarantor for one of his assistants. When this deacon subsequently absconded, Francis became liable for a large sum of money that he had to pay back over a number of years. Margaret started to give talks of a religious, though non-denominational kind, and to charge money for admission. She was a woman of dynamic energy with a natural oratorical gift; her deep, dark eyes and soft yet strong voice captivated audiences wherever she went. Indeed, her talks were so popular that she was persuaded to write a series for the *Ladies' Home Journal* called 'Heart to Heart Talks', a series that lasted over a quarter of a century. In January 1886, she and nine other New York women founded an ecumenical society called the King's Daughters, an active philanthropic organisation dedicated to the welfare of poor children.[3] The society proliferated in many American states and also in Canada, and it was highly successful at raising funds – with which it founded, for example, the Margaret Bottome Memorial Hospital in Norfolk, Virginia, open to children of colour as well as to white children.

Phyllis's father, William, was born in 1851, the eldest of four sons. He became a clergyman, although there is plenty of evidence to suggest that either he had chosen the wrong profession or that his choice of wife hindered his career. Certainly, he was incapable of securing a permanent post in England, and this necessitated frequent moves in Phyllis's childhood. Phyllis's mother, Margaret, always known as 'Daisy' by the family and born in 1853, 'was Yorkshire on both sides: her father was a Yorkshire Leathem; her mother, Rachel Pease, the sister of Sir Joseph Pease, of Darlington'.[4] Although the two grandmothers were friends, the English grandmother had increasingly become 'a dull, rich, rather narrow-mindedly religious woman'.[5] Daisy had been partly brought up with her cousin Beatrice, an only child who was a great heiress and who later married the Earl of Portsmouth. Daisy was beautiful, with blue eyes and a clear white skin, and she, too, could certainly have made a good match in society terms.[6] Although born into a Quaker family, at fifteen she had insisted on being baptised into the Church of England; the Church was not only her mainstay, but, as Phyllis describes it, also her 'first Romance'.[7] She chose to marry William Bottome, who, sadly, failed to live up to her romantic ideals of what an Anglican clergyman should be, and almost certainly she came to regret the matches that she might have made.

William, like his mother, was a brilliant preacher, 'earnest, eloquent and with a voice of great power and beauty'.[8] He was jovial and open-handed to all, a man who enjoyed a drink and a game of cards. This made him popular with his parishioners but not with his wife, especially as, like his father, he was not clever with money. Daisy may always have been delicate in health, but it seems too that she made a 'career' of invalidism to avoid any tasks she saw as onerous. As Phyllis expressed it in her autobiography, 'No clergyman's wife I ever knew so sedulously avoided any contact whatever with her husband's duties', and this withdrawal of support must have hindered her husband's career at a period when there were specific expectations of a clergyman's wife.[9]

Phyllis was born on 31 May 1882 in Rochester, Kent. She had two older sisters, Wilmett (born in 1876) and Mary, fourteen months younger than Wilmett, and a younger brother, George (born in 1887). Daisy's role as a mother is perplexing, for even in a household with several children to care for, there is a curious absence of presence and even emotional vacuity. Although there were nannies and other household staff, it seemed Wilmett assumed a large amount of responsibility for her younger siblings. Phyllis, in her turn, tended to look after baby George, even though she was only five when he was born. Although closest to George, increasingly she came to feel sorry for her elder sister Mary, towards whom her mother had taken a dislike, possibly because she had hoped her second child would be a boy. But the most significant sibling relationship for the young Phyllis was with the elder of her sisters, Wilmett, whom she hated 'with a fervent passion', even though she admired and envied the courage with which she stood up to a cruel nanny.[10] Phyllis regarded Wilmett as bossily overbearing, although in retrospect she came to realise that it was Wilmett's fate, and not her fault, that had led her to step into the vacuum left by the unmotherly mother.

It seems that Daisy Bottome suffered from particularly difficult pregnancies and deliveries. Disappointed that her second child was not a boy, she 'could not nurse' Mary, and when her third child, the desired boy, died at sixteen months, she never wholly got over it.[11] Daisy may have suffered from post-natal depression, a condition not clearly recognised then, though it is also possible that her chronic invalidism was a survival strategy adopted to avoid sexual intercourse and its concomitant pregnancies. When Phyllis was nine, she asked her mother how a woman knew when she was expecting a baby. Daisy, instead of telling her matter-of-factly the little that a nine-year-old need know, unrolled

> before my horrified eyes, an amazing – a most complicated and a wholly tragic – picture of the life between the sexes. The pains of childbirth – the greater physical strength of men – their far from greater moral strength – the white slave traffic – nothing was spared me. Even worse than the alarming pictures her words evoked, was her obvious terror of the facts that she was relating to me. It was her fear and evident repulsion that shook me to the foundations of my being.[12]

This incident suggests that although Daisy genuinely suffered in pregnancies, what had begun as real pain had developed into a neurotic retreat. Certainly she succeeded in making all three of her girls afraid of the physical aspects of heterosexual love.

The endless moves of Phyllis's childhood were largely related to the state of Daisy's health and nerves. She persuaded her husband to give up his living in Berkshire as she regarded it – with the collusion of her doctor – as too damp and bleak a place in which to recover her health. The family rarely stayed anywhere longer than two years and William's career cannot have benefited from the endless moves of parish. Considering that William was an Anglican vicar, they led a remarkably unsettled life. Daisy's plaints about her husband's fecklessness ignored her own role. She had made a profession of discontent, which, in turn, destroyed any hope of career advancement for William.

Children, however, at least when small, take their own family life as normal. When in 1889, they moved to the parish of Over Stowey in the Quantock Hills, Somerset, Phyllis was delighted. The rectory had a huge garden with a magnolia tree, and a paddock for Fanny the donkey. They had an Airedale dog called Laddie to accompany them on walks, and were allowed a fair amount of freedom for middle-class children at that time. Phyllis adored going mushrooming at dawn, led by Wilmett over 'the sweet-scented, dew-swept earth', or being taken trout-fishing by her father.[13] The church was just across the road, and her father, as ever, was popular in the parish. Like his mother he had the knack of employing parables to make his point in a vivid way in sermons of no more than twenty minutes. Phyllis was never badly behaved in church; sometimes she imbibed her father's narratives, but if the argument became too complex she studied the faces of the congregation, inventing stories about them in her head. As she wrote in her autobiography, 'I think I may truthfully say that I became a successful novelist at the age of four or five.'[14] It is certainly the case that Phyllis's evocations of English country life were to draw strongly on this epoch: 'The beauty of the waterfalls and streams, the deep, red earth, the strong, wiry bracken, the low heather hills, the fragrant drenched woods full of moss and ferns; these were the masterpieces of my childhood's world.'[15]

Phyllis did not care very much for the family of the local squire – the Stanleys – because she perceived that they regarded her father as their personal property. William naïvely assumed that his relationship with the Stanleys was one of friendship, not patronage, and was sorely disappointed when they dropped all acquaintance the moment he left the parish. Another conscious encounter with the rigidity of the English class system, albeit operating in the opposite direction, was Phyllis's experience of being prevented from playing with a little girl called Hannah, when her nurse forebade her to associate with 'a village child'.[16] Although Phyllis's American father was insouciant about class distinctions, her mother backed the nurse, using as an excuse the fear that Phyllis might catch head lice from the working-class child. Although Daisy was charitable, in approved upper-middle-class style – sending out soup for the poor from her kitchen, and the family's cast-off clothes – Phyllis early on began to recognise and dislike semi-feudal social arrangements.

When Phyllis was nearly seven, Wilmett and Mary were sent to boarding school eleven miles away in Taunton, a significant distance at a time when they were travelling by horse and cart. Prior to that the two elder girls had lessons from a governess, and Phyllis had sat under the schoolroom table to listen. Phyllis was left untutored, but her godmother sent her Andrew Lang's *Yellow Fairy Book*, with the strict instruction that no one should read the book to her. Faced with this provocation, Phyllis taught herself to read: 'It had most beguiling and enchanting pictures; yellow was my favourite colour. I asked everyone in the house to read it to me [but] nobody ... would yield to my most impassioned persuasions. In a fortnight I had read the Yellow Fairy book from cover to cover; and after this I practically did nothing *but* read for the rest of my life.'[17]

Once she could read, *Alice in Wonderland* and *Through the Looking Glass*, *The Swiss Family Robinson* and *Masterman Ready* were soon devoured.

Although Over Stowey seemed something of an idyll to small children, William Bottome was horribly bored. He was living in a semi-feudal society with little intellectual stimulation, limited by the restrictions of an 'invalid' wife. His parents came over to Britain to see what had stalled their brilliant son's career. Phyllis was thrilled to meet these exciting American relatives:

> My grandmother I only remember on this first occasion as a Presence, something large and fiery, and full of the most stimulating sense of drama, but always benevolent and pleasing dramas; gales of laughter beset her path; her eyes danced and flashed with beneficent lightning; her deep, emphatic voice seemed a kind of human thunder with no ill effects. My grandfather was on an altogether smaller scale; but to an over-sensitive child he was probably more reassuring ... He had very blue eyes like fine flax, silvery white hair and pink cheeks. He spoke in a low voice, took me long walks and taught me to look at every flower we passed.[18]

Not surprisingly they urged William to return to his home country and make his career there.

Consequently, in February 1890 part of the family left rural Somerset behind and sailed to New York. Phyllis wrote in her autobiography that her first memory of America was the Statue of Liberty and a feeling of freedom:

> It was mixed up with pigeons, blue sky and a marvellous smell that I shall remember to my dying day, as if lake water and peanut brittle had been happily blended together ... here on this soil my rebel spirit knew once and for all that America belonged to its people. It was a land newly won, creatively occupied, raw and unfinished in my childhood, but oh how tinglingly alive![19]

Phyllis adored New York – the skyscrapers, the noise of the cable cars, the energy of the people on the streets, the squirrels in Central Park; she felt that she had

> reached ultimate Paradise. Nor, for the six golden years that lay ahead of me on those hospitable shores, did I ever change this opinion for as much as sixty seconds ... The brisk agents of my Paradise were three American uncles, who stimulated, taught, protected and endowed their nieces through a series of miracles. They were – as memory paints them – lovers without drawbacks. Behind them stood rows and rows of smiling beneficent women. Sometimes they were engaged to the uncles: and sometimes they were not – but they were all beneficent.[20]

Meeting these energetic women, who did not seem to see life as all trial and misery, had a liberating effect on Phyllis.

Having left Wilmett and Mary behind in boarding school in Bournemouth, William, Daisy, Phyllis and George moved to a post at Yonkers, at this time a little country town on the banks of the Hudson some distance from New York. The house had 'mod cons' not known in England, such as a bath with hot and cold running water, whereas at home they were used to portable tin ones. The thrill of this innovation, however, wore off when the bath one day filled with the contents of the cesspool, and Phyllis ended up very ill with diphtheria.

In England, Daisy had never had to run a house with fewer than three servants; she had, in effect, been waited on from birth. Now, she had less help, and although the younger children were out of the house from nine o'clock until seven, she still could find neither the energy nor the will to engage with any parish work. After six months Wilmett, now aged fourteen, and Mary, now aged twelve, rejoined the family, and the already-existing divisions in the family began to reveal themselves with more deadly force. William loved America, unsurprisingly, as he felt completely at home there, but Daisy hated it. The children were pulled on to sides – Wilmett and George took their mother's side and Phyllis and Mary took their father's. As Phyllis put it:

> My father took to golf as a sort of escape from the baffling disappointment of his home life. My mother made her health an increasing alibi against social life. Not that she – before her children – ever disputed with my father nor even refused outright what he demanded; but we knew she opposed him; and even if she hadn't, her headaches did. She never had headaches before our life at Yonkers. But once they had started, they were used to incapacitate her, at intervals, from carrying out any social task laid upon her by my father. There were no outward signs of the conflict and disorder in my parents' relationship but my father took to golf, and my mother to headaches, because they no longer took to each other.[21]

Such was Daisy's dissatisfaction that a move was made at the end of the first year.

The post William accepted was as pastor of Grace Church, Jamaica, at this time a small town in Long Island, not far from Brooklyn. Phyllis went to a day school in Jamaica, Miss King's Academy for Young Ladies, where she was befriended by two young women teachers. Many years later, one of those teachers, Miss Dunn, wrote to Phyllis, having read one of her novels:

> A great many years ago when I was less than half as old as I am now and you were in pink pinafores – a darling child who looked like a gay little Shetland pony, you used to come for supper to a tiny house in Jamaica, and two of your teachers made you recite to them again and again ' 'Twas brillig and the slithy toves'. Then they left Jamaica, but never forgot the vivid little creature who had been to them like a piece of coral found in dull sand. I was one of those teachers, and Miss Burnett was the other.[22]

It may be that the two teachers sensed that all was not well with the Bottome family. William played cards for small stakes and drank whiskey with his male cronies in the evenings. Once in a blue moon, as Phyllis put it, he drank 'to an unwise extent', and at home he was under a semi-permanent domestic cloud.[23] As Phyllis remembers, 'I was puzzled by the fact that outside my home my father was a glorious and adored being, praised and admired by everyone I met; while under his own roof he was an outlaw, and at times, even a criminal.'[24] At least part of their domestic difficulty was that William was unfussed by niceties of social class and was at ease talking to anyone and everyone. Daisy – although she had fallen out with her own family – retained some of their ideas about class distinctions. She accepted almost no invitations in Jamaica as, apart from a very few chosen friends, she considered there was nobody worth visiting. In short, Daisy made no attempt to fit in, and consequently gave her children no help in their own necessary adaptive processes. Fortunately, William's brothers came to the children's rescue, buying the girls party dresses that met with approval in Jamaica. The kind uncles had overheard Wilmett praying, 'Please, God, make us stylish. Our clothes are all wrong.'[25] They also pampered the younger two, buying Phyllis and George such treasures as toboggans and roller skates.

American summers were taken very seriously in those days, with families taking to the seaside for the best part of three months when schools were closed. The extended Bottome family went to Quogue, Long Island, with father returning to his parish at weekends. Phyllis adored everything at Quogue, especially paddling in the salt water of the Atlantic Ocean and being offered books to read that Daisy would not have allowed, had she been consulted. Phyllis, aged nine, was already a prodigious and precocious reader. That summer she devoured Charlotte Brontë's *Jane Eyre* and Olive Schreiner's *The Story of an African Farm*. As usual the uncles – George, Frank and Harry – provided generous amounts of sarsaparilla, root beer, candy doughnuts, and sugar almonds. Phyllis's favourite uncle, the youngest, Harry, played croquet with the two younger children and took them crab fishing. The uncles also provided endless entertainment through their flirtations with young women on the island.

Phyllis was reminded of where all this could lead, however, when her mother suffered a five-month miscarriage on their first visit to Quogue. Frank, now a physician, almost certainly saved Daisy's life. Unfortunately, Daisy's dependence upon the doting Frank roused the antipathy of Wilmett, who did not wish to share the role of sole support to her mother. Every summer at Quogue, Frank patiently attempted to work out a cure for Daisy's supposedly weak heart, until he realised that to be delicate was – above all – the role she wished to preserve. There was, however, another near-death incident, when William accidentally overdosed his wife with digitalis, something he was never allowed to forget.

However, for Phyllis, an unexpected and enormous bonus came out of Daisy's miscarriage. The girls' shared room at Quogue was needed for a nurse. So William's friend, the American marine and landscape painter George Herbert McCord, offered to take in Phyllis and Mary at his house in Morristown, New Jersey.[26] This was a wholly different milieu to the Bottome girls' own home life. The mother was a fine pianist, so discussions about music and art were central to their lives. They were also delightfully cosmopolitan. McCord had travelled widely, living and painting abroad for substantial periods of time. His family had accompanied him to Venice and Paris, and two of his daughters were to become accomplished artists. It was during this visit that Phyllis perceived that these intellectual pleasures were something she needed and desired. She was to enjoy a lifelong friendship with the McCord sisters, Betty, Georgie and Maida, and they always supported her in her bids for freedom from her own bewildering family.

Unfortunately, Miss King's Academy suddenly closed, after Phyllis had attended for about a year. Wilmett decided she was too grown-up to attend school any longer, and Mary, Phyllis and George were sent daily to a hopelessly inadequate local teacher. Overall, the Bottome girls received only a patchy, haphazard education. As Phyllis put it:

> We knew we were expected to earn our own livings but it did not occur to any of us at the time that we were not being trained to carry out this purpose. Wilmett was extremely musical and had a beautiful singing voice. Music was, therefore, considered to be her special

> province, and something or other, though seldom the best thing, was usually done to help her develop her gift. Mary was a good scholar and had a particular aptitude for teaching; but nothing was ever done to help her develop her gift. I was too young for my tastes to act as guides to my education, but it was obvious that I had an overwhelming interest in books, and it was supposed that I might develop, if left to myself, some connection with literature.[27]

It was, on the other hand, 'naturally' assumed that the only boy, George, would have a more serious education, and he did in fact later go to public school and to Cambridge. Poor Phyllis, like Maggie Tulliver in George Eliot's *The Mill on the Floss*, envied the education automatically offered to her brother.

Just before Phyllis's eleventh birthday, following the death of gentle Grandpapa Bottome, it was decided that the whole family would spend a summer with her maternal grandmother, now Mrs Rachel Fowler, in London. Having been widowed at twenty-six and still very attractive at forty-six, she had recently made what was regarded as an advantageous marriage. She was happy with her second husband, who doted on her, although she had inherited two grown-up stepchildren – 'Uncle' Kennie and 'Aunt' Jo – whom she didn't much care for. The Fowlers lived in a rather grand house in Grosvenor Square, with a footman to open the door and thirteen servants. Each evening at six o'clock, the adults would dress for dinner, and the butler would lay out rosebuds, to be worn as corsages or in buttonholes, on a table in the hall for those coming down to dinner, formally announced by the ringing of a gong.

Dinner did not include Phyllis, who was banished to the nursery at the top of the house. The formal dividing line seemed to be the age of twelve. Phyllis was used to the lively companionship of her American uncles, but here strict codes of association were applied. Step-uncle Kennie was no longer allowed to offer a dry peck on the cheek to any of his 'nieces' over the age of twelve. Phyllis said that at Grosvenor Square she was 'nearer to a mental breakdown than at any other time in my life'.[28] Although she does not detail why she felt so desperate, it may be that her growth spurt at eleven, when she reached her full height of five feet six inches, and the corresponding early onset of menstruation was part of this crisis. As she wrote later, 'Unfortunately, the body, its habits and its powers, were practically taboo in the minds of my parents.'[29] In a Victorian household, the maids who changed the sheets on the beds would be the first to know of intimate bodily functions, and probably the first ones to explain to her how to manage the situation. Certainly, Phyllis described being 'superintended by strange and ignorant women' in the nursery, and appears to have been initially hysterical with shock.

Feeling vulnerable, she was befriended by Kennie Fowler, 'a sad, delicate, portentously serious man', then in his late twenties.[30] Phyllis said that neither he nor his sister ever 'told me they disliked their home, resented another's control, and would have given anything to escape it; but I both shared and sensed the bleakness of their outlook'.[31]

They, too, were suffering under Victorian convention. Although they had their own income it would not have been considered *comme il faut* for them to leave home and set up separate establishments, until or unless they married. Kennie had no profession; his major pleasure was reading, and in the unhappy young Phyllis, he found a like soul. He was much more comfortable in her company than he was in the company of seventeen-year-old Wilmett, who had turned into a dazzling beauty with clear olive skin and huge dark eyes. She was besieged by suitors, but Kennie was not one of them. He was a 'confirmed bachelor', a useful phrase that need not be enquired into too closely.

There seems to be a pattern here; in every household Phyllis would locate the one person who could feed her intellect. Kennie allowed Phyllis unrestricted use of his library. She read the novels of George Meredith and Thomas Hardy, and the poetry of Shelley. In particular, she adored Shelley, whose poems she learned by reciting them out loud until she had them by heart. This shared love of literature united Kennie and Phyllis in a small rebellion *à deux*, as this literature was considered quite unsuitable for young girls in late-nineteenth-century England.

The Bottomes' return to America was inevitably tinged with sorrow, as all the family were still mourning the death of Grandpapa Bottome. Phyllis was sent, on her own, to a boarding school run by Anglican nuns, a branch sisterhood of St John the Baptist in New York. She studied there for two years, and this was probably the most sustained period of formal education she experienced in her youth: religious instruction, English (grammar, composition and rhetoric), mathematics and music were the core subjects. During the last few months of her time there, as a pubescent twelve-year-old, she also experienced an intense romantic friendship with a sixteen-year-old schoolgirl, a Southern belle called Claude. The nuns clearly regarded it as unhealthy and tried to split them up. As Phyllis recalled, 'It is difficult to say where friendship ends and love begins in a child's mind. I was unconscious of sex or sexual impulses, too deeply unconscious of them, perhaps, to understand the difference in quality between the friendship with Claude and any other friendship I had yet known.'[32] In any case, the friendship did not survive the end of school, and turned out to be merely the first of a series of adolescent crushes.

During Phyllis's absence, Uncle Frank Bottome had become significantly more concerned with the state of Wilmett's health than with her mother's as she suffered from repeated and prolonged attacks of influenza. Grandma Bottome rescued her with a trip to Egypt and then delivered her back to Grandma Fowler in London.[33] This did not suit Daisy at all, who resented the 'kidnap' of Wilmett by the two grandmothers and wanted to reclaim her. Daisy's doctor conveniently pronounced that she could not live if she remained in America. It is almost worth a treatise in itself to consider the ways in which well-off women patients persuaded their doctors to support them in their desires. Once again, William resigned his living, though he predicted that it would be the end of his career, saying to Phyllis that 'it's like death'.[34]

In 1896, the Bottomes returned to England and continued to lead their unsettled life; from May to October they went to Burnham-on-Sea, chosen by her father largely because of its good golfing. Phyllis herself went to a 'horrible old-fashioned girls' school where the children lay on their backs on the floor to improve their figures. I found these children morons – and rough morons at that – and insisted on being freed from their grisly activities.'[35] William then managed to find a locum position at St Luke's Camberwell and so the Bottome family regrouped in lodgings in a rather seedy part of Earl's Court, convenient at least for Wilmett to continue with the singing lessons she had been taking while living at the Fowlers'. This area, close to the railway station, was the haunt of prostitutes, who attracted Phyllis's horrified attention:

> It was … considered the 'fallen women' preserved their more fortunate sisters' virtue – at a somewhat heavy price. Our fellow man apparently in those days was so easily tempted that practically nothing prevented him from running amok and raping right and left, except for a holocaust of girls and women secretly set aside for the purpose, by a policy of poverty and starvation. What was thought of those girls who fell we have only to read Dickens' account of 'Little Emily' in *David Copperfield* to realize. Even as late as 1914 in Queen Charlotte's lying-in hospital unmarried girls were not allowed visits from their own mothers, while their more fortunate 'married sisters' might see whomsoever they liked … These secret tragedies of the poor and the outcast beat in on my child's mind with a persistent ferocity.[36]

When spring came the family were on the move again, this time to dreary lodgings in Bournemouth. Phyllis as usual grabbed any chances of education she could get; she was allowed to go part-time to the local grammar school for lessons. There a young French woman teacher, Mellie Darius, introduced her to French literature, and, again, Phyllis entered into an intense female friendship. This worldly young woman – through their discussions of French literature – at least did Phyllis the favour of making the business of sexual relations seem a little more light-hearted than had previously seemed possible. Phyllis also seized the opportunity of attending a series of Oxford Extension Lectures on Renaissance art. Her sister Mary, though perhaps not quite as clever as Phyllis, was certainly also bookish, and had obtained a job at her former school in Bournemouth as a pupil-teacher; George was now away at boarding school during term-time.[37]

Around this time, Daisy's first cousin, Beatrice Pease, married to the Earl of Portsmouth and herself childless, offered to chaperone Wilmett through the London season, and have her presented at Court, taking on all expenses. This would have been a tremendous opportunity for Wilmett, who was as beautiful as her mother, to make a 'good' marriage in Fowler terms. But, 'restored to each other after their long parting, Wilmett and my mother closed together into an intimacy of heart and mind which shut out the rest of the world'.[38] Daisy was entirely unwilling to part with her, and, in Phyllis's estimation, it was thus that Wilmett's last hope of 'health and happiness' was lost.[39]

Like a lot of budding writers, Phyllis kept a commonplace book. Mary gave her one with a beautiful marbled cover for her fifteenth birthday. Inside are transcribed poems by Elizabeth Barrett Browning, Robert Browning, Shelley, Kipling, Alice Meynell, Christina Rossetti and Robert Louis Stevenson.[40] A second, undated, commonplace book has excerpts from Tennyson's *The Princess* and poems by Christina Rossetti copied out, as well as scraps of ideas for short stories. Bit by bit, her father's parables and her own store of reading were forming a literary loam to be drawn on when her writing career began in earnest.

The third winter in London at last seemed to be opening up the possibility of some career training for Phyllis.[41] Ironically, the stalling of William Bottome's career seems to have opened up a glimmer of freedom for Phyllis. Some of his friends, near where they were living on Campden Hill, opened a private Shakespeare Club, to which all the family were invited. These friends were impressed by Phyllis's remarkable ear and retentive memory and encouraged her parents to send her for training to an American elocution teacher, Fanny Mason. Phyllis joined her class and it was soon clear that she could recite both prose and poetry with equal sensitivity. A career either on stage or in giving public recitations was envisaged. Fanny Mason offered to finance her for the first two years while she was making her way. She helped Phyllis prepare twenty-five different programmes of prose and verse that she learned by heart and would be able to take on tour with her. Phyllis had trained her memory with the endless reciting of Shelley, and she now discovered that she had a real talent for comedy. Fanny Mason encouraged her to write comic monologues to act out on stage, and although she said that she was too young to do this well, nevertheless, this was her first 'professional', albeit unpublished, writing. She wrote: 'I never was nervous enough to break down, nor, once started, did I fail to enjoy the quiet attention of my audience and gain from it an added zest in the pleasure of my work. I really loved what I learned and hoped to make each appreciated point an equal pleasure to my audience.'[42]

Aged sixteen, she was offered a part in *Charlie's Aunt* on a tour of the provinces at a salary of three pounds a week. Sadly she could not take up the offer – although her early training both as an actress and as a writer would prove invaluable in a variety of ways – because it was just at this point of possible escape from oppressive family dynamics that Phyllis's own health gave cause for alarm. She had suffered from painful menstruation until she was seventeen, when she had an operation to alleviate the problem.[43] Immediately following the operation, in a weakened state, she caught measles followed by pneumonia. Her physician then told her, to her utter despair, that with her weakened lungs she must give up dreams of a career on stage. The American Bottomes tried to rescue Phyllis from the role of companion to her mother, just as they had successfully rescued Wilmett for at least one epoch. Her American grandmother offered Phyllis a home with her, and Phyllis longed to return to the democratic country, but at this point Wilmett, who had managed to achieve a little psychological independence during the time spent away from her mother, made her own bid for freedom. Wilmett insisted on staying in London for her singing lessons, and found a lodging for herself in West Kensington. She had a striking mezzo-soprano voice, and at this point seems to have found the strength to start pursuing the training for this career. Daisy persuaded Phyllis that – in the absence of Wilmett – she could not possibly do without her, and Phyllis was not ruthless enough to 'put the Atlantic Ocean between me and her [mother's] pleading eyes'.[44]

So Phyllis, a reluctant prisoner of her mother's neediness, was an integral part of the next family move. William had been offered temporarily, because the incumbent was ill, a parish in Kent, between Dartford and Gravesend, largely inhabited by cement workers: 'There was very little to be said for Swanscombe. It was inundated with smoke from seventy-two chimneys – its inhabitants were chiefly migrant workers without traditions and totally indifferent to all ideas of religion. The place, however, was dry, the stipend adequate. There was a house of convenient size. We didn't know what else to do, so we agree to at least a nine months' try-out.'[45]

Ironically, Swanscombe proved to be the parish that kept hold of William until his retirement.

At seventeen, Phyllis was allowed to put up her hair and wear long dresses; she was considered to have left her school years behind her. So she had now to take up her role as a young lady – in effect, awaiting marriage. In the meantime, Phyllis was expected to occupy herself in the ways typical of middle-class girls at that epoch – playing a little bridge, attending tea parties and tennis parties – but she found no satisfaction there. More to her taste was helping her father in his parish duties. Running clubs for working-class girls was an unexceptional form of mild social work undertaken by young women of her class before marriage. Mary started a girls' club and Phyllis, owing to her father's lack of a curate, more unusually started a club for boys between the ages of thirteen and eighteen. Phyllis and Mary helped two young women teachers, and so for the first time they were frequently in the company of professional women, rather than in the company of gentlewomen.

The boys in Phyllis's club variously had jobs in the quarries, in the factory or loading and unloading, either at the docks or on the river barges, and they worked long hours, facing danger and hardship on a daily basis. At Swanscombe, she attempted to write a book, provisionally entitled *The Sorrows of the World.* She did not manage to complete this although the material was not entirely wasted: a few years later, she would publish a book called *Raw Material: Some Characters and Episodes among Working Lads*, which was essentially a reworking of that failed attempt at a novel.[46] Phyllis writes in the first person as the fictional Edith Mallam, the daughter of a vicar in a place very like – though not called – Swanscombe. But this was only a framing device; the 'chapters' are more like individual free-standing sketches. This anecdotal, episodic format allowed her to write linked short stories; the sketches are by turns comic or sentimental and are not subtle. They include rather dated, almost Dickensian attempts at dialect, but they also contain nuggets of alertness to the human cost of poverty. As Marilyn Hoder-Salmon points out, 'class oppression, alcoholism and the abuse of women and children' are unflinchingly portrayed, even though the 'hard' information seems somewhat at odds with the chosen 'soft' format.[47] The first of the sketches features an indefatigable district nurse, and it seems likely that this character is drawn from observation of a real nurse in the community. This scrutiny must have brought with it a recognition, however unwelcome, of how little Phyllis's mother did, in stark contrast with how much work this trained woman did, to alleviate misery within the community.

Wilmett's period of escape from the suffocating family dynamics did not last long. In 1900, after a prolonged bout of influenza, little lumps appeared on her neck. This caused great alarm, because swelling of the lymph nodes of the neck was an early indication of tuberculosis.[48] Although J. A. Villemin had in 1865 established that tuberculosis was caused by a specific bacillus, 'curing' it at the start of the twentieth century was largely a domestic matter.[49] Good food, lots of rest and fresh air was the usual remedy prescribed by doctors to middle-class families. Grandma Fowler promptly rescued Wilmett from her London lodgings and carried her off in her carriage and pair to the most expensive hotel in Eastbourne.

Phyllis was at this stage not unduly worried about Wilmett; she was too busy with her own life. For the summer of 1900 her father accepted a six-month *locum tenens* at Betchworth, Surrey, and there Phyllis worked on the novel which would be her first to be published, *Life, the Interpreter*. This summer also contained a special blessing as Phyllis formed a lasting friendship with Elena Gurney, a woman in her mid-fifties, who turned out to be a very distant relation of Phyllis's great-grandmother, Emma Gurney. Elena, when orphaned, had been raised by the wealthy Quaker banking family of Russell and Emilia Gurney. Russell Gurney was a judge and the Recorder of the City of London; although politically a Conservative, he was a strong supporter of women's suffrage and had, in 1867, presented a suffrage petition to Parliament from women householders.[50] His wife, Emilia Gurney, was a member of the executive committee that had founded Girton College, the first university-level college for women in Cambridge.

Elena was to prove a significant presence and mentor in Phyllis's young life: 'she was tall and austere-looking, but still rather beautiful. She had an innocent and guileless look; and there was in her character, plainly influenced as it was by a practised religion, a great steadiness, as strong as iron.'[51]

Although Elena was a staunch Anglo-Catholic, a form of religion that would influence Phyllis for a few years, she also believed that 'art, beauty and the culture of living were all part of religion itself'.[52] Elena, a little like the McCords, brought Phyllis into contact with a different world. Elena had had drawing lessons from Ruskin and had known Christina Rossetti. She retained something of the aura of the Pre-Raphaelite era and to Phyllis, whose love for Tennyson's *Idylls of the King* was supreme, this added a kind of glamour to her new friend.

Elena Gurney, although singling out Phyllis for her special love, was one of several adults around the young Bottomes who attempted to rescue them from their intense and punishing family situation, at least for intervals. Grandmother Bottome took Mary off to America for a year and when she returned to England she tried to give Phyllis a treat too. She took her to visit Grandma Fowler in Grosvenor Square at the height of the coming-out season. At first, Grandma Fowler offered to have her maid rework a grey silk garment of her own into a gown for Phyllis. Grandmother Bottome protested, arguing for buying material for an entirely new gown, saying, 'You're far too generous to want to limit the child's pleasure!' As Phyllis dryly noted, Grandma Fowler, 'who had never been accused of generosity before', succumbed to the flattery.[53] Phyllis was sent out with Peckham, Grandma Fowler's maid, an excellent dressmaker, and they came back with yards of daffodil yellow silk, with white chenille for the trim. It was Phyllis's first grown-up dress, in her favourite colour, and she was utterly enchanted by it.

That winter, the Bottomes seemed even more scattered than usual. William had returned to Swanscombe, as the parish priest there had been unable to renew his duties. Mary was in America and George was in his penultimate term in preparatory school. Daisy, Wilmett and Phyllis were in lodgings in London. Wilmett needed to seek medical advice about a new lump, which had appeared just above the breast by her right arm. On the day of the visit to the surgeon, Arthur Sheilds, Daisy had a neuralgic headache, so Phyllis went with Wilmett. Usually they travelled in a horse-drawn omnibus, but on this day Phyllis travelled for her first occasion in a hansom, through 'a pea-souper of the most appalling blackness'.[54] At the consultation, Wilmett was told that an immediate operation was imperative. A three-week spell at a nursing home followed the operation, during which Phyllis visited every day because Daisy considered herself too unwell to go.

Meanwhile, Phyllis took over the management role in her family vacated by Wilmett, unpacking the family belongings in Swanscombe once again before bringing her mother down to the newly organised vicarage. Yet again she worked with her father as an unpaid 'curate' and was so busy that she had almost forgotten that she had left the manuscript of a *Life, the Interpreter* with A. P. Watt, the first professional literary agent in London.[55] However. 'a mysterious and heartening letter reached me from Andrew Lang, who was at this time reader for Longmans, Green & Co. He had read *Life, the Interpreter*, he told me, with great interest. Was he right in surmising that it was a first book?'[56] In 1902, to Phyllis's great delight, the book was published in a pretty yellow cover scattered with violets.

This first novel fitted into a genre usually called the New Woman novel. From the 1890s on there had been a proliferation of books which explored issues such as the problems of education and work for middle-class women, the double standard regarding sexual matters and the validity of marriage. Like many first efforts, it is not brilliant but something of a finger exercise for her later, more polished novels. Its plot-line echoes one of the themes of George Eliot's *Middlemarch.* It has an upper-middle-class heroine, Muriel Dallerton, who, like Dorothea in *Middlemarch*, has an independent income and wishes to do good works. Muriel buys three houses in the slums of Stepney and turns them into a settlement for workers. This is an urbanised version of Dorothea's plan to make ideal workers' cottages for agricultural labourers in *Middlemarch*. Another similarity to George Eliot's plot is that the large-souled central character is contrasted with an empty-headed but accomplished little charmer. However, Phyllis's original sharp wit is already in evidence; she wrote that it had been said of Gladys 'that if she were left alone in the desert she would flirt with a camel'.[57] Some of the best touches of the novel are the sardonic comments about Gladys, and women like her, who find it ridiculously easy to fool men by their feminine skills. The man Muriel loves is easily kidnapped by Gladys's pretence: 'hats of a certain shade cast sincerity in a becoming glow over an upturned face'.[58]

However, given that *Middlemarch* was set back in the 1830s, there are some new elements in Phyllis's novel. If Muriel represents an old model, that of the philanthropic upper-class woman, she is contrasted with the New Woman, in the figure of Dr Cynthia Grant. On the other hand, the portrait is undercut by the fact that Cynthia's original professional aim was to be an artist, and she seems to have become a doctor only to be a helpmate to her brother. Maternity finally appears to be her true vocation. Both Muriel and Cynthia are rewarded by the love and recognition of men who are not beguiled by the angle of a hat, and recognise their worth. Although it is something of a literary *smorgasbord*, containing elements of novels she had read, it is interspersed with astute observations of upper-class life in Grosvenor Square, and of aspects of working-class life she had encountered in Swanscombe. It is also a page-turner; early on, Phyllis developed the skill of making the reader always want to turn the page to find out what was going to happen to her characters. In otherwise rather dark days, Phyllis had the consolation that she might be able to make her way in life as a professional writer. She was only twenty years old when this, her first novel was published; she had found her own vocation early.

In between the offer to publish and the appearance of book itself there were dark moments. Wilmett's doctor pronounced that he could do no more to save her. Wilmett, who had enjoyed several flirtations, was by this stage engaged to a young man called Arthur, an American friend of their youngest uncle, Harry Bottome. Arthur broke off their engagement, returned to America, and, almost indecently swiftly, married another young woman. The letter bearing this news broke Wilmett's heart, and she gave up her struggle for life. Returning from a convalescent holiday in Broadstairs, Wilmett shocked them all by her appearance; she was terribly thin, her skin seemed nearly transparent, she was overwhelmingly fatigued and she suffered from spikes of high temperature and hot sweats in the evenings. She was in the grip of the rapidly progressive form of tuberculosis known then as 'galloping consumption'. Huber, in 1906, described the clinical course of this disease by saying that patients with the 'galloping' form

> become progressively very weak and much emaciated. Their hearts

> beat rapidly and they are apt to have a pink flush on their cheeks, which is quite unlike the blush of health, but which is in reality an indication of the fever that is consuming them. The rest of their faces is very placid and thin and is suffused with a clammy sweat. Their cheekbones are prominent; and their eyes have a quite unnatural brilliancy, seeming large and beautiful. But their lustre is not of health but rather of disease, and too often of death. And the consumptive spits blood sometimes, and is short of breath, and has a persistent, hacking cough, that harasses him dreadfully, and will not let him rest.[59]

A nurse was engaged to do what she could, which, by this stage, was only to manage the patient in the sense of keeping her as comfortable as possible. Following Florence Nightingale's strictures, Nurse Hilton kept the windows open because fresh air was considered vital. A nutritious milk-based diet liberally laced with cod-liver oil was fed to the poor patient, who had diminishing appetite. During the nurse's off-duty hours, Phyllis kept Wilmett company, reading tirelessly to keep her entertained. During a desolate Christmas, the family exchanged presents in Wilmett's bedroom under the little tree she had asked for.

Yet she was inexorably fading away. By the time Mary reappeared in May, having enjoyed a wonderful time with her American grandmother and bearing presents for all the family, she found the household wholly absorbed in witnessing the inevitable death. At the beginning of November 1901, aged twenty-three, Wilmett died. On receiving the sad news Grannie Bottome wrote to Grandma Fowler in England:

> I wrote to [Wilmett] this week, fully believing that she was getting better, and now comes your letter. It was a big wave that rolled over me. I love the child! I have known her better – than most have known her. I crossed the ocean with her. I can see the beautiful girl now kneeling on the floor of her state-room, when I did not think of kneeling. She was a beautiful girl with splendid possibilities … Poor dear Margaret, for her it is dreadful. Oh what a daughter she was! She was a *strength* to her mother. I really think Wilmett was her idol. Phyllis was her little, *is* her little Bird that nestles down, but she was so proud of Wilmett; and she had reason for being proud of her … [60]

The already uneasy family constellation resettled in a new pattern. Phyllis had already begun to take up Wilmett's place, looking after her 'invalid' mother and helping her father with parish duties. Daisy continued to dislike Mary, and was permanently critical of her, but Mary, emboldened by her year away, was more able to resist her mother's manipulations, and, indeed, was actively critical of Daisy. George, away at public school, appeared to be relatively unconcerned, but, in any case, he was safely out of it.[61]

Almost inevitably, after such a long period of strain, Phyllis fell ill with influenza, and when the local doctor was called he told Phyllis that he feared for her lungs. He had forbidden the family to kiss Wilmett, as tuberculosis was understood to be contagious, but this had frightened poor Wilmett so much that Phyllis had continued to kiss her to the end.[62] The family doctor referred Phyllis to Sir Douglas Powell, who was attached to the Brompton Hospital for Consumption and Diseases of the Chest. This was the oldest and most prestigious of the four London hospitals dedicated to the care of consumptives. Sir Douglas was Physician-in-Ordinary to the Queen and consequently was much in demand as a consultant in thoracic disease. He diagnosed a 'very slight tubercular infection' in her right lung and regarded the smoky atmosphere round the cement works in Swanscombe as completely impossible were she to have any chance of getting well.[63] Most of the patients who had private consultations with him were wealthy, so he blithely recommended that Phyllis should go to the Swiss mountains for the winter. Her parents pronounced that they could not possibly afford it.[64]

An initial rescue was made by Elena Gurney, who bore Phyllis off to Sheringham on the north-Norfolk coast where she had rented a house with a delightful garden. Organising long garden chairs with rugs and cushions, she installed Phyllis in one so that she could enjoy fresh air for as many hours of the day as possible. While Elena painted, Phyllis could continue her writing and, with any luck, might 'cure'. Before the advent of antibiotics, fresh air was pretty much the only prescription. At the very least, Elena looked after Phyllis rather than demand that Phyllis look after her. As Phyllis said: 'I was always happy with Elena. Both of us had escaped into a relationship which we equally needed.

Elena told me once that I had fulfilled her frustrated longing for motherhood, while she gave me, even though at nineteen I thought myself long past the age of it, a sense of the irresponsibility of childhood which I had always missed.'[65]

At Sheringham, Phyllis wrote *The Master Hope*, which she dedicated 'To Wilmett, in hope and love'. Its epigraph was by William Watson:

> Ah, if indeed there be,
> Beyond one darksome door, a secret stair
> Which, winding up to the battlements, shall lead
> Hence to pure light, free air,
> This is the master hope, or the supreme despair!

Phyllis's first agent, A. P. Watt, did not manage to place the novel for her, and at some point she decided to try another agent, James Pinker, who was more interested than Watt in representing emerging, rather than established talent. Pinker did manage to place it, and her second novel was published in 1904.

Phyllis was still an apprentice writer: she was trying out different forms, looking for her own voice. The novel had rather more sub-plots than she quite had the skill to manage at this early stage of her writing career. It is most interesting perhaps for the insight it gives us into all the disparate elements that she was trying to deal with at this point in her life. Daphne is the pretty, flirtatious heroine, with three men vying for her affections, as was the case with Wilmett before she fell ill.[66] The vicar of the story is an idealised version of her father, and the vicar's wife is depicted as emotionally careless of her little daughter, who is dying of tuberculosis. Some of it is convincing, but there is a difficulty with a kind of Galsworthy-and-water melodramatic scene in which one of the suitors attempts to seduce the heroine forcibly in a drunken rage. This seems more redolent of an undigested reading of the *Forsyte Saga*, with its shocking scene of marital rape, than of anything that Phyllis genuinely understood. However, there is always at the centre of her novels the conviction that women must take or at least *share* some of the responsibility for the situations in which they find themselves. The man Daphne finally marries, although he rescues her from the attempted seduction, tells her firmly that some women's behaviour can put men into near-impossible situations. Reggie, who has loved Daphne from childhood, tells her: 'Flirtation is a repulsive system of theft; you take all you can get, real things mind you, not names, and you give worthless trash back, for your part of the bargain.'[67]

While in Sheringham, Phyllis experienced another intense friendship, this time with a local nurse. Although Elena warned Phyllis against this 'inordinate affection', rather as the nuns had warned her about her passionate friendship with Claude, as being exaggerated and harmful, it has to be admitted that it helped with the representation of a nurse's working life in the novel. And the romantic friendship between the two women in the novel rings true, whereas the interaction between men and women seems less convincing. Essentially, this is because Phyllis had experienced the first kind of relationship, whereas she had had no direct experience of heterosexual relationships with adult men. Indeed, poor Phyllis seems to have been warned off men by her mother, and warned off women by Elena. Perhaps literature seemed the only safe place to be.

Nevertheless, there are some felicities in the portrayal of Daphne and of the collision of real life with her narcissism. Daphne's prettiness has always assured her of male attention, and this passage, at the beginning of the novel, when she is leaving London and going to stay with her uncle, marks the first portent of the changes that Daphne will have to face:

> The stillness and sweetness of the April world broke upon Daphne like a discovered continent. The country had been silent to her before. She had passed from house-party to house-party all through the golden summers of her life, and nature had seemed a picturesque setting – a background for well-dressed humanity; she wondered now how she had dared to point out 'views' as if they were Academy pictures and patronise roses by arranging them in vases. She realised, as the bustling Paddington train took her through mile after mile of fields and woods and hills, that nature is an element, not a convenience.[68]

This is the opening hint, and a very neat one, that Daphne will need to learn that she is part of nature, and cannot control it. Death is already stalking her small cousin, and that will have to be faced and understood. Everything else changes its significance in the face of this absolute.

Despite Elena's loving care, Phyllis's health did not significantly improve and Dr Schacht once again impressed on her parents that she must be sent abroad for the winter if she was to live. At this point, Elena generously offered to take her to Switzerland in September and to the Italian lakes for the early winter at her own expense. So Phyllis set off on what, despite the anxieties about her health, was a great adventure; to go to Europe with an older cultured woman friend, who was devoted to her, was a treat that ironically only the threat to her life could have produced.

CHAPTER 2

St Moritz and the White Death

> For psychological reasons I have written rather more fully about these years of frustration and ill-health than many people may think desirable.
>
> PHYLLIS BOTTOME, *The Challenge*

Phyllis, like her sister Wilmett, was facing a great trial. Tuberculosis killed 'men and women of all ages, but especially the young: it wrecked hopes, it broke courtships'.[1] Although men and women at any stage of life could contract TB, it primarily attacked young people between fifteen and thirty-five. Sufferers faded away, inexorably losing weight until they died. It often wasted years, transforming their lives as they waited for a cure. Tuberculosis had been known since ancient times and was a disease that did not attack any one particular organ, but inflicted damage on a variety of organs and tissue. This is the reason why so many names have been applied to it. Phthisis (a Greek word meaning 'wasting'), consumption and scrofula were among the most common. Another, more metaphorical, name was the 'White Death', as sufferers were almost invariably anaemic. At the turn of the twentieth century it was the chief killer of young people in the western world.

Phyllis, despite the fear instilled by witnessing her sister die of tuberculosis, still had belief in the future. Elena Gurney had arrived like a fairy godmother when she most needed someone to parent her. She also had a realisable ambition, to be a novelist, and she had the excitement of European travel to sustain her hopes. Phyllis's parents' initial assumption that she could rely on her writing to provide her with an adequate income once Elena returned to England was, it turned out, unrealistic. After Phyllis had paid a typist to prepare manuscripts to send to the publisher, her first two novels only brought her in about three pounds each. Fortunately, a patron of her father's, Mr White, contributed fifty pounds towards Phyllis's expenses so that, in response to the doctor's advice, she could over-winter in St Moritz. After their shared autumn sojourn at the Italian lakes, at Elena's expense, Phyllis would have to leave her behind when she went up to St Moritz. Elena could not accompany her as she was considered to have a weak heart and her doctors thought that she should not go so high above sea level, but for Phyllis, it was considered the best hope of a cure; the white snowscape might defeat the White Death.

One of the leading physicians studying tuberculosis, Jean-Antoine Villemin, had noticed that the disease rarely flourished at high altitudes. Some doctors falsely concluded that tuberculosis was caused by the failure of a small and weak heart to pump the blood forcefully enough to prevent the spread of tubercles in the patient's body. In the second half of the nineteenth century doctors thought that the heart would not have to struggle so much if the patient could live for as long as four years at precisely regulated altitudes. Although this idea was never proven, it lingered on in the imagination because German Romanticism had embodied the notion of spiritual and physical renewal in the mountains. In 1854 the first sanatorium dedicated to the treatment of pulmonary tuberculosis had been set up in the village of Gebersdorf in the Bavarian Alps. Davos in the Swiss Alps was the most fashionable resort from the mid-1860s, frequented by more affluent consumptives from all over Europe. There was a boom in the building of inns, *pensions* and hotels, all styling themselves on sanatoria; the most expensive were, in all but name, luxury hotels. Nearby valleys and villages also started to develop as sanatorium resorts, St Moritz becoming the second largest after Davos.

In November 1903, Phyllis parted from Elena in Chiavenna at the head of Lake Como and travelled up to St Moritz in a horse-drawn sledge. She was sad to leave Elena after their contented months together, but as the fog dropped away beneath her and the white snow peaks shot up into a pale blue sky, she could not help feeling excited. She was twenty-one years old, and ready for adventure. Her arrival in St Moritz, however, was not auspicious. At this time there was one main village street and a square containing the Poste Inn. There the sledge driver dumped her things. She arrived in the late afternoon with the sun retreating behind the mountains, and the air was so cold that she could feel her own breathing.

The patients in St Moritz were predominately British until after the First World War. The doctors attached to the luxury establishments were usually either owners or co-owners, so tuberculosis, for them, was a highly profitable business. For the less well-off, clusters of cheaper chalets grew up like mushrooms on the slopes behind the expensive hotels. As Phyllis's family had very little money, even with Mr White's fifty pounds, cheap lodgings were essential. The plan devised was that Phyllis would board with some British ladies – two sisters, Hilda and Annie, in their early thirties – who ran a small *pension* and teashop in St Moritz. As Phyllis would be unchaperoned, which was not *comme il faut* for middle-class young women at the turn of the century, the presence of these ladies made the arrangement quasi-respectable.[2] Kennie Fowler regularly spent part of each winter at the luxurious Kulm Hotel, and hence Uncle Kennie's own doctor, Dr Holland, offered to take Phyllis under his care. The Bottome parents assumed that Mrs Holland, spoken of as Kennie's devoted friend, would act as Phyllis's social sponsor, which again would guarantee respectability to an unchaperoned girl. Mrs Holland, however, showed no inclination to bother herself with a girl without money. In essence, the richest patients went to the Kulm and the very poorest patients went to an Invalids' Home that was largely run on private charity. The betwixt-and-betweens, like Phyllis, who had a little money, improvised their own arrangements. Mrs Holland stayed firmly in the Kulm (meaning summit), looking down her nose at the poorer inhabitants from her eyrie on the hillside above St Moritz.

On that first day, when Phyllis located her accommodation, which she had fondly imagined would have a south-facing balcony, she found instead a small, rather squalid flat which received no sun at all as the Poste Inn kept it permanently in shade. It should be noted that her room cost nine francs a week while the very cheapest room at the Kulm cost thirteen francs a week. There were two other boarders, one of whom was a photographer, a Mr Brown. His room did have a balcony, and Phyllis managed to persuade him to let her write in half of his balcony, on the strict proviso that she didn't disturb him by talking to him. The other boarder, Ethel, was a woman of thirty-five who had a bad reputation for taking lovers. The effect of living, or, more often, slowly dying, away from one's family, often had a loosening effect on social behaviour and etiquette. The consumptive patients even looked different:

> Sanatorium doctors instructed male patients to shave off their beards and trim their moustaches to a thin line in order to avoid catching phlegm from their cough. This seemed the more radical since one reason for growing bushy beards in Victorian times was partly to guard the chest and to make it easier to draw breath. Consumptive women were told to bob their hair, wear lighter dress material and raise their hems above ankle level to avoid gathering dust. It was a welcome change.[3]

Given that most patients suffering from tuberculosis died within fifteen years at most of being diagnosed, there was a curiously unreal feeling to life. Some became gloomy and hopeless; others, like Ethel, determined to live hectically until the very end.

Phyllis clearly wrote cheerful and upbeat letters home, and the news that her health appeared to be getting better circulated around the extended family. Grandmother Bottome wrote comfortably to Grandma Fowler just before Christmas 1903:

> I am so happy after the news that has reached us that dear Phyllis will get well ... there she is, our snow-bird. Nothing – she writes – between her and Heaven. Her nature is simply delicious to me. She is spiritual, and there is so much religiousness that has so little spirituality. I can understand her like a book, as we say. She is very remarkable to me, and if she lives she will make her mark.[4]

Indeed, whether she would live or not was in the balance. Shortly before Christmas, Phyllis suffered a haemorrhage. Dr Holland descended godlike from the Kulm and ordered her to stay in bed and not talk at all until she recovered. He bullied Hilda and Annie into giving her a better room with some light and air. And from there, for several weeks, Phyllis could only watch the outside world like a kind of ghost:

On New Year's Eve all St Moritz was in the streets, every hotel – even our own little Pension – was empty; and every outlying farmhouse or distant mountain village joined the St Moritz visitors, to listen to our bells ring in the New Year. I was alone, strictly prohibited from speech or movement, but from an attic window, where I crouched in the dark, I could look into the heart of the festival. Red flares lit the campanile from within, and through its loggia arches the great bells swung out, above the newly fallen snow. I could see each individual bellringer on the high platform of the bell-room, clinging to his bell rope; and shooting backwards and forwards against the pull of the bell. The dark bee-like figures were as fixed in their rhythm as the notes of music in a fugue; their bodies were caught up into the bells, while the force of hidden music shot back into their bodies. Only the tower and its leaping shadows, were visible; but I knew that the mountains were there – immovable presences – behind the black, heaving figures and the blood-red tower. All this human flurry and sound were held within the silent ramparts of their frozen cup. As I sat entranced – watching the flying bells – I was suddenly aware, with all the intensity of youth, that this New Year, rung in so gallantly, might be my last.[5]

Fortunately, after a few weeks Phyllis's health began to pick up. Part of her illness had been brought on by trying to help her landladies at the *pension*. This was now absolutely forbidden by Dr Holland, and so the harassed pair were greatly relieved when they found a young woman who would undertake part-time work in return for paying half-board.

This was Hope de Lisle Brock, whom Hilda immediately condemned as a young woman who wore make-up, implying that she was no better than she should be. Lislie, as she liked to be called, was the next, and most deeply-felt, of Phyllis's female friendships. This relationship would last until Lislie's death twenty years later; it was a friendship that Phyllis describes in her autobiography as 'deep, harmonious, unimpassioned', implying that it was a more mature relationship than any of her earlier passionate female friendships.[6] This may well be true, although there was a level of interdependence which was to prove difficult to manage on occasion; Lislie did not fall in love till she was twenty-seven, and she never married. As with the case of the nurse in Sheringham, Elena was to warn Phyllis once more that 'friendships such as yours and Lislie's ... are apt to be deceptive and even dangerous. You do not only think well of each other; but there is always the fear that you may think – because of the other's admiration – too well of yourselves.'[7] It is true that the two young women formed a mutual admiration society, writing home to their respective families about the marvellous qualities of the other.

Phyllis describes her first sight of Lislie rather as one describes a lover:

> She had just come in from a walk, and the icy air had whipped a lovely rose colour – which had nothing to do with cosmetics – into her cheeks. Lislie had large hazel eyes with very clear whites to them, under naturally arched eyebrows. These smooth brown arches gave her face a questioning look rather like a pansy's. She wore a short musquash coat, and fur cap, a shade lighter than her hair. She carried a copy of the Spectator under her arm, and held a bunch of scarlet and purple anemones in her hand which she had bought to give me.[8]

In some ways, there was a parallel between Lislie's family and her own. Lislie's father, Charles, came from an old Guernsey family, originally wealthy, but, as the money was divided among a large number of children, the inheritance had dwindled away. Dr Brock was a good physician with a largely working-class practice near Tooting where he was too kind to chase poor patients for money they owed him. This frustrated Lislie's mother, Carita, who wanted a more expansive social life than her husband could afford. Although, by contrast, Phyllis's mother wanted none, the two mothers shared a sense that their husbands had in some way let them down. And in both families, the cost of supporting a child through the potentially long period of a tubercular illness made financial matters a critical issue.

Phyllis and Lislie talked about their families, and observed and discussed the inhabitants of St Moritz. Phyllis was an extrovert like her father, and all her novels were built up out of her own experience and by excursions into the lives of others. Not as pretty as her mother or her sister Wilmett had been, she was tall and stringy, with a mass of untidy hair, and her face had a stronger nose and chin than was considered appropriate for conventional prettiness. But she had huge dark eyes, an expressive face and voice, and the kind of personality that Italians call *sympatica*. Both men and women tended to tell her things that they would not usually discuss with other people, let alone a young unmarried woman. So, although her tuberculosis held her life – almost literally – on ice, she was simultaneously gaining insights into many other people's lives.

Once Uncle Kennie arrived for his winter sojourn, matters improved; he enjoyed the company of these two young women, as he never felt threatened that they would want to marry him. He was not so keen on the company of another friend of Phyllis's, Julia Farrer, an experienced nurse, who had once been secretary to Florence Nightingale. She, like Kennie, was in her early forties and was beautiful with 'lovely chestnut hair and large cool blue eyes, with clear-cut features', but Kennie was rather afraid of her.[9]

Phyllis began to enjoy the bright winter sunshine and crystal-clear air, in stark contrast to the fog and drizzle of English winters. Kennie took Phyllis to watch curling and ice-hockey matches followed by afternoon tea at the Kulm. Neither she nor Lislie were allowed by their respective doctors to take an active part in any of the winter sports; they could only watch. However, the forbidden tobogganing run on the north side of the Kulm proved an irresistible temptation, and on one occasion Phyllis and Lislie defied their doctors:

> Once on a moonlight night we succeeded in flying on a toboggan down a long snow run. Snow runs were not as fast or as dangerous as ice runs, and as we did not fall off, no distinguishable harm followed. However, we looked on this sally as an immoral incident and did not repeat our adventure. Instead we enjoyed what we could vicariously of the St Moritz sports, watching with particular ardour the Cresta Run, and hockey on the ice.[10]

The thrilling sensation, not only of speed but also of the intimacy of holding closely on to young men, is depicted vividly in the one novel the two young women wrote together. It was an epistolary novel based on experience of life in St Moritz, and their observations of the inmates of the Kulm Hotel. Although *Crooked Answers* was not published until 1911, it arises directly out of the period spent at St Moritz, so its place belongs here. Its heroine, Patricia Lance, suitably chaperoned by Mrs Mottley Engladine, is staying at the Hotel Kulm for the winter-sports season. Patricia writes to her friend Aline, who is staying with her mama at a resort on Lake Como, and also to her father, Professor Lance, back in England. The professor is an idealised version or amalgam of the best qualities of Phyllis's and Lislie's fathers. It is a *jeu d'esprit*, with elements of Richardson's epistolary format, Austen's comedy of manners and Meredith's *The Egoist* all thrown into the mix. The humour is centred on Patricia's failure to recognise in the aptly named Peter Hope, whom she dismisses as dull and dependable, her perfect mate. It is only when he unexpectedly turns out to be a dare-devil on the Cresta Run, that she starts to see that he is more interesting than the other young men swarming around her and with whom she is flirting. Meanwhile, Aline has been enchanted by an entirely selfish young man and now has to recover from a broken heart. The comedy lies in the 'unconscious' revelations of each girl to the other, unaware of the workings of their own hearts, and punctuated by the wry, more sophisticated observations of Professor Lance, who, as his name suggests, punctures the inauthenticity of his daughter's view of the world. Although it is great fun, one or two sharp observations of the St Moritz world emerge. Patricia describes to her father the 'quantities of the vulgarest-looking hotels, and the most palpably anglicised institution to be found out of an English watering place' with 'ill people drifting about like shadows under a doom, in this land of strength and glitter and laughter'.[11] It is a reminder that Phyllis and Lislie were at St Moritz to find out whether they were to live or die, and their efforts in keeping up each other's spirits were both admirable, and necessary.

The two young women had little control over their fates; doctors were like gods and the patients were victims of altitude, being sent up and down the mountain as though they were on a potentially fatal switchback ride. At one point Lislie's health took a sharp turn for the worse and her mother came out from England, purportedly to look after her. As Phyllis wryly commented, 'she was one of those mothers who live the lives of their daughters as a hobby'.[12] Much to her surprise, Phyllis found out that Carita's interpretation of tending her daughter amounted to being escorted by Phyllis to every possible entertainment, while leaving Lislie in peace. In spring 1904, Carita took Lislie, on doctors' instructions, to Thusis. Phyllis, left behind, would have loved to have accompanied Uncle Kennie when he left St Moritz for a tour of Italy, but he was a stickler for decorum, at least in public, and without a woman chaperone, he dared not take her. He was not a blood relative and, as he pointed out to Phyllis, in Italy 'niece' was often used as a courtesy title for young women who were anything but nieces.[13]

So she was fated to be shepherded down the mountain alongside all Dr Holland's other patients to stay at the chief hotel in Ragatz. There she began writing short stories, which were apprenticeship efforts, not to be published, but at least 'they began to crystallise themselves into the shape of crucial instances'.[14] A strict class (or more accurately wealth) hierarchy was maintained: the Kulm patients had the best rooms, the best tables and the best service, whereas *hoi polloi*, like Phyllis, were lumped together in inferior quarters with a communal dining table. There was little communication between the two social groups. At least conversation with a Dr Andrews in the 'lower group' provided her with some intellectual challenges. He lent her books by Darwin, Herbert Spencer, Nietzsche, Schopenhauer and William James. Although her faith had been recently rekindled by Elena's Anglo-Catholicism, she was 'completely shaken out of all anthropomorphic religion' by this reading programme.[15] Separated from Lislie, suffering from influenza and her loss of hope for a supernatural future, Phyllis became depressed.

Her father came out to join her and was predictably subversive in the face of the class distinctions operating in Ragatz. It was a moment when the two might have found a new understanding, but they failed to seize this opportunity. As Phyllis put it, 'forty-nine and twenty do not move to the same time sequence'.[16]

Phyllis recognised that her father was deeply demoralised, having never recovered from a sense of guilt following Wilmett's death, and he regretted having been persuaded to leave America. Now, he found himself incapable of dealing with the hostilities that had broken out between Daisy and Mary at home. He blamed Mary and indicated that Daisy was becoming increasingly afraid of her daughter, pleading with Phyllis to come home and make the peace. Once again, there seems to have been a failure of the adults to take responsibility for difficult situations, the 'child' being asked to resolve the difficulties of the parents. Phyllis went back to Swanscombe with her father, despite her doctor's dire warnings of the dangers of the cement-dust-filled air.

In Swanscombe, Phyllis continued to work on the sketches for *Raw Material* and caught up with old friends – and possibly asked herself whether one of them might be more than a friend. Phyllis's first heterosexual romance had been on the family's return from America, when William had taken them to Burnham-on-Sea. At her previous school, Claude's tales of flirting recklessly with dozens of suitors had aroused Phyllis's romantic curiosity. Aged thirteen, at Burnham, Phyllis had enjoyed a mild romance with Harry, a Sandhurst cadet, who was six foot one, blue-eyed and handsome. However, as soon as the beautiful Wilmett joined the party he had immediately transferred his affections and tried to kiss her. This disgraced him with the older Bottomes, especially because he was about to leave for India for five years and was thus not in a position to offer marriage. Phyllis, always sorry for the downtrodden, had taken him back into her confidence, and they enjoyed tête-à-têtes which both families put a stop to when they became aware of them. As they had largely consisted of Phyllis reading Henry James out loud to him – enough to put anyone off reckless action, one might think – it was all entirely harmless. No doubt Phyllis was more in love with Henry James than the flesh-and-blood young man in front of her. Nevertheless it was her first practice run at romance. Her second romantic encounter had taken place during a stay with Elena. This had been an entirely one-sided story, as Phyllis had been sympathetically listening to the woes of a young curate recovering from a broken heart – and she had not observed that the young man had blithely transferred his attentions to her. But this summer at Swanscombe, a five-year-long friendship with Gerard Coleridge ripened into a romance, albeit of an innocent kind. Gerard was at Cambridge, and, in a similar fashion to her previous admirers, first and foremost he offered her intellectual companionship. He also provided her with some insights into aspects of sexual life of which she had hitherto been quite innocent. A fellow undergraduate of Gerard's arrived at Swanscombe, and to her astonishment, Gerard warned Phyllis to keep him away from her brother George, now a good-looking boy of sixteen. Phyllis was given to understand that 'the Blackadder', as Gerard nicknamed him, 'was a belated offshoot of the already-waning period of decadence started by Oscar Wilde'.[17] Phyllis was horrified at the idea of older boys or young men preying on younger boys. Once again, a particular vision of male sexuality shocked her, and she was to remain hostile to men she recognised as homosexual for some years. The relationship between Gerard and Phyllis remained at the brother-and-sister level, even though they always felt a special *tendresse* for each other.

The other significant encounter of the summer for Phyllis was a visit to Lislie's uncle, Henry Melvill Gwatkin, who was Professor of Ecclesiastical History at Cambridge. In 1874 he had resigned his college fellowship in order to marry Lucy de Lisle Brock, as this was a period when Cambridge Fellows were not allowed to marry. Phyllis was enchanted by this romantic tale, and was delighted when the Gwatkins 'adopted' Phyllis as an honorary niece. Although partly deaf and poor-sighted, Uncle Melvill was a brilliant teacher, who regarded the history of the Church as one part of history in general, and he had the gift of making his subject come alive. He, in turn, delighted in Phyllis's sharp mind and regretted that her lack of formal schooling ruled out the possibility of her attendance at one of the two women's colleges in Cambridge.[18] His own daughter had attended Newnham College, and he was a champion of university education for women, willing to teach women students at a time when many dons were not. He referred to them as his 'Newnham men', which sounds like an affectation, but it implied that he treated the women as though, just like the men, they were full members of the University.[19] He and Phyllis had fierce debates, and by treating her as an intellectual equal, Uncle Melvill was paying her the highest compliment that he could.[20]

Phyllis returned to St Moritz for her second winter, late in 1904, this time staying, as arranged previously, with a Yorkshire couple, Molly and her brother Herbert, whom she had met the previous winter. They had a large new villa, where Herbert took paying pupils; he had six that year. He had done rather well at Oxford but, then, unfortunately, had contracted tuberculosis. At St Moritz, however, it had never got any worse than when he arrived. Consequently, he was one of Dr Holland's 'pets', which is to say that, because, in reality, no doctor had a cure for tuberculosis, a patient who seemed to recover, or at least not worsen, could be 'advertised' as an example of Dr Holland's skill. Molly ran the household and it was she who had invited Phyllis to join them for her second winter. The arrangement was that Phyllis would have a south-facing room with a private balcony for her writing and she would pay no more than she had been paying at the tearooms, where she had had no balcony at all. In return she would help Molly if any of the boys were ill, and would stay in to 'babysit' on evenings when she and Herbert were invited to social events at the Kulm Hotel.

Phyllis's health was improving this winter so that when, in November, the lake froze solid after several hard frosts, two of the boys from the villa taught her how to skate. After so many months of not being allowed to do much except 'cure', it was a delight: 'Never in my life had I known such joy in movement. A swallow, tossing away the air from the knife-blade of his wings, could not have felt more sure of the sense of flight. A fiery sunset cut crimson and gold swathes out of the zig-zag pass, the valley spread in an apricot mist before us. The reeds were bright orange fading into spectral gold.'[21]

And it was just at this high point in her health that Ernan Forbes Dennis came to stay at Herbert and Molly's villa. The evening that Ernan arrived, Phyllis happened to be wearing her favourite yellow dress, and Ernan was immediately struck by her vivaciousness. On her side, she saw 'a tall young man with wavy dark hair, lighter than his thick straight eyebrows, and very dark eyes'.[22] They were attracted to each other immediately; she was more knowledgeable about literature but he was a fine musician, and played the piano at the villa with great flair and delicacy.

His mother was staying at one of the smaller hotels associated with the Kulm. Because Ernan was a patient of Sir Thomas Barlow in London, Dr Holland was keen to do everything for him, even though the family was not as rich as most of the Kulmites. Ernan had had several chest illnesses and because his eldest brother Ralph had died of tuberculosis, his mother had been advised that he should spend a winter at St Moritz.

Ernan and Phyllis were thrown together because each of their doctors had advised them to take walks in the afternoon. They shared confidences, and exchanged stories about their respective families. The Forbes clan came from north Aberdeenshire. Ernan's grandfather, Sir John Forbes, had been a cavalry general in India for half of his life and was treated by Queen Victoria as a personal friend. He had married Miss Drummond of Megginch, a beautiful if extravagant wife, when she was only thirteen and together they had had nine children. Ernan's mother, Maimie, was the eldest of the five Forbes sisters, the others being Lilla, Emily, Katie and Chattie. Only Maimie and Lilla had married, perhaps as a consequence of small dowries. Maimie had married George Dennis, who was from an old and distinguished, although somewhat impoverished family with an estate in Bridgerule, Devon. George had intended to become a clergyman, but instead, following a crisis of faith, had decided to make his living from farming the estate.

Ernan, as the youngest of four brothers, was to be the unluckiest of them in terms of the financial affairs of the Dennis family. His eldest brother, Ralph, his mother's favourite, was up at Oxford University when he contracted tuberculosis and died, aged twenty-one. Ernan's father had shortly afterwards taken a lonely walk over the Cairngorm Mountains and had died of exposure; it seems likely that it was an unadvertised suicide. The second brother, Stanley, had gone out to join an uncle, Gordon Forbes, in South Africa, who had found him a job in the diamond mines. The third brother Fred had made a career in the army, and had fought in the Boer War.[23] Ernan, aged thirteen, was the only son available to take charge of the farm estate, for which he had neither training nor aptitude. Removed from his school in Oxford and given responsibility beyond his years, at nineteen he seems to have suffered from a nervous breakdown. Such was his desperation to escape from the farm and go to Oxford University that he had run away to London where he had consulted Ralph's physician, Sir Thomas Barlow, and pleaded for his help in persuading his mother that he should be allowed to do so. Sir Thomas, seeing that Ernan was physically and emotionally exhausted, and concerned that he, too, might be suffering from the first symptoms of tuberculosis, had recommended a winter at St Moritz. He had also hoped to get Ernan away from his mother, but she was determined not to be left behind.

Ernan and Phyllis were two lonely young people, close in age, and with similar, if not identical, intellectual interests, so it was almost inevitable that they would fall in love. Almost immediately an uncomfortable interlude ensued when it transpired that her 'host' Herbert was in love with Phyllis and had been intending to propose marriage. He was furious when Ernan unexpectedly cut in. Indeed, Herbert was not the only person to watch their developing relationship with censorious eyes. As Phyllis herself wrote:

> the preoccupation of falling in love is so intense that though it is probable a lover never uses his eyes to so much purpose, he may be accounted blind, since his eyes are wholly absorbed in one particular vision. They may explain the incredible blindness which hid from me, and I think from Ernan, what our small world thought of our increasing friendship ... We were too young, too delicate, too resourceless, to think of marriage. We were thinking of love and death. Habitation and incomes had as yet occurred to neither of us.[24]

In particular, Ernan's mother, used to having her boy to herself, was singularly irked by Ernan's new fascination.

In March 1905 Phyllis went down the Maloja Pass once more to meet Elena at Chiavenna and travelled with her for a six-week stay in Florence. Daisy, at last, came out in May to join Phyllis at the Tiroler Hof in Innsbruck. Ernan was anxious to join Phyllis and to be introduced to her mother, but Mamma constantly invented reasons to prevent him. She insisted that Ernan stay with her while she took the baths at Baden and it was with the greatest difficulty that he managed to escape from her clutches to join Phyllis for her birthday on 31 May 1905 at the small wooden Post House at Toblach in Südtirol. It was there in a pinewood that Ernan proposed marriage.

Phyllis wrote:

> We kept our secret for that day to ourselves; but I felt that my mother must be told before we slept; and Ernan felt with equal

> emphasis that his mother must not be told for a long time. He had been her whole life for seven years, since the death of her eldest son Ralph, and our engagement was bound to be a severe blow to her. We must, he explained, break it gradually after she had learned to care for me, a process in which Ernan, at the moment, saw no particular difficulty.[25]

Phyllis's mother accepted their engagement with equanimity. She liked Ernan and assumed that he would easily be able to make a career in the Diplomatic Service, or become a clergyman with a chaplaincy on the Riviera, which might be health-giving for both of them. Ernan's mother, however, regarded any potential engagement as an unmitigated disaster. She was horrified that Ernan had set his heart on this stray girl – nameless, penniless and half-American. She seemed to assume that Phyllis was some kind of adventuress, which, as Phyllis was extraordinarily innocent, is especially ironic.

At first, Mamma did not fight Phyllis openly, but used the tactics of passive resistance, refusing to fall in with Ernan's travel plans and making it difficult for him to keep his arrangements with Phyllis and her mother. Eventually Ernan managed to persuade Mamma to travel to Cortina to meet Phyllis's mother. The meeting was a disaster: Mamma hardly came out of her room and was as cool as she could get away with to both Daisy and Phyllis. Mamma had been hoping that while she used delaying tactics, the danger would pass, but when it did not, she moved to more active sabotage. She told Ernan that she found both Phyllis and her mother's opinions 'arbitrary' and pronounced that Phyllis's clothes were ill-chosen and her favourite hat 'common'.[26] As she grew increasingly afraid of Phyllis's hold over her son, Mamma became increasingly less subtle in her attacks and more openly hostile.

At the end of the summer, Phyllis started to suffer from what Dr Holland called 'an overstrained heart', and he insisted that she must move to a lower altitude than St Moritz, advising Davos. Daisy, in her usual fashion when trouble struck, immediately decided to return to England, leaving Phyllis to move to Davos alone. The manners of the day meant that Ernan was obliged to escort Phyllis's mother to Innsbruck, as a middle-class woman did not expect to travel in Europe unescorted. This put Ernan in a position where he was forced to own up that he had become secretly engaged to Phyllis so that he could reasonably insist on leaving Phyllis with Mamma. Phyllis, ill and distressed that her own mother had abandoned her, was left with 'a woman who disliked me more than she had ever disliked anyone'.[27]

As Phyllis describes it in her autobiography, she and Ernan both had impossible mothers – and to add to their problems – their mothers hated each other on sight. Daisy recognised that Mamma did not think her daughter good enough for Ernan, and any mother, even the strangely careless Daisy, must have resented this on behalf of her child. But it was also the case that both women had made a career of being 'delicate'. Phyllis could see that Ernan's desire to protect his mother was a significant problem; she also recognised that although Daisy was equally selfish and manipulative, at least she was not against the marriage. At this point, it was Ernan's mother who was the major obstacle: 'Self-sacrificing, generous and intelligent as Mamma was, it must be confessed that she had clutches; and that she lived not only *for* Ernan but *on* him … I already knew only too well what living with a devoted, neurotic invalid involved.'[28] As Phyllis expressed it in her autobiography:

> If we had been able to marry within the year of our first engagement, while nature was still prepared to work her faultless miracle with our connivance, our marriage might have been, if not more successful, much simpler in its workings. We were not only both of us deeply in love, but we were malleable and eager to take our lessons from each other. Our ideals and our habits were strikingly similar, even our childhood frustrations had been the same.[29]

Mamma knew she was beaten on the engagement front, but then changed tactics, insisting that Ernan and Phyllis should live with her after their marriage, so that they could pool their resources. Whereas this might have been efficacious from a financial point of view, it could never have worked – 'Mamma was willing to give Ernan everything she possessed – but at the price of possessing him.'[30] In short, Ernan desperately needed to get away from his widowed mother in order to begin his own life, but he was not ruthless enough to do so.

During the winter of 1905/6, Phyllis was staying in the Bella Vista Hotel in Davos. Of course, Mamma came to Davos too, albeit staying in a superior hotel. There, Phyllis and Ernan consulted Dr Huggard about their respective states of health and the possibilities of marriage. Ernan was told that he would get completely well in a year's time or less. Phyllis, on the other hand, was told that her 'cure' would take longer, and therefore she should not consider marrying for another four or five years, but by then it might be possible for her to bear a child. Phyllis was prescribed a regime of 'curing' for nine hours a day on her balcony. This she did religiously, tucked up in a sheepskin-lined sack sent out to her by Grandmother Fowler. No sports were allowed. Ernan, on the other hand, was told that he must spend at least three hours a day on snow sports, so he was busy skiing and skating – though not tobogganing, which for some reason was not seen as a sport but merely as a recreation. Fortunately for the young couple, Mamma was told she could not remain in Davos after November, as she was too arthritic and sensitive to drops in temperature. She was to go to the Riviera with a friend, leaving Ernan and Phyllis to be chaperoned by Lislie, who would be coming out from England to join them. Phyllis was getting on with writing and 'curing'; Ernan was staying in a German *pension* learning German with a view to entering university and subsequently earning his living. At this point, despite everything stacked against them, they devoutly believed in a future together.

Phyllis, besotted with Ernan, wanted to be near him, and, without consulting Lislie, took two rooms at the Kaiserhof, a hotel near Ernan's *pension*. The Kaiserhof was exclusively inhabited by Poles and Germans, who turned out to be hard-drinking; as Lislie had no aptitude for foreign languages, she was understandably furious that her comfort had been put in second place by Phyllis. Ernan and Phyllis were working between four and six hours a day, he on his French and German, while Phyllis, armed with a hot-water bottle to unfreeze both her fingers and her fountain pen, wrote on a wooden board on her balcony. Lislie had expected to be in the Bella Vista and was cross at finding herself in a remote hotel, far from her English friends. When she did manage to catch up with them at the skating rink, they informed her in no uncertain terms that the Kaiserhof had an unsavoury reputation. Phyllis realised that, as a consequence of her selfish arrangements, Lislie's 'whole prospect of social entertainment for the winter was left in the lurch. I might have understood better what I was asking Lislie to sacrifice had I ever had a social life, but it was an advantage of which I was entirely ignorant. We passed through terrible hours; but our friendships held firm.'[31]

Lislie and Ernan both had to accommodate the shift of Phyllis's romantic friendship with Lislie into a new triangular dynamic. As Phyllis wrote, 'to my intense relief … [Lislie] found that she *did* like Ernan; and he had from the first moment generously accepted her. Both of them made adjustments so handsome and so entire that I doubt if I ever knew what it had cost either of them.'[32] Lislie found that she lost some of her conventionally-minded friends, who disapproved of the lack of chaperonage (which is to say that it was not considered *comme il faut* for one young woman to chaperone another), and they disapproved especially of 'Ernan skipping in at all sorts of times so much'.[33] And Lislie, who was more wedded to conventional social life than Phyllis, hated to be disapproved of; but, finally, Phyllis's company always meant more to her than anyone else's. Writing home to her mother, she said:

> Phyl is such a dear, I love her more and more, & oh she's *so* amusing – I long for you to hear her talk sometimes, I know you would like it so – it is difficult to repeat – things thrown into a conversation which strike one as clever at the time are apt to fall rather flat if dished up again. … [Phyl] met a woman at tea yesterday, and was telling me about her in the evening. 'She thinks she's rather a racy talker, doesn't she?' I said – 'Well I don't know,' Phyllis said, 'she may race but she doesn't win.' These kind of remarks strewn about the conversation like leaves in autumn, do light up life![34]

Notwithstanding their laughter, people around them were dying; that winter they lost three friends. One was Winnie Thomas, who had been a famous hockey player before the onset of tuberculosis; another was a young mother called Gwen Smeaton; and the last was a young boy Phyllis had met the previous winter at the Invalids' Home in St Moritz. Briefly, this plunged Phyllis into depression:

> I was prepared to face death for myself, or thought I was, but not to face the loss of my two companions. I felt that I might physically survive them, but the loss of my lover would have killed all that I meant by joy: and Lislie was at once my conscience and my sister. I felt sure that there was no one in the world to be compared with either of them; and I had so fastened my identity into their personalities, that I could see nothing over the rim of their lives.[35]

In the late spring of 1906 Ernan rejoined his mother at Zürich and then they travelled to Geneva, where he was to live with a French professor's family, studying French, while Mamma rested in her hotel. Here Ernan, recovering fast, and enjoying swimming, fencing and mountain climbing, made lots of new young friends, one of whom, a highly talented young Viennese violinist called Robert Pollak, was already offering master classes at the Geneva Conservatory.[36] This friendship was to be lifelong.

The power relations between Phyllis and Ernan started to shift. She was two years older than Ernan, and, having found her vocation early, was already a published novelist. At this point, however, she was clawed back into Bottome family life, spending the summer of 1906 with her mother and Mary in a pilot's cottage in Southwold, Suffolk. Her own health was poor, and was not helped by the incessant fighting between Daisy and Mary. William, as usual, took refuge in golf. Betty and Maida McCord came over from America to visit, and although their company was usually a delight, on this occasion unexpected drama ensued. Betty was determined to break free from her family entanglements – her mother was dead and her father remarried – and she wanted to set up home in Paris where she could study painting. Meanwhile, Phyllis's brother George, just nineteen and due to go up to Cambridge at the end of the summer, fell madly in love with Maida. The Bottome parents put a stop to it, on the grounds that George was far too young.

Phyllis, watching helplessly, began to see her own romance as doomed, suspecting that in her absence Ernan's mother would be plotting to sabotage their engagement. She had lost Ralph to tuberculosis, Stanley to South Africa and Fred to the army; she was not likely to give Ernan up without a struggle. In a letter to Ernan on 14 August 1906, Phyllis suggested gently that Mamma's expecting him always to be available as her companion at social events was unreasonable. She pointed out that this also distracted him from his studies, and that he could not hope to earn a living unless he persevered with these. Writing to Ernan in the odd way that she adopted of speaking about herself in the third person as 'girl' and referring to Ernan as 'Baby', Phyllis tried to persuade him that Mamma would have to resign her control of him to some degree:

> My own Sweet-heart, I do grieve for Poor Mama – and wish so I could see her settling down by some lovely church in England with one of her sisters and in reach of Fred; since, however, she *cant* do this, we must accept for her the *pension* and her nearness to you. I am sure she lives in your life as she would have done in Ralph's and – for him as well as you – the inevitable growing away from her would have come – she thinks not – but death mercifully stepped in to keep for her that illusion. The love of a son for his mother is one of the deepest things in life – but it can never be his occupation – Ralph would have had his work – and then some girl – like Baby's girl – would suddenly have caught at his heart – and Mama dethroned would have felt all that unforgettable bitterness of compulsory renunciation.
>
> We will be to her what we can – girl promises him never to forget all that his Mama has been and is to him – and to allow for her fears and her needs as far as she feels it to be right for *him*, tho he should come first.[37]

Phyllis was recuperating from minor surgery, following a tooth abscess, and writing to Ernan every day, desperate to keep the thread of connection. Her letters to him, addressing him as 'Baby', 'My own Precious', 'My own Sweet Honey', 'My Heart's Darling', 'My Own Princeling', are cloying in the extreme, but reveal her fear that Ernan is not in fact hers at all, but that he still belongs to Mamma.

In Southwold, Phyllis was working away on her third novel. *The Imperfect Gift*, first published in 1906 by John Murray, was the first of her novels to achieve commercial success as an American publisher picked it up.[38] It is dedicated to Lislie, and is not without interest, despite oddities of construction, as it draws on many of her recent experiences.[39] It is, on the one hand, a kind of reworking of the Cinderella story, where the least promising sister wins the prize, but, on the other hand, it includes one or two more subtle investigations into the complexities of relationships. The novel opens in a lake town in northern Italy, drawn from Phyllis's sojourn with Elena, where Mrs Delamaine, a young widow, is living with her two daughters, Evelyn and Marjory. Evelyn is so strikingly beautiful that all men's eyes are drawn to her, whereas the younger daughter is dreamy and lost in books. Aged about sixteen, Marjory suddenly realises that her sister is beautiful and she is not:

> She ran upstairs and looked in the looking-glass. She had never done this before except to see if her hair was tidy. Now she looked at her face – it was long and pointed; her hair grew low on her small forehead; her thick level eyebrows nearly met; under them large, dark, stormy eyes gazed back at her with all the determined tragedy of youth. The nose was straight and rather long; the mouth large but expressive; her chin was an uncompromising feature and revealed a singular will.

Immediately following this moment, Marjory starts to consider the prospect that she may never marry and therefore will have to earn her own living. Despite the artificiality of some of the plot, this scene chimes on the pulse as a felt experience. Like poor Marjory, Phyllis had always been eclipsed by Wilmett's beauty.

Less convincing is a sub-plot (lifted from George Eliot's *Daniel Deronda*) in which Evelyn, having been told that she has not enough talent to become a professional musician, goes on, because of her beauty, to have expectations of achieving high social position and control over her husband. And, similarly, the section that delineates Marjory's career – taking elocution lessons and then joining Ben Armitage's acting troupe – is unconvincing because it feels like an attempt to adopt and adapt some incidents out of George Moore's 1885 novel *A Mummers Wife*. It also accounts for some unevenness of tone. Moore wrote in the naturalist style, more usually seen in writers such as Zola and Ibsen. However, it is interesting because it fictively enacts the fantasised career which tuberculosis had denied Phyllis. It also gives an indication of the almost impossibly high standards that Marjory/Phyllis expects of a beloved young man. Within the text at least, having first broken off her engagement to Ben Armitage because she doesn't like to come 'after all the rest', Marjory finally gives up being something of a prig, and accepts him as her 'imperfect gift'. The most authentic notes in the novel are sounded in the account of the relationship between the young Marjory and her middle-aged mentor Miss Perry. Even though Miss Perry in the text is an intellectual but impoverished ex-governess, this, surely, is a fictive *hommage* to Phyllis's own relationship with Elena. As described in the novel, 'a companionship of spirit had swept away the barrier of years between the two women; they were deeply and earnestly friends. In the heart of the elder, a maternal yearning added to her love; and in Marjory's affection the element of a deep respect detracted nothing from the easiness of their relation.'[40]

A constant in all Phyllis's writing was her sensitivity to natural beauty, which had been nurtured in her childhood by Grandpapa Bottome. A Romantic sensibility distinguished all her novels. *The Imperfect Gift* opens:

> A gentle haze spread over the town in its hollow nest of hills; the fading sunlight lingered upon the scattered villas till they gleamed with the lustre of pearls against the immemorial background of black cypresses. Lower down by the lake-side, a campanile ruled the grassy promontory, ringing out across the water the attenuated music of the Angelus bell. Over the whole scene hung the unmistakable Italian atmosphere, impalpable and arresting – the lifted curtain of a golden hour.[41]

This leads the reader towards the figure of the widowed mother calling out for her two daughters to come home to her. Phyllis learned early exactly how to invite her readers into her novels.

And even if Phyllis had not yet securely found her own writing voice, it should be noted that her three earliest novels were all written in an age of transition. In societal terms, the middle-class were still puzzling away on whether it could be entirely respectable to allow young unmarried women to live unchaperoned, and in literary terms, the Edwardian-country-house novel was in the process of giving way to the New Woman novel. This era, from the *fin de siècle* to the First World War, could be described as an awkward age for women writers. Around this time, Phyllis sent Lislie a copy of Henry James's *The Awkward Age*, which is itself an enactment of the tensions between various available views of how society should accommodate those young women awkwardly betwixt and between the schoolroom and marriage.[42]

Ernan and Phyllis had been separated for six months at this stage, albeit writing to each other every day. Their reunion in Davos, towards the end of October 1906, was not a success. Because Lislie had suffered a bout of illness, Phyllis had to be chaperoned by her older sister, but Mary disliked all sports, and also vehemently disliked being a third spoke in the relationship. Fortunately, in January 1907 Lislie was well enough to come out to Davos so Mary was able to leave. But Lislie, too, felt *de trop* to the Phyllis–Ernan dyad, even though the engaged couple were not happy with each other. Ernan, in particular, was increasingly scratchy and neither of them recognised the tension between them for what it was. Phyllis candidly admits in her autobiography that part of their problem was that they were both sexual innocents.

> Neither he nor I knew that long engagements physically affect men differently from women. Not could I realise into what prison of his childhood I was driving him back. Free at last from his own ill health as I was not yet free from mine; denied the natural relationship of love, while in constant nearness to its object; trying to carry the burdens I had thrust upon him as well as his own, Ernan felt himself once more chained to an adored and adoring invalid as he had been all his long childhood to his mother.[43]

In the midst of all this unease, a cable arrived from South Africa announcing that Ernan's brother Stanley had died of pneumonia. Ernan rushed to Lugano to rejoin Mamma, while Phyllis and Lislie remained in Davos together. As Stanley had seemed to embody the best prospects of rebuilding the family fortunes, this was a bitter blow. There were no letters from Ernan for some time.

In April 1907, a telegram arrived asking Phyllis and Lislie if they could join him at Lugano, and Phyllis and Ernan began to recover their lost happiness. Ernan had still not met her father, despite being officially engaged to Phyllis, a circumstance which was not *comme il faut* in Edwardian families. William Bottome was persuaded to take a holiday at Fécamps, then a picturesque fishing town in Normandy, in order that Ernan could leave Mamma in Zürich and come to join them. While William got on with his golfing, Phyllis and Ernan wandered together along the high limestone cliffs, once again full of hopeful plans for their future. Their immediate plan was to spend the winter in St Moritz, where Ernan could work as a teacher of French and German at the Villa Adrian with Herbert, while, as a *quid pro quo*, Herbert would help Ernan get ready for university entrance. Herbert wished to leave St Moritz when he was fully well, so there was the possibility that he might be persuaded to sell them the villa, which Ernan could run as a school. But this plan was about to be dashed.

Ernan wanted Phyllis to return with him to Mamma, but she knew this would displease her own family. In November 1907, only a few weeks after they had parted, Ernan's mother died. A heartbroken letter arrived:

> Little Mum was just as peaceful and happy when I went to say good morning to her as when I left her in the night. And now I have placed some tall white lilies in her darling hands – and some white roses above her head – and she will rest – rest for evermore like a beautiful, deathless flower herself. Oh darling, how I do love her – and how I remember her fragrant presence when as a child I waited for her good-night kiss – those hands were so very beautiful – they were more like her than the darling face.[44]

Ernan brought her body back to Bournemouth to be buried next to her son Ralph. Although Phyllis rushed to Bournemouth to be with Ernan, she had not been with him at the crucial juncture of his Mamma's death and the Forbes Dennis family immediately closed ranks against her.

Phyllis felt helpless, not least because she was suffering from a renewed outbreak of tuberculosis, the symptoms of which she was desperately trying to hide. Ernan's older brother Fred was very kind to her, although he was not fooled about how ill she was, so even he, the most sympathetic of that family, believed that Phyllis's state of health could only result in a stressful, even tragic marriage.

The arrival of Frank Lascelles to console the family simultaneously reinforced the plot to shut Phyllis out. Frank had been a friend of Ralph's at Oxford, and although the Dennises seemed to have taken him on his own evaluation, he was in fact largely self-invented. Born as Frank Stevens in 1875, the son of the vicar of Sibford Gower in Oxfordshire, he was to die as Frank Lascelles, Lord of the Manor, living in a 'manor house' that he had himself created. Having been the leading light of the Oxford University Dramatic Society, acclaimed for his Romeo, he had joined Herbert Tree's company at His Majesty's Theatre in London where he had enjoyed a few good parts. Frank was an extraordinary, flamboyant and charismatic creature who desired a larger stage for his talents.

The area he made his own was that of staging historical pageants; it is now virtually a lost art, but before the First World War there was a considerable vogue for 'pageantitis'.[45] Pageants told the history of the place in which they were staged, from ancient times until the present day. They were held outdoors at the site of the most historical interest in the town. Most pageants used few spoken words, but were largely dependent upon music, dancing and spectacular staging. Pageanteers were usually volunteers from the local community, with occasionally a few professional actors to raise the standard. When Frank appeared in Bournemouth he was flushed with the success of having staged a successful historical pageant in Oxford that had made his name as a pageant-master.

Combined with his supreme self-confidence was a dangerous devotion to the cult of mother worship. When Frank's mother died, he had made a pageant out of her funeral procession to Sibford Gower Church and an alabaster shrine to her within it. Rushing to console Ernan, eleven years his junior, Frank encouraged him, too, to think of his own dead Mamma as the ideal love. Phyllis, who had already had to fight this tendency in Ernan, was now faced with an even more deadly enemy, for Frank was a kind of Pied Piper whose charisma could persuade people of almost anything he wanted them to believe. Much later, Phyllis was to write about the mothers who liked their sons to be quasi-lovers, though conveniently with no element of sex in the relationship, saying how well she recognised the psychological syndrome of: 'Boys dominated more or less unconsciously by deeply spiritual mothers, with a compulsive hatred of sex ... The asceticism of the High Church Movement made an overwhelming appeal to such mothers and was passed on to both sons and daughters. The sons often became frustrated celibates ... '[46]

The Edwardian straitjacket of convention worked against Phyllis. She became so ill that her doctor said that she must leave immediately for Davos. Frank and the hostile Dennises persuaded Ernan that he would ruin her reputation if he travelled out with her without a chaperone. Consequently she travelled alone and by the time she arrived was extremely ill. With the sixty pounds earned from her writing, Phyllis paid for Lislie to come and join her, hoping that Ernan would soon follow.

But Ernan was not immediately at liberty to come out to join her, as he and Fred needed to wind up the family estate. And Ernan's doctor, Sir Thomas Barlow, strongly advised him that the engagement should be brought to an end because Phyllis showed no signs of 'curing'. Prospects of marriage looked dim. Ernan arrived in St Moritz as previously agreed, but Phyllis's doctor would not allow her to go up the additional thousand feet above sea level to St Moritz. Ernan wrote suggesting that the only possibility of a future for them was a *marriage blanc*; he was afraid that pregnancy might injure her, and in any case he had no secure income to support them. Phyllis replied, as usual adopting her odd way of talking about themselves in the third person, that she

> agrees with him that they had better be married 'companions' for a couple of years anyhow. They will be able to see how expenses can be met, and yet have all the comfort of each other through the difficult places – and get better and better all the time – this is just as he likes, for he knows that anything he wants becomes at once her heart's desire – but she does feel that any path in life together would be less of a strain to both.[47]

Desperate to speak face-to-face with Ernan, Phyllis attempted to join him at St Moritz but became severely ill in the attempt and had to retreat with Lislie down to Lake Como. Once the scene of a happy stay with Elena, it was there that she received the news that Elena, aged sixty-one, had died.

At this terribly low ebb, she received a telegram from Ernan that filled her with despair. Frank Lascelles' ambition had now turned to the Empire as a broader canvas for his talents and he had asked Ernan to go with him to Canada. There, Frank was to organise a pageant to celebrate the foundation of Quebec by Champlain three hundred years before. Ernan would make a useful secretary to Lascelles, because he now spoke fluent French; to be cynical, one might also add that Ernan had just inherited some money from the family estate. Frank was notoriously careless with money; although he earned a lot, he also spent a lot.

Grieving over the now idealised version of his mother, and believing that Phyllis might never be well, Ernan seized his chance of escape from this emotional cul-de-sac. Although he eventually came down from St Moritz to discuss it with Phyllis, and did not break off the engagement, he was devoured by the desire to escape with Frank. She could only accept, heartbrokenly, that Ernan was determined to go out into a wider world, leaving her behind. She was struck by the irony that Ernan's study of French, which she had encouraged in the hope that it would lead first to a job and then to marriage, was, instead, to take him away to Canada. She wrote to him, 'I have lost everything that made me a woman – and hardest of all for a woman I have lost my confidence in my power to please.'[48] At the beginning of December 1907, Ernan set sail on the *Kaiser Wilhelm II* to Ottawa; it was a fairly honourable escape from an intolerable situation.

CHAPTER 3

Unfinished Symphony: The Years without Ernan

It seemed to me in London that the only important thing was to get out of that Edwardian straightjacket.

PHYLLIS BOTTOME, *The Challenge*

Phyllis regarded the eighteen months following Ernan's departure to Canada in December 1907 as 'the longest and most unpalatable of my life'.[1] Formally, she was still engaged to Ernan, but he was on the other side of the world, enjoying new experiences. Phyllis was worried, among other things, that the small amount of money he had inherited after winding up family affairs in Bridgerule, which they had presumed would see Ernan through an Oxford degree, was being absorbed by Frank. Phyllis herself was so unwell that she earned nothing from her writing during those first eighteen months. This failure to provide for herself depressed her hopes for the future.

Although Phyllis lived with her parents in the summers she needed healthier air in the winters. During the winter of 1908/9 she and Lislie stayed in lodgings in Bournemouth, Phyllis continually urging Ernan to write more often. This dreary period was enlivened by a two-month visit from Uncle Melvill, who, saddened by her circumstantial inability to acquire a university education, attempted to be a one-man educationist. He demolished the tiny shreds left of Phyllis's Anglo-Catholicism. Phyllis had been strongly drawn to what she saw as the beauties of Newman's prose, and Elena had reinforced her High Church leanings, but, following her reading of Herbert Spencer and now Uncle Melvill's intellectual challenge – 'An untruthful mind *has* not beauties' – she wholly gave up the remnants of her Anglo-Catholicism. She had, however, nothing to put in its place; Ernan wrote to her urging her to turn to Christian Science as he had, but this struck no chord with Phyllis, so she was doubly bereft.

Her doctor's view of her health was increasingly grave. In May 1909, Phyllis was quite seriously ill again; writing to 'My Beloved Boy', she tells him, 'I have had a slight lung breakdown – first a little blood – spitting – and then pleurisy.'[2] Ernan's response to this letter shows his fears that than she would never be well:

> Well Phyl mine, so this old enemy still pursues us! He drove us to the mountains – he drove us together – he drove us apart – and now I think he would like to drive us to despair ... does she know he sometimes wishes she might have passed him by unnoticed on the big road – because then he wouldn't have so big a load of pain to carry – pain which he gives not receives – for he feels that she cannot understand him, that she finds no comfort in his clenched hands – and yet he can't – can't – can't stretch them out somehow – He feels as tho' he had made her ill – perhaps killed her – but no! nothing so kind as that. Oh dear dear Lamb – I feel as though I might be writing to a grave ... [3]

This could hardly have been reassuring; she wrote to him at Christmas 1909, quoting the Lady of Shallott, 'I have grown old in waiting ... My vitality is being slowly sapped by suspense – always some new postponement – always less and less of your presence. Take me or leave me now.'[4]

Dr Schacht organised injections that Julia Farrer could administer and during the winter of 1909/10 Phyllis went to Santa Margherita on the Italian Riviera with Julia as her nurse. She was exceedingly unwell and sent Ernan a pathetic stream of letters pleading with him to set a date for their marriage that summer, saying that it was only this hope that could help her get well. They had waited five years since their engagement, which was long enough. Some of her letters are practical, saying that her parents, following the death of Grandmother Fowler, had inherited some money and could therefore help them set up home. But finally she challenged him directly by writing explicitly, 'If you don't want me you'll have to say so quite plainly like this: "Phyllis I no longer love you!" then I should understand.'[5] Ernan dithered on, avoiding giving her a plain answer until 24 July 1910, when this letter effectively extinguished all hope:

> I do love to know that I have your love ... And I do feel that we shall sometime – somewhere – come together again. But I don't want it to be now – I don't think we should be happy ... I needn't tell you how much I realise I owe you – or how much I hope you will be better and free always for your work – you know that.[6]

Phyllis was grief-stricken and terribly humiliated. With supreme irony, it appeared that when Ernan finally left her and she would have been only too happy to die, her health slowly started to return. That spring, when Julia had to return home, Lislie and Uncle Kennie came out to join her, and they travelled by easy stages to Lake Garda. Some German ladies they met *en route* encouraged Phyllis to try the spa at Bad Nauheim, north of Frankfurt. Her parents could now afford such pamperings, so gave her their blessing. Even though, on arrival, Phyllis was still sufficiently ill to have to be carried to the baths, after a couple of months she was remarkably restored to health.[7]

Phyllis's various doctors now agreed that so long as she could spend the winter months out of England for the next few years, she might have a reasonable chance of a full recovery. Both of her parents joined her for a Swiss tour, and when William went home, Daisy stayed on with Phyllis at Vevey on the slopes of Mont Perin. When Daisy finally returned home, remarkably, the Edwardian straightjacket of chaperonage that had previously been rigorously insisted on, and which had made the courtship of Ernan and Phyllis so complicated, was suddenly abandoned. Whether the Bottome parents simply assumed that, at twenty-nine, Phyllis was an old maid who had missed her chance of marriage when Ernan escaped, is hard to say. But it is the case that Phyllis went back to the familiar Hotel Metropole in Santa Margherita alone. There 'deprived of the two greatest intimacies of my life, I felt unable to take more than a superficial interest in those around me; but with increasing health, I managed to keep at bay the icy sense of inner loneliness from which I had not recovered.'[8]

Phyllis, however sad, was an extrovert and could not stay locked in herself very long without taking an interest in those around her. She made several new women friends, but the most significant new friend of this period was a man who had a haunting physical resemblance to Ernan, albeit, at thirty-four a much more experienced and worldly man.[9] Charles Paul Frèrejean was a charming young French pianist, probably a man with no great depth, but he quickly appealed to Phyllis's tender heart by describing how he was trying to recover from a nervous breakdown. He told her that as a boy he had been sexually abused by a priest, and that his father had killed himself in a *maison de santé*; he himself was terrified of inheriting the same tendencies and gave Phyllis his revolver to safeguard. On a lighter level, during the course of an animated conversation with him about Shelley, Phyllis realised that these 'were the first ideas I had exchanged with anyone for months'.[10] They decided to write a book together, with Paul providing the French background out of his experience as chief accompanist and private secretary to one of the world's most famous retired singers and the most famous of its singing teachers.

Paul, though not destined to be her new great love, was extremely important to her at this juncture. Above all, he persuaded her to be adventurous; they went to Rome together and then to Capri, not as lovers, but as fellow-workers. It is clear that Phyllis did the lion's share of the writing, but at least he introduced her to a world where the sun shone, artists and writers lived in bohemian casualness, and homosexual as well as heterosexual partnerships pertained without comment or scandal. In fact, his casual attitude to sexual matters – he was almost certainly bisexual – went some way towards softening her still somewhat judgemental views, although she continued to dislike overtly effeminate homosexuals. She found herself living a life in Italy in a more bohemian society than she could possibly have enjoyed in England.

The three months that Phyllis spent in Rome and Capri, Lislie spent in Davos, sending a letter each week keeping them in close emotional contact. In January came news that Lislie had an admirer, a soldier, twenty years older than she was. However, after Lislie had fallen in love with Wyn, he told her that he had a wife and three sons, although his marriage was a hollow shell. Phyllis, perhaps influenced by Paul, was quick to advocate John Stuart Mill on divorce: 'He was stiff reading, but convincing; and he burned through and through with respectability and release.'[11] But Wyn had no private means, and a divorce would impact badly on his military career. When they arrived together in Capri, Paul was amazed that Lislie would not sleep with Wyn, any more than Phyllis would agree to sleep with Paul, even though she was attracted to him: 'How you mismanage these things, you arrogant Anglo-Saxons! ... Nature arranges one thing – and you arrange another – and then you are surprised that it hurts!'[12] Wyn sorrowfully departed back to his family, and when Lislie's Aunt Lou Gwatkin came out from Cambridge to join the two women, Paul decided that it was time for him to move on too. Their joint book, *Broken Music*, was finished. But before leaving, as she wrote in her autobiography, Paul

> said to me, 'I have never asked it of you, but *now* I want to see a photograph of that ghost who has stood between us – all these months. Please show me this Ernan, to whom you were – for an eternity – engaged!'
>
> I had destroyed my photographs of Ernan, even those Mamma had given me; all but one which I could not bring myself to destroy and this I now produced from the bottom of my trunk, where I had kept it hidden so that no one should think I had not fully recovered from my broken heart.[13]

Many years later, after Paul had committed suicide, Phyllis wrote, 'He was indeed a strange being, full of delightful superficial qualities and apparently endless charm, but as hollow as a meringue beneath it. I must say he did me a wonderful intellectual turn, for which I shall never fail to feel deeply grateful to him, although it was not exactly what he set out to accomplish.'[14] From Paul's point of view, he had failed to seduce her, admonishing her for what he called her 'cold, intellectual gaiety', but Phyllis's gain was that he had made her feel a sexually desirable woman again.[15] Following Ernan's rejection this was significant: 'Paul's affection for me ... had helped to restore my courage ... I no longer felt robbed of all feminine attractions.'[16] Indeed, he was driven to propose marriage, but this she could not contemplate.[17]

Overall, Paul had done her a good turn; he had, among other things, made a European of her. Like Ernan's Mamma, he did not approve of her style in hats. On one occasion, he 'seized my best hat, tore the trimming out of it, and rapidly proceeded to make a far smarter new one, by turning the trimming upside-down and cutting the hat in half'.[18] He did his best too with her clothes, attempting to transform her from a gauche Englishwoman into someone looking *mondaine*. But, importantly, he had provided a point of reference and a motivation for her to take up her writing career once more. *Broken Music,* although not deeply serious, indicates that no matter what her personal troubles were, she could always turn the materials to hand into saleable work. She described it as a 'bridge book' and she felt that she had moved – in the course of the three months she spent with him – from an amateur to a professional writer.[19]

Broken Music was an experiment in style, and it has a new freedom and energy that makes reading it an invigorating experience. It was written by a technique of absorbing and recounting Paul's experiences and using his memories for a *mise-en-scène* of which she had no direct experience. In her Preface she wrote that 'the actual characters are not, as children say of fairy tales, "true", but many of them belong to that system of parallel cases which runs side by side with the truth.'[20] The novel is largely the story of an innocent and musical young man, Jean D'Ucelles, leaving the French countryside and facing the entanglements and corruptions of Paris. Madame Torialli is the *femme fatale*, who finds that male secretaries who are simultaneously lovers serve her interests well. Jean finds a position in an *atelier* that specialises in exploiting rich young women with poor voices, finding them jobs that should have gone to poor women with good voices. Some of the book works rather well, though the representation of the French working-class girl is somewhat unconvincing. Paul himself had so much more experience of older sophisticated women-lovers than of young innocent ones that it is hardly surprising that Phyllis's second-hand representation is a bit more Mimi from *La Bohème* than wholly convincing. A character whom she succeeds in bringing vividly to life, however, was an invention of her own – Romain, an upper-class *flaneur* – successfully Gallicised by Paul. Century & Co. expressed tentative interest in publishing, but only if she would change its ending – Phyllis originally had Jean D'Ucelles departing for Russia without a love interest, resolved to follow Music as his Muse – or write a sequel. Determined to earn money, she wrote the sequel in three weeks, bringing the neatly conceived Romain and his nephew Jean D'Ucelles to London, where French assumptions about relationships clash with Anglo-Saxon ones. *The Common Chord*, as the sequel is called, has, once again, a plot driven by competition for Jean between a diva – on this occasion a ballerina – and an intelligent young Englishwoman. The two books taken together are sometimes derivative, but even at this early stage in her writing career there is a keen note of observation that strikes the reader as 'true'. Jean is described as 'not by nature a vain man; he was more dangerous to women than that, he was intuitively perceptive'.[21] This seems a likely enough description of the real-life Paul. The literary critic, Nicola Humble, has made the case that some 'middlebrow women's fiction of this period indulged in a curious flirtation with bohemianism'.[22] This observation seems to fit not only how Phyllis was writing here, but also reflects her bold experiment in lifestyle. Living freely as one artist among others, no longer chaperoned in Edwardian style, was an unexpected liberation.

Shortly after this Uncle Kennie asked his great friends, Lilian Beit and her sister Marguerite Carter, to invite both Phyllis and Lislie to visit them at the spa at Bad Nauheim. In spring 1911, Phyllis was due to go there for her 'final' cure; her doctors now considered that, although she should stay out of England for the four worst months of winter, she could probably spend eight months a year there without undue trouble. Although Phyllis and Lislie were initially rather nervous about meeting such grand folk, these sisters swiftly became their most loving and generous friends. At the smartest hotel in Nauheim:

> We found, sitting upon a sofa, shoulder to shoulder, two of the loveliest young women of our time. The Carters had originally come from Virginia, but after the disaster of the Civil War, their suddenly impoverished family had broken up, and one branch of it had moved to New Orleans. The deep south was in them, with its sense of privilege, its high acceptances of obligation and its exquisite courtesy.[23]

In 1897 Lilian had married Otto Beit (1865–1930), a Jewish financier; it was a match which the Carters considered a terrible *mésalliance.* However, after his older brother Alfred's death in 1906, Otto retired from business and devoted his energies to philanthropy, for which he would be knighted in 1920. No doubt this shift in status helped the Carter family to overlook what they perceived as his 'unfortunate' Jewishness. Phyllis and Lislie were to enjoy many invitations to the Beits' London house in Belgrave Square, and to their country house, Tewin Water, in Welwyn, Hertfordshire. Beit was an unassuming and reserved man who unostentatiously became an art connoisseur and collector. Up to this point, Phyllis herself seems to have had traces of unexamined anti-Semitism common to her class, but her friendship with Otto Beit stopped this in its tracks.

Lislie's family finances, unlike those of the Bottome family, were getting worse. She made up her mind – as she was not a writer like Phyllis, who could write anywhere – that she simply must get a job at home. She became a secretary to an American lady, who was struggling with her sight and needed a daily companion. In the winter of 1911 Phyllis went to Valescure alone, and stayed at the Hôtel des Anglais. There she edited and rewrote *The Common Chord*, dedicating it to 'My Friend and Comrade Charles Paul Frèrejean'. Almost her only friend was a Lady C who was such an inveterate gambler that she had been removed from Monte Carlo by her family and was maintained as a sort of cosseted prisoner in Valescure. The other guests were terrified of her, but she liked Phyllis, primarily because Phyllis was an excellent bridge-player. Lady C asked Phyllis to accompany her to tea at the villa of her friends Colonel Call and his wife. This was meant as a treat for Phyllis as Colonel Call's wife, Laetitia, was the daughter of Shelley's friend Edward Trelawney. But Colonel Call was a close relative of Ernan's, so Phyllis felt that it could only be an embarrassment on all sides and declined. As she herself had written about her young hero in *Broken Music*, 'Jean began to discover that it was not very easy to give anyone up. He had always considered memory a pleasant faculty belonging to the old; he found now that it was a relentless spirit which pursued the flying soul even of the young.'[24]

Uncle Kennie, apparently no longer so hidebound by convention, joined her for the last few weeks of her stay at Valescure and towards the end of March Lislie was able to join Phyllis for a month in Venice, because Lilian Beit had given her the necessary money as a present. They stayed at La Calcina on the Zattere, the *pension* where Ruskin used to stay. They visited Isola del Deserto, the island of St Francis, where he had founded a convent. Phyllis wrote a short story inspired by this visit, and already, her sure sense of place makes the story shine before our eyes:

> It was a sunny morning, and I was on my way to Torcello. Venice lay behind us a dazzling line, with towers of gold against the blue lagoon. All at once a breeze sprang up from the sea; the small feathery islands seemed to shake and quiver, and, like leaves driven before a gale, those flocks of coloured butterflies, the fishing boats, ran in before the storm. Far away to our left stood the ancient tower of Altinum, with the island of Burano a bright pink beneath the towering clouds. To our right, and much nearer, a small cypress-covered islet. One large umbrella-pine hung close to the sea, and behind it rose the tower of the convent church.[25]

The story is of Brother Leo, the youngest of the Brothers, all of whom have taken a vow of poverty. They live simply on fish they have caught, vegetables and figs that they grow, and black bread, or a little macaroni in the winter months. All the other monks have lived in the world, except for Brother Leo, who was adopted by the monks as a child when his parents died of cholera. He had been content until a day spent at the lace-making island of Burano had shown him the poverty that makes people unhappy, and he wonders whether he should go out into the world to try to help. The Father Superior feels that before he fully commits himself to a life as a *poverelli* he should have one day in Venice, to see if he would indeed prefer a life in the wider world. Leo marvels at St Mark's and at the Bellini *Madonna* in the Frari, but he is shocked at the sight of beggars amid so much wealth. He cannot understand why the rich do not simply share their money with the poor. At the end of the day he decides to return to his fellow brothers, as he has decided that: 'if money had been the way to save the world, Christ himself would have been rich. It was stupid of me. I did not remember that when He wanted to feed the multitude, He did not empty the great granaries that were all His, too; He took only five loaves and two small fishes; but they were enough.'[26]

This story was the first of many that Phyllis's formidable agent James Pinker sold to the *Century Magazine*, and it marked the beginning of her acclaim as a much-loved writer in America.[27]

By the turn of the twentieth century the professionalisation of the literary market was fully in place, because of the development of international copyright acts during the late nineteenth century. Consequently, the literary agent had become a major player, acting as mediator between author and publisher in arbitrating and evaluating literary property. Pinker had begun his career as a reader for a publishing company, and then set up as a literary agent. His skill in negotiating rights and contracts for authors in both the American and British markets made him one of the leading literary agents of his time. Although he represented authors with established careers such as Arnold Bennett, Henry James and John Galsworthy, he also sought out untried new talent, such as someone like Phyllis, and went out to do battle for them in the marketplace. With Pinker as her agent, Phyllis was beginning to find her feet professionally.

On this trip to Venice, it was Lislie, rather than Phyllis, who was faced with decisions of the heart. Wyn had suffered another lung breakdown and desperately wanted to see Lislie again. Phyllis thought that such a visit could only result in a horrible upset and advised her not to meet him. Two years later Lislie would read of Wyn's death in *The Times*, and Phyllis would guiltily wish that she had not interfered.[28]

For eighteen months, Phyllis and Lislie had saved to spend a winter in Rome, and in 1912 they were at last able to fulfil this dream. Almost immediately, however, Lislie became ill with 'Roman Fever',[29] complicated by her weak lungs. On the doctor's advice they moved to a hotel at Frascati, and a concerned Uncle Kennie came to join them for a month. There they met the painter Lady Butler (Elizabeth Southerden Thompson, 1850–1933), who had trained at the Female School of Art in South Kensington, London, and had had to study the naked male at a private life class, before achieving fame as a painter of battlefields. She talked to Phyllis and Lislie about these feminist struggles and the freedom women needed if they were to be creative.

> The subject was one that Lislie and I had been discussing all winter long, without having come to any positive decision. 'If there's one thing', Lislie used to say, 'that I hate more than a suffragist, it's an anti-suffragist!' Deprived of half our years in England, and limited by ill-health, I suppose we should not have been able to play an active part in the struggle even if we had understood it. We knew no one who fought on either side, and as the newspapers were in the hands of men – sometimes highly skilled and intelligent men – we saw only one side of the question.[30]

Whereas, encouraged by Uncle Melvill, they both considered themselves feminists, their key interest was in the higher education of women and the opening of all careers. They were afraid, however, that the suffragettes' political aim might harm that objective. But Lady Butler convinced them that getting the vote was the key to all freedoms.

She was the sister of their favourite poet, Alice Meynell, and she invited them to meet Alice in London in June.[31] Alice held Sunday-afternoon gatherings, to which they had open sesame after their first meeting. She, like Lady Butler, was a staunch supporter of women's suffrage. Due to the proximity of their ages, Phyllis, not surprisingly, became closer to her daughter Viola, who was a novelist. Phyllis attended these afternoons as a professional writer; indeed she had the same agent as Alice Meynell. In this circle she met and became friends with the novelist May Sinclair, who was about twenty years her senior.[32] May and Phyllis shared a love of the writings of the Brontë sisters, and saw their heroines as pioneers of modern feminism. Their other connection was that May had earlier been a protégé of Lislie's beloved uncle, Henry Melvill Gwatkin, and, similarly to Phyllis, had been the beneficiary of his informal tutorials.[33] Like Phyllis, May had not had a great deal of formal education but had found it where she could. After she had been only a year at Cheltenham Ladies' College, her father's shipping business became bankrupt and her life dramatically changed. She, too, had experienced the death of siblings: she had nursed four brothers dying from inherited heart disease. May was a member of the Women Writers' Suffrage League and her novels frequently centred on the sexual difficulties women faced, as well as the social and political ones. At a party given by May in her flat in Edwardes Square, Kensington, which Phyllis found rather dull because the guests were 'both earnest and apathetic at the same time', she had one sudden pleasure. May introduced Phyllis to her protégé, the young American poet Ezra Pound:

> he made the impression on me of an electric eel flung into a mass of flaccid substances. Physically he was a tall, slight, nervous young fellow, with the face of a scholarly satyr, red-gold hair, and a pointed beard of the same colour. Leonardo da Vinci might have used him equally well as a model for a cynical Christ with his eyes open; or for a spiritual and not wholly covetous Judas. Ezra was an intensely uncomfortable young man, even to himself, but he was most stimulating. He never sat still for a moment; he endangered every chair he sat on: he had a most irritating staccato voice, and a short unnecessary cough which he wielded like a weapon.[34]

Ezra had come to Britain specifically to meet W. B. Yeats, whom he admired greatly, though later he became a greater fan of T. S. Eliot. He was an ardent propagandist for the new in contemporary writing, trying to convince Phyllis that she must bring her mind forward. In his London years, Ezra could be described almost as the stage manager of the emergence of at least one branch of modernist literature. As Helen Carr phrases it, he was a 'flamboyant poet and polemicist, already viewed by literary London with mingled amusement and alarm'.[35] Ezra felt that Phyllis was lagging at least a quarter of a century behind his ideas; he accused her of being 'a modern without a foundation; and a romantic without a roof!'[36]

Whatever else, he gave her 'the first unbiased and objective literary criticism' she had ever received and which she never forgot. Ezra taught her:

> [1] A work of art is the honest reproduction of a concrete image. Imagination is the faculty which finds out every fact about this image, and never the revelation of the feelings aroused by it.
> [2] Why are you not content with saying that a man stepped intentionally on a kitten? Surely it is not necessary to add that he was a humane man?

> [3] If you think rightly you will act rightly. It is never honest to have a thought that does not become a part of your experience.[37]

Although Ezra criticised Phyllis's work, he also helped her career by getting her stories placed in *The Smart Set*, a monthly magazine founded in 1900, of which he was a sub-editor.[38] One of these was 'Rose', in which Phyllis's eponymous heroine was a straightforward young English girl who meets an amoral and louche Frenchman, Leon, drawn closely from her experience of Paul Frèrejean. After marriage they go to Capri, where he almost immediately engages in an affair with a married woman. Unexpectedly, Rose outwits the machinations of her more sophisticated husband, and takes him back rather than running home to her family in Somerset. It is worldly in the sense that sexual infidelity does not capsize the marriage, although there is a 'moral' ending, in the sense that marriage to a good woman is offered to modify the behaviour of the erring husband.[39]

It was one of the most attractive aspects of Ezra's personality as a young man, this zeal in rushing to help anyone whose work he admired, but who he thought needed 'modernizing'. Phyllis also wrote what she thought one of her best stories, 'The Liqueur Glass', under Ezra's influence, a deceptively simple tale where a bullied wife decides to murder her husband:

> Henry's idea of marriage was very direct; he knew that he had done his wife an enormous favour. She was penniless and he had the money; she was to come to him for every penny and all she had was his as a matter of course. She could do him no favours, she had no rights, and her preferences were silly. It had occurred to Mrs Watkins in one awful moment of early resentment that she would rather be bought by a great many men than by one. There would be more variety, and some of them, at least, wouldn't be like Henry.[40]

This early short story was – much later – to be chosen as one of her best twenty-five by her friend Daphne du Maurier in the year that Phyllis died (as was 'Brother Leo'). As du Maurier wrote, 'When she chose this form she did so deliberately, knowing that her thought could be transmuted in no other way, for only in this sudden brief exposure to the light could the essence of her idea be captured.'[41] Indeed, her short stories are exceptionally resonant, and if Ezra Pound helped her towards this cryptic pared-down style, then we owe him a debt of thanks.

Ezra also influenced the way she wrote *The Captive*, which Phyllis described as 'the first of my novels which really became mine'.[42] This may seem like a contradiction in terms, but she means that not only had she internalised his three golden rules, but also she had found her voice. In particular Ezra advised her to avoid padding, but instead to allow events to stand for themselves, without too much authorial explanation. He probably still thought her hopelessly old-fashioned, but there was a sense of development in skill in this novel.

The Captive was dedicated to her sister Mary and published in 1915 by Chapman and Hall. In it, a young society woman called Rosamond Beaumont decides that she wants to be an artist rather than marry one of the suitable young men from their set that her mother is hoping for. She persuades Maisie Brent, a painter living in a studio in Rome and working for a living by selling her paintings, to let her come to stay. Rosamund is selfish in an unreflecting way, hardly noticing all that Maisie does for her, and not realising when her beauty captures the heart of the Irish painter, Pat, whom Maisie loves, that she has 'robbed' her kind friend. Maisie's friends resent the intrusion of this worldly creature, but Maisie defends her blithe unawareness, arguing that Rosamund's whole life 'has been a kind of smothering'.[43] The marriage to Pat is doomed. Rosamund has no talent, and her art teacher, Mammelli, after trying his best to teach her the terms of art in dicta very similar to those that Ezra Pound had given Phyllis, tells Rosamund that she is hopeless and must give up painting. However, what is worse, she does not value, because she does not have even the talent to recognise, the genius of her husband Pat; she would prefer him to paint fashionable items that would sell well and allow her to live comfortably: 'Rosamund didn't mind fighting. It was to her, indeed, the natural condition of things between a man and a woman. She didn't want Pat as a comrade; for comradeship, if she wished it at all, she still went to Maisie, but she liked an opponent to live with, an opponent who was in love with her, and whom she could reduce, from time to time, to an amenable semi-slave.'[44]

Disillusion sets in; Rosamund's smothering family reclaim her.

Following a divorce, after a decent interval she marries her first suitor, the one her mother had thought right for her all along. Mammelli, the art teacher, pronounces, 'She is a captive, that is the price they pay – these Princesses who cannot see.'[45] Although Maisie the independent woman is clearly the heroine of the story, the one Pat comes to recognise as his soulmate, sympathy still exists for the young woman from a conventional upper-middle-class family who had made a brief break for freedom but could not shrug off her innate need for bourgeois comforts.

Phyllis at this time also had a less challenging and, for that reason, a more comfortable friendship with the Irish writer Ethel Colburn Mayne, fifteen years her senior, who had written biographies of Byron and of his wife. She had also written a handful of novels that had fallen out of fashion and said to Phyllis, 'You and I … are like St Paul. We are born out of due time; we can't belong to the Edwardians – we're too truthful – and yet we aren't callous enough to be modern! So we must just stay where we are.'[46] This is an interesting point in view of Phyllis's uncertain posthumous reputation; she is not easy to categorise as belonging to one specific group of writers. But it does not relate accurately to Phyllis's sure-fire response to the specific *zeitgeist* of the times she lived through.

In contrast to her flourishing professional life, Phyllis's domestic life remained fraught. At the parental home in Swanscombe, things had long been tense; George was busy preparing to become a chartered accountant in London and was rarely at home. He had recently become engaged to Marjorie and was looking for a home for his new bride. Phyllis's father became increasingly ill from prolonged bouts of bronchitis, and his doctor blamed the dust-laden air from the nearby cement factory. His friends had shrunk to the small flock of parishioners whom he had served for fourteen years, and his most significant relationship was with the district nurse who looked after him with a tender attachment entirely missing in Daisy. In the rainy summer of 1912, too ill even to escape dull care on the golf links, he resigned his parish, and the Bottome parents moved to Bromley in Kent. Much to Daisy's jealous anger, into a nearby street moved the devoted nurse, so the home was hardly harmonious. William died aged sixty-one on 26 May 1913, having just read Phyllis's 'Brother Leo' in the *Century Magazine* as almost his last conscious action.

A newspaper obituary alerted Ernan, who sent Phyllis a letter of condolence via her publishers, suggesting that as their engagement had so long been broken, they might meet simply as friends. Phyllis was immediately thrown into a state of turmoil; she had not, *au fond,* ever stopped loving Ernan and was not at all sure that she could simply meet on the basis of friendship. At first she did nothing. In September George got married and this too was announced in the newspaper. On this occasion, Ernan sent her a spray of white heather and lilies of the valley; it may be noted that in terms of the Victorian practice of choosing flowers for what they symbolise, the flowers he sent indicated that 'wishes will come true' and 'return to happiness'.

Phyllis was at this time buckling under the weight of her mother's expectations. Daisy had made it clear that when George married she would rely on Phyllis to be her 'guardian angel for the rest of her life'.[47] But not only had she tasted freedom, by this stage Phyllis's feminist ideas were increasingly in conflict with what her mother saw unequivocally as Phyllis's duty. Ironically, her older sister Mary escaped these expectations precisely because Daisy disliked her so much. Phyllis, advised to spend her winters abroad, took her mother to Rome, and had a dreadfully gloomy time. Daisy was not interested in all the art treasures, not did she wish to engage with fellow travellers:

> It was during this interminable and sunless winter that I had finally to admit to myself, my discovery growing in painfulness with my understanding, that my mother refused, and would go on refusing, the two things on which my heart was set – human fellowship and the pursuit of the imagination. My social activity horrified her; my work-life she brushed aside, as she had my father's. What she wanted, and what she failed to get, was a nurse-companion sufficiently delicate to share all her exclusions. What she got instead was a creature active as dynamite, who wanted to exclude nothing that adventure prompted.[48]

Phyllis resigned herself to living with her widowed mother, but made it a condition that they should live in London, so that she could take up her place more fully in the literary world. They moved into Brunswick Gardens near Kensington Palace, whereupon Daisy insisted that she was too delicate to suffer visitors. Ezra, in particular, was outraged that Phyllis should feel obliged to live with her mother and be governed by her whims like some kind of domestic slave, and he urged her to escape. Surely, he challenged Phyllis, she did not want 'to go down to posterity as an example of filial piety'?[49] But, despite chafing under her mother's passive-aggressive regime, Phyllis still saw it as her obligation, while simultaneously being wholly out of sympathy with her mother.

As Phyllis could rarely offer hospitality at her home, this limited her encounters with fellow writers to occasions in other people's drawing-rooms or in restaurants. At least this meant that Ezra introduced her to delicious meals at the Tour Eiffel restaurant in Percy Street, off Tottenham Court Road, and at Belotti's in Soho. Ezra was bohemian, flirtatious and charming, and Phyllis delighted in their meetings and their conversation. But Lislie was almost as threatened by Phyllis's new intellectual friends as Daisy, afraid that Phyllis would leave her behind. So between them Daisy and Lislie restrained Phyllis from taking full advantage of 'living among the youngest and keenest minds of my day and sharing their adventurous outlook'.[50] Although, conversely, as she was to concede later, if she had stayed with Ezra and his crowd, 'I should have lost the larger life I was to have in Europe and the deepest of my human relationships.'[51]

So, what had been happening to Ernan in the years following his bid for freedom, swept up in the wake of Frank Lascelles' grand ambitions? Although he had not immediately broken off their engagement, it had seemed inevitable that their long-distance relationship could not survive. Phyllis was not paranoid in regarding Frank with alarm. Frank had been very close to Ernan's older brother, Ralph, when they were both at Oxford. Even Ernan's mother had warned Phyllis about him, telling her: 'Frank ... is selfish and I don't trust him. He was bad for Ralph and he is worse for Ernan. Be very careful that you do not let him spoil your lives.'[52]

Unsurprisingly, Phyllis at first took this warning as simply an example of Mamma's dislike of any rival for Ernan's affection. However, she also had a trace memory of seeing him when she was fifteen, in Bournemouth. Her friend, the senior curate at St Peters, without explanation, had refused to introduce her. She remembered him as gorgeously handsome, with 'large brilliant blue eyes, chestnut curls and the carriage of an emperor'. He was a brilliant actor, and in many ways his finest role was the one he invented for himself. He had enormous flair and drive which ideally suited him for his career as pageant-master. When invited to run the Quebec pageant he had naturally regarded Ernan, who spoke good French, as his perfect aide-de-camp, and this had led, at least in part, to the end of the engagement.

The background was this. In 1904, Earl Grey, the Governor General of Canada, had been under:

> instructions to do whatever he could to bring Canada more closely into line with British thinking on imperial defence matters, and on naval policy in particular ... The problem as he formulated it had two facets: Canada's lack of self-esteem, and French Canada's indifference to the empire ideal. Canada needed some kind of symbolic representation of its nobler self as a nation in order that it might escape the petty internal disputes that made any wider involvement in the world contentious.[53]

Initially, Louis Parker, the originator of history pageants, had been approached to stage a pageant as part of the tercentenary celebration. As he was already committed, they had turned to Lascelles.

In Quebec, Frank had found a divided town: the French-speaking and English-speaking communities did not get on. His speech to the assembled burghers of Quebec was a plea for 'greater sympathy and a greater pride in your common heritage'.[54] Grey enlisted Lord Strathcona, a Canadian businessman and politician, to head the Canadian financial appeal, and he himself led the way by making a thousand-dollar contribution of his own. There were huge difficulties in raising the money, and some elements of the Canadian press persisted in believing that Frank and Ernan had been making a small fortune out of the pageant in surreptitious ways. This is especially ironic as Ernan would be in debt for years following his unfortunate entanglements with Frank's affairs.

Frank had great powers of persuasion; he had theatrical vision, and an astute sense of what he needed to bring his visions to life. He was very good at charming society women, and quickly drew in the English-speaking contingent, but he needed Ernan's fluent French to tap into the French-speaking network. Once they had charmed the women, the women in turn would persuade their menfolk to contribute money, and even to dress up and be trained to act. And the women organised all the costume-making. Typically, Frank had not factored in the cost of the dresses, and the commissioners had to make good this financial oversight. By June 1908, the wealthy élite and the bishops were persuaded to give full backing, and a cast of thousands had been recruited. Rehearsals were stressful, with Frank barking out orders through a megaphone in English and Ernan repeating them in French. In July the pageant was presented and artistically it was a huge success; Frank was the master of spectacular effects. Somehow Frank and Ernan had managed to pull off a pageant that was simultaneously very French and very Catholic and yet was also acceptable to the English-Canadian section of the audience.

On 29 July, Frank held a party to thank the only paid actors. These were principally Iroquois and Ojibway Indians. They had been an essential and energising part of his pageant, singing, dancing and simulating combat. They presented Frank and Ernan with magnificent headdresses of eagle feathers and decorative pins, watched by two of the society women – Ethel Chadwick and Lola Powell – who had attached themselves to the two men.[55] After the pageant was over, these four went on a journey down the St Lawrence. This seems to have been a rather odd occasion as the more attention that Ernan paid Ethel, 'the more withdrawn and moody Lascelles became'.[56] Frank liked the company of society women, but only when they adored him, and he did not like it when one of his 'disciples' paid marked attention to a woman. As a gay man he did not himself want any sexual dealings with women, but on the other hand he did want to be the gravitational centre of any social group. Ethel was a great flirt, who probably didn't take Ernan seriously; she was also a devout Catholic so it is unlikely that this relationship could ever have become serious. Nevertheless, he presented her with the pin the Iroquois had given him as a memento when they parted, so, despite the fact that he had not formally broken off his engagement to Phyllis at this time, it seemed he had become increasingly detached from her.

Ernan was at this time primarily under the influence of a flamboyant gay man with a magnetic character who seemed effortlessly to attract and hold court to a circle of devoted 'disciples'. Phyllis's earliest letters expressed her distressed sense that Frank was a kind of Pied Piper, ineluctably drawing Ernan away from her. Writing on 16 April 1908 to her 'Little Brush-Wood Boy', she had commented that she felt 'that Frank is a big sponge that absorbs him all and leaves her a few chill rivulets down her spine'.[57] But it remains an open question as to exactly how she interpreted Ernan's devotion to Frank, and whether she wondered why she was being demoted from fiancée to friend. Certainly, Ernan would know only too well Phyllis's intolerance towards homosexuality. She had, early in their relationship, castigated him for recommending *De Profundis* to her, claiming that it was 'black' and 'perverted' and that Oscar Wilde's apologia killed souls.[58] There had seemed no possible meeting of minds between them in this area. It is also the case that to be a practising homosexual was a criminal offence under the law, and a successful prosecution could lead to penal servitude with hard labour. In the 1890s, Oscar Wilde had served two years in gaol and had ended up bankrupt. Homosexuality laid men open to blackmail and, although, especially in public schools, a blind eye might be turned to experimentation among adolescent boys, generally it was regarded as a 'sickness' that boys should struggle to 'grow out of'. Thus there was a lot at stake.

When, in 1911, Frank and Ernan were back in London organising the Pageant of London as part of the Festival of Empire and Imperial Exhibition held in the vast grounds of the Crystal Palace, Phyllis did not dare to attend, even though she would have been one of thousands and the chance of bumping into Ernan would have been negligible. She was too heart-sore to risk meeting him, so she missed one of Ernan's triumphs, albeit with Frank Lascelles' name on it as Master and Ernan's merely as Secretary. The pageant was in its way magnificent: made up of four parts staged over three days, it involved fifteen thousand voluntary performers recruited by borough in over forty scenes. There was a military band and a choir of four hundred voices. In the Crystal Palace grounds were three-quarter-size replicas of the overseas dominions' parliament buildings, containing exhibitions of the wares of each country. The pageant was hugely successful; one commentator said, 'Though we have books, we have them in excess, and the value of the pageant, in such directing hands as those of Frank Lascelles, is that it picks out great events for us, makes them alive again, and impresses them on the mind.'[59]

What Ernan had not told Phyllis, when she was pushing him to marry her, was that during the course of these adventures with Frank, his financial affairs had become almost irrevocably sunk. As Phyllis described it later:

> The Festival achieved all it set out to do, on a scale of the utmost magnificence, although its guarantors had to be called on to the full. Two unforeseen financial burdens were forced upon its producers. One was the great transport strike, which involved the cancellation of heavy provincial bookings; and the other was the death of Edward VII in 1910, just before he was to open the Festival. This not only caused fresh expense, but a year's postponement.[60]

Frank, however, was so cheered by its splendour that he now promulgated a grand plan for an Empire Theatre Project, which he believed could support and strengthen ties between the Commonwealth dominions. To his own financial detriment, Ernan did two years' unpaid work on this project, persuading influential people whom he met to invest in it. But the potential investors in England insisted that Canada should make the first investment, and the death in 1914 of Lord Strathcona, who had promised to underwrite the share capital, therefore brought an abrupt end to the scheme.

Out of the Pageant of London experience, a new and significant friendship arose when the seventeen-year-old Ivor Novello was employed to compose some of the music.[61] Ivor's 'Mam', Clara Novello Davies, a singing teacher in charge of the Welsh Ladies' Choir, had promoted Ivor's career from his birth. She was certain that he was a musical prodigy and in this she was proved correct. In 1903, Ivor had effortlessly passed an exam to enter Magdalene College School as a chorister. His boy-soprano voice was superb, and he was almost immediately given all the solos to sing in the Chapel Choir. He was also exquisitely beautiful and frequently in trouble. In December 1907, the Dean of Divinity at Magdalene had complained to the parents of three of the choristers about their sons' inappropriate behaviour.[62] One of these three was Ivor, who had been caught in the chapel behaving inappropriately – clearly a euphemism for some kind of sexual behaviour – with another boy.[63] As one of his many biographers comments: 'Ivor was conducting romantic liaisons with his fellow choristers, some of them quite as handsome in their fresh-faced youth as he was, and all of them desperately attractive in the pretty gowns. Eighty years later one of his choirboy lovers could still remember Ivor's irresistible methods of seduction. No one that he knew of, he recalled, had ever said no.'[64]

But, probably because of his overt homosexual behaviour, the school would not give Ivor a bursary to continue his education and he left 'under a cloud'.[65] This must have seemed like a sudden ejection from paradise. As his parents could not afford to send him to university, he made a scrappy living from giving piano lessons and composing and writing songs; in 1910, he managed to get two songs published, 'Spring of the Year' and 'The Little Damosel'. Ernan, to do him credit, immediately recognised Ivor's enormous talent and had great hopes that he would become a renowned composer. Phyllis wrote later that Ernan:

> himself deeply musical, yearned to see Ivor become a future Schubert or even Mozart, and urged him towards serious musical composition, but a strange flaw cracked the jewel of Ivor's composer talent. The more he concentrated upon the technique of composition, the swifter the power and sweetness of his melodies evaporated. Something within himself winced away from the intricacies of construction. He made music as a bird sings, not as a thinker thinks. His was the genius of the troubadour.[66]

Frank Lascelles, now an internationally acclaimed pageant-master, was busy rushing round the world, to Cape Town in 1909 and to Calcutta in 1912.[67] He had new enquiries from Toronto and America, and wanted Ernan to set about the preliminary investigations, as even Frank, for all his prodigious energy, could not be in two places at once.

When Ivor's parents' marriage briefly foundered in 1912, he was caught in the middle of their domestic war and ended up excluded from each of their homes: 'Ernan's address was not known to him, but he managed to abstract it from a club porter; and with tear-stained cheeks turned up at midnight on Ernan's doorstep. Ernan was staying in the home of his mother's oldest friends, two *grandes dames* of Norman decent and rigid Victorian conventionality.'[68]

The Miss Malets were not best pleased by this outré behaviour, but reluctantly admitted him overnight. Ernan set about trying to reconcile Ivor's parents, which was no easy task. Ivor persuaded Ernan, or 'The Bear' as he had nicknamed his new friend, to take him along on the exploratory trips to America and Toronto, as the plan was for Ivor to write the music for any forthcoming pageants.

Therefore during the winter of 1912 Ernan took Ivor with him to New York for three months. There they stayed in the Home Club, and met Ricardo Martin, the Metropolitan Opera tenor, and his wife, who lived at the Club. They also met the actress Constance Collier, then in her thirties, with whom, much later, Ivor was to collaborate. Ivor had a wonderful time in America and Canada; he was away from quarrelling parents, with a man nine years older and thus able to look after him, whose company he adored. All of the friends Ernan had made on his previous Canadian trip welcomed his protégé, and under Ernan's guidance, Ivor began to write in a more disciplined way. He wrote an operetta called *Fickle Jade*, which, although never published as a whole, had within it some songs that would become moderately successful. It is clear that Ernan hugely enjoyed his role as aide-de-camp to both Frank and to Ivor, both of whom had enormous talent. However, his prolonged negotiations with financiers trying to establish Frank as master of a potential Toronto pageant came to nothing. Much money had been expended and none was immediately returning.

In the spring of 1914, and living in London, Ernan and Phyllis began to see each other once again, notionally just as friends. It was an uncomfortable period. Phyllis had long since ceased to be the centre of Ernan's universe, as she had been when they first met. His home was now Frank's mock manor house at Sibford Gower, near Banbury, a country retreat created with 'a history fashioned from his own imagination [and established as] a memorial to his mother'.[69] The house fabricated the past quite as much, albeit in a different way, as did the pageants. Frank had turned the barn into a huge medieval-style hall with a minstrels' gallery at one end and a huge pipe-organ. Undoubtedly, this was a homoerotic environment; there was overwhelmingly 'a sense of male pleasure in the physical presence of men, or even sometimes in their spiritually or ethically masculine qualities'.[70] Frank had studied Greats at Oxford, which had licensed him in a kind of philosophic exploitation of Platonic ideas to justify close and loving relationships with boys.[71] Frank always liked young boys around him, and his man-servant, Ewart Bodfish, the son of his gardener, accompanied Frank in his travels. Frank's self-creation as a fantasy lord of the manor could certainly be described as an extravaganza of camp sensibility, upwardly mobile in pretension. Not only his pageant-making but also the Shakespeare plays he put on in his *faux*-Elizabethan garden gave endless opportunities for dressing-up and cross-dressing.

When Ernan and Ivor had returned to England in 1913, the professional orientation of them both was towards the liberal, tolerant milieu of the theatre. Ivor moved back in with his mother, who had taken a flat in the roof of the Strand Theatre at Number 11, Aldwych, and there he pursued his dreams of becoming a great actor-manager like Herbert Beerbohm Tree. Ernan himself took drama lessons with Rosina Philippi and appeared in several small parts at the Old Vic. There was a certain irony in all this, in that Phyllis had originally trained to be an actress, but ill health had prevented her from pursuing this career. Now it seemed that it would be Ernan at the centre of the theatrical world. He was also, according to Phyllis's autobiography, 'emotionally involved in the sentimental attachment of two devoted women. The elder was wildly in love with Frank, the younger with Ernan.'[72] She does not name them, but these ladies were Lady Jane Kenny Herbert and her daughter, Ora. Some society ladies were permitted into Frank's charmed circle and he adored them rather as he did his mother, especially if they dressed exquisitely. These women were, of course, doomed to disappointment if they deceived themselves into thinking that Frank might marry them. Ernan was another matter; and at this time he seems to have been equally emotionally involved with both Ivor and Ora, whom he saw as two pet lambs needing his protection. The whole of this circle wished to keep hold of Ernan and not lose him to Phyllis. A terrible competition for Ernan's loyalty took place. There seems a question, at the very least, about Ernan's sexual orientation in this epoch. He was living in what David Cecil describes as the 'heavily perfumed atmosphere of homosexual flirtation', but an admirable insouciance towards homosexuality does not of itself prove that Ernan was himself a practising homosexual.[73] It has to remain an open, if intriguing question.

While all these micro-politics were ongoing, in the larger world there were more ominous developments. The old empire of Austria–Hungary maintained an enfeebled, but still oppressive sway. On 28 June 1914, Archduke Franz Ferdinand, heir to the throne of Austria–Hungary, and his wife, the Duchess of Hohenburg, were assassinated by a Serbian nationalist while driving in an open car through the streets of Sarajevo. Despite conciliatory messages from Serbia, Austria–Hungary at once declared war on Serbia, the beginning of a chain of events that led to the Great War. On 29 July Russia started to mobilise troops; Germany responded by threatening to mobilise unless Russia demobilised within twenty-four hours. On 1 August, Germany, because her ultimatum had been ignored by Tsar Nicholas II, declared war on Russia. On 3 August, the Kaiser declared war on France. Germany's invasion of Belgium, in violation of Belgian neutrality, on 4 August, brought Great Britain into the war. The two European camps, the Triple Alliance and the Triple Entente, were brought face to face on the battlefield.[74]

As second in command to Frank, Ernan had spent some years play-acting battle scenes. Now he was to join the real theatre of war.

CHAPTER 4

World War I

With no greater responsibility ahead of him than death, Ernan felt that he could afford love.

PHYLLIS BOTTOME, *The Challenge*

Phyllis was condemned to the role of many women during the First World War. She could only worry over her beloved and wait for letters to let her know that he was safe. Ernan's romantic schoolboy notions of chivalry, and belief in empire, typical of his class, were now brought sharply from fantasy to reality. Ernan bombarded the War Office with demands to be sent to the front immediately, emphasising his proficiency in languages. The War Office set him French and German tests that, unsurprisingly, he passed at A1 standard. In September 1914 he was ordered to report to Marseilles, where he was appointed interpreter to the 34th Poona Horse, 9th Cavalry Brigade, recently arrived from India. Ernan's grandfather, Sir John Forbes, had been a commander of one of its squadrons, the Bombay Cavalry, so he felt both connected to and proud of his family tradition. His rank was that of second lieutenant.

Before leaving England, Ernan passed his last few days with Phyllis and her mother at 15 Brunswick Gardens, and made Phyllis formally his next of kin.[1] After all the vacillating in their relationship, when he headed off for war, Phyllis, rather than his brother or any other close friend, was the person identified as his significant other. Daisy, perhaps surprisingly, had made no objection to Ernan's renewed presence in their lives, despite its undefined nature.

Ernan's early letters to Phyllis sound more like those of a friend than a lover; there are no terms of endearment, more a tone of frank comradeship, and they were usually signed 'Your Trooper'. The Poona Horse

Company was in the trenches at Festubert, although Ernan could not tell her this; all letters home were checked by censors to make sure that no sensitive information was given away. And soldiers were asked to destroy their letters at frequent intervals (in case the enemy overtook their position and could gain some benefit from them). Consequently, only Ernan's letters to Phyllis and not her replies have survived. In the half of the correspondence extant, his letters attempt to be light-hearted and entertaining; they include various tales of his black horse, 'Peter the Hermit', nicknamed because he did not like other horses. There is a series of thank-you letters for things Phyllis sent out to him: a yellow chamois waistcoat, a lamp, spare batteries, a balaclava, cakes, oatmeal biscuits, dates, sardines, plum puddings, cigarettes, muffler, handkerchiefs, rubber wading boots with cork socks inside, Jaeger socks, newspapers, books and a chessboard. Ivor was also sending out gifts to Ernan: toothpaste, shoelaces, shaving soap, cocoa and matches.

But despite Ernan's attempts to avoid burdening Phyllis with distressing information, the difficulties of life at the front could not be entirely hidden. One of Ernan's jobs was to keep the dressing station running, using horse-drawn ambulances. His work involved burying the dead, cutting the muddy clothes off the injured soldiers so their wounds could be dressed and sending hopeful cases on stretchers behind the firing lines to the field hospitals. In November 1914, he wrote to Phyllis: 'I am glad that you will never see what I saw … after a time I found I couldn't talk to anyone – I could only have cried.'[2] And in another letter, he wonders: 'What was it really for? Was there anything to be purchased at such a price that the world could afford to buy it? If Kings and diplomats could pass a night in a crowded dressing station could war take place?'[3] Ernan worked alongside Gurkhas, Sikhs, and Pathans, as well as the British tommies, in trenches filled with foul black water, in some places knee-deep or even waist-deep, because the clay soil trapped and held the rain.

He spent much of his energy and time, up to six hours a day, finding and buying food, firewood and coal and getting it up the lines on mule carts. As Phyllis was to write to her publisher many years later: '… I get on very well with animals, though my husband is even better. They used to give him in the Army all the ill-tempered mules and horses to handle because he immediately found a good relationship with them.'[4] The reality of war turned out to be a long way from the noble fantasy of imperial pageant. So much of his time was spent in provisioning everything – from camp beds, files and boots to mineral water – that he thought after the war he might easily embark on a career as a house agent or house mover. His language skills were crucial as he foraged and acted as interpreter for two squadrons, and he was permanently semi-exhausted.

Back in Britain in 1914, there was initially a comfortable assumption that the war would be over by Christmas, but the retreat from Mons put paid to that illusion. Phyllis's sister Mary left for Egypt with her great friend Margaret Sampson, who did voluntary work in the East End of London and was deeply involved with the Anglo-Catholic Movement of the Church of England (she later became an Anglican nun, under the name Sister Margaret Clare). The two women were trapped in Cairo for the duration of the war. Phyllis's brother George, now happily married to his Marjorie, was in France, according to Phyllis, undertaking 'an arduous war job'. She does not define what it was, though possibly he was using his accounting skills for some purpose.[5] Both Lislie and Phyllis felt that they must make some contribution to the war effort in the ways that women could, although neither of them was strong enough to volunteer for nursing or landwork.[6]

Lislie at this time was working each morning as secretary to a West End doctor, Dr Des Voeux, usually referred to by his initials as DV. Following Germany's invasion of Belgium on 4 August 1914, trainloads of Belgian refugees started to pour into Cannon Street Station from Dover. DV acted as treasurer of the Fund for Belgian Refugees, so Lislie was able to add to her responsibilities by keeping the books for this fund. Less fortunately, perhaps, Lislie fell in love with the clever Irish doctor, who was married to an invalid wife. Although DV had no intention of leaving his wife, he had lots of love affairs and would willingly have included Lislie on his list of inamorata, but she was not willing to betray his wife.[7] It is interesting to note that although Lislie twice fell in love, first with Wyn and then with DV, in both cases there was an insuperable problem that prevented the relationship being consummated. Considering these cul-de-sac relationships, it is hard not think that Phyllis, more than any other human being, was the real love of her life. There seems a strange synchronicity in that although notionally Ernan and Phyllis form the heterosexual dyad, in each case there was, in effect, another 'beloved' – Ivor in Ernan's case and Lislie in Phyllis's.

One curious note is that, around this time, Lislie sent a sample of Phyllis's handwriting to a graphologist and this was the report.

> The writer has hypersensitive feelings quickly excited and emotional. All externals affect her, owing to her keen sensibility. This makes her suffer more than she need, & perhaps heightens her pleasure, though pluck and despondency seem to be having a tussle. She is too much swayed & governed by her feelings, so, though clever in several directions she does not regulate her powers to the best advantage. She is very affectionate and sympathetic, is capable of tender, devoted attachment, will be demonstrative and might be jealous. There is enough self-love to make her try to look after her own interests; but she has a generous outlook, is inclined to extravagance, & also to an impulsive benevolence; is probably imposed upon.
>
> The writer is go-ahead, & often precipitate in speech & action, though prudence is always tugging as an afterthought. She should try to be more deliberative. Her mind shows some originality, bright ideas flash into it, but her thought is not sufficiently clear & analytic. She has imagination & sentiment & a full power of language … [8]

This analysis seems a remarkably accurate assessment of Phyllis's personality at this time.

Phyllis herself was stationed at Hammersmith Town Hall, which had been charged with looking after three thousand Belgian refugees posted to the Hammersmith and Shepherd's Bush district. She wrote in her autobiography:

> My part of the job was to find – and keep – the Belgians suitable lodgings, to translate for them in difficulties, and to take them to hospital when they required medical attention. I had to deal with any incidents that turned up on my visits – shocked or irate landladies were the form that these incidents usually took … Some of our problems came from dubious passports, some from secret funds

> while claiming grants; and among our very fine average of industrious and decent workers there was a handful of remarkably black sheep. I had several memorable interviews with the police about these tough propositions.[9]

Phyllis worked eight to ten hours a day, and Ernan's letters frequently urged her not to work too hard with her 'Belgees' but to stick to her writing.

After eighteen months she was rescued from this exhausting job by John Buchan (later Lord Tweedsmuir), who, in February 1917, was put in charge of the foreign propaganda section of the new Department of Information (renamed the Ministry of Information at the end of the war).[10] His department was an annexe of the Foreign Office and 'its business was to collect information on the political situation and the trend of feeling and opinion in the different countries'.[11] Although Buchan cultivated the persona of the gentlemanly amateur, in reality he was 'a tough and professional propagandist'.[12] He made a distinction between news and literary propaganda and a key focus was on the importance of Anglo-American relations. Phyllis worked for him for two years, and many of the things about propaganda that she learned at this period – for example, the use of writers, and of war-artists and filmmakers – were to prove a significant preparation for her future activities in this field during the Second World War.

Despite the almost daily letters passing between Phyllis and Ernan, there was still no defined relationship between them. In early March 1915 he spent time with Phyllis, greatly admiring her new fawn hat, but he also spent an equal amount of his leave with the Sibford Gower friends. On his return to duty, Ernan was appointed ADC to General McAndrew and was moved to the St Quentin area, where he acted as paymaster for the billeting of troops. Phyllis used her Department of Information influence to get a travel permit to share with him his one-week leave in the Boulevard Arago, near Montmartre in Paris, *chez* the McCord sisters. Writing to thank her for the wonderful week, he signed it 'Your Trooper's Love', but he also apologised for his horrible restlessness. Ernan managed at various times to spend some of his leave in England with Phyllis and Lislie, once at Tintagel (just before Phyllis starting working for John Buchan) and once on the Sussex Downs. Slowly they were reforging their relationship: in March 1916 Ernan wrote to Phyllis to say that 'what we want is a good long quiet time together – which we haven't had at all since we have reached our present state of development'.[13] They managed a few days together at St Ives in April 1916, during which, among other things, they had an intense conversation about religion. Phyllis no longer had any time for organised religion, whereas Ernan was still searching for a set of beliefs with which he could feel at home. He was writing seemingly contradictory letters. On the one hand, he was saying that he had 'failed in and muddled everything' and had 'only bankruptcy to look forward to'.[14] On the other hand, he was telling her, 'I could get three weeks leave, by getting married! If the war isn't over by end of September it must be considered.'[15]

Ernan's involvement in Franks Lascelles' affairs remained a huge area of difficulty; he had run through his inheritance from his mother and was deep in debt from acting as guarantor for Frank's various pageant and theatre schemes. He was being chased by solicitors' letters, which might easily have rendered him bankrupt. (Frank's insouciance towards money matters meant that he himself was to end up bankrupt and to die in poverty, although this was a long way in the future.) Although Ernan's affairs were in a sorry state, he at last had the wit to put them in the hands of a competent Scottish solicitor called William Fairchild Greig. Greig promptly set about organising a coherent and realistic repayment scheme.

On Phyllis's side, things were improving financially. In 1916 her novel *Secretly Armed* was published in England where it received hardly any reviews, but it was accepted as a serial under a new title, *The Dark Tower*, in the *Century Magazine* in America and there it was a huge success. She therefore, more optimistically, saw Ernan's financial problems as thoroughly irritating but not something that should stop them from moving towards marriage. However, Ernan's fierce Scottish pride made it hard for him to accept the notion of having his debts paid off by Phyllis.

Phyllis's breakthrough novel, *The Dark Tower*, is in part a fictionalised version of Lislie's aborted first romance with Wyn, a man who had told her, rather late in the day, that he was married. In the novel, the hero, Winn Staine, comes from a family where all the men are in one or other of the services. He is a thirty-five-year-old major who has served long years on the Khyber Pass and is a natural leader of men. Unfortunately, he does not really understand women and so is easily fooled by a pretty kitten-like creature whom he marries without really knowing her. The Staines family are drawn with superb comedic strokes, though simultaneously Phyllis makes a series of explorations of false and true loves, both romantic and familial. Winn is a man who takes his physical strength for granted and is aghast when diagnosed with consumption. Going to Davos for a cure, he meets a young woman with whom he falls deeply in love, and his love is reciprocated. His code of honour requires that he should not harm her reputation, though this is represented as a severe struggle for them both. Ultimately, he is rescued from his emotional cul-de-sac by the start of the First World War; once again he is with his men, in a situation he understands. Phyllis sent out draft versions to Ernan, so that he could check her trench-warfare scenes for accuracy; consequently, after some corrections by him, they have the ring of authenticity:

> It came very quickly and confusedly toward dawn. The silence was rent across like a piece of torn silk. The crash of bombs, the peppery, sharp detonation of rifles broke up the sullen air. Out of the dark, vague shapes loomed, the trench filled with the sound of deep breathing and scuffling, and the shriek of sudden pain. Death and mud and darkness closed together. It was all over in half an hour, the attack was driven out, and the men moved uncertainly about, trying to discover their dead, and relieve their wounded.[16]

It is noteworthy that in this novel Phyllis represents the English doctor in Davos as quietly picking up intelligence about what the Germans were up to, and equally quietly passing it on. This detail may well be due to insider knowledge from the Department of Information. As usual, everything that Phyllis observed in her life was turned swiftly into fiction.

This is also true of the other novel she wrote during her time at the Department of Information, *The Second Fiddle*, published in 1917, which tells of a young woman, Stella, working in a town hall as secretary to the town clerk. Stella works so hard that she become indispensable to her boss; as she says, 'a secretary is a kind of second fiddle'.[17] The details of eating in cheap cafés, full of Belgian refugees, where the ham sandwiches were so horrid that the taste needed disguising by mustard, all have the ring of authenticity. The realism of this part of the writing is in slightly uneasy contrast with the depiction of Stella's romance with the upper-class Sir Julian, an injured war hero (more precisely he has suffered injuries as the result of intelligence work undertaken immediately before the war). But as usual, she investigates the complexities of love; Julian's pride – he has been crippled – gets in the way of his accepting Stella's love, which he views as the sacrifice of a girl who does not know what it means to love a man. Stella retorts that he must learn to regard women as human beings, not merely creatures to be protected: 'Human beings have a right to their own risks. They know their own mind, they share the dangers of love!'[18] It is hard not to see these novels as, among other things, a way for Phyllis to express to Ernan her own position: the society woman the hero falls for first is always revealed to be an empty vessel morally, while the heroine is always a working woman in some form – an artist or an office worker – and they always take the moral high ground. It could be regarded as wooing by stealth.

From about June 1917 there is a series of letters from Ernan, which – among other things – seem to indicate that Phyllis was pushing him towards a decision on marriage. He is trying to face up to her request for certainty:

> I have spent every night going round the outposts – examining wire – machine-gun posts – observing – taking other officers round. I have dug for vegetables in deserted gardens to save the mess bill – and it is all to no purpose – the cursing is more complete and bitter. The gen[eral] refused to touch his breakfast and his lunch one day and then nearly died of rage! ... Your letters make things possible – I feel like a man in a fever, your letters are the cool drinks which keep him in touch with life! ...
>
> I must say the thought of a cottage and a garden and a piano with

you, all unplanned and unfurnished, is at the moment the most attractive possible prospect – but then I never know about myself – at the end of a month some horrible restlessness might make me unbearable.[19]

It seems likely that she sent a pretty cross letter to him about the situation his indecision leaves her in, as he reply sets out his position more frankly than romantically:

I doubt if anything short of feeling it an over-riding necessity should persuade one to 'take the risk' [of marrying] – I mustn't do it because you want it – I must do it because I want to – and you must do the same – the risks vanish according to the intensity of the wish – I quite understand that – Well, I don't see as many risks as I did – I can say that. Don't ever think I am unconscious of the awkwardness of your position with your Mother, your friends, the annoyance of waiting for decisions from vacillating neurotics – of course I am conscious of all this – but it is what I try to forget – because I don't think it should have any weight in the matter really – I don't intend to marry you to make you more comfortable – I want it to be the most selfish thing I've ever done.[20]

Meanwhile, the war continued unabated. In October 1917, Ernan's adored brother Fred had been badly wounded in his side, and one of his oldest friends, Douglas Hope, had been shot and blinded. Pushed by Phyllis to stop shilly-shallying, Ernan finally decided that he would use his next leave to see all his friends and relatives and to tell them of his decision to marry her. Phyllis feared that his family would once again unite against her, and she also knew that there would be strong opposition from the Sibford Gower group. This was not paranoia but an accurate assessment of events. The Forbes family, related as they were to the Duke of Atholl, had a strong sense of their social standing, and it is clear that they regarded Phyllis as not quite what they would have liked for Ernan. She was not 'gentry' but a woman who worked for her living. Aunt Emily began her interview with Ernan by telling him that she thought he had decided to marry largely because he had been depressed by Douglas Hope's condition, and that he had become afraid of disablement and poverty. She reassured him that she and Aunt Katie (his mother's sisters) would never let him want; they had no idea, however, how deeply in debt he was.

The Sibford Gower folk were utterly horrified at the news of Ernan's impending marriage. Initially there was silence; Ernan wrote to Phyllis in September to say that he had still had 'no news of his two poor lambs whom he has left unshepherded and abandoned'.[21] By his two lambs, Ernan meant Ivor Novello and Ora (Doreen Kenny Herbert), to whom his renewed relationship with his ex-fiancée came as a complete shock. Ernan had been living his life in separate compartments, and the collision was painful. He felt like a criminal and was utterly wretched, which can hardly have been reassuring to Phyllis. A bizarre exchange of letters then occurred between the key players. Phyllis wrote to Ora, to see if they might be friends. A letter from Ernan to Phyllis followed:

> Ora asks if I shall mind her not writing to you – I shall of course say 'no' – but she hadn't had your letter which was as perfect as anything could be – as you say it is pride that can help one a little – she wrote very frankly and generously – but my plans went wrong and she could not get in touch with Ivor who was away for the night – and she was terribly worried about him – I feel as if I should never get over it or feel quite the same again – as though I had fired shells into my own compound – but I know I shall – If only whatever pain I have given them may be weighed out in happiness to someone else. But they seemed so helpless – Ora has so little in her life – Ivor cannot deal with pain of any kind.[22]

Ernan continued in his effort to persuade Phyllis not to be so 'rigid' in her lingering dislike of camp homosexuals.[23] Unfortunately, Ivor blindly hit out at Phyllis by sending Ernan a very unpleasant letter about this forthcoming marriage. It was addressed to Ernan, but somehow Ernan managed to include it in one he sent to Phyllis. It is the sort of accident that might have interested Freud, but, in any case, Phyllis was horrified by the content of Ivor's letter. Essentially, Ivor accused Ernan of marrying Phyllis out of a false sense of duty, because he had been stringing her along for too many years to be able to retreat with honour. All of this indicates that Ivor believed that in some sense he possessed Ernan, though at this distance in time it is not possible to tell whether the irresistible Ivor had ever sexually seduced Ernan. In a way, it is irrelevant, but what is clear is that Ivor was 'broken hearted' when Ernan insisted that he intended to marry Phyllis.[24]

Certainly, at this stage in his life, Ivor no longer *needed* Ernan as he had when he was a teenager. Financially, he was far better off because one of his songs, 'Keep the Home Fires Burning', published by Ascherberg Hopwood and Crew, had become the anthem of the First World War and had earned him fifteen thousand pounds.[25] When Ivor went to the front as a member of a concert party, it was this song that the troops called for more than any other. Undoubtedly this was the best kind of war work he could do. In June 1916, he had enrolled to be trained as a pilot at Chingford, but, although looking incredibly dashing in uniform, he twice managed to crash planes. In fact, he was so utterly hopeless that his friend Eddie Marsh, Private Secretary to the Prime Minister, hurriedly suggested that Ivor would be more useful for propaganda purposes and got him transferred to the Air Ministry in London.[26] Indeed, Ivor had by now several friends who were far more powerful and influential than Ernan. It may not be coincidental, however, that it was in the same year that Ernan announced his renewed engagement to Phyllis that Ivor fell in love with a young actor called Bobbie Andrews. Although Ivor had many lovers – Bobbie would stay by his side for the rest of his life.[27]

Perhaps to reassure Phyllis that he really did intend to marry her this time, on 17 October 1917 Ernan sent her a cheque for an engagement ring, which he hoped would be an emerald set prettily. Lislie rushed about and managed to find just such a ring for her. But money troubles were still strongly in Ernan's mind; he implored her not to put an advertisement in the *Morning Post* about their forthcoming wedding: 'It would mean bills and misery and precipitated bankruptcy! My address here is unknown, as it is I live in oblivion – but advertise me shamelessly and they'll buzz round – that was the beauty of being married abroad.'[28] After the long years of waiting, Phyllis could hardly have been pleased that, whatever the stated reason, Ernan wanted their wedding to be a sort of hush-hush affair.

Nevertheless, encouraged by Lislie, and despite an air raid, she bought material from Marshal and Snelgrove to be made up by a good dressmaker. She was to wear 'a terracotta costume with a long coat, a velvet picture hat of a darker shade, and an apricot chiffon blouse with hand-painted butterflies on it'.[29] In October she set off for Paris to stay with the McCord sisters at their apartment on the Boulevard Arago to await Ernan's marriage leave. In wartime, the bureaucracy for serving soldiers' marriages was simplified. All that was needed, as Ernan had explained to Phyllis, was 'to write to the Secretary in Foreign Affairs asking for leave to be married without notice or residence in Paris – they wire "yes" to the Consul and whenever we roll up we get married – no licences, no nothing'.[30]

Phyllis left an England that was half-starved to arrive in a frozen Paris. She wrote that

> Betty and Maida were able to procure only a few green sticks for a fire, and the gas we cooked on at the lowest of pressures was only turned on for three and a half hours a day. As the bitter winter progressed we went to bed at five o'clock to keep from freezing. A shell dropped from Big Bertha every quarter of an hour, preceded thirty seconds earlier by shrieks from two clipped seagulls, who shared our garden.[31]

The only formality that remained was for Ernan to be granted marriage leave, but all leave was suddenly cancelled because of the Battle of Cambrai, the British effort to penetrate the Hindenberg Line.[32] This last delay was not Ernan's fault, but at this point Phyllis must have remembered one of Christina's Rossetti's poems, 'The Prince's Progress', a study of infirmity of purpose in a dilettante bridegroom, and wondered whether she too might die still waiting.[33]

Finally, however, Ernan got his leave and arrived in that dark December the day before the wedding. A blizzard struck the city and the long-awaited bridegroom finally appeared, powdered with snow and carrying a bough of white lilac, an interesting choice as, in the language of flowers, lilac symbolises both love and reluctance. Nevertheless, Phyllis, who had waited a full twelve years since their initial engagement for this moment, was irrepressibly ecstatic. She did not care about a wedding reception, but Maida insisted that there must be one, and rushed Phyllis around trying to get as much food as could be mustered in wartime: 'Maida and I walked though [the snow] on pavements like rivers of ice. One of us fell down every few moments. I do not know what Maida felt; but my sensations were those of complete invulnerability; it was as if I walked on air, and fell, when I had to fall, on a substance softer than a cloud.'[34] Betty and Maida stayed up all night decorating the studio and organising the best wedding feast they could manage.

On New Year's Eve 1917, aged thirty-five, Phyllis finally married her first and only love. Phyllis described the wedding day:

> We began to get married very early in the day at the Mairie in the apache Quarter, swept there by friendly Americans in a big car. This was followed by a second civil ceremony at the British Consulate on the right side of the river, and we finally wound up with a celebration in the Embassy Church, still lavishly decorated in red and white flowers for Christmas. It was New Year's Eve and though all day long it poured with icy rain, I felt as if it were a day in June. It was a pity, we thought, that we could not go on being married in order to prolong the sensation.[35]

As Lislie had been refused a passport, Maida took on the role of bridesmaid, and Betty acted as Best Man. Discovering, on the way to the Consulate, that Ernan had not bought Phyllis a wedding ring, she dashed off and managed to locate one, thrusting it into Ernan's hand seconds before the crucial moment.

At midnight the newly married couple boarded the Riviera Express to Hyères but ran into a snowdrift at Valence that held them up for twelve hours. However, the ever-resourceful Betty had provided a picnic basket with *pâté de foie gras*, sticks of bread, chocolate and a superb bottle of wine, a Château Yquem 1870. Before the wedding a series of discreetly worded letters from Ernan indicates that Phyllis, still a virgin, had raised some questions about sexual matters. Her mother was not the person she would have turned to, as Daisy had always made it clear that sexual relations were distasteful. Ernan advised Phyllis not to worry about it, saying simply that 'it is the old question of not allowing things to overstep their limits'.[36] He suggested that she should go to see a Dr Niall in Arlington Street, opposite the Ritz Hotel, presumably for sexual information and possibly for contraceptive advice, as there is some discussion in the letters about temperatures for douches. Honeymoons where one of the pair is uninitiated can be grizzly affairs, yet it seems, after all the delays and uncertainties, that the honeymoon was a delight. As they travelled south, the snow melted:

> Next day at sunset we found ourselves under a sky of sapphire and apricot, and heard the chattering of palm leaves. Night dropped on us as we drove to Hyères, out of a sky blown clear by *mistral*, and furnished with enormous stars. We had been given Queen Victoria's former drawing-room at the Hôtel Costabelle, a magnificent apartment full of crimson brocaded furniture, with a big balcony overlooking sea and garden.[37]

Phyllis's description of her husband is telling. He looked, she wrote, 'like the prince out of a fairy tale … five foot eleven in height, broad shouldered and slender waisted … With great physical strength, Ernan united extreme gentleness of manner.'[38] The most revealing comment of all is that, after the honeymoon, when Ernan had to go back to the front after their three-week honeymoon, she felt bereft: 'I had never had my nature fulfilled before [so] had never known so blank a sense of frustration.'[39]

Ernan returned to his job as aide-de-camp to General McAndrew, and Phyllis stayed on in Paris with the McCord sisters so that she could be as near to him as possible and could share his leaves when they came. None of this suited Daisy; she had expected the marriage to take place in October and for Phyllis to come back to live with her immediately after the honeymoon. Instead Phyllis stayed in Paris, trying to finish her novel, which was to be published as *A Servant of Reality*. Very few women writers had the necessary direct experience to write about war; they were more likely to write about the gulf that opened up between the men who had been in the trenches and their families back at home. It amounted almost to a new genre for women's novels.[40] Started before her marriage, it had initially focused on the feelings of a prisoner of war returned to his homeland. The novel starts with an interesting psychological study of a young surgeon who had been previously self-confident and somewhat aloof. However,

Captain Anthony Andrews had been a prisoner of war in Germany for two years and on his return to England he was suffering from what we would now call post-traumatic stress disorder.[41] At dinner the first evening back in his parents' home he becomes disturbed when his father asserts that the Germans are not human beings, and answers: 'It's very funny your saying that, Sir … They struck me as very human always, and very like some of our own people. It occurred to me that we might be treating Germans just the same, if we thought of them what they thought of us. I often used to wonder if we weren't. War makes people's minds untruthful.'[42]

Anthony slowly comes to terms with the horrible experience of war and achieves – painfully – a new moral code.

In each of Phyllis's wartime books, it seems as though it is England itself that exerts a healing process on the stricken returnees, and this novel is no exception:

> Every morning he woke at dawn to listen to the country sounds. The earth stirred at three o'clock in a faint, grey light – a light which was like the mere absence of darkness. All the birds moved in their nests at its approach, and shook out a sleepy protest before they sank into their last short sleep. A wind sprang up suddenly and passed across the fields with a faint shuddering of shaken leaves; sometimes a brief shower fell, a hurrying small shower, leaving behind it the sweetness of the visited earth … Anthony drank in the sounds of life, the little regular country sounds, with a quickened sense of reassurance and returning energy. The mildness of England sank into his being, not all at once, and not with the ecstasy he had expected, but at last it came.[43]

Following her honeymoon, Phyllis found that her original impetus in writing the novel had shifted. She tries to imagine the kind of woman who might attract her hero and describes her as half tart and half luckless innocent. To some extent her entry into the narrative distorts the focus from the prisoner and his progress in returning to useful life as a doctor. Nevertheless, Phyllis 'uses' her sexually promiscuous heroine to provoke questions about the double standard operating at this period:

> The female sex was permanently divided into two classes: those who 'did' and those who 'didn't'. It was assumed that the women one met in 'decent' society' lived on a plane of such exalted virtue that the slightest allusion, however obscure or oblique, to the functions of the body was an insult; and it was equally assumed that elsewhere, on another plane, was a class of women who were not so ethereal and not so restricted in their conversation.[44]

It was permissible – especially in wartime – for men to consort with women from either 'class', but no woman could move freely across this divide. Indeed, once a woman got a reputation for being fast, society was quick to condemn. Phyllis attempted to tackle this in the novel.

Although Phyllis was rightly not entirely convinced that she had wholly succeeded in pulling together the two 'halves' of her novel, it received respectful coverage. The *Times Literary Supplement* of 30 October 1919 remarked that even the title indicated that the book was gloomy, but recognised that Phyllis was tackling the way war recast identity. The Century Company always issued novels with vivid illustrations, so that all their books were appealing as material objects. *A Servant of Reality* quickly became a best-seller.

Phyllis was highly suspicious when a Hollywood film called *Dark Victory* appeared with a script she felt was wholly lifted, without acknowledgement, from her novel *Secretly Armed*. She took legal advice and only reluctantly decided to let it go when advised that a suit might cost a fortune and there was no guarantee of winning. This experience, though extremely frustrating, may have given her the first intimation that perhaps one day she might be able to negotiate screenplay rights for one of her novels.

In this new hopeful period, Phyllis was eager to have a baby. Ernan was more doubtful. In a detailed letter sent in February 1918, he laid out the cons and pros, in that order, once again adopting the slightly odd third-person way of speaking about themselves that was characteristic of many of their letters:

> a) Risks are of course her health at the time of having a babe – the normal risk one accepts – with her the special one owing to heart and

lungs and possibly the old troubles & operation she had when 14 or 15 ... Her age will be against her of course

b) Then comes the risk of permanent invalidism for her – and perhaps more or less giving up her work – Will there be enough money for her to be properly looked after & the Babe in this case? He mustn't be counted on as it is war-time & anything might happen to him

c) She says it is favourable in some ways – the time of year – her present health etc. – against that come the troublesome times we live in – the question of actual food conditions for her – air raid anxieties and general strain.

As to pros:

a) the joy it would be to her to have a Babe – I cant estimate this but I take it that Nature would not clamour so loudly without some corresponding satisfaction arising for carrying out her desire. The whole thing hangs on this – for I do not care a hang what I go through if it is worth while to you – I mean if it is a tremendous thing to you to have a babe – it is worth a corresponding risk to both of us – It's not worth while risking death (of pain I say nothing – I know her courage) & forfeiture of health and work, unless the gain is a supreme one

b) there is always the possibility if things go well of a great gain to her health

c) if anything happened to him; he would be very happy to think of her not alone.[45]

Ernan made it clear that he felt he now had everything he needed in her, and did not want a baby for his sake. He went on to say that it was imperative that she should take medical advice before any decision was made. It seems that Phyllis did this immediately and was advised against it, because only two days later, a commiserating letter from Ernan says:

He's so grieved for her – if she's sad over the dashing of her hope – So far as he's concerned he must wickedly confess to finding an exceedingly great relief! Not that he wouldn't most gladly have

> shared with her every kind of hardship to get what she wanted … But all the same you know almost anyone can have babes & hardly anyone can make books.[46]

To Phyllis the months after the Battle of Cambrai were the most depressing months of the war. In Paris she and the McCord sisters could hear the guns when the wind blew that way, and knowing that Ernan was not very far away, but facing appalling dangers, was hard. Every day the papers published devastating casualty figures. On Easter Sunday 1918, Phyllis went to High Mass at Notre Dame and the congregation was almost entirely composed of women in black, crying quietly; the few men there were all mutilated ex-soldiers. Phyllis could only thank her lucky stars that Ernan's cavalry division was about to be moved to Egypt, where she felt his chances of survival would be increased. But then she received a great shock; Ernan wrote to say that he had decided not to accompany General McAndrew to Egypt, but instead to join his brother Fred, then Lieutenant Colonel of the King's Own Scottish Borderers, for the spring offensive at Arras.[47] His chances of dying in the trenches would go up exponentially.

Phyllis was horrified, and tried to get him to change his mind; nevertheless, in March, Ernan transferred from the Indian Army to the British Army. She tried to take comfort in the idea that Ernan's older brother would somehow look after him. Fred was the first of Ernan's family to make her welcome, and she had come to love and respect him. That was all she had to hold on to, to keep fears at bay. Almost inevitably disaster struck. In the spring offensive at Arras, Ernan was trying to

> form a defensive flank with a broken and retreating platoon from another battalion. The men had lost their officer and ran past him like broken leaves, blocking the narrow communication trench. The only way of reaching the head of the column was to jump out of the trench and run across the open ground in view of the advancing Germans. This Ernan did and was shot down. The stretcher bearers, who eventually picked him up, wanted to carry him immediately to the dressing-station. Ernan, however, refused and made them carry him to Fred at his headquarters to report on the situation.[48]

On 28 March 1918, Fred sent Phyllis a note from the front:

> Dear Phyllis – You will probably have had a wire before this to say that Ernan is wounded. It looked a nasty one in the side, and I am trying to get news about him but it is hard in these times. He was an old brick about it. The men were full of his praises (they are judges and seldom make a mistake!) He walked down without any help. It was a hard fight and I could not give him the individual attention I should have liked. Let me know your news please.
>
> Your affectionate brother-in-law[49]

On 1 April, Phyllis received a telegram from Lislie's mother, Carita, telling her that Ernan was now in a hospital in London. The Channel ports were closed to any but officials; Phyllis persuaded the British Embassy to give her a letter, authorising her to travel, to give to the Intelligence Officer in Le Havre. She stayed the night with Ernan's godmother, Mrs Dora Delano Forbes (Franklin D. Roosevelt's favourite aunt), then living near the Gare St Lazare, in order to catch the 5 a.m. train to Le Havre. Arriving in the pouring rain, she went straight to the docks to see if she could find a way to get to England. After a miserable twenty-four hours, she managed to get aboard a ship carrying fifteen hundred Australian troops for an exceedingly dangerous thirteen-hour voyage. Arriving at Southampton at night, she was only able to get on a train to London at 6 o'clock the next morning. Lislie met her at Victoria and told her exactly where to find Ernan.

Sir Herbert Samuelson was the chairman and treasurer of University College Hospital. He and Lady Samuelson had bought a house at 58 Grosvenor Street and had refurbished it to include a gold and white ballroom on the ground floor. Once the war started, however, the house was converted into an officers' hospital, with the ballroom serving as a hospital ward. Phyllis found Ernan lying face down, with a wound so deep that 'the surgeon could get his large hand into it', and he was exceedingly weak from loss of blood.[50] Ernan had been admitted there on 30 March, and on Phyllis's arrival all he could say was, 'Why didn't you come sooner?' He had no inkling of the appalling journey she had gone through to be by his side. Ernan had been 'lucky' in that the bullet, which had entered his back just below his shoulder blade, had just missed his spinal chord. Initially he was coughing up blood, because the bullet had scraped his lung, but fortunately had not destroyed it. He had also suffered a gutter wound on his right side, where a bullet had grazed his skin leaving a channel in the flesh, but this was a less serious matter.[51]

Ten days after Phyllis had arrived at his bedside, his condition took a sharp turn for the worse when general sepsis set in and his temperature spiked to 105 degrees. He was delirious and closer to death at this point than at any other time. Thanks to a radical treatment given by Major Stewart, Ernan survived, and turned the corner towards recovery. During the crisis stage, Phyllis visited Ernan every day, but as he started to convalesce, unresolved difficulties inevitably emerged. The hospital-visiting rota was arranged so that the Sibford Gower friends did not have to encounter Phyllis. Ernan had long managed his world by keeping the two sections of his life in wholly separate compartments and he still wished to do so.

The Sibford Gower set, in part society women and in part gay – in both senses – theatricals, who circled round Frank Lascelles and Ivor, continued to cold-shoulder Phyllis. On a day when she was not visiting him, Phyllis wrote instead, trying to make him see that a life in which Ernan effectively lived in two separate camps could not possibly work. She said, in particular, that she was not against Ivor *per se*, but against his efforts to separate them, 'which he would always consciously or unconsciously try to do'.[52] Writing as usual in their odd third-person way, Phyllis pointed out that:

> Ivor completely struck at her outstretched hand – and then ignored her existence – Can there be an intimacy formed out of such materials? And if not – is boy prepared to exclude girl from what he calls the 'deepest intimacy of his life'? – One which includes a different manner of living – and Ora and Jane and Frank? Or is all this to go on in his heart and life *without* her presence – and in active enmity against her? And Boy to give himself to it *away* from her? Oh Darling think *clearly* – *act* clearly ... She is always – His wife[53]

Phyllis was not indulging in paranoia about Ivor's behaviour: she was correct in perceiving him as potentially dangerous. Earlier biographies of Ivor were little more than hagiographies, but in any case would have had to be cautious until homosexuality ceased to be a crime in law. Post-1967 biographies have been more candid about Ivor's busy sexual life; of most interest here, perhaps, is Ivor's seduction of Christopher Hassall. When Christopher married, his wife seemed to have unhappily endured a similar pattern of behaviour to that which Phyllis complained about in the early days of her marriage:

> [Christopher and Ivor's] relationship, a deep and professionally rewarding one, continued after Hassall's marriage and caused much distress to the latter's wife. Ivor would ring up and have long conversations with him while she, unable to avoid overhearing what passed, would flinch at the passionate terms of endearment that were used ... [Hassall's son said of Ivor] 'He had no scruples about taking whom or whatever he wanted, instinctively, and possibly guilelessly, and without a qualm.' So the marriage teetered on from dispute to dispute as Chris, forever torn between Ivor and his wife, could not make up his mind which to choose.[54]

In the end, Hassall's wife felt that Christopher was more firmly married to Ivor than to her, and divorced him. She then suffered a mental breakdown, but Phyllis was made of sterner stuff.

Initially Phyllis thought that if she consented pro tem for Ernan's friends to see him without her presence she would be seen as offering an olive branch to them. When Lady Jane asked if she might call on Phyllis, she eagerly accepted, thinking that this might be the start of a *rapprochement*. When Lady Jane arrived at Brunswick Gardens, Phyllis discovered her to be about the same age as her own mother, and a woman who had obviously been a great beauty in her youth. Phyllis was horrified when Lady Jane launched into an attack, which she described in her autobiography: 'My visitor told me that I had married Ernan under false pretences. He had never loved me and had, indeed, been in love with another member of their circle, and she had every reason to believe he was still in love with her.'[55]

Phyllis discreetly does not name the supposed inamorata, although it must have been Lady Jane's daughter, Ora.[56] Ernan was eventually backed into a position where he had to choose either Phyllis or the Ivor, Frank, Lady Jane, Ora circle. Ernan chose Phyllis, but it was a huge loss for him. Although Ivor would eventually come round to acceptance of Phyllis, the others were irrevocably lost to Ernan.

Older friends of Ernan's, from a completely different set, such as his blinded friend, Douglas Hope, and Seton Henry, had initially been prejudiced against her by the Forbes family, but they and their wives swiftly came to accept Phyllis. Ernan's brother Fred had taken the trouble to go and re-meet Phyllis before the marriage, and no doubt his approving reports meant that – at the very least – the Forbes family could hardly continue to regard her as some kind of adventuress. During Ernan's five-month stay in hospital, Phyllis managed to write and place a whole series of short stories; she was the major breadwinner, and they were still paying off Ernan's debts. Phyllis, as ever, was steadily earning her own living. Phyllis was reassured that the Forbes family had finally come to accept her when they gave her permission to wear a Forbes clan tartan cloak. Indeed, Colonel Lachland Forbes, 'whose crusty manner covered the kindest and most generous of hearts', came to tell Phyllis personally that Fred had been killed in action.[57] This was sure to be a dreadful blow to Ernan, and he thought Phyllis would be the best judge of how to tell him.

After weeks of being made to lie still, until the surgeon could be absolutely sure that his spine was undamaged, things were finally beginning to look positive. Phyllis wrote: 'It had been arranged for Ernan to sit up for the first time. With their usual beautiful consideration the Samuelsons had insisted on his being given a private room, so that he might see me alone for the first time. I found him full of joy that we could be alone together. I knelt beside him, and for a few minutes I could not tell him that Fred was killed – but at last it had to be told.'[58] Indeed, Phyllis could not put off telling him, because he would have seen it on the Casualty List the next day.

By the time Ernan came out of hospital, and despite the fact that he and Phyllis had not been wholly alone together since their honeymoon, they had new responsibilities – Fred's widow Louise, and her two children, seven-year-old Dorothy and five-year-old Nigel.[59] Fred had tried his fortune in South Africa, fought in the South African

War, and then had settled in Southern Rhodesia. The only property Louise owned was a farm in the wilds of Rhodesia, which she was incapable of managing on her own. While considering what best to do next they took up lodgings in adjoining properties in Cornwall, and ran their households in common. Ernan was thirty-four years old and he was still suffering from a war wound that made any movement of his back and chest painful. He had lost one circle of friends, and felt responsible for his widowed sister-in-law and her children. As it was to turn out, Louise, a singularly beautiful young widow, who was inclined to disappear to London rather frequently, leaving her children in the care of the Forbes Dennises, would shortly solve her own problems.

Ernan's wound, although classified as very severe, was not considered likely to incapacitate him permanently. In August 1918, the Medical Board included a note that he would be considered for employment under Military Intelligence when he recovered,[60] but pronounced that he would need six months to recuperate before he could go back to the front. For the rest of the summer, they rented a cottage at East Harting in Sussex for themselves, and for Daisy and her two maids. Lislie visited at weekends, and Nigel joined them for his school holidays. Phyllis was happy with all the people she loved best close to her; Nigel she regarded as the child she could not have herself.

Ernan had decided to pursue formal qualifications in French and German through the medium of a Cambridge extension course; Phyllis was busy writing *The Kingfisher*. She chose the title for her new novel from 'the flash of unmitigated joy passing across our chequered lives, so like the flight of this dazzling and infrequent bird'.[61] Ernan had long urged her to reprint *Raw Material*, but she preferred instead to excavate from it the experiences of working with boys in Swanscombe in order to write a new novel. In it, Jim, a boy born into a working-class family where the father's drunkenness makes weekends an uneasy nightmare, attempts to protect his mother from a beating, but in hitting his father with a poker, kills him. After serving three years in a penitentiary, he emerges at seventeen, and starts to work on a barge, where the beauty of nature starts to soothe his sorrows:

> It was incredible to wake in the early mornings to the easy sliding motion of the barge, and to look into a free world brimming over with light. A buttercup field by the waterside came upon Jim as suddenly as an act of creation, the thick, wet green of the grass loosened to let the light of the flowers through – each cup a glistening yellow world. The elms above the little cups broke in a mist of green parted by sudden breezes, and the sunbeams fell through in shifting showers of gold.
>
> Heavy coral buds on high pink loose strife lined the river banks; the bulrushes whispered incessant secrets; meadow-sweet wound down to the water's edge, spreading its fragrance far and wide. Blue forget-me-nots burned in ardent patches of colour under cool green reeds, and flat-headed, wide, white cups of water-lilies floated out serenely upon the surface of the stream …
>
> Jim left the barge and strolled down the towing-path under the lifting sunbeams. His eyes rested vaguely on a weeping-willow across the stream, when something splendid and vivid, which made him hold his breath for an instant, darted out upon the river. He could not see plainly what it was. It passed in a flash, but he saw that it had wings, and was blue. It was like watching a sapphire tossed from bank to bank in the sun; only this creature was more alive and more entrancing than any jewel.[62]

Phyllis remained in some ways a Romantic writer, describing nature, in similar terms to those of the Romantic poets she loved, as a maternal, even educative force. The novel focuses on Jim's reclamation through education of various kinds, including sentimental education. He becomes a union organiser and wins the love of an upper-class woman, Viola Egerton. Even though this seems a slightly unlikely match, it is true that the Great War broke down class barriers to some extent, and that Phyllis both approved of this and wished to represent this new world.

Phyllis and Ernan had begun to believe that the war would be won before too long, and that Ernan would not have to return to the front: 'Foch was about to make his great united frontal attack, when the Siegfried line was broken, and with America coming into full action at St Mihiel, victory leapt into sight.'[63]

But their peaceful interlude came to an abrupt end when the Medical Board pronounced Ernan fit to return to the front. Once again they were plunged into a state of acute anxiety. At the beginning of September, Ernan was sent to Claremorris in Ireland to join the 3rd Reserve Battalion and train a new draft of soldiers. He wrote to Phyllis to tell her that: 'Louise sweetly gave me boots, puttees and an almost new pair of corduroy riding breeches of [Fred's].'[64] Folk at Claremorris told him how like his brother Fred he looked, and there is a strong sense of his stepping into his elder brother's shoes figuratively as well as literally. He asked Phyllis to send 'my revolver belt – it hangs from the shoulder and has little corrugations on it to hold cartridges – & also Fred's big overcoat which stupidly I couldn't find'. Ernan was still being chased for money: 'a letter from Hill Brothers on September 11 1918 comments, "I'm again asking your attention to our account … we have refrained from troubling you for some time in the matter owing to the present state of affairs, and in view of the fact that you have been on active service." '[65]

On 18 September, Ernan took a test paper and an oral exam in French and underwent various interviews and background checks preparatory to being seconded to the Intelligence Corps. Having successfully passed his exams, at the beginning of October 1918 Ernan was sent out to Intelligence headquarters at Marseilles. When the time came for embarkation, Phyllis went down to Folkstone docks to see him off, and there witnessed an officer broken down from shellshock having a hysterical fit at the prospect of being returned to the front. She wrote: 'It was as if his shame had been taken from him and had become ours.'[66]

She was tremendously relieved that Ernan was not going back to the battlefields. Nevertheless, 'Marseilles was a stamping ground for smuggled goods, sent over the Spanish border, and an international hide-out for spies, who came and went in all directions, usually escaping recognition … Ernan's new job had a dangerous "cloak and dagger" side to it.'[67] His commanding officer was the general of British troops for the area, and, after an initial probationary period, Ernan was confirmed as an intelligence agent and made a captain.[68] He was then directly in charge of forty British sergeants who liased with various French controls to bring in 'intelligence'.

Sailors and soldiers from all parts of the world came into and went from Marseilles, and the docks stretched for miles, so there was endless opportunity for clandestine arrangements. Ernan, although Phyllis did not know this from his letters, always carried a revolver when he left his office.

Military regulations forbade wives from joining their husbands in this sector; there was a fifty-mile exclusion zone, though as Phyllis wryly noted, this did not stop women 'with less formal relationships' achieving immediate right of entry.[69] In France, brothels were well-advertised to the soldiers. Indeed, Phyllis, ever resourceful, turned this into a short story called 'The Vocation', which features an ex-nun turned sex-worker, servicing the troops at Amiens: '[It was] explained that the Government gave certain permits for women of her profession – that the men needed them so much. They came – she told me – out of the battle and murder and hideous danger – wild to forget – forget the sights they had seen, the friends who had fallen, and all the evils of war – they could only forget in the arms of a woman.'[70]

The war was finally moving in the direction of an Allied victory; it had been greatly prolonged by the rough balance between the two sides. Although in 1917 the Allies had seemed on the verge of losing the war, the entry of the United States had provided enough support in the form of abundant supplies and hope of final victory to keep the Allies fighting. Finally, on 11 November 1918, Germany signed an armistice and the war was over. Ernan sent Phyllis a letter saying, 'I can hardly realise that we stopped killing and maiming one another yesterday at 11 o'clock – and that Alsace and Lorraine are French again.' In total, eight million servicemen had been killed; even greater than the huge military losses was the estimated number of ten million civilian deaths, principally from starvation and disease. Everyone hoped that it would be the war to end wars.

Back in England, Phyllis persevered with her writing and was selling stories as fast as she could go. A long-short story called 'The Victim', which she wrote around this period, had as its hero an elderly American inventor who has lost his only son in the First World War. His dearest wish now is to spend his declining years with his younger daughter Elise and her husband in the English countryside: 'Mr Brett had gone on steadily with his inventions and his adaptations, but when he sat under the yew tree and watched the bees in the fuchsia hedge, the sunshine and the flowers had a trick of fading out and leaving in their places a shell-swept muddy hillside under a low grey sky.'[71]

Unfortunately, his elder daughter, Hermione, is determined to wreck this idyll and has built a life of semi-invalidism to inflict her will on her family. She is a monster of egoism, and Mr Brett can only save his younger daughter's marriage by agreeing to live with Hermione in Paris. It is Mr Brett, and not Hermione, who turns out to be the real victim indicated by the title.

It is interesting that at the time she was writing 'The Victim', Phyllis was finally facing the fact that her own mother would be – if allowed – a similar, if more subtle, destroyer of happiness. Daisy was busy complaining to George, that Phyllis and Ernan exploited her for their financial benefit. Phyllis was furious when her brother demanded that she spell out her financial arrangements with their mother. They were utterly straightforward: she paid a pound a week to Lislie to type up her work and a pound a week to Daisy for household expenses, plus she shared the rent on the house. However, she was sensitive about the issue of Ernan's debts, which she did not want George to know about. She was relieved to receive a sweet letter from him reassuring her that he now realised that Daisy had misrepresented the situation. As Phyllis wrote to Ernan, it was not George's fault that Daisy was 'such a "victim" and men get readily taken in by victims'.[72] It is clear that by this stage in her life, Phyllis recognised that Daisy's victimhood was a chosen and malicious role.[73]

In December 1918, Phyllis went down to Sibford Gower to reclaim Ernan's furniture from Frank Lascelles' house, arranging with a removals company to have it packed up and delivered to the house she shared with her mother. Frank was in Canada so she had only to deal with his older, and utterly devoted, sister, Rosa Stevens, to whom, naturally, Phyllis made no critical comments. Lady Jane Kenny Herbert did her best to interfere in these arrangements, because they clearly signalled Phyllis's victory in claiming Ernan's loyalty. Phyllis, however, was in no mood to put up with any nonsense from either Lady Jane or her daughter.

Ernan was still wondering what he would do in peacetime; should he become a commercial traveller, for instance? He wrote to Phyllis, 'so little seems to me really worth while – which I suppose is the worst confession that a human being can make. The steady drive and recurring routine of life, instead of seeming beautiful – appears bleak, blank and unnecessary. Rather like a quicksand which involves you so persistently, that finally you disappear altogether.'[74] Phyllis suggested that he sought advice from his Uncle Lachie about what to do after demobilisation. Lachie advised him that the government was bound to need representatives in Germany and that his language skills would aid a career in that direction.

The two of them could not be together for Christmas, nor for their first anniversary, but Phyllis bought her husband a picture of Hyères for a present.[75] Ernan wanted Phyllis to join him for his January leave, but Phyllis was determined to clear Ernan's debts. Greig told them in February 1919 that if they could raise a lump sum of seven hundred pounds, they could clear pageant debts going back to 1912.[76] Phyllis managed to sell a 'long short' called 'The Worm' – a fairly pedestrian story about two rather weak-willed characters, who eventually marry and between them withstand a bossy one – and that had replenished her coffers to some extent. She was delighted when she managed to sell 'The Victim' to *Harper's Bazaar* for three hundred pounds and thought that if she could just stay put, finish the second half of *The Kingfisher* and sell it for a good price, then they might be in a position to clear all Ernan's debts at one go. And then, as she wrote to Ernan, at last 'we could start life afresh *without* liabilities – it would be such a *heavenly* thing! I feel sure we shan't have a happy moment till we do – because we *can't* spend with a free conscience … also it would handicap you *most* unnecessarily to go though the courts. Once we get the whole thing settled we are free to live where we like … [77]

Ernan was irritated with her response:

Now if you start worrying about 'Jews', I shall at once get a divorce – I only married you on condition that you wouldn't do so! – And you are not to think that you cannot do as you like with your own money until they are squared … if you feel I ought to have done more [to

> pay off debts] even during the war (as I could have in small ways by not taking leaves etc etc) you should have told me so ... the debts were not 'deliberate' – but caused by speculations which always had possibilities in them – until Strathcona died – after which no more were contracted.[78]

Phyllis, however, was resolute.

Ernan's 'job' at this stage was to take part in the kind of mopping-up operation that comes at the end of a war. At thirty-four he still did not know what career he should undertake when this came to an end. Writing to Phyllis, he complained: 'He so hates work which is office & business, and is so unfitted for work which *isn't*, by reason of his lack of education, that he feels unless he leaps into a job at once he will float away to nothing for ever.'[79] Phyllis's preference was to live in England if he could get a good job there because she believed that Louise, Nigel and Dorothy needed them. But, as it turned out, Louise had her own plans. In 1920 she was to marry Fred's best friend, Fitzroy Griffin, and the whole family returned to Rhodesia. Phyllis was somewhat shocked by this, although it is hard to imagine what else a woman untrained for a profession, with two children to support, could otherwise have done. But they also suspected that Griffin, a man with great charm, had a serious drinking problem, and were desperately concerned for the two children. Louise took her daughter Dorothy back to Rhodesia with her, but left Nigel in a little school in her house run by her unmarried sister, Adelaide Bosanquet, with the arrangement that he should spend his holidays with Ernan and Phyllis. This arrangement held for about three years, until Louise sent for him to join her in Rhodesia. During this time, when he was between five and eight years old, as Phyllis said, 'Nigel entered deeply into our hearts and lives ... to me he was the child we could not have ourselves.'[80]

They continued to discuss Ernan's old dream of being a schoolmaster, but for this he would need to prepare himself, perhaps by a correspondence course, for entry to qualify at London University. But Ernan felt sure that it was best to remain out of England until he had cleared his debts:

> Remember you took me with these disadvantages when you married me – no work and embarrassments, so you mustn't expect me suddenly to become a free agent and able to settle where I like ... it is something of a handicap having reached middle-age without real business experience or training or professional qualifications – so please don't expect very much of me.[81]

Most young men of Ernan's class would have gone to Oxford or Cambridge. Ernan, however, had no formal qualifications. Under Phyllis's guidance he had managed to undertake something close to a university-standard literature course during the war. When he was in the trenches, there were days and nights of terrible exhaustion and danger but there were also long periods of inaction and potential boredom. Phyllis endlessly sent him books to fill in his literary 'gaps'. On 30 April 1916, Ernan had thanked her for sending him *Le Père Goriot* by Balzac: 'He fills up the blank places between Shakespeare and Henry James ... '[82] She sent him E. M. Forster's *Howards End*, which he liked even better. Next he read *War and Peace*, Gibbons' *Decline and Fall of the Roman Empire*, Tolstoy's *Anna Karenina* and Voltaire's reflection on *Pensées* by Pascal, and read Flaubert in French. Lislie sent him Yeats's poetry, which delighted him, and Phyllis sent him Donne's poetry too. A career as a schoolmaster had seemed a possibility while he was educating himself in the trenches.

Phyllis's sister Mary arrived back in Marseilles from Egypt on 5 March, and Ernan went to meet her. As Phyllis was determined not to spend money visiting him, he took his week's leave at the end of March 1919 to come to her. Of course, Ernan pressed his wife to return and live with him in France; Daisy did not want to lose Phyllis, and insisted that Phyllis should not abandon her when she was so ill. To be fair, Daisy had begun to suffer from urinary problems at this stage of her life, but weariness with her mother's long-adopted role as a *malade imaginaire* meant that Phyllis's sympathy had run out. Jealous of Phyllis's great affection for Lislie, Daisy had started to be nasty to her. This helped Ernan's cause, because Phyllis reached snapping point. She found Daisy a smaller house in Woking near to George, moved her into it with the help of a good nurse, and that was the end of their common home. Phyllis had reached the stage where she could only feel thoroughly relieved to be free of her mother.

But parting from Lislie was another matter; Lislie was bereft at the thought of their separation. Ever since they first met in St Moritz, Phyllis seems to have held pride of place in her heart. As Phyllis wrote in her autobiography, 'perhaps she had always spared me too much. She stood with her bared heart between me and every threat to my life.'[83] Carita blamed Phyllis for what she foresaw as Lislie's loneliness, and told Phyllis bluntly, 'Your friendship with Lislie has done her a great deal of harm. She has lost her older friends and become intellectual, which nobody likes.'[84] It seems true that Lislie had become over-dependent on Phyllis, something that Elena had tried to warn Phyllis about many years before, but it begs the question of whether Lislie ever really wanted anyone in Phyllis's place. However, her situation was now painful. She had neither a lover, nor a vocation and she was about to lose her most intimate friend.

Lilian Beit and her sister Marguerite Carter with exquisite tact invited their two younger friends to spend their last weekend together with them at Tewin Water. Lislie promptly became ill, having one of her attacks from a lung abscess, and pleaded with Phyllis to stay with her for just another week. Phyllis semi-reluctantly stayed on, feeling as though her 'heart was cut in two'.[85] It seemed more like the parting of lovers than of friends, although with the loss of so many young men in wartime, many women led single lives where a woman friend was their most significant other. Lislie's letter to Phyllis, in effect resigning her claims and handing her over to Ernan, says:

> My own Precious Dear … before I let you go I want to remind myself as well as you, that however long it may be before we materially meet again – there is no real separation, death itself cannot destroy that which never dies; – and that is Love – bodily separation is an ache – and one misses, ah how one misses the daily sweet companionship – but it is not the real separation the separation of the soul – and that can never come between you and me – any more than it can come between you and him.[86]

Phyllis was initially racked with guilt about the 'hollow ache of loving' that she knew her departure meant to Lislie.[87] But she was simultaneously eager to join her husband in their new life. Not stopping in Paris even to see the McCord sisters, Phyllis jumped straight on to a train heading south, anticipating a joyful reunion: 'At last the laggard train fumbled its slow way into Marseilles and I met my punctual husband, who had been waiting for my delayed train for several hours. I found him furious with me. His fury was, as I eventually found, perfectly reasonable and even complimentary – why had I not come before? Weeks earlier I was free to come – and hadn't.'[88]

Perhaps not surprisingly, Ernan, having been long separated from Phyllis – apart from a brief one-week leave – and having himself been required to give up his whole circle of friends, was furious at these extended delays. However, they were soon reconciled. Phyllis wrote:

> I suppose Marseilles may be a vulgar town, and I was often told that it was a dangerous and a wicked one; but I was to spend five months in it lost in a fairy tale. I loved Marseilles from the first moment that I heard its high-pitched, clattering, jazz-bound soul pouring into tumultuous sound. I loved its smell of coffee, tar, myrtle, dust and disinfectants. I loved the dry papery palms, the spotted trunks of plane trees, and the welcome shade their leaves threw across the Rue de Rome. I loved too the crammed and jostling, gay and luminous Cannebière – where everyone who was not sitting in the white dust and drinking *sirop* under striped awnings was staring at those who did.[89]

Ernan's job in Marseilles had its dangerous moments, although much of what he was doing he did not share with Phyllis. There was one occasion when he had to brief her, because he asked her to act as a 'disguise' for a White Russian who had been spying on the Bolsheviks in Paris. He had been betrayed and Ernan's job was to get him away in a gunboat to Malta, and then to Constantinople. This experience is fictionalised in 'The Little Red Band', where the fictive White Russian explains the desire for revenge arising from seeing his wife and children murdered in front of him by the Bolsehviks. He has now come to ask himself whether the 'evil I set out to kill is a new evil about to overwhelm the world, or but the result of an old evil which has already overwhelmed it. Perhaps there would have been no Red Band if life had been less easy, less opulent, less cruel? Think! If what I set out to kill was what I myself had made? This thought has struck me – was the Red Band their murderer, or was I?'[90] Among other things, the story is a small reminder that the British saw Communism as the great threat to world peace at this time, and it indicates, even at this early stage, Phyllis's interrogation of politically conservative assumptions.

This period in Marseilles was especially productive for Phyllis's mastery of the craft of short-story writing.

> Short stories should [not] be too lightly undertaken, or manipulated for mere relief, out of a fagged mind. No – the real short story should spring like a tiger on the back of its victim; and in no time of my life was my back more favoured by tigers springing than in this halcyon Marseilles period, week by golden week.[91]

Several of the stories that she wrote around that time drew on the turbulence and atmosphere of the months she spent in Marseilles.[92] In 'The Tug-of-War', for instance, a hard-headed British general spends his leaves with the beautiful, supposedly divorced, Madame Nibaud, who lives in style in the Ritz Hotel in Paris and discreetly receives gentlemen callers. In between their sexual encounters, she tries to find out when the next great offensive will be. Finally, the general's ADC is forced to warn him that this woman is a spy.[93] 'The Residue' is the tale of the enduring friendship of two Frenchwomen. One of them had lost her son at Verdun, the other had found out that her first husband, who had abandoned her years before, had tried to sell France to her enemies, and had been executed at Vincennes.[94]

They left Marseilles on All Soul's Day, 1919; Ernan was moved briefly to Passport Control in Paris, where they stayed once more with the McCord sisters. But their world was about to change once more, when Ernan was offered a choice of Vienna or Rome for his new posting. They chose Vienna, in order to take advantage of Ernan's facility in German. They had survived the Great War, were newly and happily married, and had high hopes for the future.

CHAPTER 5

Vienna and Old Wine

None of us had ever before lived in a city mortally struck by war.

PHYLLIS BOTTOME, *The Goal*

For Phyllis and Ernan, the five months they had spent in Marseilles had been a magical time. Finally they were married and able to live together. They had at long last escaped the stranglehold of their over-bearing mothers and Phyllis had retrieved Ernan from his possessive friends. Ernan had chosen her, had committed to her, and perhaps the distance from England helped them both to make a fresh start. Phyllis always regarded the five months at Marseilles as one of the happiest periods of their life. In the late summer of 1919 Ernan was able to take a holiday from his job and they enjoyed a second honeymoon:

> We snatched our short August leave in the mountains above Marseilles. No holiday was ever like it; from dawn to dusk we wandered over mountains covered with wild lavender and little golden bees … All day long we shared the golden solitude where only butterflies intruded, each one as lovely as if it had been carved out of a rainbow.[1]

Notwithstanding their personal happiness, however, the political out-comes of the Great War meant the situation they were to find in Vienna was not auspicious for a brighter future:

> Our happiness was not only based upon our confidence in each other but upon a world we believed had been set free for democracy, a world that would be for ever, by the price our generation had paid

> for it, at peace. What, however, we found was a chaotic, disrupted, frustrated world, each country competing wildly for what was left of its self-rifled treasures. Germany and Austria, 'les deux cadavres de l'Europe' as a French friend called them, surrounded by a ring of suspicious and irritable victors, unable to decide how to dispose of the bodies. Not much later on, Hitler made the decision for them.[2]

Ernan's job in Vienna placed him at the nexus of the extreme difficulties created by the aftermath of a world war and the collapse of the Habsburg Empire. When the long reigning Habsburg emperor, Franz Joseph, had died in 1916, he had no direct successor.[3] Nearly thirty years earlier his son Rudolf had died with his mistress in a double suicide at Mayerling. The emperor's nephew, Franz Ferdinand, had been assassinated, and, as his marriage to a non-royal woman was morganatic, the Habsburg crown fell to Franz Joseph's grandnephew, Karl. He had attempted to preserve the empire as a federation of nationalities and, in spring 1917, had tried and failed to negotiate a separate peace with the Allies. But after the war the Allies firmly established Austria as a republic.

Under the terms of the treaty signed at Saint-Germain in 1919, the territory was sliced up. The newly founded republic of Austria was, in effect, the German-speaking remnant of the dismembered Habsburg Empire; certain regions were formed into the new states of Yugoslavia and Czechoslovakia, while others went into the newly independent republic of Hungary. In 1920, in Hungary, Admiral Nikolaus Horthy had seized power, established himself as regent and declared Hungary a kingdom with the throne vacant. 'Legitimists' continued to plot Karl's return from exile in Switzerland, where he had retreated after his forced abdication in 1918. All in all, the political situation in the region was highly unstable.

But it was not just the regional political situation that was dangerous. The predicament of the Jews and the varying levels of anti-Semitism that existed at this period were also part of the volatile mix. Balfour, when British Foreign Secretary (1916–19), had been sympathetic to Zionism, and his Declaration of 1917 had stated that the British government favoured 'the establishment in Palestine of a national home for the Jewish people', on the understanding that there should be no disadvantage to 'the civil and religious rights of existing non-Jewish communities in Palestine, or the rights and political status enjoyed by Jews in any other country'.[4] The British government had been increasingly perplexed by the question of its role in the Middle East as the Ottoman Empire disintegrated. Initially, British policy was shaped by a desire to put a barrier between the French in Syria and the Suez Canal, but as the First World War progressed the support of Jews in America and Russia became important. As the historian A. J. P. Taylor sardonically puts it:

> Palestine was at this time inhabited predominantly by Arabs, a fact which the British government brushed lightly aside. Apparently it was assumed that the Arabs would gladly abandon Palestine to the Jews in gratitude for receiving some sort of national existence in the other Ottoman territories. Or maybe Lloyd George and Balfour merely took their knowledge of Palestine from the Bible, which in this respect happened to be out of date.[5]

Of the many outcomes of the First World War, this one was perhaps to cast the longest shadow, and continues to be troubling today.

Into this maelstrom Ernan arrived, in the spring of 1920, to join the British Legation in Vienna. His job was Passport Control Officer (PCO) to Austria, Hungary and Yugoslavia. This title was a semi-transparent cover for an intelligence officer serving at the British Embassy. The PCOs were supposed to spend the majority of their time collecting intelligence, leaving the junior officers dealing with routine administration of visas. However, during the First World War the Military Intelligence Department had operated a system of surveillance of alien passports by means of visas and this was no longer a straightforward matter. Indeed, it was a demanding job, as the PCO was, on the one hand, a public bureaucrat, but was required, on the other hand, to provide cover and resources for active members of the Secret Service (SIS) or MI6.

When Ernan first arrived in Vienna, his office was woefully short-handed, but he at last obtained, as his second in command, the services of Aylmer Macartney, a man with a thorough knowledge of German and an exceptional understanding of Central Europe and the Balkans. He recommended to Ernan that he took on a former helper of his in Prague, Miss Margery Bates (always known as 'Bill'), who had worked in counter-espionage in Switzerland. With Evelyn Graham-Stamper as its fourth member, this team had to deal with a wide variety of political problems following World War I, while also controlling large numbers of 'stringers' (the nickname for unofficial providers of intelligence). Further, Ernan's office was flooded by a tide of Jews trying to emigrate to Palestine and there were only certain categories of Jews for whom he was allowed to issue passports. Ultimately it was up to the individual PCO on the spot to interpret existing rules and regulations according to his own discretion; visa decisions had to be made on the spot by the PCO.

When Ernan first set off for his new posting, Phyllis was not instantly able to accompany him. Unexpectedly she had to return to England because she was suffering from intermittent but sharp pains. Dr Des Voeux diagnosed a grumbling appendix, which was removed, and she then stayed in England to recuperate. During her convalescence, she wrote a novel called *The Crystal Heart* (published in 1921 by Century, with black-and-white illustrations by Norman Price). Briefly, the plot centres on Joy Featherstone, who nurses her youngest sister, Rosemary, when she becomes terminally ill, the loving but self-absorbed parents curiously inactive in the face of this danger. This section of the book is fairly convincing in its psychological study of a young girl, growing up fast in order to assume responsibilities that would more usually fall to the lot of a parent. Somewhat less convincing is the second half, where Joy is faced with the sexual overtures of a blackguard, Owen, married to her best friend. Owen usually has sexual affairs with working-class women, and is rather inclined to blame them when they get upset: 'There is always a great deal to be said for a man who has been too popular with women … Women had been selfish with him. They had taken his charming manner too seriously.'[6] The ending is somewhat melodramatic and unconvincing, as Joy descends into insanity and death. It is fair to say that several of Phyllis's early novels have this fault: they begin with great psychological acuity, but then give way to melodrama. It may be that in this novel Phyllis was attempting to deal with and work out resentments of her own and perhaps, at some level, it worked as a necessary exorcism.

By the end of the First World War, Vienna had ceased to be the seat of an imperial court ruling over fifty-five million people, and instead had become the top-heavy capital of a tiny, landlocked, mostly alpine republic with a population of seven million. Its few industries and farms could nourish only a fraction of its population, so Vienna's two million people existed in a state of near starvation. Although the armistice had ended the fighting, the Allies kept in place the harsh blockade that they had imposed during the war, so people of all ages were dying from malnutrition-related diseases. The city was further reduced to destitution by ruinous currency inflation, inevitably leading to a thriving black market.

Ignoring the advice of her doctor, Phyllis joined Ernan just as soon as she could travel. Arriving at the Westbahnhof in Vienna, she was shocked by what she discovered:

> I found the square grass-grown. A single horse-drawn Victoria stood on the vast, empty space awaiting an unlikely passenger. The great city spread before my wondering eyes, motionless and silent as a dream. A few starved people, mere walking shadows, crept here and there. Notices were put up asking foreign drivers to drive slowly, since the people could not move quickly to get out of their way, on account of the starvation. There were no cars but foreign ones; a few battered creaking old yellow trams crawled and whined their way from district to district. On our first walk together, we saw a ragged woman sitting under a tenth-century shrine in one of the small and picturesque stone alleys that intersect the main streets of Vienna. She had an enormous baby stretched across her lap, I thought he must be six years old at least, but she told us that he was only two. It was hunger that had softened and stretched his bones so that he looked like a plant run to wood, too tall ever to flower. She was trying to feed him from a bowl of soup, but her claw-like hands trembled so with hunger that we stopped to help her. We tried to give her hope but we knew that there was no real hope for either of them. The hospitals of Vienna were at this time subsisting without fats or meat,

> mostly on carrots and turnips boiled in water. The patients drank coffee made out of acorns. The bread was terrible and there was little of it. Bandages were made of paper. The currency sank so low that the equivalent of four hundred pounds a year could provide its owner with one loaf of bread a month.[7]

Ernan was alarmed that Phyllis had arrived before the end of the doctors' advised convalescent period, and did not think that the small and simple flat that his old friend Robert Pollak had found for him in the Barnabitengasse was suitable. But she loved it; it had not changed for a hundred years, and stood in a cobbled courtyard off a street leading from the Mariahilferstrasse, just above Haydn's old church.

Despite the terrible penury in Austria, Ernan and Phyllis themselves were for the first time in their married life comparatively well off. Phyllis's heroic writing efforts and good sales had cleared Ernan's debts, and he himself was on a decent salary. Ernan's job involved a certain amount of diplomatic entertaining; initially, they took guests out to eat at the Restaurant Schoner in the Siebensterngasse and, on special occasions, at the famous restaurant run by Anna Sacher. A habitué of the Sacher Hotel was Princess Stephanie von Hohenlohe, who was only on the outer fringes of their circle at the time, but whom they were to encounter later in their life. Although Jewish (née Richter), she always claimed to be of purest Aryan descent, and managed to reinvent herself several times over. In her early twenties she had become pregnant by the son-in-law of Emperor Franz Joseph I, but this had been hushed up by a swift marriage to another Austro-Hungarian prince, Friedrich Franz von Hohenlohe. She had taken Hungarian citizenship but divorced in 1920. Ernan's office regarded her as a *femme fatale* politically as well as sexually.[8]

As Phyllis quickly realised, in Vienna cafés were the focus for all social and intellectual life, and each of them had their own distinct character. Phyllis's favourite was the Café Central, just beyond the old town square, which was the particular favourite of the writers and poets. Phyllis naturally gravitated towards creative people; it was there that Marcel Fodor, the Hungarian-born correspondent of the *Manchester Guardian,* introduced her to his protégée, the American newspaper journalist, Dorothy Thompson. Dorothy, then only twenty-eight, was full of boundless energy, enthusiasm and talent. She was a remarkable young woman who had been born in upstate New York, the daughter of a Methodist minister. After graduating from Syracuse University, she had taken a job as spokeswoman for the Woman's Suffrage Party at its headquarters in Buffalo. After a period in New York City writing publicity, she became foreign correspondent of the *Evening Post,* for which her first assignment was to Vienna. And through Dorothy, Phyllis met the American poet Edna St Vincent Millay, a tiny childlike figure with a mass of Pre-Raphaelite red hair, who was then travelling through Europe on a contract to write articles for *Vanity Fair.* As Phyllis commented in her autobiography:

> It was perhaps remarkable that we three Anglo-American women should meet in Vienna at this epoch of its tragic close. Poet, journalist, and novelist, each in her own way voicing Vienna's immediate history. For there is no doubt that Edna took to the full into her heart the tragedy of broken Europe, nor that Dorothy Thompson expressed with sure and courageous utterance knowledge she seemed to pick out of the air; and in my turn *Old Wine* was a personal record of what Vienna meant to the observer in 1920 to 1923.[9]

Phyllis especially enjoyed her friendship with the two women because, in Vienna, she was second fiddle to Ernan, and these were essentially literary friendships. However, although she was to remain friends with Dorothy for many years, her friendship with Edna was to putter out. This was because she took Dorothy's side in a bitter quarrel with Edna. Early in 1922 Dorothy married her lover, the Jewish-Hungarian writer Josef Bard. He was strikingly handsome, suave and philandering, and although Dorothy overlooked his peccadilloes as irrelevant to their grand passion, she did expect a degree of loyalty from her friends. Initially she was delighted when Edna agreed to rework, in verse, Josef's translation of Hungary's leading poet, Andrew Ady. Dorothy, Edna and Josef went to Budapest together, where Edna was busily occupied in entertaining two lovers. Notwithstanding Edna's voracious sexual appetite for both women and men, Dorothy assumed that two lovers would be enough to keep Edna busy, and was unconcerned about leaving Josef and Edna behind when she had to return to Vienna. However, Edna simply could not resist seducing Josef, although to be fair to her, seducing him was much like shooting fish in a barrel.

Dorothy was furious with Edna, feeling betrayed by her friend. Years later, Dorothy would write in her diary:

> She was a little bitch, a genius, a cross between gamin and an angel … She sat before her glass and combed her lovely hair, over and over. Narcissan. She never really loved anyone except herself. Very beautiful with her little white body and her green-gold eyes. 'Dotty, do you think I am a nymphomaniac?' she asked.[10]

Dorothy's pride helped her to put a brave face on it, but, unsurprisingly, she did not trust Edna after that. Phyllis, who loved Dorothy, was loyal to her first friend in Vienna. Although Phyllis recognised that Edna was attracted to women even more than to men, she seemed unaware that Dorothy, too, had lesbian affairs alongside her relationships with men, so that marriage could never be a simple affair. Phyllis always liked Josef, but Dorothy insisted that loyalty to her meant breaking off any friendship with him, compliance with which demand Phyllis later came to regret. Wholly unfairly, Josef blamed Phyllis for Dorothy's determination to leave him.

Phyllis was deeply fascinated by 'Vincent', as Edna chose to be called, this *femme fatale* who bewitched women and men alike. Frequently attracted to triangular relationships, Vincent left a trail of collateral damage in her wake. Unfaithful husbands' wives attempted suicide; discarded female lovers had breakdowns. Phyllis was puzzled by Vincent's casual cruelty, regarding it as similar to the cruelty of a child. Vincent had suffered from a horrendous abortion, which meant that she could not herself have children, and Phyllis considered that this was one contributing factor to her oddly vicious behaviour towards others. But she never underestimated Vincent as a poet. Phyllis fictionalised Vincent in her short story 'Blue Clay'. In it, the narrator is a worldly, second-rate writer who goes to the rescue of a woman poet, whom she comes across naked, drugged and drunk, about to be thrown out of a hotel as a result of creating a huge disturbance with two men. She takes her to stay with some nuns where she can dry out and pays the nuns for looking after her. Although the narrator is unfailingly kind, she senses that the poet dislikes her, and is puzzled that she seems to prefer the nuns and their strict moral code. The narrator, not unnaturally, rather resents this, but the Mother Superior explains to her, 'She prefers us because we are dedicated, and your little poet friend is also dedicated ... ' Sadly, the narrator observes, 'Both the poet and the saint had rejected me. I was not even that blue clay out of which diamonds shine.'[11] Phyllis was undoubtedly right to recognise Edna's genius; in 1923, she was the first woman to be awarded a Pulitzer Prize for her poetry.

Like Dorothy Thompson, but for different reasons, Ernan needed to have an ear always receptive to political currents. Once he was convinced that Phyllis had recovered from her operation, they moved into a larger apartment that they could use to entertain and gain access to a wider cross-section of society. Consequently, in Vienna, Phyllis enjoyed the fullest social life she had ever experienced. Initially, she was inclined to get dress codes and social codes all wrong as the situation was completely outside her previous experience. The embassy had a box at the races and another at the State Opera, adjacent to the royal box. There they enjoyed performances such as Richard Strauss's *Der Rosenkavalier*, starring Lotte Lehmann and Elisabeth Schwarzkopf, and also witnessed the remarkable Maria Jeritza in *Salome*. Around this time, Phyllis wrote a rather odd long-short story, 'The Perfect Wife', perhaps partially inspired by the plot of *Der Rosenkavalier*, where an older woman gracefully withdraws to allow a younger woman to take over her partner. In Phyllis's story, the older woman, who is childless, hands over her husband, making no fuss, befriends the new wife and maintains a friendship with the new couple. Her perfect, civilised behaviour disguises the fact that she has not really let go of her husband. She had made of him a substitute child and is bewildered when his new wife does not treat him in the same way. In Phyllis's narrative, the older woman has made the mistake of putting everything into her marriage, until there is nothing left of herself.

In all matters of Viennese social etiquette, Phyllis was ably advised by two friends, Dr Schumpeter, who had been a counsellor to both Franz Joseph and the young emperor Karl, and Baron Höfflinger, the chief legal advisor and man of affairs to Count Berchtold. Setting themselves the task of grooming her into an acceptable version of a 'Viennese' lady, they often despaired. Democratic by instinct, Phyllis treated her servants like friends although her advisors warned her repeatedly that they would regard her – and exploit her – as a fool. It appeared, unfortunately, that this advice was accurate, as Ernan's chauffeur, Rudolph, treated Phyllis with great contempt until Ernan had a stern word with him. On one visit to the opera, although Schumpeter and Höfflinger had advised her on the purchase of a magnificent evening dress of emerald-green velvet, Phyllis horrified them by wearing the dress with snow boots, and then whipping them off inside the private box to reveal bare feet. But they persisted in the challenge, and took her to the best couturiers and hat-makers in Vienna. Irene Spierer, a superb milliner, made her beautiful hats, and it is clear that Phyllis's new-found pleasure in and taste for well-cut clothes and stylish headwear date from this period.

The Forbes Dennises' new home was the Palais Reitzes, a large and beautiful flat five storeys above Ernan's office. Phyllis commented that

> The great front windows looked over half the city towards the rounded hills of Kahlenberg and Leopoldsberg, standing up like warning fingers in the wide Danubian plain. Beyond them again was the distant blue of the high mountains.[12]

The building was situated opposite the Votivkirche, an exuberant assembly of steeples, pointed windows and arches, topped by two crocket-covered spires. As this flat was part of the official diplomatic base, with it went 'the second-best cook in Vienna', so that they could hold dinner parties for a dozen 'carefully selected guests' at a time.[13] During their weeks in their smaller flat, Phyllis had discovered that Austrian aristocrats would not willingly dine with Jews; nor, it turned out, did her Jewish friends enjoy dining with aristocrats. As she wrote, 'there seemed to be walls of ice on both sides and nothing I could do melted them. In the end, and very reluctantly, I had to give different [dinner] parties for each, though it made my heart sore, and my blood boil to do it.'[14] Only at their big embassy parties, which they threw in their huge music-room with its Bösendorfer grand piano, could she insist on an eclectic mix of legation colleagues, old Austrian aristocracy, Jewish intelligentsia, journalists, artists and musicians of every kind. Robert Pollak, whom Ernan had first met in 1906 in Geneva, played the violin with tones of fire and velvet, and would entertain their visitors while Ernan accompanied him on piano. On other occasions Ernan would play the accompaniment for the Viennese dancer and choreographer Albertina Rasch, who would dance for the assembled company. Of Polish-Jewish descent she had studied at the Vienna State Opera Ballet School and had worked in the United States as a ballerina at the New York Hippodrome before the First World War, and toured with Sarah Bernhardt.[15] Much later, Phyllis would draw on Albertina's accounts of Bernhardt to write a short story loosely based on her.[16]

Ernan was in his element. He organised a Christmas fancy-dress party in the embassy flat that was remembered for decades afterwards by everyone who attended it. Ernan, as host, was resplendent in an eighteenth-century costume and wig.[17] Ever since his pageant days, he had enjoyed any excuse for dressing up, and his favourite company was that of musically gifted people. He was therefore especially delighted to be able to enjoy once more the friendship of Robert Pollak. Three weeks before the start of the First World War, Robert had been appointed professor of violin at the Moscow Conservatory of Music. On the outbreak of hostilities, he had been made a civil prisoner, although, during his four years of detention in Russia, he had been asked to give master classes at the Moscow Conservatory.[18] Phyllis was delighted that this old friend of Ernan's was keen to be friends with her too, and much later she was to fictionalise Robert's experience in Russia into a short story called 'The Point of Vantage'.[19] Having returned to his native Vienna after the armistice, Robert had become head of the violin department at the Vienna Conservatory. He had recommenced a career of concert tours all round Europe, sometimes as a soloist, sometimes as a member of a quartet, and sometimes he acted as guest conductor of symphony orchestras.[20] To have such a distinguished musician play at his soirées was indubitably a social coup for a diplomat, especially as it was known that he performed at the Forbes Dennis flat for friendship's sake. This was a very successful epoch in Ernan's career.

Phyllis had an odd relationship with her two chief Austrian 'advisors', as she was fascinated by them but did not entirely trust them. Baron Höfflinger had survived the currency crisis in Vienna by exchanging his kronen for diamonds, and consequently he continued to live well. It is unclear where Schumpeter's money came from but as political economist of Franz Joseph's regime and finance minister to his successor Karl, he was no doubt very shrewd in speculations. Sometimes Phyllis found it hard to stomach the way they unabashedly enjoyed their beautiful horses, their beautiful carpets and Mercedes cars when much of Vienna was starving. Phyllis recalled that Baron Höfflinger 'only once left Vienna while I knew him, to pass a few weeks in Venice, but returned promptly by the next train. "I could not stand the sight of the post-war world," he told me. "It seems to me chiefly inhabited by people from the Balkans who eat with their hands and their feet." '[21]

Yet these two men were representatives of the old Habsburg Vienna that had largely disappeared and, as such, provided an important entrée into another world for her.[22] They were sophisticated and well connected, arranging dinner invitations for their British friends to schlosses where they were on first-name terms with the hosts. They openly had mistresses, whom Phyllis met – and discreetly studied – at the races. Politically, of course, they were a million miles from Phyllis and Ernan, whose political sympathies lay with the Social Democrats.

In Vienna, inflation ran riot until finally curbed in 1924 by a hard-currency loan, guaranteed by the major foreign powers, and a switch to a new currency, the Austrian schilling. But before that:

> International plunderers as well as stupidly heartless traders took cruel advantage of Austria's helpless financial chaos. Crooks with nine cheque books and no consciences juggled with the exchange; and not all of them were professional crooks. *'Haifisch'* as the Viennese called them, Austrians as well as foreigners, cornered food supplies, bought land, historic castles, household treasures for a song, cheating and disheartening the starving population by their rapacity.[23]

In this unstable situation, the leaders of extremist political parties found new adherents, which would later lead to crisis. But, in the period when Phyllis and Ernan were there, Vienna had become the first great metropolis in the world to put its municipal government in socialist hands. 'The Vienna municipal administration did its valiant best, out of small resources, to meet the needs of its workers and their dependants. Houses were requisitioned, factories were taken over and run for the benefit of their workers as well as for the consumers. Laws were passed to check the Exchange and other semi-legal robberies ... '[24] 'Red Vienna' lasted from 1919 to 1934. From 1922, the city, which held a third of Austria's population, constituted a *Land,* or province, all on its own with wide powers of taxation.

For Phyllis and Ernan, it was an exciting time to be in Vienna. The vision of Austrian socialists differed from that of Russian Bolsheviks precisely because the Austrians saw culture and education as the transforming agents that could bring about a just society. This period of Phyllis's life led her to form her left-leaning liberal political views, which were entirely different from the conservative ones, at least on her mother's side of the family, with which she had grown up. Ernan, similarly, had long struggled to sort out a religious-cum-political system of belief which made sense to him; writing to Phyllis towards the end of the First World War, he said: ' ... For me there was an arch-socialist who founded the Christian philosophy – but apart from that I am not sure to what extent it can be administered externally. Though I suppose obstacles can be removed by governing bodies – & people can be educated or rather children can – '[25] Both Phyllis and Ernan were idealists.

In this turbulent period, humanitarian aid filtered into Vienna from her former enemies: 'Save the Children' arrived first, though some British people thought feeding the children of the late enemy misguided. Phyllis wrote to one such objector that if she could only see the children 'green with hunger and so thin that they looked as if you could slip them through a wedding ring', she would be sure to offer her own dinner.[26] The Dutch Red Cross, the American Red Cross and Quaker organisations were all trying to help. When Phyllis and Ernan first arrived in Vienna, seventy per cent of children under two were dying, but after two years' work by these organisations they had managed to reduce child mortality to a near normal rate.[27]

Phyllis was directly involved in fundraising for two organisations. The first was the Friends' Mission for Children, whose head, Dr Hilda

Clarke, she had met at one of her husband's dinner parties. The other was run by Valerie Adler, the wife of a Viennese banker. One day, when sitting alone in a café, Phyllis was approached by a small Jewish woman who, after introducing herself, asked Phyllis to join her on a small working committee to run a Warmestuben. The literal translation means 'warming-up room', and it was a refuge providing both shelter from the cold and hot food. The plan was that those who could pay should pay a small amount but those who could not, need pay nothing. Valerie wanted especially to make use of Phyllis's skills as a writer, getting her to draft the appeal and act as unpaid fund raiser. Phyllis was happy to comply, with the support of her husband's office, sending out the appeal to everyone in the British Embassy and to foreign missions in Vienna. She personally sent persuasive letters to potential donors in Britain, including Otto Beit, the millionaire husband of her friend Lilian. And Phyllis's favourite uncle in America, Harry Bottome, legal counsellor to the New York Life Assurance Co., sent a handsome contribution – the winnings of a poker party.[28] That first winter, the kitchens were able to feed six hundred daily. By the second winter the numbers had dropped to four hundred, and by the end of the third winter, the republic was on its feet, and these emergency measures were no longer needed.

The chief surgeon of the Children's Hospital, Dr Spitzer, approached Phyllis to see if she could get him surgical rubber gloves. She did so by telegraphing her London doctor, Dr Des Voeux, who sent them twelve dozen pairs by return and put an advert in *The Lancet* for more. Ernan, too, was active in organising aid. He had heard on the diplomatic grapevine that the USA was withdrawing an over-supply of food and medical supplies from Belgium and asked if some could be diverted to Professor Wenckebach, chief of the Vienna General Hospital. In short, both Ernan and Phyllis were engaged in relieving hardship in whatever ways they could.

In the autumn of 1921, a more immediately personal cry for help came from Lislie. She had fallen ill once more and came out to join them for a period of recuperation. Lislie and Phyllis had not seen each other for fifteen months, the longest period that they had been apart during their long and intense friendship. Phyllis had always maintained to Lislie that loving her husband would never mean that she loved

Lislie less. This was true in theory, but in practice, when Phyllis left England to join Ernan, first in Marseilles, but more absolutely in Vienna, they were no longer sharing their lives. Phyllis had new and exciting friends in Vienna, and she was alarmed to find when Lislie came out to join them that she seemed like a faded sepia print of how Phyllis remembered her. Lislie no longer seemed to have any enthusiasm for new sights and new experiences, as she used to do in their shared times in Rome and Capri.

Phyllis asked Professor Wenckebach, a close friend since Ernan's intervention in getting the American base to send medical supplies to his hospital, if he would attend Lislie and consider her case. At this time there was an upsurge in more active interventions in the treatment of tuberculosis in Germany and Austria. Collapsed-lung theory was the idea that underpinned this new approach to pulmonary treatments. The theory was that by artificially collapsing a lung, and therefore depriving the TB bacilli of oxygen, the bacteria would either die or go into a state of suspended animation. Following this procedure, 'the inflammatory and immune responses of the normal tissues around the lesion are given a chance to arrest their further spread. Scar formation is encouraged.'[29] Wenckebach advised an operation on the phrenic nerve, followed by pneumothorax injections, as a preliminary to the new Saarbruck rib operation. All of these treatments were aimed at collapsing the lung.[30] Professor von Eiselsberg, considered the finest of the Viennese surgeons, was to undertake the first operation. Eiselsberg told Phyllis: 'It is not an easy operation, one can give no general anaesthetic for it, and she will be conscious all though it. There will be no pain, but she will feel pressure. Also the operation is tricky – on no account must the patient be frightened during it and breathe quickly, or she might die on the operating table.'[31]

Eiselsberg asked Phyllis to be present and to tell Lislie a story to take her mind off the operation and to keep her breathing steadily. Phyllis held Lislie's attention by telling her the plot of a thriller she was thinking of writing, arising from a story Dorothy Thompson had told her. During her recovery after the operation, Lislie spent part of her summer at a sanatorium in Kaltenleutgeben, then a beautiful village in the foothills of the Vienna Woods, with her mother Carita as her companion.

Until she had helped Lislie through this crisis, Phyllis kept secret from Ernan that she, too, was ill. Her doctor had warned her that there was fresh TB activity in both of her lungs.[32] Once she had 'confessed' to Ernan, he arranged for both women to rest at a Kurhaus at Semmering. Together, Phyllis and Lislie relived their experience at St Moritz – the peace of the mountains, the first snows and the sunshine on the pine trees. Ernan phoned every evening and came up to visit when he could, although that winter there was renewed political tension to contend with. While Phyllis was rendered *hors de combat*, the political situation took a new and dramatic turn. In autumn 1921, Karl made an attempt to reclaim the Hungarian throne. It was said that following his failure, Karl and his wife Zita were being held incommunicado in the Esterházy Castle in Tata. Dorothy Thompson commandeered a Red Cross badge and a car with an American flag flying, in order to bluff her way into the country and find out whether this rumour was true; thus began the legend of the intrepid girl reporter. That winter, too, in Vienna hungry mobs rioted, looting fashionable hotels and shops.

Sometimes Ernan brought Robert Pollak up with him to visit Phyllis and Lislie in Semmering, where Robert would give impromptu concerts for the patients. He always finished with Beethoven's *Frühlings* Sonata, which seemed to promise a new spring, a new life. That particular spring, Phyllis reported, 'came with a rush. I never saw pear trees so white, or the wild cherries among the dark, denuded mountain pines so thickly "hung with snow".'[33] By May, when Lislie had completed her course of injections, Phyllis was able to move her friend to Salzburg, where her mother Carita was to look after her for a month. Phyllis herself was feeling much better, so she and Ernan escaped their various duties to enjoy a magical and much-needed holiday in Venice. They stayed at La Calcina, Ruskin's old *pension*, where Phyllis had originally stayed with Elena and subsequently with Lislie. They then returned to Vienna to resume care of Lislie, helped – in entertainment terms – by their close circle of friends. Albertina Rasch told Lislie scandalous stories about the New York Opera House, Höfflinger and Schumpeter dropped by to amuse her and Evelyn and Bill from Ernan's office were unfailingly kind to her.

Lislie was booked into the Loew Sanatorium, where a young German surgeon, Sparmann, from the Saarbruck Clinic in Munich performed the *plombage* or rib surgery, which involved making a cavity below the ribs in the chest wall and introducing various substances to induce the lung to collapse. Ernan then moved Lislie and Phyllis back to the Kurhaus in Semmering. But the characteristic nightly spikes of temperature indicated that the tuberculosis had returned, and Lislie was persuaded to undergo a second rib operation. The Collapse Theory was one thing, but in practice this was an exceptionally gruelling operation for someone as weak as Lislie.

Phyllis and Ernan brought Lislie back to their flat to nurse her with the assistance of a trained nurse, Maria Teresa. For the next ten weeks Lislie was slowly dying, and as neither of her parents regarded themselves as fit enough to travel to Vienna in the winter weather, Phyllis and Ernan were her sole 'family' support. Ernan was inevitably tied up with the turbulent political events and needed to absent himself for trips to Budapest. Phyllis tried to keep Lislie entertained by reading to her; Max Beerbohm's essays were the only entertainment Lislie could enjoy by this stage. Listening to Phyllis reading 'Going Out for a Walk' made her smile when for the last time she was fully conscious.[34] Maria Teresa kept her out of pain with injections of morphine every two hours, and eventually Lislie slumped into a drugged semi-sleep. Lislie's doctor was increasingly anxious about Phyllis's health, and warned her to keep dosing herself with disinfectant. But Phyllis was no more likely to pull away from her beloved woman friend than from her sister Wilmett, so many years before.

> It was a long and hard delivery that I was watching but I would not have been anywhere else for the world. Sometimes I would ask Maria Teresa, kneeling on her other side, if she was sure that Lislie was not conscious. Maria Teresa would test her fixed eyes with light and tell me, 'No, she knows nothing! She does not suffer.' Once she seemed to be struggling to say my name, 'Phil – Phil,' over and over again ... at last Lislie's difficult breathing ceased, and her burning hand in mine grew cold.[35]

Lislie died on 21 February 1923 and they buried her at Kaltenleutgeben. Albertina Rasch, who had come every day to stand in the snow outside the Palais Reitzes to see if the blinds were drawn, planted a lilac tree on Lislie's grave. A letter from Lislie's mother Carita says, 'My dear Phyllis, I simply cannot picture you without your best friend.'[36] Phyllis and Lislie had been devoted friends since they had met in St Moritz almost twenty years before. In snow Phyllis had met her, and in snow she had lost her.

Ernan was extremely distressed. More than Phyllis he needed some religious faith to sustain him; in Vienna he went both to the Christian Science Church and to High Mass at St Stephen's. Phyllis's doctor warned Ernan that his wife would fall gravely ill again if he did not take great care of her, and, having just witnessed the slow and excruciating death of Lislie, Ernan asked to take his holiday a month early. In March 1923, they went to Rome where Phyllis had been so happy with Lislie and which Ernan had never visited. They discussed what needed to be done to save Phyllis's life; the doctors had advised Ernan to send her to a sanatorium in Davos. They both knew from experience that such a 'cure' might never come, but they still believed that she might survive if only she could live in cold, dry mountain air. Ernan could not bear the thought of being separated from Phyllis again. In the first instance he rented an Austrian friend's house at Bad Hall, whence he could take a long and tiresome train journey into Vienna on Mondays and return on Fridays to spend the weekend with Phyllis. To keep her company while she worked Ernan bought her an Alsatian puppy named 'Luchs', whose energy distracted Phyllis from being wholly bowed down with grief over Lislie's death.

Phyllis found that she had to lay aside her work on *Old Wine*, as the only story she felt drawn to write at this juncture was the one she had used to entertain Lislie when she was undergoing her first operation. *The Depths of Prosperity*, signalled as being co-authored with Dorothy Thompson, explored a new genre for her, that of the thriller.[37] Set in New York, the plot centres on a socialite, Mrs Irvine St Clair, who lives solely to win male admiration, and who sets out to destroy her only daughter, Hilary. Mrs St Clair is jealous that her seventeen-year-old daughter will in time take all eyes away from her own beauty, and conspires with her doctor to marry her off to a dissolute young Englishman. When Hilary runs away from him and returns to their Park

Avenue home, the doctor allows her to become more and more addicted to veronal. Mrs St Clair is a Lady Macbeth figure, who outwits almost everyone except a young nurse, Nancy Beck. It is an extraordinarily convoluted plot, involving domestic abuse, unscrupulous physicians, an attempted murder and, finally, a happy ending. Although not formally satisfying, it marks one discrete area of Phyllis's work – that of portraits of psychologically disturbed people. Mrs St Clair evinces the toxin inherent in women whose only sphere of influence is that of the control of men through the exploitation of their 'feminine' charms. Phyllis shows how this manoeuvre inevitably brings such women into deadly competition with all other women, including their own offspring, and the extent to which the apparent charm masks ruthlessness. For all its faults – it is a book that hasn't wholly caught hold of this unfamiliar genre – it hits various feminist nails on the head. The woman who wins out is the young nurse, yet again in Phyllis's oeuvre an example of a professional woman who takes her place in the world because of her acquired skills, not because of her skills in flirtation. The novel, however, did not make her much money. This was largely because Phyllis's agent, James Pinker, had died in the very same week that she lost Lislie.[38] Previously, he had successfully sold the serial rights of her novels and all her short stories to the *Century Magazine*; then, as now, America was the place to make real money for a writer. To lose her agent at such a moment, when she was both ill and mourning Lislie's death, was doubly unfortunate, because it had a direct impact on her capacity to earn.

Ernan did some research, and then – despite Phyllis's protests – gave up his diplomatic post. He was determined to live with her in the mountains if that was where she needed to be. She wrote later:

> The sacrifice my husband made was heart-breaking for him and for his office, and I felt appalled to be the cause of it. [He had been offered a permanent] post of attaché to the Embassy. But my husband had turned his back upon Vienna now and nothing could shake his determination. His mind and heart were set upon my recovery. He knew that my will had been stretched too hard in a losing fight, inch by inch for the last eighteen months, and he doubted whether I had

the strength to fight another battle for my own life, alone, and in our youth-haunted surroundings.[39]

Ernan had, for the first time in his life, been highly successful in his career. Unless he was a saint, he must have felt that the fates were especially unkind; he had once before left Phyllis because he had been persuaded that she would never get well. Now he had seen Lislie die and could only wonder how long he would be able to keep Phyllis. In October 1923, they sadly packed up the Viennese flat and moved to Mösern, a mountain village above Innsbruck.

Phyllis had already started work on *Old Wine*, which was the first of her books in which her life-experience and her apprenticeship in her craft came together to form a fully realised and wholly accomplished novel.[40] This was as a result, as she said in her autobiography, of 'the direct outcome of the freedom and strength I had gained from my marriage; and perhaps also from the intensity of my grief over Lislie's death'.[41] In mourning the friend of her youth she poured some of her sorrow into the picture of the breakdown of values in Vienna after the First World War. Both the grim reality of post-war Vienna and its sophistication had moved her forward into a different world, a more grown-up one. This novel, *Old Wine,* was of an entirely different order from anything she had previously written. She vividly portrays the social shambles of Vienna in the 1920s, the fallen aristocrats, the independent professional women among the American and British relief workers and the position of Jews in that volatile society. It was this novel that would establish her critical reputation when it was published in 1925.

The *mise en scène* of Vienna is beautifully realised, and what the places and things mean to the inhabitants. To the fallen aristocracy, Vienna is not Vienna at all without the opera, the races and meals at Anna Sacher's restaurant. To Count Otto Wolkenheimb, his family estate at Trauenstein must be preserved at all costs; in the end he sells his honour to save it.

The novel opens in autumn 1918. Baron Eugen Erdödy tells Otto and their cousin Franz Salvator that the emperor has left for Switzerland and that the Habsburg way of life is finished. All three of them will need to marry 'foreign money' if they are to survive. In the event, only Otto actively attempts this, when he proposes to a young American woman reporter, Carol Hunter (inspired to a large degree by Dorothy Thompson), mistakenly believing that she is heiress to an American fortune. He had hoped that by marrying her, he could save his beloved estate, which is under threat.

> His peasants no longer revered and admired him. They claimed as rights what he would have given them as privileges if he had been rich enough to afford his own instincts of generosity. What Otto disliked most about the new order of things was the way in which it upset his sense of his virtues. He knew that he was a generous and considerate landlord; but when he was suddenly pinched and driven by the loss of more than half his fortune, was it the moment for his peasants to rise up and chivvy him into allowing them the same indulgence which (in the goodness of his heart) he had conceded them in the days of his prosperity?[42]

He knows that as he can no longer live off his estates – almost all the timber has been felled and sold – and as his fortune has disintegrated with the collapse of the krone, he must find a way into business affairs. As he explains to his cousins:

> 'I have made rather a study of history – and in history there are many parallel occasions. Moments of chaos like this, for instance. We have spoken of the world as dead; but worlds don't die, they change their fashions of life. One sign of vitality still exists, even in this dismembered city. There are a few hundred Jews in Wien who will regulate our new-found freedom and starvation to fill their own pockets. They will survive.'[43]

Otto assumes that, as a man of the world who has had many successful affairs with women, the easiest way into this business world would be to seduce Elisabeth Bleileben, a thirty-eight-year-old married Jewess. His research tells him that it is she who has the business brains in her marriage; she has promoted her husband's career, but she is bored, and has just found out that her husband has a mistress. She is in charge of the Austrian relief charities, and supplies food from Julius

Mandelbaum's wholesale groceries. She does not exactly rob the charity but she does find ways of making sure that she and Mandelbaum get some personal profit.[44] The critic Phyllis Lassner comments: 'Her scheme to profit from a Red Cross milk delivery to starving children demonises her not only as a Lilith who rejects motherhood, but also as a female conflation of Shylock and Fagin … '[45]

Otto invites Elisabeth to his large apartment in Vienna; it is the first time he had ever entertained a Jewish guest, and 'for the first time Elisabeth saw what luxury was like. Not the luxury that can be procured for large sums in first-class hotels, but a luxury evoked by centuries of cultivated habits.'[46] The deal is struck: she will bring him money, in the form of letting him in on speculative business deals, and he will transform her social style. The first time he meets her she is wearing a violent orange dress; he takes her to the best shops and encourages her to wear sophisticated black and white. Otto's arrogance is such that he feels sure that he has control of his 'funny little Jewess'; he is used to taking up mistresses and dropping them again after a couple of years when he gets bored with them.[47] But he underestimates Elisabeth; after all, he may be witty, but that is not the same as living by his wits. He is a baby in commerce, and she is an experienced and bold business-woman. He has also paid no attention to bourgeois morality; he has insolently assumed that he could drop Elisabeth when he had what he wanted, which was an entrée into the business world. But – in her world – a Jewish woman facing divorce for adultery is disgraced and outcast. Elisabeth becomes an avenging fury, very like Salome in the opera she and Otto separately attend; she has control of two mortgages on his property and evidence of his shady dealings. He is in her power and not the other way around. As Elisabeth says, 'What fools the old lot are! They deserved to lose an Empire!'[48]

By the end of the novel, Otto is not much more than a gigolo. Although Elisabeth is not an attractive character, she is carefully painted as neither ridiculous nor grotesque. Loving Otto makes her vulnerable; and there is a fierce integrity in that, if not in much else. Shakespeare created in *The Merchant of Venice* a marvellous evocation of a city and also a psychologically explicable account of why the Jew, long-spat-at, might one day want revenge. Phyllis's novel, too, negotiates this difficult terrain. Baron Eugen Erdödy, Otto's cousin and most devoted friend, feels that their marriage will be a battle of wits, in which they won't be bored, at least. Speaking of Elisabeth he says, 'She is like the rest of us – this Jewish lady – a mixture of bad motives, strong emotions, and a certain confused sense of justice and duty.'[49]

Instead of clinging to the old world, two other characters in *Old Wine,* Franz Salvator, fresh from the defeated army, and his sister Eugenie, try to embrace the new world. She is a widow, who has ploughed what money she had into a hospital for the orphaned children of soldiers, and she nurses there, trying to save children dying of starvation and pneumonia. Her superior there is Carl Jeiletes, a Jewish doctor; before the collapse, no aristocrat would willingly be in the company of Jews. Eugenie organises meetings for intellectuals fortnightly at her house, with the hope of working out what the new Austria needs to be. Franz is initially horrified that his sister has invited Dr Jeiletes into their home, even though she has worked with him for four years:

> 'One is not obliged to make friends of people one works with,' said Franz stiffly. 'I teach the sons of grocers in the Berlitz schools, and I am on cordial terms with them, but I don't ask you to receive them socially.'[50]

Eugenie thinks that they must drop outdated ideas of caste; why, she asks, should she exclude from her group of intellectuals 'the picked brains of an intelligent race which has become part of us'?[51] Eventually Franz begins to see that his sister's rejection of the supremacist order is right:

> 'We must lift Austria by changing – not by lamenting change! It will not be a great Empire again with the most brilliant Court in Europe, but if it becomes a self-respecting small country like Switzerland, which pays its way and keeps its culture, its universities, its sense of beauty and art, it will not lose its soul! It is the integrity of our work that Carol [the American journalist] most admires. She says we are a country of artists, that we make hay and pastry with the same perfection with which our musicians make their symphonies and

> sonatas. Perhaps it is true. And what we have to give to Europe is a higher standard of beauty.'[52]

Taste, however, is not as important as integrity, although in Franz's model the two are brought into harmony. In Otto's model – and this is his fatal flaw – appearances are everything.

The other major relationship that needed to be readdressed in order for Austria to move forward into its new future is that between men and women. As always in her work, Phyllis considers gender and social-class relations. Baron Eugen has a mistress in his working-class cook; he treats her with courtesy but he would not for a second have considered marrying her. Into Vienna sweep the British and American women who are free and independent; they do not expect to be protected by men; they do not require the false courtesy that is the flip side of contempt. Eugenie's marriage has taught her that impeccable manners in public may mask brutality behind closed doors. She begins to recognise that the comradeship and respect between women and men that the British women seek may be preferable. Dr Jeiletes cares for her but cannot imagine that a Magyar princess would ever consider him – a Jew – as a husband. Jane Simmons, the businesslike head of the British Relief medical section trying to bring food and medicines into his hospital, sees into his heart:

> 'We live in a broken world,' said Dr Simmons thoughtfully, 'but misery has this advantage, Dr Jeiletes, the line between those who desire to heal it and those who desire to profit by it becomes unusually distinct. You and the Princess belong on the side that heals. No other difference counts in the same scale!'
>
> 'No! no! You are not right!' said Dr Jeiletes. 'It is too deep, this caste system.'

When there is great political turmoil, some will adapt and survive and some cannot. Eugen believes that Austria can only be saved by the return of the emperor, though his cousin Eugenie has come to believe that Austria can save herself. Consequently, when he knows that the Emperor Karl's attempted return has been squashed, and that Otto has betrayed that cause in order to keep in with Horthy's regime, Eugen shoots himself. His code of honour has been shattered, and he cannot live without it. And, Eugenie, although she has always looked to Otto as the Head of her House, and has loved him since childhood, finally turns away from him, saying, 'My House has fallen.'[53] At the end of the novel it looks as though the way is clear for a (love) alliance between the young American journalist and Franz Salvator, and – if not marriage – a deep friendship between Eugenie and Dr Jeiletes. They represent the future. The novel itself is an intricate balancing act, significantly more sophisticated than any previous novel Phyllis had attempted.

Ernan's abrupt departure from Vienna caused dismay in the embassy, which would have been willing to retain him in a less demanding role. Evelyn Graham-Stamper, having been on leave in England, had missed the moment of Ernan's resignation. Returning to Vienna, she sent Ernan a letter at the end of August 1923 expressing her bitter disappointment:

> Dearest Beloved Herr Chief – Monday here again and nearly a week since you left Wien ... I hoped till the last that you would be able to come to some arrangement even though it would be difficult if dear Mrs Forbes Dennis had to go to Switzerland. I knew, of course, you could not leave her alone, but thought you might be able to pay us short visits. However, now I see the futility of such hopes and my heart is very sore.
>
> My heart is *very* sore. I know everybody simply hates you going ... One thing I have simply got to say and as I know you would be off through the door before I had two words out – I just have to write it; I am so inexpressively grateful that I have had the privilege of working with you and *under* you. It is *not* a little thing to win the respect and affection of those working under you, you know Herr Chef. We know that a man is not a hero to his valet, how much less so to the cold dispassionate judgement of his staff!!!
>
> Because I have known you, because of the loving respect I feel for you, all my life I will be just a trifle more gentle to the rest of humanity – the sort you are nice to, who make me impatient ... the rich Jews without manners ... will try to look at them through your eyes.

> Funnily enough I think I have always liked and admired you most when I have felt desperately impatient over your protégés! Do you remember rounding on me one morning because I had urged you to be impatient with that horrid little secretary of the Rothschilds? Your sleep was affected by it, and you were quite cross with me, but what you said to me about impoliteness being inexcusable under any circumstances whatever fell on fruitful soil … and when you pointed out that it might be as difficult to be a rich unpleasant Jew as a poor one, you made me see things in a different light …
>
> With every loving thought to you both and my most humble salaam . . . [54]

This letter encapsulates Ernan's deep-rooted sense of *noblesse oblige* and punctilious courtesy even in the face of provocation. He had found a career that matched his talents – an aptitude for foreign languages and an ability to lead others by modelling good behaviour – and so he made a heart-breaking renunciation in giving all this up. By making this decision and giving his whole care and protection to Phyllis over the next two years, he may well have saved her life. But this sacrifice was to give rise to some bitter feelings in the future.

Phyllis herself had gained a huge amount from these three years in Vienna: a new *savoir faire,* and, more importantly, a grasp of the complex politics of Austria and its neighbours following the Great War. It also led to her first serious consideration of the position of Jews in Europe. An ominous wave of violence was convulsing the continent. In Italy, Mussolini's inexorable rise to power, aided by his black-shirted fascist shock troops, continued unabated. The old liberal regime in Italy seemed powerless to resist. By October 1922, Mussolini had assumed dictatorial powers in Rome and set about controlling the minds of the people. This was a significant and horrendous portent of events yet to unfold in other parts of Europe.

CHAPTER 6

Mösern, Kitzbühel and Meeting Alfred Adler

> The science of Individual Psychology was not at all literary. It was not even a philosophy. It was a new way of living – and like life itself, it was personal, confusing, and hard to learn.
>
> PHYLLIS BOTTOME, *The Goal*

In September 1923, Ernan's search for a suitable place for Phyllis to cure was rewarded with a perfect find. He discovered a small mountain village above Innsbruck with a southern aspect and an altitude and climate as good, he thought, as anything in Switzerland. There were no hotels in Mösern, only an inn and nine peasant families who lived and farmed on the meadows nearby. Ernan arranged to rent rooms from the Spiegel family; they were small farmers who supplemented their income with summer visitors, but were not used to taking in winter guests. Ernan persuaded the Spiegels to take them in; the money they were offering was no doubt generous at the time. Arriving at the railhead of Seefeld, they were brought to their new home by the eldest son, Joseph Spiegel. The couple mounted a shaky horse-drawn Victoria while their goods and chattels were transported on an ox-cart:

> Our next door neighbour and most constant friend, the Hohe Munde, met us at the turn of the road, his great round head sparkling with new fallen snow, while his seven smaller sisters sank away from him peak by peak into the valley. Behind us rose the majestic cone of the Reiterspitz, and across the valley, a mere stone's throw as it seemed from the Mösern meadows, was the Hocheder, an eleven-thousander, highest and mightiest mountain of them all.[1]

1 *Phyllis's beloved grandmother, Margaret Macdonald Bottome*

2 *Wilmett, Mary and Phyllis (centre) as young children*

3 *Ernan aged nineteen, when Phyllis first fell in love with him*

4 *Ernan's Mamma thought that Phyllis and her hat were rather vulgar*

5 Ezra Pound. Phyllis made friends with the poet in London around 1910

6 Ernan's friend Frank Lascelles; the pageant-master became a threat to Phyllis and Ernan's relationship

7 The young Ivor Novello (left) with Ernan, whom he nicknamed, 'The Bear'

8 Ernan in the uniform of the 34th Poona Horse; he acted as interpreter for the regiment at the start of World War I

9 Nigel Dennis became the almost-son of Ernan and Phyllis, following the death of his father in World War I. Here he is aged nine, in Rhodesia

10 In 1919 and 1920, starving children in Vienna had no resistance to the influenza that swept across Europe in the aftermath of World War I

11 Phyllis Bottome in Vienna

Anna, their cook, and Lena, the maid, who had accompanied them from Vienna, took one look and fled back to civilisation. There was a trap door up to the Forbes Dennises' rooms, but upstairs there was no water supply, electric light or lavatory. Nor was there a kitchen, nor any shops in the village from which to buy food, so it is hard to imagine what role these Viennese servants could have played. Fortunately, Maria Spiegel, the eldest daughter of the house, took it upon herself to bring 'these mad English folk' food up on trays from the kitchen on the ground floor, where the Spiegels themselves, their cows, their pigs and their chickens all lived. Once settled in, they sent back to Vienna for Ernan's Bechstein grand piano. The piano was sent in a huge packing case to the railhead, and brought up on the ox-cart in the falling snow. It took father Spiegel, the only son, Joseph, one of their near neighbours and Ernan himself to get it up to their sitting-room.

> The re-assemblage of a carefully packed grand piano is always a serious business even for experts – but here were three men who had never seen a piano before and one who had never unpacked one, but held it dearer than a Ming vase, and just as frail. Shouts, groans, moments of tense silence, rapid footsteps, sharp admonitory barks from Luchs, reports from Maria and occasional frightened hoverings on my part in the doorway to uplift and reassure, ended in complete triumph. All the legs were on, and in the right places. There was only one faintly adverse mark, invisible to any but a very searching eye, and the piano was truly and rightly assembled in the best position, avoiding equally draughts from window and door. All listened in silent awe while Ernan made it speak.[2]

They were to live in Mösern for four seasons; Luchs left a strong trace of his presence by fathering puppies all over the mountainside. During this time Phyllis, sitting out on the balcony in her comforting sheepskin sack, was able to finish writing *Old Wine*, which she regarded, correctly, as her first grown-up book. Vienna, she felt, had thoroughly jerked her out of her Edwardian world. Observing the complex political and social nexus in Vienna had sparked both the desire and the necessity of tackling much more complex work.

In 1923 they celebrated their first Christmas in Mösern. Phyllis and

Ernan held a party for the village children, of whom there were twenty-five in all, as they heard that no one in the previous few years had been able to afford presents for them. They decided to give each child a warm garment, a toy and a bag of sweets – and an orange, a rare delicacy which had not been available since before the war. Ernan had gone down to Innsbruck on his skis, with two rucksacks and a detailed list of all the gifts to be purchased. Father Spiegel went into the woods and cut down a tree for Christmas that they decorated with the prettiest ornaments Ernan could find. Maria produced a wonderful spread, largely from foodstuffs purchased by Ernan. The result was a party the children never forgot and Phyllis and Ernan felt fully part of this alpine community.

This remote mountain village was a magical retreat for a writer:

> There were no hotels, no telegraph poles, no links with the outside world, no shops. It was under snow for seven months of the year, sometimes cut off entirely by drifts from either Seefeld or the Inn Valley for weeks at a time, except for ski runners. The road was, if not impassable, liable to degenerate into a torrent in the spring, and an exiguous pathway between snowdrifts in midwinter. We were self-subsisting, hardy and self-engrossed ... There was no crime because everybody knew what everybody else had; and there were few shocks. If telegrams arrived at Seefeld, as from time to time they did, they might be brought to us by an enterprising child of six who was a constant wayfarer and messenger between Seefeld and Mösern; and he would then be rewarded by a lump of sugar; which was an unheard of delicacy.[3]

The story of their life in Mösern was not written until much later. Sailing from America to England in 1940 she was to write *The Heart of a Child* in one burst of inspiration.[4] As it draws so directly on the four seasons they spent in Mosern, I will outline its story here. Set in the third year of the First World War, in the fictive village of Feldmuss, it centres on Karl, the eldest son of the Spiel family, and his love for his St Bernard dog, named Luchs. Phyllis dedicated the story 'To the memory of Luchs, Our Friend and Wolf-Dog'. The Spiel parents, who run the only inn in the village, are somewhat brutal, especially the father. He considers a beating the best way to make his children work for him, and they fear him but don't love him. When he gets ill, the local doctor says that Father Spiel must have meat in order to recover. His wife argues: 'How on earth are peasants to buy meat during the third winter of the war, or kill the cows that the farm depends on near Christmas when there are no calves? The pigs and sheep too must all be sold, except those to breed from, when the moment comes to take them down to market.'[5]

The doctor says the dog should be sacrificed. Young Karl is faced with conflicting ethical problems; the priest says to him that a man has a soul – even his brutal father – and a dog does not. Defiantly, Karl steals money from the church offertory box, and goes on the longest journey of his young life to take Luchs to live with a kindly veterinary surgeon in Innsbruck.

Karl, at eleven years of age, feels that he is almost a man; he looks after his younger brothers and sisters, as well as herding and milking the cattle that the Spiel family owns. But alone in the big town, having handed over his faithful dog, he feels for the first time that he is, after all, only a little boy: 'There was the hoot of an ambulance car from the Front, for instance; or soldiers shuffled by in small weary detachments, to and from their camps; or perhaps far more predatory and alarming still, came the sudden spurt and the flash past of lean long armoured cars, manned by machine-guns and filled with tin-helmeted officers.'[6]

When Karl returns home he is so badly beaten by his father that the whole village threatens to boycott the inn, and the Catholic priest, Father Wissenheit, says he will remove the boy from the Spiels' 'care' should it ever happen again.[7] Although the priest realises that Karl has stolen money from the church to pay for this train journey to Innsbruck and back, this same priest 'because he was sensible as well as good, put his mind, or tried to, into the heart of a child'.[8]

A major theme of this story is that of hatred, and the need to let it go. All through the war the villagers had been taught to blame their enemies, in particular the English. But as soon as the war ends English Quakers enter Innsbruck, helping to feed the starving children. And furthermore, two of these English come to stay in the village and give a Christmas party for all the children. This is a barely fictionalised account of the Forbes Dennises' own party in Mösern, including a description of the Englishwoman as a 'white-haired smiling lady'.[9] Karl's Christmas present is, of course, his beloved dog, returned to his love and care. The story is, in effect, a parable, albeit as always in Phyllis's work, drawing on a real experience.

Even though they could live very cheaply at Mösern, neither Phyllis nor Ernan could manage indefinitely without an adequate income. Ernan was earning nothing, and Phyllis's thriller, *Depths of Prosperity*, was only likely to sell well if she could go to America to promote it. This her new publisher, Doran, strongly urged her to do. She also needed a New York agent, as successor to the formidable Mr Pinker.[10] Her doctor reluctantly agreed that she should go, provided that she returned to the mountains for the winter. Phyllis was tremendously relieved, as Ernan had become increasingly restless in the confines of Mösern, cut off from the exciting international world of Vienna.

Phyllis went first to visit her family in England and then attended Betsy McCord's wedding to Lendall Pitts in Paris. She rejoined Ernan in Southampton in late September 1924, and they sailed together to New York. Phyllis was especially exhilarated as America had always represented to her a land of free spirits, even freedom itself.

> The whole of my childhood came to meet me as the light fog lifted and I saw dimly glimmering through the morning mist the Statue of Liberty with its splendid, still partially unfulfilled promise. Suddenly the skyline was crowded with the glittering towers that make the new profile of New York. These high and shimmering beehives were wholly new to me, but the scent of the air was the same. I drew in long, rapturous breaths of that lake-water-and-peanut-brittle smell that had haunted my happy childhood. This New World, no matter how it disguised itself by speed and size, I knew by heart.[11]

Waiting to meet them was her youngest uncle, Harry Bottome, who had faithfully corresponded with her ever since the death of her father. He had recently remarried and was keen for Phyllis to meet his new Southern bride and his friends. Ernan was able to resume friendships with Delanos and Roosevelts that he had made during his 1912 New

York visit and to introduce Phyllis to them. They also visited his Forbes cousins in Boston, who made them both welcome. In America, unlike England, Phyllis was a celebrity, as the *Century Magazine* had been serialising her novels for seven years. Phyllis always felt completely at home in America as though the six years she had spent there as a child had given her a double birthright.

Were it not for her necessary obedience to doctor's orders, they might well have made a life in America. But he had ordained that she must winter in the mountains, so they returned to Mösern. Once again spending many hours on her south-facing balcony in her sheepskin sack, Phyllis was soon busily engaged in a major restructure and redraft of *Old Wine*. Although the trip to America had caused no setback in her health, the threat of an attack of tuberculosis remained. Their biggest problem was to find a way for Ernan to make a living in a place where Phyllis could continue to 'cure'. Their original plan in St Moritz days had been for him to become a teacher; he was already fluent in French as well as in German, which had improved immeasurably during his post in Vienna. Consequently, it was decided that he would study as an external student for the London University Teacher's Certificate.

The plan was that Ernan should set up a school to take adolescent boys between fifteen and twenty, mainly English and American, who wanted to learn French and German. In time, he hoped to attract French and German boys who wanted to learn English. Together, the couple were committed to developing, 'on however small a scale, an international spirit in the new generation that might place a brick in the invisible structure of World Peace. This had been a dream of our youth even before the 1914 war, and now that we saw, in 1924, how little progress had been made since, we were even more anxious to put our early dreams to the test.'[12]

They needed to find a place where the climate would be good for Phyllis's lungs and where they could find a house to rent suitable for setting up as a boarding school. They chose Kitzbühel, a picturesque, sleepy little Tyrolean market town, 3,000 feet up in a windless valley. It had existed almost entirely as an agrarian economy until the arrival of the train in 1875; after this, a stream of winter sports enthusiasts had started to arrive, mostly Austrians, with a smattering of English visitors too. There was the beginning of development with tourists in mind: a Grand Hotel had been built to house the fans of skiing, tobogganing and curling. But it was still all fairly low-key in the 1920s. The cobbled streets and inns were charming; on Saturday mornings, the farmers set up stalls in front of the Rathaus, selling bread, cheese, hams, honey and jam as they had for hundreds of years.

For the winter of 1925 they rented the Villa Waldschutz under the Hahnenkahm; Phyllis was writing a novel that contemplated, in fictional form, that extraordinary creature, Edna St Vincent Millay. Clearly, before Dorothy Thompson had insisted on a break in the friendship, Phyllis had listened closely to tales of Vincent's life in Maine and in Greenwich Village, New York. The conceit running though *The Messenger of the Gods* is that the protagonist, Imogen, is a modern-day maenad. Maenads in Greek mythology are divine spirits who follow Dionysus, who love to dance and who are amorously free; they are murderous to men if driven to fury, but paradoxically they also excel as nurses. All of these elements are to be found in the novel, cleverly woven into an otherwise realistic tale of a talented young poet trying to find her way in the world. After reading Shelley's 'Ode to the West Wind' as a young girl, Imogen says:

> 'What's a Maenad, Dr Luke? I don't quite get that bit:
>
> > Like the bright hair uplifted from the head
> > Of some fierce Maenad.
>
> Shouldn't you just say she was a lady with a lot of hair that moved about in a high wind?'
>
> Dr Luke ventured. 'A classical lady maybe, and tempersome? I don't think there can be many left nowadays: that breezy life must have taken it out of them considerably.'[13]

From this moment on Imogen is determined to become a poet, and this burning ambition underscores everything else. The metaphoric underpinnings perhaps slightly over-determine the plot, as the ending when Imogen is redeemed morally by her nurse-like devotion to her lover, who is dying from consumption, rings less true than all the earlier parts. But the realism of three-quarters of the novel must have come direct from tales of Vincent's early life; like Vincent, Imogen lives on the coast of Maine, at the tide-line of the sea in the poorest part of the town. Similarly, Imogen has a father who has been thrown out by the mother, a forlorn and lost soul, who is, nevertheless, loved by the daughter. As in Vincent's own life, a rich woman from New York, in the novel a Miss Chester, discovers the girl's gift for poetry when staying in a hotel for summer visitors where the girl works.[14] The patroness takes her back to New York, buys her smart clothes, introduces her to smart society and shows her off as her poet-child. Miss Chester wants to take credit for Imogen's achievements, but disowns her once her wild side is revealed. Some of the most vivid scenes in the book must have come directly from Vincent's stories about such things as the costume ball in Greenwich village, which she attended dressed in some Turkish-style pyjamas. Similarly a drunken episode in which Imogen collapses into blue hydrangeas has the ring of remembered truth.

In the novel, Imogen learns to flirt early, and at seventeen becomes pregnant following a romance with a rich young summer visitor, holidaying with his mother. Although this ends in a miscarriage, which is hushed up by her doctor and her mother, Imogen comes to realise that she is now irrevocably a 'bad girl', whom no decent man would wish to marry. She resents the double standard:

> She and Maurice had done the same thing, but it was only upon Imogen that this darkness fell. She had a moment's sharp resentment against Maurice; the overwhelming antagonism of sex broke upon her dismayed heart. Why should she have a separate burden? Their pleasure had belonged to them both, but this terror was all her own.[15]

Following this early sexual experience, Imogen is reckless, and has a habit of fascinating men both young and old, until she is eventually pushed out of rich New York society for bedding another young woman's fiancé.

But Imogen is always true to her poetry. Her first boyfriend, Maurice, considers it crude and not decent. She tries to explain to him how she comes to write what she writes:

> 'There's the sea now,' Imogen went on reflectively. 'I can see it as it is – a great weight of water awfully cold and choking or like a whipped forget-me-not. The same with seagulls. Watch one flying overhead! It's like a little cloud taking life. Then it comes close, a chunky, greedy brute, with flat eyes like a codfish! Poetry's getting them both together; it's the air which they can move in, side by side, without hindering each other. Their truth is both beauty and ugliness. One has to go far enough to find it out.[16]

Maurice's failure to understand or appreciate Imogen's poetry provokes a maenad fury that leads to his death. By contrast, the lover who becomes significant to her is the one who understands what she is trying to do with her poetry:

> 'You like those poems?' she asked in a low voice.
>
> Derrick looked up at her with his flickering laughing eyes. 'I know what they're at,' he admitted. 'They don't fumble, and they don't spatter nature with cheap scent. I rather like the way they handle ugliness.'
>
> 'Beauty isn't everything,' Imogen said more softly still. 'Ugliness is just as important really. Beauty – she's been on the streets too long. Ugliness is worth having if you can strip her clean of mud.'[17]

If we take it that this portrait of Imogen is in some way Phyllis's *hommage* to Edna St Vincent Millay, it is worth noting that she recognises in her not only the strange arrogance of genius, but also that Vincent is true, if to nothing else, to her craft.

While Phyllis was busy working on her novel, Ernan was testing his theory that the boys in their school would learn a new language quickly and most thoroughly if they had two teachers, one who spoke English and one who spoke the language to be acquired, in this case, German. Ernan taught pronunciation and grammar, and the local teacher, Peter, worked on conversation and written work. This system seemed to work well. Ernan was a naturally gifted teacher, and at some level he seemed to help the boys grow up as well as learn. The boys were made to work hard at their studies all morning. In the afternoons they were free to go skiing or walking, Ernan often accompanying them as he was a fine skier and an indomitable mountain walker. They returned home for outdoor tea on the balcony, followed by preparation for the next day's lessons before supper. During the first winter they had only a handful of boys, two of whom were Cyril Egerton and Warren Martineau. A letter from Warren many years later gives a nice sense of how he remembered his time with Ernan and Phyllis:

> My days with you both at the Villa Waldschutz when I was a gauche, exceptionally ignorant teenager, fresh from a hospital bed, were the happiest of my life ... [I remember] Fritzel, the little old pony in his little sleigh from Innsbruck, Mariacher the driver with his huge horses and stream of children, 'Celie' the pretty maid – our evenings of reading near the best of stoves 'Bunker Bean', *Wuthering Heights* (I still treasure the copy Phyllis gave me). My survival from blood poisoning due to the devoted nursing, day and night, by you and Phyllis, 'Becky', Luchs and Peter.[18]

This establishes something of the pattern: if a boy were to be ill, then Phyllis herself would nurse him; she was a good nurse when occasion demanded, as she had acquired a great deal of experience looking after first her sister and then Lislie. Reading in the evenings in Phyllis's part of the house was something treasured by all the Kitzbühel boys.

Unfortunately, after their first winter, the landlord wished to sell the house, and as they could not afford to buy it, they rented a larger chalet on the opposite side of the valley. The Villa Tennerhof was set in an apple orchard on the south-facing side of the valley on the lower slopes of the Kitzbühler Horn, facing the Hahnenkahm. It was an old farmhouse dating back to 1679, with three tiers of balconies that they used to fill with scarlet geraniums and purple and white petunias, a local custom that has been preserved to this day. Because of its location, the Tennerhof farmer's traditional duty was to act as a weather forecaster. When a thunderstorm seemed imminent in harvest time, he would hoist a white sheet on the roof. This became Ernan's responsibility while the Tennerhof was their home.[19]

Financial constraints meant that they all lived together as a sort of extended family. This must have had disadvantages for Ernan and Phyllis, but had enormous advantages for the boys. There were no rules other than the decorum of courtesy. Boys were expected to turn up on time for meals and to treat servants – Becky the cook and Celie the housemaid – with due respect. Other than at mealtimes, the big dining-room was used for table-tennis, and for playing records on a gramophone. After supper, the boys usually went up to Phyllis's workroom, where they could play cards, or read, or tell ghost stories they made up. Phyllis, endlessly inventive, had devised an imaginary dining club, and the boys were encouraged to imagine a banquet with exotic foods. She had been used to entertaining her younger brother George and she found this an infinitely transferable skill. She had also got to know all the interesting characters in Kitzbühel and would tell stories about them.

Indeed some of them were colourful enough without any embroidery. In the nearest schloss to the Tennerhof lived the Gräfin Lamberg and her daughter Paula, the most famous woman ski-jumper in the world at that time. Her daughter-in-law, Gräfin Martha, and her children lived in Schloss Kaps on the other side of the valley. Martha's dissolute husband had left her and his three children, and lived with a mistress, 'a canary-headed lady, who had formerly worked at a Kitzbühel photographer's; they were therefore generally referred to as the Graf and the Photo-graph'.[20] Gräfin Martha, with whom Phyllis became close friends, sensibly ran her schloss as a *pension*, though unfortunately this resulted in a feud between the mother- and daughter-in-law, as running a *pension* was considered déclassé, though exactly how the deserted wife was supposed to support herself and her children otherwise was less than clear. Phyllis's closest friend of the Kitzbühel days was Luischen ('little Luise') Thaler, the district nurse, who had worked with the Friends' Mission in Innsbruck after the war. She spoke excellent English and, with Phyllis, she set up a Shakespeare Society, which Kitzbühelers wishing to improve their English could join, alongside the Tennerhof boys.

Having a working writer in the house spurred several of the boys to try their own hand at the art, and Phyllis would always read and critique stories that they had written for her. In this way, at Kitzbühel, she mentored the apprenticeship writings of Ian Fleming, Nigel Dennis and Ralph Arnold (novelist and publisher).[21] They could also listen to

Ernan playing on his beloved Bechstein grand, now almost as seasoned a traveller as the Forbes Dennises themselves. Ernan was a fine musician and Phyllis was a professional writer so these adolescent boys found themselves living in close company with two intellectuals, who were keen to give them everything they could. As well as learning languages they were encouraged to think, reflect and write. It was hugely more than a 'crammer'.

Childless themselves, they poured love into their charges – rather too much, felt Robert Pollak, who was concerned that they were throwing pearls before swine: 'Those young cabbages, of what use will they be to you in later life for all your interest and care? When they are grown up they will forget all about you, and you will never hear from them again'.[22] This may well be the fate of teachers generally, but it was not the case with any of the Kitzbühler boys who never forgot the Forbes Dennises. Ernan gained a well-deserved reputation for being able to handle delinquent upper-class boys.

In the spring of 1926, Ernan went to visit Robert Pollak in Vienna, and while there, talked over the various problems of his adolescent charges. Robert advised him to consult Dr Alfred Adler, who, he said, was currently 'turning Viennese education upside down in the Hauptschulen, by teaching the teachers how to produce a good human being'.[23] Adler was a member of the faculty of the Pedagogical Institute in Vienna, in the division of therapeutic education where, beginning in 1924, he gave a series of lectures on 'The Difficult Child'.[24] Consequently, Ernan visited Alfred Adler, then aged fifty-four, in his consulting-room in the old quarter of Vienna; he was not immediately impressed:

> All I saw was this funny, tubby little man who offered me a cigarette and asked what I wanted. I tried to explain and he asked me whether I had read any of his books. I said, 'No. Have you written any?' And he pointed to a shelf above his head. When I'd scribbled down a few titles he told me to read them and come back in a year's time. That was my first interview with Alfred Adler.[25]

Despite this somewhat inconclusive first meeting Ernan began to read Adler's books, translating them for himself from the German in order to understand the main concepts. He quickly recognised some of his own personality traits as he read Adler's *The Practice and Theory of Individual Psychology* (1913) and became increasingly interested in his work. He also saw that Adler's theories about the discouraged child could help a teacher to turn that child around, so long as he took great care to understand what was making the child afraid to learn and to achieve.

Adler had received a medical degree from the University of Vienna in 1888, and after initially practising as an opthalmologist, had gradually shifted to neurology and psychiatry. Although he had already started his own theoretical work, he was interested in Freud, who had become known in Vienna for his approach to hysteria. In 1902, Adler became one of the first members of Freud's inner circle, and was viewed by Freud as his heir-apparent, as shown by Freud nominating Adler as the first president of the Vienna Psychoanalytic Society in 1910. They had a famous falling out, the crux of which was that Adler dissented from Freud's insistence that all neurosis stemmed from repressed sexual instincts. Freud never allowed direct challenges; anyone who did not accept his psychosexual theories was expelled from the group. Jung, Bleuler and Adler all suffered this fate.[26]

Initially, Adler disagreed with Freud's hypotheses in three key areas. He did not concur with Freud's view that aggression was only the sexual drive (which Freud called *libido*) disguised. Nor did he believe, as Freud claimed, that it was suppressed desire for the opposite-sex parent that caused children to harbour murderous wishes against the same-sex parent. Adler's view was more 'Darwinian' in the sense that he thought children were to some extent 'hardwired' to operate according to an instinct that could better be understood by thinking in terms of the survival of the fittest. Although Adler believed that aggression was the core drive, in so far as it related to the child's physical and psychic survival, in survival terms it would make no sense to murder the parent. Adler also challenged Freud's notion of penis envy, and called the repression of women the 'carcinoma of our culture' in a 1911 article specifically criticising Freud's psychosexual theories.[27] Adler considered that in society as it stood at that time, there existed in men an internalised misogyny (which he called 'Masculine Protest'), which caused the repression of all things deemed weak and feminine.

Freud would not tolerate Adler's challenge to his theories, and expelled him from his group; Adler was then free to develop his own social psychology. Adler's experience of working with his 'pupils' – he did not call them patients – led him to believe that the disposition to neurosis lay not so much in unconscious sexual desire, but in feelings of inferiority. Adler evolved the notion that all children experience a sense of inferiority because of their relative size and dependence on others. In turn, inferiority can lead to attempts at overcoming the perceived weakness ('compensation'); this process is motivated by the generalised drive which Adler called striving for superiority. Some individuals are so overwhelmed by early feelings of helplessness that they develop a lifelong sense of inferiority and this he called the inferiority complex. Others attempt to overcome their sense of weakness by pretending to feel superior, when inwardly they lack self-esteem; this Adler called the superiority complex. In other words, we construct an ideal self in which we are big, strong and on top. In unfavourable circumstances, the feelings of inferiority are extreme, yet our ideal self becomes godlike.

Although both Freud and Adler agreed that the first five years were highly significant, Freud always saw the child competing with the parent of the same sex for the attention of the parent of the opposite sex (the Oedipus or Electra complex). Adler, on the other hand, considered from his observations that siblings competed with each other, in order to win greater parental investment. In consequence, he believed that birth order was significant: the first-born's place in the family was secure, until the arrival of the second-born; after that, there was a competition for each sibling to find a niche within the family in which he or she could feel secure. Although Adler regarded this as normal, sibling rivalry could also turn poisonous, and children within a family often chose a *gegenspieler,* a person to compete with at all costs in an endless neurotic duel. This particular concept must have leapt off the page at Ernan, who had been unconsciously engaged in just such a duel with his older brother, Fred. When Fred had gone off to war, then so must Ernan. When Fred had been sent to the most dangerous frontline position, nothing would do but that Ernan must join him (which had meant getting himself transferred, with difficulty, from a company about to be sent out of harm's way). Fred had died, a hero, with a DSO;

Ernan had been obliged to make do with a near-fatal injury, and had then tried to make himself responsible for Fred's widow, Louise, and her two children.

No sooner had Ernan started to grasp Adlerian theories in relation to his own life, than he had a marvellous opportunity to test them out in his observations of two brothers, Peter and Ian Fleming. Later on in his career Ernan was to become a psychologist, and to treat some famous people. However, Ernan's case notes, rightly, have an embargo on them until 2022, so his explanations to Ian Fleming's biographer give us our best clue to how he started to make use of Adlerian theories – in the first instance, as an aspect of his teaching.[28] Phyllis and Ernan met the younger Fleming brother first. Ian had been almost expelled from Eton; he had kept a car against the rules and would often truant in it, always having an assignation with a pretty girl. His mother removed him just before he was formally expelled, and having heard that Ernan had done a good job with Lord Ellesmere's nephew, Cyril Egerton, sent him out to Kitzbühel for the summer in the hope of keeping him out of mischief. Ernan went down to meet him at the station:

> my first impression of Ian was that he was very good-looking, very arrogant, very Etonian and very prickly. What the French call *difficile*. It was almost impossible to get through his defences, and he showed no great inclination to work. We were reading André Maurois's *Ariel* in French, and Ian made a great show of not liking it. I learned later that he wrote to his mother complaining that he was being worked far too hard.[29]

Ian regarded Kitzbühel simply as a summer vacation, swimming in the Schwartzee, climbing the Horn and chatting up pretty girls at the Café Reisch was his idea of what he wanted to do. His mother intended that on his return to England, he should do officer training at Sandhurst. Even the kind-hearted Forbes Dennises were frankly somewhat relieved to see the back of him.

In August 1926, Phyllis's mother died, aged seventy-two, of heart failure.[30] Phyllis had come to view Daisy with distaste, as someone who had put neither her husband's nor her children's welfare above her own selfish needs.[31] However, these must have been very uncomfortable feelings to process and it may well have been that Adler's arrival in her life was especially opportune in helping sort out her conflicting emotions.

In the summer of 1927, Adler came to visit Ernan at Kitzbühel, on his way to an educational conference at Locarno, which Ernan was also to attend. Phyllis had read some Freud, whom she considered a wonderful writer, but she was, unsurprisingly, more drawn to Adler's more 'feminist' standpoint. Initially, Phyllis was unimpressed and even a little disappointed by Adler. She said in her autobiography that Ernan had led her to believe that she would be meeting 'a Socratic genius, who would plunge us all in the depths of psychology'.[32] It might also be, however, that she liked to be the intellectual leader in their relationship, and in this case it was Ernan who had 'discovered' Adler.

When Adler arrived at Kitzbühel he was fifty-seven years old, and his love of Viennese cakes and pastries had caused him to become rather rotund. Initially he seemed more *gemütlich* than intellectual, and he listened more than he talked. Phyllis acknowledged, however, that his attention spread a curiously warming effect over them all. She later described her first impression:

> Instead of the stimulating and awe-inspiring psychologist whom I had been looking forward to meeting, I beheld a small, stout, active man, abstemious, unrigid, full of the love of living, his twinkling eyes like those of a Paris gamin. Only, his great brow was the brow of a sage. Adler sat on a high, straight-backed chair, his feet swinging off the floor, as if only a joke could hold him there. Our boys, one and all, delighted in him. I found, after Adler's departure, that no one in our large household had failed to feel drawn to him. He had spoken what seemed like a chance word of encouragement or good fellowship to everyone.[33]

They took their meals altogether outdoors under the trees; Adler was interested in the life of everyone: Phyllis and Ernan, the boys, the local women who worked for them. Even their dog, Luchs, liked to rest his head on Adler's knee.

On the last evening of his stay, Phyllis and Ernan, on this occasion without the boys, took Adler out to supper. Sitting under a flowering chestnut tree outside the Café Reisch and gazing out on to the village street, Adler spoke about his experience in the First World War, and of how he had treated shell-shock cases. He spoke frankly of

> the artificial humbug that had to be kept alive in order to continue the wholesale slaughter, and the deadly effect of so much falsity and violence upon the human mind. As he talked, we seemed to see the naked structure of war, and to understand how so much suffering inflicted by each country upon the other must destroy – as indeed we now know that it did destroy – the standard of living for generations. In those hours, I ceased to think of Adler as ordinary: I knew what I was looking at, and listening to, was a great man.[34]

Now, it seems, Phyllis as well as Ernan sensed they were in the presence of a kind of genius. In this conversation with Adler, she found that although he wore his scholarship lightly, he had formulated some of his key psychological theories from Aristotle's concept of *poiesis*, or the creative force of the human being. Whatever the variables of a person's life, Adler said, it should be possible to create a workable whole. From Seneca he had adopted the view that what happens to us is not so significant as how we view it. Phyllis's understanding from the conversation that evening, that Individual Psychology was less focused on the libido than on encouraging each individual to engage with society, chimed with everything she believed. She had learned from her grandmother, and even from her flawed father, that looking out, rather than in, was the best definition of a good life. And, although Adler did not follow Jewish religious practices, he embodied what might be called Jewish ethical values, particularly the concept of *tikkun*, the healing or repairing of the world.

That same summer, Ian Fleming's older brother, Peter, aged nineteen, arrived from Christ Church ready to brush up his German. The contrast to be observed between the brothers was striking. As Ernan put it: Peter had a 'wonderfully disciplined intelligence which went through German like a razor through butter … Peter was the sort of thoroughbred who comes out of the stable glossy, confident, superior to all the other horses, a natural winner. Whereas Ian had been the sort of horse that arrives sweating and nervous at the starting-post, more likely to throw its rider than win its race.'[35]

Shortly after Peter had returned to England, Ian was in trouble again, for exactly the same truanting activities with cars and girls that had got him in trouble at Eton, and, facing a punishment of six months confined to barracks, he quit Sandhurst. His despairing mother was considering buying him a one-way ticket to Australia – sending the errant son off to the colonies, a rather nineteenth-century response.

Ernan suggested that she pack Ian off to Kitzbühel for the winter and he would see if he could do anything with him. Having studied Adler's theories and having had the opportunity to observe Peter Fleming, Ernan felt that he was beginning to get a handle on the crux of Ian's problems. Both Peter and Ian had a dead hero for a father. In 1917 Valentine Fleming had been killed by a shell, the same year that Ernan had nearly been killed. Peter, although less than twelve months older than Ian had responded by taking up the role of the male head of the family, applying himself with great seriousness to every task. At Eton he had won all the prizes, whereas Ian had been merely Fleming Minor, never able to live up to the godlike brother. As Ernan saw it, Ian had found his niche as the disgraced younger brother, a role to which he had become neurotically addicted. Ernan said:

> He was like a weathercock as one mood chased another. He couldn't give himself a chance. He had no workable aim at all to his life and all the usefulness had been squeezed out of him. He was immensely frustrated – who wouldn't be after trying to compete with an unbeatable brother like Peter? There he was, caught between his burning ambition and his constant disappointment. By the time he came to us, all he could really do was make a nuisance of himself. For he was a rebel, like most second sons ... I could only suppose that it was the father who was originally responsible – unconsciously, of course. That, after all, is usually the pattern you get in these cases of a family with an outstanding elder son. The father tries to make up for the mother's devotion to the eldest, and in Ian's case the father's death when the boy was nine must have made it worse.[36]

There seems little doubt that Ernan turned Ian around at a time when he might otherwise have gone completely off the rails. Ernan was a gentleman of Scottish aristocratic ancestry, which made him seem to

Ian a little like the male Flemings, and, further, he had been tested in war. Like Ian's father, he could be regarded as a war-hero, and Ian came to see Ernan as an idealised father-figure.

Following Adler's theories, Ernan saw that he had to replace Ian's self-defeating goal of being a failure with a new goal that could lead to success. He encouraged Ian to work towards being accepted by the Foreign Service, and it may well have been that Ernan's work in military intelligence made this seem a rather glamorous option. The Foreign Office examination was highly competitive and only a few candidates from the best Oxbridge colleges were normally accepted, so Ernan had set him a challenging goal:

> but for someone with Ian's extreme ambition it had to be an important aim or nothing. At the same time as I advised him on his syllabus I picked on as many subjects as I could in order to get him interested in educating himself … The choice of subjects you could offer for the Foreign Office examinations was very wide, and as I advised Ian I tried to give him subjects which would complete his education and also suit his temperament. So I centred his reading on the idea of studying the struggles of the individual throughout the ages to improve himself and better his conditions of life.[37]

Once again, Ernan was almost uniquely well-placed to advise Ian: neither he nor Phyllis had attended university but both had educated themselves in a kind of long-running reading group of two. Their own range of reading was eclectic, and they were very much European, rather than merely English, intellectuals. As Ian was to say later:

> I remember in those days before the war reading, thanks to the encouragement of the Forbes Dennises, the works of Kafka, Musil, the Zweigs, Arthur Schnitzler, Werfel, Rilke, von Hofmannsthal, and those bizarre psychologists Weininger and Groddeck – let alone the writings of Adler and Freud – and buying first editions (I used to collect them) illustrated by Kokoschka and Kubin.[38]

Despite some improvement, Ian continued to get into scrapes. He craved excitement, and after learning to ski, would ski dangerously rather than skilfully. He drove extremely fast and made a near-fatal misjudgement when he drove his car across the level-crossing near Kitzbühel and had the front of the car sheared off. Ian miraculously escaped injury. His amorality with girls and women continued, which is hardly surprising, as his mother had endless sexual liaisons and in 1926 had introduced into the family an illegitimate daughter sired by the artist Augustus John as an 'adopted' child.[39] After one of Ian's many scrapes, he compounded the problem by being rude to Phyllis. Ernan, though remarkably patient and empathetic with Ian, had a chivalrous attitude with regard to how men should treat women. He threatened him with expulsion and Ian's abject letter to Ernan assumes that he is about to be sent home in disgrace:

> I see now, Ernan, that everything good that I have done, everything that I have thought good, that I have thought generous has been a sham. I had thought that there were one or two things I had left to pride myself on. But they go now the way of all the rest. You have shown me today and I have added my realisation that everything of any merit I have ever done has been a spectacular gesture, in the hopes that someone would see it – a gesture which would save me the trouble of ever being anything genuine, of ever having an emotion which contained more than words. You perhaps realised this when first I came here. You tried to help me, you gave me everything, your time, your affection, and, I think, some of your health. I took them all and thought it enough to feel vaguely thankful and be pleasant when it suited me and when I hoped it would be noticed. I shirked my work when I could, and I thought fit to be rude to Mrs Forbes Dennis when she was kindest to me, and I thought to myself – now I've got a friend, and a friend who will work out my troubles for me, and who will do anything in the world for me – good, let it be done – let my work even be done for me, and if I imagine I am grateful it will be sufficient payment. And you, Ernan, you saw this going on and you suffered for, God knows why, you liked me, and you spared my feelings and you put yourself to greater efforts, and I was the same, and I began to feel intensely grateful to you for being my friend and for making

something of me, but now I realise it was only a surface change and concealed better the blasted spectacular sham which I choose to call my character. Intelligence I may have but what was its use when it all went to perfecting this sham – what is its use now when it makes me realise my rottenness. God knows I hope it will one day produce something which I can show you and make me more worthy to ask for forgiveness.

This letter may seem an exaggeration – I only wish it was – at any rate, please believe that there is something in me which makes me hope that one day I shall be able to ask your forgiveness.

IAN [40]

Ernan insisted on his apologising personally to Phyllis, and after 'a tearful repentance scene' he was allowed to stay.[41]

In the spring of 1928, Mrs Fleming wrote asking whether Ernan really felt that he could turn Ian into a suitable candidate for the Diplomatic Service; his reply was succinct:

Ian's qualities are considerable; his general intelligence is above the average; he has imagination and originality, with the power of self-expression. He has excellent taste, a love of books, and a definite desire both for truth and for knowledge. He is virile and ambitious; generous and kind-hearted.

But he is nineteen and going through the most difficult period of his development. With unusual physical and intellectual maturity he has not yet acquired mental discipline or working philosophy.

He therefore lacks stability and direction. His ambitions are considerable but vague. He has not yet learnt to enjoy work or to subordinate his impulses to his permanent aims, nor has he yet grown out of the schoolboy's fear of authority and the mental dishonesty which such fear often produces. This coupled with the strength of his desires, often makes him fall below his theoretically high standards of conduct.

These facts should not cause dismay. He requires time to learn to handle a complex personality.[42]

The confidence with which Ernan 'analysed' Ian had certainly come from his readings of Adler. Having met Ian's mother and having categorised her as a dangerous *femme fatale*, he felt sure that settling Ian into good work habits was an imperative first step. In this he succeeded, and Phyllis, naturally, was brilliant at encouraging the boys' imaginations.

At dinner she would tell them tales set in the village, often turned into a kind of gothic soap opera that could be carried on each evening. All the boys loved these stories, and several joined in with their own characters. Ian's contribution was a tale of Graf Schlick who committed terrible crimes and perpetrated unspeakable tortures. She encouraged the boys to write them down, and 'Death, On Two Occasions', critiqued by Phyllis, was the first fiction he ever wrote.[43] After a year working with Ian, Ernan suggested that, given his aptitude for languages, and to improve his chances of a career in the Foreign Office, he should study Russian. Ernan arranged for him to become an external student of Munich University, living with a German family there, in order to make sure that his German also continued to improve. Ernan urged Ian to undergo an Adlerian analysis with Dr Leonard Seif while in Munich and even set up a meeting, but this Ian refused. Ernan encouraged him to continue to think psychologically, however, writing to Jung on Ian's behalf to obtain written permission for him to translate Jung's lecture on Paracelsus from the German. In short, although regarding Ian as a sort of 'half Faust, half Byron', and worrying about him a good deal, the Forbes Dennises continued to love him. The love in the relationship worked both ways. Ian said that the Forbes Dennises were 'father and mother' to him 'when he 'needed them most' and that his time in Kitzbühel was always a golden time in his memory.[44] Although frequently ruthless in his relationships with people, Ian was unfailingly generous in later life in all his dealings with the Forbes Dennises.

To their great delight, another of the boys who came to the Tennerhof was Ernan's nephew, Nigel. The Forbes Dennises had acted almost in *loco parentes* for three years following the death of his father, Fred, but when he was eight his mother Louise had taken him with her to live in Rhodesia. In 1927, Louise wrote to say that he 'had rather outgrown his strength', and that it would be a good thing if he could come and live with his uncle and aunt in the mountains.[45] When he arrived, aged sixteen, to join them at Kitzbühel, they immediately felt that there was something more seriously wrong with Nigel than a growth spurt, and following a visit to a specialist, he was diagnosed as suffering from epilepsy. This was one problem. They also had to integrate Nigel into a school filled with English public schoolboys, which he found very difficult. He wanted to enjoy the privileges of a nephew in a context where it was necessary that he should be treated on exactly the same terms as the other boys. This situation proved extremely difficult to manage, but it was clear to Phyllis that Nigel, like Ian Fleming and Ralph Arnold, had a talent for writing: 'All the boys wrote occasional essays for me to comment on, upon their own subjects. I realised when I read Nigel's that he was a born writer. He had that raw eye and direct gift of observation only to be found in writers.'[46]

This talent, she encouraged with great pleasure.

The next book Phyllis wrote, *Windlestraws*, turned back to thinking about British social life. It revealed among other things that, following her years in Vienna, her political positioning had moved a long way from the conservatism with which she grew up. By 1928, women in Britain could vote on the same terms as men, and if they had contributed to National Health Insurance, were eligible for a pension at sixty-five. Although the novel, set in a country house, has a slight sense of the Edwardian about it, its frankness about sexual matters is modern. Her original name for the novel was 'Rose Garden'; she imagined a young woman, exquisitely beautiful, first seen by her heroine in a rose garden. But the beauty of Beatrice Falconer only serves to distract the eye of the beholder, like the rose she resembles, from her deadly thorns. The heroine of the novel, Jean Arthbuthnot, goes to the beautiful Tudor house, 'Windlestraws', to act as secretary to Reggie Falconer, to help him in his campaign to become a Conservative Member of Parliament. Jean, whose father is an academic, and who has herself achieved a first in History, helps Reggie to write his speeches, even though she is not in sympathy with his politics. Accompanying him to his meetings:

> Jean heard again and again the same short views on privileged life, the same genial selfishness, the same assured conviction that the power, honour, and glory of England lay with one particular class, and that whatever anyone else claimed in any other class was bad for them and worse for the country ... Reggie didn't want people to suffer. He wanted the lower classes to be docile and well cared for by their betters; although it had never occurred to Reggie himself to be docile or that he had any betters. He saw no reason why the qualities his own manhood rejected shouldn't be gratefully accepted by nine-tenths of the manhood of his county.[47]

The patriarchal element inherent in the ideology of the landed gentry is paralleled in the complicated emotional set-up. Beatrice is an unhappy *femme fatale* who captivates men and is careless of the pain she inflicts on women. But, although the two men in the novel (Beatrice's husband Reggie and Reggie's best friend Ian Ramsay) are shown as having been heroes in the First World War and having their own code of honour, nevertheless there is a kind of moral bankruptcy in the Conservative mindset. On her first evening at Windlestraws, Jean is moved to discuss a play she has recently seen performed, Strindberg's *The Father*, that goes to the heart of the tangled relationships she sees in front of her:

> 'Strindberg made the wife in his play a fiend dragging her husband's mind to pieces; but the husband admitted with complacence that she was to have no control either over her own child, or over her own money, or over herself.' There was a curious silence in the room, as if Jean's audience were not only listening to her, but to each other's inaudible comments on her words. 'I thought it the greatest Feminist play I ever saw,' Jean went on a little nervously, 'though I'm sure Strindberg didn't mean to defend women. He made the play out of hatred of his wife; but even the hatred of a great genius has a flash of truth in it!'[48]

Although the representations of both men seem more sympathetic than that of Beatrice, nevertheless Phyllis brings out the facts that Beatrice had been more or less married off at nineteen to Reggie, a man she did not love. Perhaps as a direct consequence, she finds sexual relations with him repulsive, but her side of the bargain is to produce an heir for Windlestraws, which is not merely a house, but a landed estate. Once she has produced a son as her third child, her husband agrees to leave her alone sexually. But whereas he is free to take mistresses, if she breaks the marriage code she will be thrown out of what has become her home and will lose her children. However repugnant Beatrice is, in her social class she will pay more than her husband, according to the laws of the country. She has her compensations, and generally these are a cruel use of her beauty. It is a twist on the old George Eliot theme that women may become poisonous if constantly thwarted. Although Jean feels sorry for Reggie, because, despite everything, he still loves his wife, in the end he is revealed to be a 'windlestraw', an insubstantial man. This novel does not have anything like the immediacy of her writing about Vienna; she is drawing on a sense of England that is slightly archaic, as she has not lived there for almost a decade. It was not to be one of her best-sellers.

A series of events served to unsettle Ernan's plans for the future. Phyllis always had her career as a writer, even if she suffered from bouts of TB. Ernan's career was always constrained by what Phyllis's health could stand. A new possibility had opened up for him as a result of the visit to the Locarno conference he had attended with Adler. There he had met Beatrice Ensor, the foundress of Frensham Heights, a co-educational school in England, who had encouraged Ernan to apply for the headship. He was short-listed for the job, and went for an interview, but in the end the trustees decided to appoint someone who had had experience with girls as well as boys. Ernan was more relieved than disappointed; he had not felt sure that he could make a success of it. Writing from Frensham Heights on 1 January 1928, he said, 'I am more than ever convinced that I am the wrong person ... I am not tough enough on the one hand or inspired enough on the other.'[49] But his lack of fixed purpose proved a strain on both of them; it is to be noted that *Windlestraws* was dedicated 'To My Husband', at a juncture when their marriage was under acute strain.

In the autumn of 1928, Ernan decided to accompany Robert Pollak to San Francisco when he returned to the San Francisco Conservatory of Music, where he had succeeded the famous violinist Franz Ondiric as the head of the violin department. One of Robert's first pupils there was the eight-year-old Isaac Stern, later to become a world famous virtuoso violinist.[50] Ernan was suffering from what Sinclair Lewis has called 'village virus'; he felt intellectually deadened and after one of his recurrent fits of restlessness he decided to look for a job in America, although it is not clear exactly what kind of job he thought he could find, or even what he was looking for.[51] Phyllis, with her beloved dog Luchs to keep her company, remained at the Tennerhof in order to continue writing and to look after Nigel.

In October, Phyllis took Nigel to the Odenwaldschule, near Heidelberg. Ernan had met the headmaster, Dr Paulus Gehab, at the Locarno conference and had visited the school for a week to decide if it would be good for his nephew. Phyllis herself stayed for nearly a week and was impressed with it; she was especially interested in its co-educational aspect, and how potential sexual encounters between older pupils were managed, or otherwise:

> If the older ones fall in love, they aren't selfish or bullying about it – which is all we can expect from love – and much more than one usually gets. As no one pays any attention to what may take place – I doubt if anything does. And anyhow if it does I don't believe that it matters! All that I ever learnt about life was wrong – and I was sheltered and indecently innocent for many years ... The whole thing was an eye-opener to me.[52]

There were two hundred and fifty children between six and eighteen years old, with eight children (four boys and four girls) living in each chalet with two adults, one male and one female, as house-parents. There was a democratic system in place, rather similar to that of Summerhill. The children were encouraged to take responsibility for their own learning and to take their share of household tasks. Nigel, initially, found this system irksome: 'I can't bear being put on my honour. You see, then I can't do what I want.'[53] Nigel Dennis is today, perhaps, most famous for his satire, *Cards of Identity*, but his first novel, *Chalk and Cheese*, a barely fictionalised account of his experience at the Odenwaldschule published in 1934, is very interesting.[54]

Phyllis had intended to go to Paris in November, but after Ernan's departure, she experienced what she immediately suspected was a return of tuberculosis. The familiar symptom of temperature spikes alarmed her, so Phyllis's friend Luischen, the district nurse, measured them and found that her nightly temperature was running at 102 to 103 degrees. A consultant at Innsbruck took X-rays and said she must go straight into a sanatorium as both lungs were affected. However, she decided to return to the Tennerhof where she could 'cure' on her balcony and where Luischen could check on her every day. Inevitably she was lonely during this period; there must have been alarming echoes of the previous time when she was ill and Ernan had disappeared to Canada and America with exciting male friends. Nor is it surprising that Ernan felt restless. On marrying Phyllis, Ernan had been compelled to give up his friendship with Ivor Novello and the whole of that circle. Ivor, by 1928, was a matinée idol of the silent screen, receiving two thousand fan letters a week. After a string of earlier film successes, he starred in *The Constant Nymph*, which was considered by critics and adoring fans alike the best film of that year.[55] By contrast, Ernan, once Ivor's most intimate friend, had been forced to give up a glamorous posting in Vienna because of the fragile health of his wife, and had found himself trapped in an alpine village. Phyllis wrote to Dorothy Thompson:

> I am quite alone in Tennerhof – empty as a shell – the whole valley given up to a few lean cats prowling over the cut fields for mice – and the sodden drop of apples. Not a soul to call a soul. Marindel [a local peasant woman] knocking leaves off trees – toothless and wise – representing life ... I feel as if, with Ernan's going, half of me – and that the better half – had fallen over a precipice![56]

She admitted in this letter that lately she and Ernan had found that their love was 'as painful as a nutmeg grater'.[57]

During this period of semi-enforced 'leisure', sleeping badly and suffering from perpetual fever, she wrote a 'long short', a term Henry James invented to mean a story of about sixty-to-seventy thousand words, a form in which she liked to work. Its title, 'Tatter'd Loving', is taken from one of Shakespeare's sonnets and is a study of a troubled family constellation. In it, Vera obtains a divorce and marries Edward, shown as her true love, but, as a consequence, is forced to leave her daughter, Ariadne, behind. When Ariadne is almost grown-up, the two women re-meet, and Ariadne asks why her mother stayed so long in an unhappy relationship with her father before leaving with Edward. Vera explains to her: ' "I had no money and no training. In those days women rarely earned their own living, certainly not women who had been brought up in a sheltered useless seclusion out of which they'd been suddenly dipped into the world, and married off at eighteen." '[58] Ariadne is ready to adore her newly found mother, but Vera is jealous of her own daughter, and very nearly shipwrecks her marriage to Edward as a consequence. It could be argued that this is the first of Phyllis's specifically Adlerian studies of malfunctioning human beings. Vera is neurotic; although superficially a beautiful woman, she is revealed as essentially a spoiled child who has never really grown up. Published in Britain in 1929, and then in America in 1930, it received very good reviews. In *Good Housekeeping* (February 1931), Emily Newall Blair said that it had a 'sparkling style, situation handled with adroitness, suspense piled on suspense, characters delineated so that they throbbed with life, yet revealed to their innermost core'.

Ernan returned to Kitzbühel in December without having found a new opening in America, although it seems likely that Robert Pollak had tried to help him. Matters were bought to a head by their landlord insisting on them either buying the Tennerhof or giving up the tenancy. Although they could just about have afforded to do it, it would have absorbed every bit of their capital. Having witnessed the joy that Robert experienced teaching gifted scholars at the San Francisco Conservatory, Ernan decided that he would rather give up the Kitzbühel school the following June and instead retrain as a teacher of piano.[59] He assured Phyllis that this would make him happy, and, of course, her strongest desire was that he should find a career that satisfied him. Initially they assumed that Phyllis would have to stay in Kitzbühel, simply taking a smaller house, but at this point her doctor appeared with the good news that, as she wrote to Dorothy Thompson, 'The TB after a pretty wild beginning has got completely "isolated" by old scars – and the mischief is absolutely arrested. I have only to be careful and go very slow for a year.'[60] Although they could honestly feel that they had helped some of the adolescent boys under their combined care, Ernan in particular felt miserably cut off from the concerts, musical shows and opera which he so loved. Kitzbühel, too, was changing. Because of the development of the winter sports scene, more and more tourists were flooding in, so the advantages for a writer were beginning to be outweighed by the disadvantages – less peace and more visitors. Another upheaval would have to be made. Phyllis wrote to Dorothy that:

> Personally I prefer Austrian life, but that is partly because I am a coward and like amiability, and also because I am too used to sunshine to do without it. But on the whole, if I had £10,000 a year and could go abroad whenever I liked, I should live in England rather than anywhere else in the world; but hand me £10,000 a year first![61]

It was crunch-time. They had gone into the Tyrol in the first place because of Phyllis's recurring bouts of tuberculosis, but, at this point, the TB seemed to have burnt itself out and her lungs were clear. They took, as it were, a deep breath and decided to leave their home of four years. The most difficult part was the knowledge that they must leave Luchs with Luischen; bidding him farewell at Innsbruck Station was painful in the extreme.

All in all, Phyllis's life in Kitzbühel was encapsulated in several short stories and most thoroughly in her next novel, *Wind in His Fists*, or *Devil's Due* as it was called in the American edition.[62] This was Ernan's favourite novel of all that Phyllis wrote. On the one hand it is a novel based on the figure of an expert woman ski-jumper, like Paula Lamberg. Phyllis knew from local gossip that Paula was much admired as one who took *noblesse oblige* seriously and also that, considering her social class, she was something of a rebel; her father insisted that she should do her amazing ski-jumps dressed in a skirt, as to wear breeches would be horribly unladylike. Phyllis knew also that there was no respect for her dissolute brother, the young Graf, and out of this local gossip she wove her story. Phyllis never herself skied; this was something Ernan did in the afternoons with the boys while she rested, but, as she said, 'the whole spirit of ski-ing lived round me for four years, and my imagination was besieged with it'.[63] It is a remarkable paean to its thrills from someone who never experienced it personally; indeed a great many closely observed portraits of people and pursuits went into this novel and made it work well. Her rogue male character, the amoral Max von Ulm, takes some of the personality facets she had observed in Ian Fleming: the love of risk-taking, the love of fast cars, the careless use of women. The evil old Graf also owes something to Ian's wild tale of the sinister Graf Schlick figure that he told at the Tennerhof. That bit of melodrama feels out of place in an otherwise perfectly observed book; in every other aspect, it is a *tour de force*.

Phyllis captures the way that on the one hand Catholicism ran deep and permeated the whole of village life while on the other the farming families made their own pragmatic relations with the Church. If the sun shone on a Sunday in harvest-time, they could not turn their back on it, never mind it was the stipulated day of rest and worship. The spinning wheels to weave the loden cloth must be left untouched on a Sunday, but they did not feel that this stopped them from preparing the wool ready for the Monday. Similarly it was not uncommon, nor considered blameworthy, to have a child before marriage, as long as a wedding to the child's father took place later on. Contrasted with the straightforward moral universe of Kitzbühel was the code of conduct of the Viennese interlopers, represented by Max and his wife, and this provided the necessary tension.

Phyllis especially loved the peasant farmers that she had lived alongside in Mösern and Kitzbühel, finding them 'a singularly hard and independent people, original in character and often full of courage, resourcefulness and humour'.[64] Her friendship with Austrians and Austria was to be a life-long affair. It was heart-wrenching to leave Kitzbühel. As Phyllis wrote, 'The mountains themselves had played a large part in our lives, and the roots planted day by day in sight of them went very deep.'[65]

CHAPTER 7

The Gathering Storm in Munich and the Study of Adlerian Psychology

Although we cannot alter facts, we can change
the way we look at them.

ALFRED ADLER

In the spring of 1930, Phyllis and Ernan, now forty-eight and forty-six years old respectively, had come to another crossroads in their lives. Ernan had discovered that although he was a gifted teacher he missed music so much that he wanted to retrain as a piano teacher. Another, even more significant development for their future lives, was that both of them wanted to learn more about Adler's theories. They spent winter near Nice in the South of France while they contemplated their next move. Adler himself now lived and worked mostly in America, but they decided to follow his suggestion of working with his colleague in Munich, Dr Leonard Seif, who lectured on Individual Psychology at the university.[1] As Phyllis expressed it in her autobiography:

> Both of us, I think, were equally interested in Adler's psychology, but our interest had as yet no form attached to it; not did it become an acknowledged purpose until it had already acted upon us. Individual Psychology, unlike its fellow psychologies of Freud and Jung, is not a series of intellectual tenets to be grasped, but a gradual retraining of an entire personality, to be slowly – and perhaps never entirely – accepted. It is indeed a form of existentialism.[2]

For the winter of 1930/1, they moved to Munich and settled into a small bed-and-breakfast, the Pension Siebert, in the Kaulbachstrasse.

Their analyses with Dr Seif were to prove the key turning point in their joint commitment to Adlerian philosophy. Both of them found analysis very painful. This is hardly surprising: as Phyllis puts it, a consequence of analysis is that 'the veils of unreality that have weaved themselves in and over the self-deceiving heart are pulled away'.[3] It is no coincidence that the slang term for a psychoanalyst is a 'shrink', although it is the ego of the patient that has to shrink. Initially, Phyllis got more out of her analysis that did Ernan, who never found in Seif the *sympatico* analyst that he had found Adler to be. Adler was a highly sophisticated Viennese man, who recognised that Ernan was 'in blood and breeding a Scottish aristocrat, a very subtle thinker, and with a pride so sensitive and entire that it could not be touched safely by any but the lightest surgeon's hands'.[4] Seif, on the other hand, came from Swabian peasant stock, was blunter in his approach, and somewhat pointedly made Ernan see that Phyllis was the major breadwinner of the couple, and that Ernan, in the face of challenge, was inclined to back away from anything that looked in danger of leading to success. A neurotic fear of failure, according to Seif, was repeatedly converted by Ernan's pride into a rapid retreat from the very thing that was about to yield success. In Adlerian theory, the flip side of an inferiority complex is a superiority complex, and although it sounds as though these two states of mind are opposites, they are, in reality, often closely aligned.

Ernan was somewhat disgusted with the way in which Phyllis accepted Seif's views as 'gospel'. Adler's oft-repeated dictum that although we cannot alter facts, we can change the way we look at them, seemed to Phyllis a simple yet precise way in which to set about purging one's thought processes of a state of merely-wishing in order to accept full responsibility for one's actions. Phyllis became an Adlerian rather as though she had undergone a religious conversion, perhaps because she had lost her conventional Anglican faith following her study of Herbert Spencer. In particular, Phyllis recognised the significance of Adler's theories about a sibling's 'place' in the family. She said:

> Adler believed that children form their secret life plan very young and are deeply influenced by their place in the family. An eldest

> child often feels the dethronement, as Adler called it, by the second child, very deeply, and it may discourage him throughout life; on the other hand an eldest child is often an authoritarian and a model child, identifying himself with the parents, and remains a conservative in all his ideas. This may discourage the second child who will then become a rebel if he is strong, or a dreamer if he is weak. A youngest *may* be like the Prince in the fairy tales – the pick of the family because he can never be dethroned; or he *may* feel overpowered by his elders, especially if they are of the opposite sex, and become too discouraged to take his full place in life. Often the youngest child seeks his success line by becoming a buffoon, or in other ways avoids full responsibility for his actions. But a courageous youngest may go very far indeed.[5]

Adler's theories helped Phyllis to understood why she had hated Wilmett so fervently, and helped her to forgive Wilmett retrospectively. They also helped her to forgive herself, to reposition herself and to redirect her emotional energy.

Following her analysis with Seif, she no longer fretted about religious dogma, but settled on the tenets of Individual Psychology – work, love and social engagement – as a sufficient framework for living. This, if not philosophically sophisticated, nevertheless served her well as a moral template. Although she had enjoyed reading Freud, she felt that the stress on the unconscious did not of itself provide a key to how to live. A Freudian analysis, she believed, could not *automatically* lead to any desire to make changes. Adlerian psychology, on the other hand, assumed that locating one's neurosis was the easy bit, which anyone with a modicum of intellectual power could grasp. The difficult part for the 'pupil' was to be challenged into a retraining of the whole personality, where implementing changes in the self would be mirrored by changes in the pupil's behaviour, not only towards the people immediately around them, but in relation to society as a whole.[6] As Phyllis would express it in her autobiography: 'The most ruthless Nazi or Communist may have, and use successfully, suicidal courage, without producing any results beyond murder; but if courage is linked with love for his fellow man, and used as St Francis used it, then it can transform all who welcome it, and truly shines "like a good deed in a naughty world".'[7]

Phyllis had found a framework that helped her to locate herself in the world, and although, in our more cynical age, it might be easy to dismiss her conversion to Adler's Individual Psychology theories as simply exchanging one set of beliefs for another, the proof of the pudding is in the eating. For the rest of her life she demonstrated a remarkable spirit of social, as well as personal, generosity.

In the autumn of 1931, encouraged by Seif, Phyllis travelled alone to America to meet her new publisher, Houghton Mifflin. Seif thought that it was important for her development that she should make her own arrangements for the trip to America, rather than have Ernan make them for her. He also recommended that Ernan should not accompany her but should stay in Munich and then go to London in January to begin training for his new career as a music teacher. He more or less forbade Ernan to find an excuse to go travelling with Phyllis. Phyllis duly followed Seif's recommendations, leaving Ernan behind. Initially Ernan was so enraged that he refused to answer Phyllis's frequent loving letters. Finally he sent her a letter telling her just how he felt:

> Seif sends his love – & says he thinks you will manage rather well. I went to him on Thursday – & told him my only feeling was of rage at being left & and that I couldn't write any letters –
>
> He said it was a frightful blow to my pride that you had left me – & I was trying to make myself feel important by saying 'No' – which was all there was for me to do by not answering letters.
>
> The dreams showed concern for your safety – at which he told me to leave you alone & not bother whether you were ill or died – he said I had no right to wish to keep you alive if it was time for you to die – it was only selfishness on my part and the fear of being left to shift for myself![8]

Ernan struggled on in Munich, giving English lessons to German students, teaching English and American students German, and giving music lessons to pupils of various nationalities. He was suffering from rheumatism in his fingers, which frustrated him because his own piano playing could never be as perfect as he would have liked it to be. He doggedly continued his analysis with Seif, although he found the process exceedingly uncomfortable. Writing to Phyllis towards the end of November he commented: 'Seif says I have deeply identified myself with Papa – the hen-pecked incapable failure – that I simply can't get free for another view of things.'[9] The Adlerian explanation of his behaviour was that Ernan had turned the suicide of his father into a neurosis; the shock was real, but Ernan's exploitation of the shock was a neurotic response.

Phyllis meanwhile was in Virginia visiting her long-standing artist-friend, Maida McCord, whose husband, George Roper, had made a fortune from the lumber trade. It was not an especially comfortable visit, as George was an obsessively jealous man. Phyllis was to write later, in an essay called 'Love and Marriage', although discreetly mentioning no surnames:

> He was jealous of every friend his wife had of either sex, indeed of any human being or even animal, who preferred her to himself. He became so jealous of her dog that she had to part with it. She replaced the dog by a parrot; but some competitive instinct entered into this bird, and though a quiet and pleasant companion to the wife during her husband's business hours, the moment the husband returned home the parrot persistently talked him down. The husband could not stand this second voice in the household, so his wife wisely parted with the parrot. However, after a time she bought a bowl of goldfish, and I was relieved to get a letter from her saying, 'George does not mind goldfish.'[10]

On this trip, Phyllis found herself appalled by the attitudes of the Southerners to their 'Negro fellow-citizens', though by the time she was writing her autobiography, she hazarded an explanation of sorts for its psychological roots: 'the people of the South in America – as in Germany [before the Second World War] were a defeated, impoverished people. Historically they had been the top dogs; now they were under-dogs and their distorted pride turned to cruelty.'[11] However, she was proud to visit the hospital for babies built in Norfolk by the King's Daughters Society as a memorial to her grandmother, Margaret Bottome. There, no colour bar existed, in respect of either patients or staff.

As ever, money needed to be earned. During the two months she stayed with the Ropers she wrote *The Advances of Harriet*, a 'long short' involving a naïve young Englishwoman who has various entertaining adventures, but ultimately has to come to terms with the fact that she has no special talent and certainly no self-discipline.[12] Phyllis said that it was considered 'the most amusing of my books but was not, I think, except on the surface, meant to be amusing ... serious problems lurked beneath it, not all of them solved.'[13] Its heroine, or anti-heroine, Harriet, is a spoiled, very pretty and wholly insensitive seventeen-year-old. Having been expelled from school and having got into a romantic scrape with the squire's son in her native Sussex village, she is packed off to Paris to stay with her half-sister, Anne, who works in the British Embassy. Anne is everything Harriet is not; she is a self-contained professional woman, used to earning her own living and having good friendships with both men and women. Harriet knows how to attract men and how to flirt with them, and is so vivacious that she soon persuades Michael, Anne's work colleague, to fall in love with her. She does this knowing perfectly well that she has stolen Anne's special friend. In short, she competes with her long-suffering older sister, and is willing to cheat in order to outdo her. Ultimately, Pierre, a sophisticated Frenchman, whose attention Harriet desperately seeks, chooses Anne as the sister to marry. At the beginning of the novel Harriet makes advances to men that end in disaster; but by the end of the novel, the advances she has made are those in self-knowledge. Even in the last line of the novel, however, the reader finds Harriet deciding to have a baby, chiefly because she would like to have a baby before Anne does.

This is all done with a very light touch, though it is clearly Adlerian in its depiction of sibling rivalry. It is neatly told, and the details of the embassy in Paris ring true, no doubt helped by Ernan's inside knowledge. The account of Anne's great friendship with her friend Olive is also deftly accomplished. One of the few instances of Harriet getting past her own ego to a moment of empathy for someone else is when she realises what Anne's marriage will mean to Olive. Harriet 'felt a pang of pity for Olive. Olive had her "married man", of course, but he had always seemed to Harriet rather a shadowy person beside the actuality of Anne.'[14] This seems an echo of how Phyllis's marriage to Ernan had affected Lislie, with perhaps, too, a new degree of self-awareness in Phyllis herself.

In New York, Phyllis was approached by Elisabeth Marbury, the first female literary agent, primarily because *Windlestraws* had been a best-seller in America. Marbury was a theatrical as well as a literary agent, and she swiftly organised a dramatist to work with Phyllis with a view to adapting *Devil's Due* for the stage. However, there was no reliable means of making artificial snow at the time, so it proved impossible. It was also Marbury who pointed out to Phyllis that the big money in those days was in converting books into films, and had not this new agent died in 1933, there might have been an earlier success in that arena.[15] Marbury wanted a new publicity photograph of Phyllis and arranged for her to visit Anselm Adams, now famous for his landscape photography but at that point in his career earning his living by commercial portraits. His description of their encounter is comical:

> Ensconced in my studio in 1930, one of my first commissions was to photograph the British novelist Phyllis Bottome. Miss Bottome showed me some soupy portraits by British photographers, remarking, 'I really don't want anything like these, you know.' I assured her my pictures would be sharp and direct, nothing fuzzy ... I made one exposure and realized I had a problem with my sitter – the dear lady was like a flaccid, graven image. As I made the next exposure, one of the flash bulbs exploded, scattering little pieces of glass in her white hair and giving her a considerable scare. After cleaning up, I continued; the subject had now assumed a certain dignity and poise, with a definite air of expectancy. While I do not recommend such fear tactics, the resulting portraits were very fine.[16]

Phyllis needed a new sharp image for the American market. Earning money was important, as Ernan was once again a student, studying in London with Professor Tobias Matthay of the Royal Academy of Music. Matthay was a distinguished pianist and piano teacher, whose most famous student was the concert pianist, Myra Hess.[17] It gives some indication of Ernan's talent that Matthay was willing to take him on at his relatively advanced age.

In London, Ernan renewed his friendship with Ivor Novello. Phyllis asked Ernan to take advice from Ivor on the possibilities of getting *Devil's Due* filmed. In 1926 Phyllis had written a book called *The Rat*, whose story was, rather unusually for her, adapted from the play by Ivor and Constance Collier, jointly written under the nom-de-plume 'David L'Estrange'. The play had produced excellent box-office receipts, albeit less than enthusiastic critical reviews. The film version of 1925, 'a custom-made star vehicle to self-consciously exploit his Celtic looks and devilish sense of humour', had made Ivor a matinée idol.[18] For someone so full of her own ideas as Phyllis, this 'borrowing' was somewhat surprising. It was written in the period when her marriage was under strain, and when Ernan was deeply missing his friends in the world of music and theatre. One has to consider whether this novel was Phyllis's 'imperfect gift' to Ernan in an effort to build bridges.[19] If so, it appears to have been successful. Ivor accepted Phyllis's gesture towards *rapprochement* in the form of her version of *The Rat*, recognising it as a kind of novelistic *hommage*. Thereafter, Ivor did his best to promote Phyllis's work, and later, once she had returned to England, she would at last experience the charm and generosity that was part of Ivor's appeal to his many friends.

During the last few weeks of her American visit, Phyllis stayed with her uncle, Harry Bottome, and his wife Marion.[20] She also stayed with her friend from Viennese days, Dorothy Thompson, and her second husband, Sinclair Lewis. Dorothy had married the Nobel Prize-winning novelist in 1928 following her divorce from Josef Bard and Lewis's divorce from his first wife Grace.[21] Lewis, always known as 'Hal' by his friends, was a literary star in the 1920s, acclaimed for his satires of middle-class pretensions in small-town America, *Main Street* being the most famous of these.[22] However, Hal had a serious problem with alcohol, and often got into fights with anyone who disagreed with him if he had been drinking heavily. On the other hand, he was charm itself when sober so it may well be that Phyllis only saw his best side. On this visit she was also introduced to their son, Michael, who was born in June 1930. After his birth, Dorothy wrote to an American friend that in the event of anything happening to them she hoped that she would assume guardianship. In the same letter, she told her friend,

'Phyllis and Ernan Forbes Dennis are a man and wife, old friends, to whom I could entrust Michael, confident that he would be brought up in a cultivated atmosphere, and in a way which we, Hal and I, could both approve, but they are English, and Phyllis has been ill for years with tuberculosis.'[23] During this same visit, Hal introduced Phyllis to his great friend Frank Adams, who wrote the literary column of the *Herald Tribune*, and to his wife Esther; they too became lifelong friends.

Phyllis also visited Dora Delano Forbes, Ernan's godmother, and through this contact enjoyed a conversation with Dora's sister, Sara Delano Roosevelt.[24] She found that the future president's mother shared the social prejudices of her time and social class against Jews, but, as Phyllis said in her biography, 'She listened with sympathy when I told her of their persecution in Germany.'[25] All in all, Phyllis felt that she had made good use of her trip to America. As she wrote to Ernan, although she had

> worked like a horse ... Seif helped me so enormously this time, because I have learned how really little it matters if a thing *is* beyond me to do. And quite happily just don't do it! There were heaps of minor things I *should* have attempted before – which this time I ignored or postponed – with nothing but good results! I have used half my strength all my life long in things which had better remain undone – and no doubt I shall continue to use up a quarter of my strength in this way. But I shall try to cut it down to a quarter![26]

Phyllis returned to Europe on the liner *Conte Biancamano* to the port of Genoa, where Ernan was waiting to greet her. They had been apart for several months and their marriage had been tested. Their analyses – and being required to function adequately when not together – had shown them both that their marriage had been based too much on the model of 'the boa constrictor and the rabbit'. This was an Adlerian description of a particular form of marriage relationship. Phyllis's 'exploitation' of Ernan had been revealed to her, just as Ernan had been made aware of the 'alibis' he adopted to make excuses for his hesitating attitude, his vacillating movements and recurrent retreats.[27] Staying for a week near Portofino they enjoyed both a wonderful renewal of their love but also a much-needed joint commitment to live together in a more equal partnership.[28]

In December 1931, Ernan received news that his beloved uncle, Colonel Lachland Forbes, who had retired to an eighteenth-century villa on Lake Orta near Milan, was seriously ill. Ernan rushed there, but by the time he arrived, Uncle Lachie had died. Writing to Phyllis, Ernan said, 'I gave a large wreath of mimosa and narcissus from you and me ... there must be some ancient, deep-rooted instinct about death and flowers – one's thoughts turn to flowers at once.'[29] Lachie had left Ernan his house and his money, which was a relatively small sum, in his will. This was the first house they had ever owned, and was therefore especially exciting for them. Their immediate plan was to spend winters in Munich and summers at Lake Orta.

Returning to England, Ernan carried on with his training at the Matthay School in London, finding the five-week Christmas break something of a setback in his progress. Phyllis borrowed a friend's cottage at Newenden, Sussex, to forge on, as ever, with her writing. At some point in the following summer, Ernan suffered from a bout of jealousy caused by her interest in a male friend. Writing to him in July 1932, she said:

> My own Precious ... If I have given you pain – I have the comfort of having shared it – for my heart is like something torn to bits – by claws! I am not concealing anything from you – if that is what you fear. I mean there is nothing between Cyril and me and never will be.[30] I do not mean I have not been to blame in that I am a whole person! If you have to suffer agony for your incompleteness so have I for mine. I am not single-minded and I have therefore impulsive divided desires over which I have insufficient control. But you are to me – and will always be – the most significant, perhaps the *only* significant relation of my life. I did not love Lislie as I love you – she knew it – and it helped to kill her – for I had not learned and did not know – how wrong the 'inordinate' entwining of our innocent love could be! You need have no jealousy of any human being – but you need have great patience with your poor old Frau, who has been – and is – guilty of waywardnesses and false attractions!

> I do no want to make excuses, but I suppose without the intensity of short desires – and long curiosities – I could not get the output of an artist. We feed on hearts, to give them to the world – not to destroy them.[31]

Despite, or even because of, the Adlerian training, there seems to have been a kind of turning of the tables in their relationship. Hitherto, Phyllis had been jealous of some of Ernan's friends; now he was jealous of some of hers. This is not surprising, perhaps, as his new career training meant that he was back at 'school', with much younger adults, which must have been somewhat galling to him. Letters from Ernan to Phyllis around this time were often signed from 'her useless lump'. From personal accounts, it seems likely that Ernan might easily have been a concert pianist if he had received early training, and maybe this was his strongest regret. In July, he passed his music test brilliantly, thereby qualifying as a music teacher.

Thus, when they returned to Munich for the winter of 1932, Ernan was equipped to give both German lessons and music lessons, and their flat acted as a base for various young people. It was beautifully situated, close to the Englischer Garten that stretched from the centre of the city for three miles alongside the swiftly flowing River Isar. Their flat was large enough to house three young girls and several of the old Tennerhof boys who came to Munich to continue their work with Ernan. It was something of a mixed household: one of the girls was a strictly-brought-up young Scottish cousin of Ernan's; another of the young women, Em, was a beautiful American who had some undesirable friends and troublesome love affairs. Phyllis's sister Mary, then in her late forties, also came to join them. She had been the unfavourite child of their mother, but had found some consolation in her Christian faith; she found more help in an analysis with Seif. Mary had brought out with her their nephew and Phyllis's godson, Phillip Bottome, nineteen and fresh out of public school.

However, while they were living in this almost idyllic spot, Hitler's grim shadow was beginning to fall over Munich:

> There he was: at first a cloud no bigger than a man's hand, and then darker and yet more spreading, till the cloud covered all the sky …

> All through 1932–1933, his raucous voice was that of a madman working himself into a frenzy – the whole nation shared it; broken, beaten, impoverished, starved, forced to accept the whole of the war guilt, though they knew themselves only partly responsible, the brave and biddable German people were only too ready to repeat their unnecessary journey into Force.[32]

Munich was the Haupstadt der Bewegung, the capital of the fascist movement, for not only was it the birthplace of the National Socialist German Workers' Party, but it also remained the party's administrative centre. Hitler had begun his career as an impoverished political agitator, but, backed by a hundred thousand goldmarks from the industrialist Fritz Thyssen, he had made his first decisive move for power in Munich.[33] Although the 'Beer Hall Putsch' of 8 November 1923, an attempt to overthrow the Weimar Republic, was defeated, Hitler regarded the sixteen Nazis who had died in the uprising as martyrs. Consequently, Munich became a kind of hallowed ground in Hitler's imagination. Imprisoned there for a few months, Hitler began to write the first volume of his political treatise *Mein Kampf*. He had been released in December 1924, and although a political ban on public speaking kept him briefly quiescent, he was busily writing the second volume of his book. It was not until autumn 1928 that the ban on public speaking was lifted throughout the German states.

Initially, Hitler had found only a relatively small core of Nazi fanatics remaining; on the other hand the cult of idolatry had intensified. The Wall Street Crash of 20 October 1929 provided the crisis that Hitler needed to draw wide-ranging popular support. No country had been more vulnerable than Germany to the worldwide depression that followed the global economic recession. In America, a despairing population elected Franklin D. Roosevelt in November 1932 and entrusted themselves to his New Deal. But in Germany, only Hitler seemed to offer strong leadership; he claimed that he would repudiate the Treaty of Versailles, provide work and food for all, and reconstruct Germany as, once more, a proud nation. Not only the unemployed were seduced by this vision; many German industrialists saw Nazism as a necessary bulwark against Communism and poured funds into the Nazi treasury. Many middle-class Germans thought Nazism the lesser of two evils, although not all of them shared Hitler's virulent anti-Semitism, which initially they tended to regard it as a passing aberration. Even assimilated German Jews themselves could be 'anti-Semitic' in their contempt for eastern Jews who had swarmed into Germany and Austria after pogroms in Poland and the Baltic countries following the First World War.

By October 1929, still backed by rich industrialists, Hitler had moved into a handsome flat at number 16 Prinzregentenplatz. He had ridden the storms of internecine warfare that had arisen within the leadership, partly by mobilising a private army, the Sturmabteilung, recruited from the thousands of unemployed young men. Usually known as Brown-shirts because of their brown uniforms and high boots, they paraded through the streets armed with horsewhips. In November 1931, Dorothy Thompson had managed to secure an interview with Hitler and published a book called *I Saw Hitler*. At this first meeting she wholly underestimated his power, writing:

> When finally I walked into Adolph Hitler's salon in the Kaiserhof Hotel, I was convinced that I was meeting the future dictator of Germany. In something less than fifty seconds I was quite sure that I was not. It took just that time to measure the startling insignificance of this man who has set the whole world agog.[34]

In 1932, Phyllis often saw Hitler lunching in his favourite restaurant, the Café Heck, which stood on the corner of Ludwigstrasse and Galerie-strasse. By chance, it was also the café of choice for the group of Individual Psychologist students who met to discuss what they had learned from their observations in Seif's Child Clinic:

> A small and insignificant figure in his brown uniform, Hitler sat alone in the corner opposite to us, with his back to the wall. I never saw him at a table in the middle of the room. His dark hair plastered across his forehead, one separate lock hanging just above his sombre, staring eyes, he bore a strange resemblance to Charlie Chaplin, but without laughter. Our group sat around a large table not far from his, talking our happy heads off. We were a heterogeneous group,

> men and women from many countries. Some of us were Seif's helpers, some were his patients, many of us were both. We were of various social status. One group contained a blacksmith, a medical student, two dressmakers, several teachers, a doctor or two and a poet. Seif was always with us, benign and beaming, a friend among his friends. None of us had priority, nobody took a special seat or even chose his neighbour. We were a society without rules; and yet there was a ruling spirit. We had begun to believe that man should really love his neighbour as himself ... There were only a few yards between us and Hitler – that gloomy solitary whose dreams were full of hate ... Sometimes a brownshirt pushed through the swing door of the Café Heck and stood by Hitler's table for a minute to ask a question or to give him a message. Hitler would bark out an order or simply shake his head unsmilingly.[35]

The IP group were learning of Adler's view that finding one's own best work is creative and life-enhancing, whereas the desire for power and domination is the false goal of the neurotic, and is limiting and destructive. It seems particularly ironic that in the opposite corner to them, both literally and figuratively, sat the man whose destructive desire for domination was about to grab the attention of the world.

Still, in contrast to the increasingly threatening political atmosphere, Christmas in Munich that year was enchanting. Every shop had a Christmas tree and wreaths of holly and mistletoe; in the butchers' windows, even the carcasses of pigs and hares had evergreen decorations tied with red ribbons to ear and tail. Endless statues of the Madonna and child with sugar lambs adorned the churches and shop fronts. It remained hard to imagine that the Nazi icon of the swastika could ever defeat these Christian emblems, striking terror into the hearts of Jews and indeed of everyone whom the Nazis deemed enemies.[36]

Just after Christmas 1932, Phyllis and Ernan joined a ten-day party at the invitation of Dorothy Thompson and 'Hal' Lewis. Dorothy needed to be in Vienna to report on European affairs, so she and Hal had rented the Villa Sauerbrunn in Semmering that winter, 'a cuckoo-clock of a house ... with Ritz comforts in beds and bathrooms and kitchens and chairs and lights'.[37] Following the stock-market crash of 1929, Hal's attention had turned to the rise of demagogues – not only Hitler and Mussolini – but also in America itself. His cautionary tale, *It Can't Happen Here*, which would be published in 1935, imagined how fascism might take hold in America. It seems likely that the conversation at the Semmering Christmas party was a key moment in kick-starting his thinking about the fragility of democracy everywhere.[38]

The party guests were lodged in the Semmering Hotel and included foreign correspondents such as Edgar Mowrer and his wife Lilian and the Hungarian couple Marcel Fodor and wife Marta. Also present were political figures, such as First Secretary Haddow of the British legation in Vienna and Nicholas Roosevelt, American ambassador to Budapest, and a scattering of aristocrats, such as Prince Paul Sapieha of Poland (and an American writer called Virgilia Peterson, who was to become his wife) and the Baron Laci Hatvany and his wife. Baroness Hatvany's *nom-de-plume* was Christa Winsloe, and she was the author of *Mädchen in Uniform,* a tale of a schoolgirl crush that ends in tragedy. This was to be made into a film, one of the first with an overtly lesbian theme, shown in America in 1932. Dorothy had a brief affair with Christa that began at Semmering. But, whatever the erotics of this eclectic group, the major focus of conversation was inevitably the alarming political situation. The Americans believed that Dorothy had woefully underestimated Hitler's charisma, and were sure that he would come to power within in a few months. They feared that

> nothing could stop him now; and if Hitler came to power, he meant war, and nothing would stop that. Probably war would stretch to England; but this we had privately hoped was their professional bias towards war in its most acute form. What a European war wouldn't stretch to, they had firmly assured us, was America. Not this time – not twice in a generation – would they be dragged in uselessly to heal the quarrels of Europe.[39]

Phyllis and Ernan returned to Munich in a sober mood, realising that they were not likely to be able to remain there for much longer. That winter, the weather seemed to be especially grim; it turned piercingly cold, with an icy wind whistling down the streets. The political news was equally chilly: on 30 January 1933, Hitler became

Chancellor. His first task in office was to dissolve the Reichstag, to call for new elections to confirm his position, and to take steps towards passing an Enabling Act that would allow him to govern without reference to parliament or president (in effect establishing him as dictator). On 27 February, a fire in the Reichstag in Berlin provided an opportunity for the Nazis to make a clean sweep of their political opponents. An emergency decree 'for the Protection of People and State' was enacted the next day, indefinitely suspending freedom of speech, of association, of the press, and of the privacy of postal and telephone communications. Hitler's Brownshirts rampaged unchecked as they rounded up communists, social democrats and trade unionists, who were savagely beaten, some to death.

The *Münchener Post*, a social-democratic newspaper, had long been a target for the Nazis. The editors had suffered death threats and accusations of being the centre of a red nest of vipers. On 9 March 1933, Brownshirts raided many social-democratic and communist institutions, including the *Münchener Post*. Their offices in Marienplatz were destroyed and their printing presses smashed. The newspaper's insurance company was made to pay for the damage, and the premises were then turned into a rest and recreation centre for the Brownshirts. On 20 March, Heinrich Himmler, at that time the Police President of Munich, opened the first concentration camp at Dachau, just outside Munich, where political prisoners could be imprisoned, tortured and killed.

Although official Nazi policy towards the Jews in Germany was to encourage their emigration, attacks on Jews broke out all over the country. They were beaten and robbed, and some murdered. A retaliatory threat of an international boycott of German goods by the American Jewish Congress led Hitler, on 1 April, to proclaim a national boycott of Jewish businesses. The German economy could not stand up to the threat of an extended international boycott, so he called it off after one day. Nevertheless, it was a portent of what German Jews might expect from the Nazi regime. On 7 April, the Law for the Restoration of the Professional Civil Service was enacted, dismissing all Jews and political opponents from the civil service (although initially President von Hindenburg obtained an exemption for those Jews who had fought in the First World War). That same month, measures were introduced preventing Jews from being admitted to the legal profession, excluding them as doctors tending patients under the national insurance scheme and limiting the proportion of Jewish children in all schools.

The frantic pace of Hitler's legislative controls continued. On 2 May, all trade unions were dissolved. On the 10 May, university faculties throughout the country witnessed bonfires of books regarded as unacceptable by the new regime. A campaign of *Gleichschaltung,* meaning a 'bringing into line' of all aspects of cultural life to fit with the Nazi ideology, meant that, among other things, control of the film industry came under the diktat of Josef Goebbels, the Minister of Propaganda.[40] Jews were excluded from almost all cultural activity, even from such things as amateur choirs. Unsurprisingly, many Jewish intellectuals started to leave Germany as soon as Hitler became Chancellor. Perhaps the most internationally famous of Munich's intellectuals, Thomas Mann, had observed in an American magazine, as early as spring 1923, his uneasy sense that Munich was becoming the city of Hitler and the swastika.[41] Indeed, that spring Himmler issued an order to take Mann into 'protective custody', but Mann, on a lecture tour in Switzerland, wisely decided to emigrate. Everywhere in the streets, the traditional greeting of 'Grüssgott' had been replaced with the 'Heil Hitler' salute. By this point, Phyllis and Ernan decided that they too must leave: '... it was no longer possible to live there without witnessing the cruel persecution of our Jewish friends, or ourselves refusing to make terms, however passively, with the controlling gangsters. "You must go now," our Consul General told us. "You can only do your friends harm by staying, and if you refuse to give the Hitler salute you will be imprisoned and I shall not be able to get you out." '[42]

Once again they had to wind up both a home and a school and in May 1933 they left Munich with very heavy hearts. Phyllis's nephew, Phillip Bottome, returned to London, but her sister Mary accompanied them to Casa Forbes on Lake Orta:

> It seemed, however, as if Hitler's long, tireless shadow pursued us. We were miserably anxious about the friends whom we had left behind us, and our future was at its lowest ebb. We arrived at our

> lakeside to take over Uncle Lachie's heritage in a wild thunderstorm, with hailstones the size of walnuts falling into the white and vicious-looking lake, to find that our house had to be altered into livable condition while we were living in it.[43]

Every day was of necessity interrupted by the sound of workmen, which meant that for Phyllis, getting on with her writing proved difficult. Although it had three good rooms, and a pretty loggia overlooking the lake it had no bathroom; a walk down to the lake for bathing had to suffice. Mary Bottome rapidly fled to England, although they were delighted to be joined by Lewis Way, one of the old Kitzbühel boys. Ernan had been looking forward to sharing the house with Phyllis, but the summer turned into something of a nightmare when both Lewis and Phyllis fell prey to diphtheria after the village drains erupted into the lake. Their Bavarian cook, Maria, whom they had brought with them from Munich, also became ill, and Ernan ended up acting as nurse to all three of them. In Phyllis's case, although she recovered fairly quickly, she fell ill again almost immediately with what appeared to be another bout of tuberculosis. As if this were not enough, Ernan received a telegram telling him that two of his aunts – Emily and Lilla – were both desperately ill with inoperable cancers. Ernan was beside himself with the anxiety of choosing which patient most needed him – it must have reminded him of the pull-and-push between Phyllis and his mother all those years ago.

Fortunately, Ernan could leave to attend to his aunts because Lewis was well enough to take Phyllis to a sanatorium at Montana, Switzerland, run by a Dr Roche, an excellent doctor from New Zealand. Prior to the availability of antibiotics in the mid-1950s, Phyllis always lived with the fear that tuberculosis would return.[44] Sometimes doctors could not tell from an X-ray whether they were looking at old fibrous scars left behind after the tuberculosis had receded, or whether the shadow they could see on the X-ray was active. On this occasion, it may have been a false alarm, and she seems more likely to have been suffering from pleurisy. Nevertheless, the 'old enemy' remained a shadow both literally and metaphorically over their lives.

While Ernan was in London looking after the aunts, rushing from one hospital to the other, Phyllis was finishing the novel that she had been writing in Munich. During a previous visit to Britain, Adler had given a lecture at Cardiff University. Dr Muriel Northcote, deputy superintendent at the Cardiff Mental Hospital, had taken the opportunity to show Adler and the Forbes Dennises around this huge state mental institution.[45] Phyllis had been very impressed with Muriel, who had given her introductions to several private hospitals where she might be able to collect material:

> I quickly decided that only a trained psychiatrist could make an accurate study of mental illness, but what I saw was within my powers was an interrelated study of doctors and their patients, since I found that in each human being there is an opportunity to become sane or mad ... Individual Psychology had taught me that the real question is not, 'How do people go out of their minds?' but, 'What do they go out of their minds for?'[46]

Initially Phyllis had intended to call her novel *The Island,* thinking of John Donne's dictum: 'No man is an Island entire of itself; every man is a piece of the Continent, a part of the main.' It was only after Phyllis had finished her analysis with Seif that she came to realise that the sane were those who successfully adapted themselves to life, rather than expecting the world to adapt to them. She chose instead to call the novel *Private Worlds,* on the grounds that

> It is our own egocentricity that cuts us off from the mainland, reducing us from individual control of ourselves to slaves of our own desires; or else, from moral cowardice, into becoming slaves to the wills of others ... *The Island*, as I now saw it, joins up with the mainland only when it ceases to be a private world.[47]

Private Worlds was published in both Britain and America in 1934, dedicated 'To Doctor Leonhard Seif and the Munich Group of Individual Psychologists – my counsellors and my friends'. Its title refers both to the disordered minds of the mentally ill and also – at certain points – to the states of mind of the physicians who worked with and for them.

As in many of her novels, she portrays a professional woman as her central character. Jane Everest has to contend with the prejudice of the new superintendent of the mental hospital, Charles Drummond, a man who considers the work unsuitable for women. Her name itself indicates the scale of the mountain that she has had to climb in order to achieve the professional position of a female psychiatrist. Against the wishes of her father and her brothers, Jane's mother and subsequently Jane's aunt had used their small private incomes to support her through her medical and psychological training. Jane is contrasted and compared with two very different kinds of women. One is Myra, a spoiled and deadly society woman, the sister of Charles Drummond:

> She had ruined his life, as nearly as it is possible for one human being to ruin another's life. But all she had set out to do, as she had often explained to Charles, was to live her own life in her own way. She had never, he knew, forgiven him for knowing the truth about her. She had called it putting the worst construction upon an innocent act. Charles had devoted his entire fortune to preventing Myra from being hanged. The revolver had somehow gone off, and Pete – her husband – had fallen backwards down the stairs: and been picked up – dead.[48]

The other is Sally, the young bride of Jane's close friend and long-time colleague at the hospital, Alec Macgregor. Sally has been neither educated nor trained for a career. She starts to suffer from an acute inferiority complex. On the one hand, she feels left out of the professional and intellectual conversations held by her husband with Jane, and on the other, she suspects that her husband is having an affair with the predatory Myra. She suffers an acute nervous breakdown, and although four months' pregnant, hurls herself down a flight of stairs. She loses the baby, and seems out of her mind for some time.

While Sally is recuperating, Jane explains to her that her profession has been her whole life because:

> The man I was engaged to was shot for cowardice in the War. I was nineteen and he was twenty. There was an attack and he ran away. They'd have let him off if he hadn't taken the platoon with him. My brother was his Colonel. I haven't been in love since then ... It was

> twelve years ago. And it made a psychiatrist out of me. That's a thing to be thankful for. I had an idea even then that it wasn't just his fault – as people like to say of a nervous breakdown – and now I'm sure of it. It was worth finding out.[49]

Sally, however, has dared to open herself to love, whereas Jane is revealed as someone who fears the loss of control implicit in a sexual relationship. Ultimately, and perhaps predictably, Jane falls in love with Charles, who is re-educated into respect for women during the course of the novel. Until awakened by her feelings for Charles, Jane had enjoyed an intense, albeit platonic friendship with Alec. This, she had persuaded herself, was entirely harmless, although in the end she comes to a different conclusion: 'It is predatory to meet people's needs – to cater to their weaknesses – and to fence them off from your own. With a pang of dismay Jane admitted to herself that her reserve had been a form of cowardice ... '[50] This is the lesson that Jane had to learn; she may be chaste in the conventional sense of the word, but her intense relationship with Alec had been damaging to his marriage. Although Alec does have a brief sexual fling with the *femme fatale*, arguably it is his relationship with Jane that has most undermined his marriage.

Jane is brought to learn this painful lesson by a recovering patient, who explains to her how he has come to see things:

> The way I look at it now is that there mustn't be any private worlds. Letting oneself be cut off by pride – or shutting oneself up completely in a dangerous intimacy – or hiding because of fear – well, those things aren't the escapes they look like. There is in all of them a sort of solitary confinement – even in the intimacy; one's got to belong to the outside world as well. Then one's all right! I don't mean that one needs to go about talking – but one mustn't keep the best of oneself up one's sleeve. One must stand open to life!'[51]

Significantly, and as though to underline the fact that sanity and insanity are not polar opposites, but – frequently – the product of circumstances, it is the recovering patient who teaches his doctor a thing or two.

There are a few melodramatic moments, which, although not entirely persuasive, are integral to Phyllis's knack of always making her novels page-turners, and the book was, in America, the overall best-selling novel for 1934, running into many editions.[52] Its Adlerian message is that mental health is not only a private, interiorised matter. As critic Phyllis Lassner expressed it, 'Jane Everest's struggle for the authority to choose love as she defines it is plotted as a political and social debate about the gendering of administrative, theoretical, and clinical authority.'[53]

As a consequence of the novel's best-selling status, Paramount bought the film rights and the film came out in 1935, under the same title, directed by Gregory La Cava and starring Claudette Colbert, Charles Boyer, Joel McCrea, Joan Bennett and Helen Vinson.[54] Walter Wanger, an independent producer, was a graduate of Dartmouth College, and an intellectual, a very different creature from the stereotype of a Hollywood producer. Phyllis's novel about mental illness appealed to him and he was proud of the film that he had made. On 24 April 1935 (the day before its première), he took out a full-page colour advert for the film that included interviews with the stars and also a long interview with Phyllis. Delightedly, Wanger sent Phyllis a review in *Liberty*: 'Lyn Starling's adaptation of Phyllis Bottome's novel, a first-rate piece of creative work in itself, deftly and incisively discloses how these characters grope their way to adjustment and happiness.'[55] The doyenne of Hollywood writers, Louella Parsons also praised it in the *Los Angeles Examiner*, saying:

> *Private Worlds*, based on the widely read novel by Phyllis Bottome, deals with a delicate and difficult subject of minds that are out of tune and dwell in their own private worlds ... Whether or not this picture will be a box-office success is doubtful. It is an experiment and an unusual picture and certainly not on a popular subject, but it is well done and ably directed by Gregory La Cava.[56]

Probably these good reviews helped, as the picture was a great success in America, with Claudette Colbert being nominated for an Academy Award for her portrayal of the woman psychiatrist. Unfortunately, the British censorship board was more hostile. Wanger's letter saying that the preview had gone well in America, quoted a warning from the censor in England about the script:

> *Private Worlds*' story in present form runs grave risk of censor

> prohibition owing to depictions of mental cases. Following scenes would never pass ... Madmen attacking doctors, Carrie Flint's unbalanced actions. Matron's coarse insinuations. Following passages doubtful. Claire's reaction to recovered mental cases. Sally's operation. Unless morbidity of background is minimised and benefit of psychiatry emphasised, subject liable to come under standard censor objection to morbid themes.[57]

The upshot of British censorship was that the film did not make very much money for Paramount because the British market was essential to financial success. Nor could it be a critical success in Britain, because, as Wanger put it, the censors had ripped 'the guts out of my picture, to my way of thinking ... '[58] Nevertheless, Phyllis believed that her novel and the subsequent film had increased compassion for the mentally ill and contributed to a debate on the improvement of treatment facilities. The novel was also broadcast in America as a radio series by United Artists and adapted as a play.[59]

Once Phyllis had recovered from her latest bout of illness and Ernan, on the death of his aunts, was no longer required for family duties, they decided to go to California for the rest of the winter. They set off from Rotterdam in January 1934 in a freighter called the *Balboa*. As they were good sailors it struck them as a cheap way to take a sea cruise through the Panama Canal to San Francisco. Unfortunately they were dogged by terrible storms, during which Phyllis wrote a short story inspired by an idea about Sarah Bernhardt that she called 'The Cup of Alteration'.[60] It is one of several portraits she made of actresses or ballerinas; she was fascinated by the extreme personalities of women who sacrificed everything else in their lives in order to become incomparable stars.[61]

In San Francisco they stayed with Cora Felton, a great friend of Robert Pollak's, whom Ernan had met on his previous trip to America. Robert himself was out of the country; in 1930, he had taken a job as head of the violin department of the Imperial Academy of Music in Tokyo. Cora was a magnificent hostess, who could provide introductions to anyone they wanted to know, and fend off less desirables. The success of *Private Worlds* (both novel and film) had made Phyllis a celebrity in America, and Cora helped her to withstand the onslaught of the publicity machine. She was a skilful telephone user, accepting on Phyllis's behalf useful press interviews and sessions with photographers, but also protecting her in her lovely house. Phyllis was enchanted with this friendly reception, as on many past occasions not all of Ernan's friends had been so agreeable.

She experienced a similarly warm welcome in San Francisco from Gertrude Atherton, whom – again – Ernan had met on his earlier visit. She was at this time as famous as Dorothy Thompson, and possessed of a similarly large personality; she shared with Phyllis a great interest in European politics. From Phyllis's point of view as a sister-writer, Gertrude 'had written the first, outspokenly modern novel, *Patience Sparhawk and her Times*; and she had followed this up with the first really natural and fact-revealing biography of Alexander Hamilton.'[62] She was a feminist who believed that the time had come for a woman president in America, and that Eleanor Roosevelt should do the job.[63] She was the doyenne of Californian literary life, writing best-sellers, and the founder of the San Francisco branch of PEN, the international organisation of poets, playwrights, essayists, editors, novelists and other literary professionals founded in London in 1921.[64] She was an accomplished networker, singularly well placed to introduce Phyllis to significant writers, and many American editions of Phyllis's books came out with a puff from Gertrude until her death in 1948.

During this American visit, Phyllis was lecturing for the Colston Leigh Agency. Phyllis particularly wanted to speak to schools, universities and educational bodies in general. Colston Leigh, on the other hand, knew that talks to ladies' clubs and public meetings paid better, so they agreed on a compromise. Ernan took on his favourite role as aide-de-camp, and liaised with Colston Leigh's office. Phyllis found that this second career as a lecturer came naturally to her. She had always been possessed of an exceptionally good memory and, way back, as an apprentice actor, had received some training on how to project her voice. These earlier ambitions had also given her an acute sense of how to grab and hold an audience's attention. So naturally did it come to her that Dale Warren, her editor at Houghton Mifflin, delightedly referred to her as the 'Speak-easy'. Starting her tour in June, Phyllis lectured in New York and Boston, including Columbia and Harvard Universities and Wellesley University, but, unfortunately, it came to an abrupt end when she was laid low by what was probably a bad bout of bronchitis. For Phyllis, it was never clear how serious any lung infection might turn out to be. Notwithstanding Colston Leigh's fury, Ernan insisted that Phyllis should cancel her later dates, and took a villa in Santa Barbara for three months to give her the best chance of a full recovery.

During this trip, Phyllis started to work out the basis of her next novel, *Level Crossing*. The idea had arisen following the kidnapping of Charles Lindbergh's baby son in March 1932. Although a ransom had been paid, the body of the baby was found in May 1932, and forensic evidence indicated that the baby had been shot and killed shortly after the kidnapping.

After Phyllis had recovered her health in Santa Barbara, they both went to New York for further analysis with Adler, who had adapted very well to his life in America following his first visit in 1927. He had already been offered the Chair of Psychology in the Long Island University of Medicine, after two and a half years of lecturing for Columbia University. Following this visit, Phyllis then recommenced touring for the Colston Leigh Agency, working non-stop from the end of October to mid-December 1934.[65] She lectured in Indiana, New York, Michigan, Ohio, Illinois and Toronto, Canada. The talks were financially rewarding even though the agency took fifty per cent, because each of her lectures effectively grew her fan base and helped sales of her books. Not surprisingly, the Forbes Dennises began to consider whether they should live permanently in America:

> The next problem we had to solve, taking it to Adler for his counsel, was where best to found our permanent home ... Looking back on our situation at the time, both financial and professional, I rather wonder that we did not do the obvious thing and decide to settle in America, while keeping in touch with Adler. We both loved Americans, and could have been quite happy in any one of our three favourite cities, Boston, San Francisco or Washington. I suppose our European commitments still seemed too vital to think of breaking them up.[66]

Adler did not tell them where they should live, regarding it, no doubt, as a question only they themselves could answer.

Around this time, they heard once more from their beloved nephew, Nigel Dennis. This was a great relief to them because there had been a bitter quarrel with his mother, Louise. She had not been pleased with Ernan's choice of education for him. After closing the Kitzbühel school, they had first sent him to the progressive Odenwaldschule, but on finding him increasingly 'immersed in Nietzsche and nursing a beard', had settled him instead in Munich, where he could continue with his German and also study Individual Psychology with Dr Credner.[67] When Louise returned from Rhodesia, she reclaimed her son, and the family started to run a small hotel in Chipping Campden called the Live and Let Live. Nigel himself seems then to have been sporadically employed: he helped in the hotel, did a bit of tutoring in Wales, and also sold ladies' garments door-to-door. But in 1934, aged twenty-two, he took a bold plunge, travelling steerage to New York and beginning a freelance writing career there. They were delighted to be reconnected with him, and sent him some money to help his fresh start.[68]

As the Colston Leigh tour had paid so well, they decided on a European trip that was more or less for pleasure, although Phyllis, as a professional writer, was, of course, always note-taking and writing. For over a year they had been out of Europe, and they decided to stay the rest of the winter of 1934/5 in Italy. They settled in a small hotel in Rapallo, on the Italian Riviera, and there re-met an old friend and made a new one.

Ezra Pound, whom Phyllis had not seen for thirty years, was living there with his wife, Dorothy Shakespear, a painter who had been part of the Vorticist group in London before the First World War.[69] To Phyllis's horror she found that Ezra had become a 'brittle Fascist', adoring Mussolini. Phyllis was utterly hostile to dictators, so she quickly found that they needed to avoid politics as a subject of conversation. He tried to persuade her that C. H. Douglas's social-credit system was the only thing that could save the world economy. Phyllis did her best to understand Ezra's argument, but she admitted that she

> was never able to grasp the place that either C. H. Douglas or the Italian Führer took in Ezra's mind. He tried hard to impart to me the glow that his partnership with C. H. Douglas in particular threw over his life. (Despairing of my prejudice against Dictators, he soon gave up the attempt to sell me Mussolini). At least I wholly agreed with him that money – and the mysterious authority it claimed over the modern world – should be debunked as speedily as possible ... the fact that I was willing to admit some complete overthrow of our financial system – though I never grasped how Douglas could replace it – did something to reconcile Ezra to my continued existence.[70]

Ezra persuaded Phyllis to give to Eleanor Roosevelt a letter from him advising the President to adopt Douglas's social credit system in America. The President politely declined to do so.

However, more alarmingly, arising from his devotion to the social credit system, Ezra had come to view usury as the Great Crime against the working man, and in a further step, he regarded usury as the special province of the Jews. He was a man possessed by rabid anti-Semitism; many of his letters to people other than Phyllis refer to Jews as 'kikes', to American newspapers as 'jewspapers', to Roosevelt as 'Jewsfeldt' or as 'ooze'. During this 1935 visit, when Phyllis pounced on the issue of Mussolini's view on the Jews, Ezra assured her that Mussolini did not particularly dislike the Jews. He must have masked his own fanatical hatred of Jews, because Phyllis and Ernan were full of talk of Adler and wanted Ezra to meet him. It is possible that they believed that Adler might be able to cure Ezra of his unfortunate fixation. But there was no hope for any such meeting of minds. Ezra regarded the Jewish Adler as a specimen of filthy vermin. It seems clear that he did not say this to these Adlerian disciples, as Phyllis innocently asked him if he would write a puff for her intended biography of Adler. Ezra curtly told her publisher that he declined to endorse syrup.[71]

On this visit, with the scenes in Munich fresh in their minds, after the initial shock of his inimical politics, they inevitably decided to stick to safer subjects than fascism. The Pounds had lived in Rapallo in an apartment above a café on the Via Marsala since 1925, and were embedded in the cultural life there. Phyllis and Ernan enjoyed the piano and violin concertos Ezra organised in Rapallo, selling tickets at the door himself and making all the business arrangements so that the musicians would receive every penny of the profits. Phyllis wrote: 'We made a very happy four. Ezra's interest in music and his organised benevolence in arranging concerts for out-of-work artists knot my husband to him, while Dorothy was as beautiful in her young middle-age as she had been in her extreme youth, and soon became my friend.'[72]

Dorothy seems to have been an extremely long-suffering wife; Ezra divided his time between his wife, with whom he had a son, and his mistress, the American violinist, Olga Rudge, with whom he had a daughter.[73] Olga had a home in Venice, but also rented a *pied-à-terre* in the village of Sant'Ambrogio, which was an hour's walk up a steep narrow mule-path from Rapallo. Although discreet, it is hard to imagine that their comings and goings were unobserved by the local community.[74]

It is also difficult to imagine that the Pounds and Forbes Dennises could have been a very relaxed foursome, or at least, they could only have been so with a huge number of things left unsaid. Both Ezra and Dorothy approved of fascism. When Italy invaded Abyssinia in October 1935, the League of Nations branded Italy an aggressor and called for sanctions against her.[75] Yet Ezra continued to condemn Phyllis's political position with the comment, 'liberalism was always green slime'.[76] Nevertheless, Phyllis continued a correspondence with him, although she did not seem to understand just how violent his anti-Semitism was. Phyllis tried to persuade Ezra that the Jews were a convenient scapegoat, saying to him: 'It is natural for lazy-brained people to hate Jews, but why should a person with a full active brain, mind any other race?'[77] Ezra, however, was incapable of hearing reason on this point. As his lifelong friend William Carlos Williams was to comment a few years later: 'The man is sunk, in my opinion, unless he can shake the fog of fascism out of his brain during the next few years, which I seriously doubt he can do. The logicality of fascism is soon going to kill him. You can't argue away wanton slaughter of innocent women and children by the neo-scholasticism of a controlled economy programme.'[78]

In 1944, when Phyllis came to write about him in *From the Life*, she explained in Adlerian terms how Ezra was an example of the 'spoiled and wilful child who makes whips and bloodshed take the place of wisdom and social interest.'[79] Despite this comment, she seems to have let him off pretty lightly, though; by the time she was writing this, Ezra was in danger of being condemned to death as a traitor to the USA.[80]

A slightly strange thing happened after leaving the Pounds in that Phyllis's dispatch case was stolen, holding the first draft of her work on *Level Crossing*. She had to rewrite it, and she told Ezra that, following her conversations with him, in the new version she had tried to show the money basis of society's problems clearly. She wrote to him that 'the frozen logic of competition is the madhouse and the gangster ... I try to show in *LC* that the characters that make a cooperative contribution finally succeed.'[81] In *Level Crossing*, Phyllis's heroine is a young pregnant Scottish wife who has married into a rich American family and is kidnapped for ransom. Deidre is finally restored to her husband, and her baby, too, is safe; the novel thus has a happier ending than the Lindbergh story that had originally sparked off her idea. Deidre recognises that two members of the kidnapping gang have become gangsters primarily because they have had no hope in life, following the Depression:

> 'Countries', Deidre thought, 'should be responsible like mothers, for their children! They should feed them and guide them! Human beings should not be left helpless, in a terrible emptiness ... '[82]

Deidre has to struggle with the dilemma of what loyalty she owes to the two members of the gang who had let her live, in balance with what she owes to the safety of the community as a whole. This is left unresolved. Influenced by Ezra, Phyllis attempts to interrogate the morality of the rich capitalists, many of whom show no sense of social responsibility. She writes flatly, 'All people who hurt other people to get what they want are gangsters.'[83] Overall, the novel consists of some melodramatic moments combined with a quasi-political attempt to critique capitalism, which does not prove a wholly successful amalgam. Her own voice seems somewhat tainted.

However, a less fraught friendship began in Rapallo following a visit to Max Beerbohm, whom Phyllis had never met before. Max, who tended not to like women writers, had surprisingly sent her a letter via their shared publisher, John Lane, admiring her work and inviting her to visit him. It had caught up with her in the sanatorium at Montana, where she was ill and therefore unable to take up the invitation. Phyllis had been immensely cheered to receive 'a letter full of that deep encouragement of a fellow craftsman'.[84] Although living in the same town, Max, having met Ezra once, declined to meet him again. It is not irrelevant, of course, that Max's American wife, Florence Kahn, was Jewish. Max was a caricaturist and writer, who had been part of the Oscar Wilde set in Oxford in the 1890s. His older half-brother Herbert Beerbohm Tree was the great London actor-manager. Max had had a series of crushes on and broken engagements to actresses, including Ivor Novello's great friend, the glamorous Constance Collier. In 1910, he had married Florence, an actress who had not had a successful career, although she had been noted for sensitive performances in Ibsen's plays. Moving to Rapallo, they lived very quietly; as Max commented later, 'I wanted to be alone with Florence.'[85]

An invitation to visit Max was an honour. Phyllis and Ernan walked for about twenty minutes up the coast road south of Rapallo to the Villino Chiaro, admiring the magnificent view of the Mediterranean three hundred feet below. The *villino* was a simple white construction, with a little rough garden planted with lemon, almond and orange trees behind. The entrance lobby was decorated with Max's caricatures of Henry James and other literati, and the cool interior was painted in soft tones of grey and fawn. Max – although transplanted in Italy – remained an Edwardian dandy. He was always impeccably dressed, carefully choosing a camellia for his buttonhole before dinner. Florence too had an air of a woman out of time; with her red hair and pale complexion she seemed like a Pre-Raphaelite painting come to life. Any meal with the Beerbohms felt like an occasion; it began with a glass of vermouth before dinner; detailed attention was paid to the food and, above all, to witty conversation. Max's conversation was never less than brilliant; he had been friendly with all the decadents in the 1890s, such as Aubrey Beardsley, Oscar Wilde and his lover, Bosie. Unlike many fair-weather friends, he had refused to condemn Oscar when scandal, court cases and a gaol sentence overtook him. There seems a slight parallel, however, between Max's life and Ernan's, in that, on marriage, they had both left a whole set of friends behind them.

Phyllis intensely admired Max's flawless essay style, and looked to improve her writing from his critiques of her short stories. He was immensely civilised, not merely aesthetically, but also, as it were, politically. Max, she wrote:

> saw, long before anyone else did, and with dreadful clarity, what awaited the land he loved ... In this world of increasing rigidity, Max Beerbohm kept his personal freedom of thought elastic, and inviolate, Among the people who visited the *villino*, those who were German Liberal-minded, or those of Jewish origin, exiled from their native land, must have felt, as they received the exquisite hospitality handed out to them – perhaps even emphasised by the deep unspoken sympathy of their hosts – as if they were enjoying a glimpse of a lost Paradise.[86]

The Forbes Dennises were to remain friends with the Beerbohms, meeting up in London in 1936, for instance, when Ivor Novello was starring in a dramatised version of Max's *The Happy Hypocrite*.[87] And, in turn, Max and his wife enjoyed Phyllis's short stories, congratulating her, in 1940, on her collection called *Masks and Faces*.[88] It is a suggestive title, as Max himself wore a 'mask' of impeccable courtesy, yet the mask was true, in the sense that his moral probity and genuine goodwill towards his fellow men matched his mask. It is also reminiscent of *The Happy Hypocrite*, whose theme is that of Oscar Wilde's *The Picture of Dorian Gray* in reverse.[89] In this case a predatory and dissolute aristocrat, Lord George Hell, falls in love with an innocent young woman and dons a saintly mask to disguise evidence of debauchery; when he is unmasked, the *coup de théâtre* is that his face has grown lovely to match his new morality.[90]

After the Rapallo visit, in April 1935 they moved on to Florence, staying at a fourteenth-century villa as the guests of two American sisters who were the cousins of Phyllis's dear friends Lady Beit and her sister Marguerite Carter. They had a standing invitation from them for the second fortnight of April. In this circle they met Alice Keppel, once the mistress of Edward VII, who invited them to her villa on San Miniato. She unabashedly kept a life-size portrait of her former lover over her bath. They were also invited to I Tatti, the home of Bernard

Berenson, the much respected art historian and connoisseur. Berenson was an American-born Jew, whose parents had immigrated to Boston from Lithuania, but after an education at Harvard he had gravitated towards Europe. His sixteenth-century villa near Florence was full of works of art, books and photographs. Phyllis did not care for him; after a conversation with his wife, Mary, who was at that time lying very ill in bed, she liked him even less.[91] Phyllis was to comment in her autobiography that 'he extended his intellectual sympathy to Hitler and Mussolini, who left him in full possession of his villa throughout the war … [he] was one of the very few Jews that I have not been able wholeheartedly either to admire or to like.'[92] There is more than a hint that she saw him as similar to the coolly malevolent fortune-hunter in Henry James's novel *Portrait of a Lady*. Indeed, his artistic reputation was later to become compromised by the substantial income he derived from certificating works of art for dealers selling to wealthy Americans.[93]

After Florence, they moved to Vienna to spend the late summer working with Adler. Phyllis observed in her autobiography:

> In 1935 the little country of music and song, irony and honesty, mixed with great friendliness – that 'soft' country as the Germans call it – was already preparing its own downfall. The sense of defeat was in the air and Adler, who loved Vienna as men love the first woman of their eager dream, saw that it was going to be defeated. 'I shall never return to Vienna again,' he told us quietly. 'It is already a dead city.'[94]

That summer Adler was staying in the Hotel Regina at the corner of the Währingerstrasse where he had lived as a child. Phyllis and Ernan took a flat in Grinzing, then a quiet little village of vineyards climbing up into the Wienerwald.[95] Adler gave two series of lectures that summer – one set of them took the form of formal lectures to medical students at the university. Phyllis wrote an article for an American magazine directly based on these lectures, called 'Human Relationships'. Adler was a charismatic lecturer, but the couple enjoyed even more the informal meetings in the large upstairs room of Adler's favourite Café Siller, where the IP students, practitioners and interested others held round-table sessions, which included getting advice on problems encountered in child-guidance clinics, for example, or within schools. The Café Siller had a fine view over the Danube, so afterwards everyone spilled out on to the little flowered tables on the café terrace, still talking. Laci Zilahi, the editor of the *International Journal of Individual Psychology*, would turn up to discuss editorial matters with Adler. It was on this visit to Vienna that Phyllis and Ernan met Adler's wife and children. Adler had met his wife, a small fair Russian woman, Raissa Timofeyewna Epstein, in a student Marxist group. They had four children, three daughters and a son: Valentine (Vali) was politically active like her mother, Alexandra (Ali) and Kurt were following their father's footsteps into psychotherapy, and the youngest, Nelly, wanted to be an actress.[96] In view of her own adulation of Adler, Phyllis noted how hard it must be for his family to have to share him with his large group of friends and pupils. Although he was a fondly affectionate father, she watched as Nelly and her husband Heinz Sternberg had to drag him away from the crowd at the Siller and take him to a café on the other side of the street in order to regain his attention for themselves.

Adler had been a socialist in his youth because of its humanistic aims, and strongly identified with the democratic tradition of Austrian socialism. He could not, however, go along with Communism following the excesses of the Russian Revolution; he was deeply alarmed by the intoxication with power. This had caused the loss of some old friends, such as Joffe, a close associate of Trotsky in pre-World War I days in Vienna.[97] Raissa, on the other hand, had remained in sympathy with the Communists until around 1935, and this had caused some tension in their marriage. Ironically, though, as Alexandra Adler later explained to Phyllis, it may well have been Raissa's Marxist sympathies that saved 'all the family's lives since we felt urged to leave earlier than Hitler's advent because our whole family had become unpopular with the Austrian Government even before Hitler came'.[98] Adler had foreseen that it would not be long before all Jews would have to leave Austria and he insisted that his children worked hard to make their English fluent, so that they would be able to secure jobs in America, when it became imperative that they should leave Vienna. He himself was already spending winter semesters there, establishing a career.

In preparation for his anticipated permanent departure to America, he had decided to sell up his property, specifically his country house in Salmannsdorf, a village an hour's drive out of Vienna, where he liked to go at weekends. At Adler's invitation, Phyllis and Ernan joined him there in the Wienerwald for a nostalgic last day. A gifted singer, he especially loved Schubert's work, and lovely old Viennese songs. This final summer, Adler had been disturbed to observe that Austrians no longer seemed to remember the words of their own lieder; they only knew German ones. Phyllis records in her autobiography, Adler's comment: ' "It is a bad sign," he said to us, "when a country forgets its own songs." ' He gave to Ernan that day his collection of much-loved Austrian songbooks and to Phyllis a bunch of roses from his garden.

By the autumn of 1935, Phyllis and Ernan were, hardly for the first time in their married lives, being pulled in two directions. Ernan wanted to stay in Vienna where he was happily studying music therapy with Dr Leonard Deutsch. Phyllis wrote to Ezra Pound proudly boasting that Deutsch said he had never had such a good pupil as Ernan. As the political situation in Europe increasingly darkened, Phyllis, unexpectedly perhaps, began to feel that she wanted to make a home in England. Ernan wanted Phyllis to stay with him until he had finished his course, but, for once, Adler intervened, and indicated to Phyllis that Ernan was always arranging for Phyllis's needs ahead of his own needs; this time she should go ahead and find them somewhere to live, leaving Ernan to continue his own intellectual and professional development. Just as Seif had previously advised, Adler insisted that it would be good for them to take on – if only for a period of a couple of months – 'the opposite role to that to which we were accustomed'.[99]

It seems clear that, to both Phyllis and Ernan, Adler was the wise, idealised father-figure, who replaced internally their own rather unsatisfactory ones. Generally, Phyllis was a decisive, even dominant woman, but with Adler she seemed to enjoy the sense of being a compliant daughter. She was beginning to work on the novel that she had been brooding over since their Munich days, a novel designed to give a clear warning of what the rise of Nazism would mean to Germany and to Jews in particular.

CHAPTER 8

The Battle against Appeasement in Britain: the Writing of The Mortal Storm *and the Adler Tours*

The Mortal Storm *will doubtless stand as the first significant novel torn out of the bleeding heart of modern Europe.*

cover blurb for the Little Brown edition

In America, Sinclair Lewis had urged Phyllis to return to her roots, telling her that 'no writer could safely give up his native land as a background for his work'.[1] However, by this stage it seemed not entirely certain, even to Phyllis, where her roots were. In many ways, especially in her political awareness, she was far more European than English. An American father, and consequently an American branch of the family, plus, increasingly, a celebrity status in America, also meant that coming 'home' to England, especially alone, was a somewhat hollow experience. Adler, being a wily old fox, had perhaps realised that Phyllis, on her own, needed to find out where 'home' was.

Coming back to England in 1935, aged fifty-three, Phyllis had left behind her the two men she loved best – her husband, Ernan, who was finishing his training as a music therapist with Leonard Deutsch, and her father-advisor, Adler. Living alone, in rented accommodation, she found starting this new phase of her life something of an ordeal:

> I had lived out of England for thirty-five years of my life and for so long in Europe that my own speech sounded strange in my ears. The fruit of my work, my professional career, with all its rewards and

> repercussions, and the nationwide contacts it had brought me in America, were left behind me. No one in England knew me, beyond my two remaining family relations, Mary and George, and a handful of old friends. I had never met my English publisher. I knew no editors or reviewers and, worse still, I had never met any of my writing colleagues. The London I had known and loved before my marriage had gone with Lislie's death. What confronted me was a wilderness of strangers … .[2]

Professionally, she was all at sea. When she had left America, the PEN Club had given a farewell dinner in her honour, where alongside her on 'high table' had been the philosopher John Dewey and Madariaga, the Spanish Ambassador.[3] In England, she had no networks. In an attempt to find a new intellectual circle for herself in London, she attended a Women Writers' Club lunch in Piccadilly given in honour of Dorothy L. Sayers, where she was on a table at such a distance from the literary 'stars' that it underlined to her that she was by no means a celebrity in England.

Politically, too, Phyllis found it difficult to get her bearings. She could not fathom why the British policy of appeasement towards Germany had persisted after the advent of Hitler as Chancellor of Germany. Consumed by what she had observed in mainland Europe, she experienced a 'stunned sickness' at what she perceived as the lack of concern she found in those to whom she spoke:[4]

> I had come from a Europe that was distraught and obsessed between Hitler and Mussolini, with Stalin waiting in the wings. The fate of six million Jews was in the balance. I simply could not believe in the easy nonchalance of London. When I met Conservatives, they stared at me in frank bewilderment. 'Oh, but we like Hitler!' they said.[5]

Phyllis's only contact with government at this point was Alfred Beit, the Conservative Member of Parliament whose mother Lilian had always been a good friend to Phyllis and Lislie.[6] Alfred warned Phyllis that she should not clutch on to people like the Ancient Mariner, but should learn to be more strategic in selecting to whom she spoke. Alfred was married to Clementine Mitford, a cousin of the more famous

Mitford sisters, two of whom were deeply enamoured with Hitler, so he must have had a shrewd sense of upper-class anti-Semitic and right-wing views. Beit, himself of Jewish descent on his father's side, had listened carefully to what Phyllis had to say. This was a thin ray of hope, but Phyllis, however politically knowledgeable, was utterly disconnected from the levers of power in her home country.

Phyllis understood that the roots of appeasement had sprung from the not inappropriate sense that the 1919 Treaty of Versailles had imposed such punitive reparation payments on Germany that it was unlikely to bring lasting peace. Of even greater psychological consequence was the 'War-Guilt' clause, which laid all responsibility for the First World War at Germany's door.[7] Englishmen visiting Germany were struck by German sensitivity on this point; many distinguished Germans objected, including, for example, the novelist, Thomas Mann. The French had wanted vengeance, and an imposed peace rather than a negotiated one; Churchill was one of several statesmen who had argued against a punitive settlement, saying, 'I have always held the view that these war debts and reparations have been a great curse ... that the sooner we could free ourselves from them and the less we exacted, the better for the whole world.'[8] During the 1920s, Britain had sought to revise German repayments in the hope of revitalising European businesses damaged by the war and, in this way, to reposition Germany as an ally. Much of the justification for appeasement was the belief that Germany, if treated well, might become a peace-loving democracy.

Hitler was a brilliant opportunist, able to exploit the sense of grievance within Germany, as well as having a sharp eye for the weakness of Western democracies. As early as May 1930, Sir Robert Vansittart, then the new Permanent Under-Secretary of State for Foreign Affairs, had warned that Hitler was a 'half-mad and ridiculously dangerous demagogue' – but Hitler was not yet formally in power, so, if anything, this should have given new impetus to making concessions to the Weimar Republic rather than letting power pass into less democratic and more grasping hands.[9]

In March 1931, the German government had proposed an immediate Austro-German Customs Union, and two months later the largest

Austrian bank collapsed. Germany was no longer in a position to pay reparations, even had she desired it. Economic depression had opened up the possibility, even the psychological necessity, for a strong leader. Whereas in America the Depression opened up a route for President Roosevelt and his New Deal, in Germany it opened the way to a monster with hypnotising rhetoric.

In Britain, towards the end of 1931, the economic crisis had led to the fall of the Labour Government. Although Ramsay MacDonald, the leader of the Labour Party, remained Prime Minister, he was the head of a National Government which was mainly Conservative, even though a Liberal, Lord Reading, was Foreign Secretary. Appeasement was not the policy of any particular party; most politicians accepted appeasement as the only policy capable of breaking the European deadlock and averting a war of revenge. At the Lausanne Conference of 1932 reparations were finally laid to rest, but this change in policy came too late to avert disaster.

It was patently obvious to Phyllis that from 30 January 1933, once Adolf Hitler had become Chancellor of Germany, any hope of democracy in Germany had ended. The evidence in her eyes had been clear: within a week the Reichstag had passed an Enabling Bill giving Hitler full dictatorial powers. On 1 April 1933, a one-day boycott had been declared against all Jewish shops, and Jews were beaten up on the streets of Berlin. In May trade unions had been made illegal, so communists and trade unionists could be arrested and imprisoned without trial. However, Phyllis found that many British people felt that all revolutions bred violence in their initial stages and that Nazism was no exception. Further, Hitler claimed to be the principal guardian in Europe against the spread of Communism, and some tolerated him on this account. On 21 June 1935, the British government concluded the Anglo-German Naval Agreement that enabled Germany to build up its navy, including its submarines. Phyllis noted, however, that Churchill strongly opposed this.

Phyllis's long sojourn in mainland Europe had given her a unique insight. From the moment that Hitler had taken Germany out of the League of Nations in 1934, and the League of Nations had failed to stop Mussolini from taking Abyssinia in 1935, she had become increasingly afraid that the democracies lacked the will to attack.[10] She perceived that Hitler had taken the same view. From her experience in both Vienna and Munich, she had no doubts at all that the rise of Hitler would mean the death of liberalism. In Vienna she had come to know Adler's closest friend, Carl Furtmüller, who, after the First World War, had been appointed by Otto Glöckel, the head of the Ministry of Education in the new Austrian Republic, as Superintendent of Secondary Education. He had implemented a progressive regime throughout the Hauptschulen, in which pupils were taught to cooperate as members of a group, rather than have the teacher as the traditional exalted authority. But with the seizure of power by the Austrian fascists in 1934, Furtmüller had been dismissed.[11] When she gave these sorts of examples to people in Britain, Phyllis found that they merely shrugged their shoulders.

She slowly realised that the British public had been lulled into a false sense of security by the damaging complacency of most of the press and the BBC. Up until 1936, the *Manchester Guardian* was almost the only honourable exception; it openly stated that anti-Semitism was fundamental to the new Germany, and not some kind of accidental extra.[12] It is no surprise that Ezra Pound had told Phyllis that 'the *Manchester Guardian* is the most goddamn lying and corrupt rag in England'.[13]

In December, after two months' separation, Ernan caught up with Phyllis in London and together they found a house that they both loved, Lonach Cottage, 46 Lexham Gardens. Despite its name, it was one of two architect-designed modern detached houses; there was a certain amount of work to be done, but potentially it was perfect:

> It was spacious, light and airy, and contained a sunken bath and a beautiful music room, with a door leading on to a stone terrace overlooking the small patch of garden. This we could use as our chief living-room, or alternately for Ernan's music pupils. A hall and dining-room opened out of it, and could be used as auxiliary sitting-rooms; while I had a little south-facing work-room at the top of the house which perfectly suited my writing.[14]

However, having agreed to purchase it, they left it in the care of the builders and both went in separate directions once more. Phyllis borrowed Viola Meynell's cottage at Gresham on the South Downs, and there wrote various short stories to sell to journals, six of which would later be collected as *Masks and Faces* (1940). Phyllis was still the major breadwinner, and worked from nine to one every day, regardless of whatever else was happening. She also found time to write a story that she donated to *Christmas Pie,* published in November 1936, to raise money for King George V's Jubilee Trust for the Youth of Britain.[15]

Aghast at her discovery that Britain was suffering from an *ignorantia affectata*, the expression Thomas Aquinas coined to describe a cultivated ignorance, Phyllis's desperate determination was to write a novel that would wake up Britain and America to the perils of letting Hitler's ambitions go unchecked. Phyllis's new agent in Britain, David Higham, approached Geoffrey Faber with her first draft of *The Mortal Storm*, when, in 1936, he started a new list of fiction writers. Faber immediately commissioned her novel and from the first Phyllis had a wonderful relationship with Geoffrey Faber; he would be the publisher of all her books published in Britain after this.[16]

While Phyllis was writing, Ernan accompanied Adler on his annual Dutch tour during the spring of 1936. Writing to Phyllis from Amsterdam, he told her that Adler had suggested that Ernan should do 'more IP [Individual Psychology] on the pupils & less music – so that one would be charging more for *treatment* rather than for lessons – He thinks one *knows* enough – and might learn to be less discouraged by working with students!'[17] Clearly, Adler was still advising Ernan to locate his own best work. Dating from this point, Ernan consistently moved towards establishing himself as an IP therapist, over and above any other strings he might have had to his bow.

Adler's first visit to England had been in 1923, when he gave one of the key lectures at the seventh International Congress of Psychology in Oxford. As he had given his lecture in German, he had not reached a wide audience. His 1926 visit to London was at the request of one or two medical and psychological societies. Alan Porter, subsequently to become Professor of Literature at Vassar College in America, founded the Gower Street Club of Individual Psychology. Another key member was Philip Mairet, who, before the First World War, had been the editor of *The New Age,* a journal extremely interested in psychoanalysis and psychology.[18] A later journal, also edited by Mairet, the *New English Weekly*, founded by A. R. Orage in 1932, was highly influential, in the first instance among left-leaning intellectuals. Orage's social philosophy, harking back to the ideas of William Morris, argued that the nation needed to find again the links with the past that had been severed by industrialisation and mass production. Everyone, he said, must take his share of both drudge-work and cultural activity. This was hardly more than guild socialism, yet in this same nexus one could find a socialist writer such as Storm Jameson side by side with Ezra Pound, who would become increasingly right-wing. As a consequence of Orage's open publishing policy, a bewildering array of left-liberal and right-wing articles could be found in his periodical's pages.[19] By 1931, Adler had insisted on being disassociated from the Gower Street Club, as he did not want the concepts of Individual Psychology adopted or indeed contaminated by political factions and power struggles between left-wing and right-wing groups.[20] As Phyllis wrote, 'Adler objected to Absolutism in any form, partly as a dogma without means of progress, and partly as an unnecessary support for those who were afraid to explore their own potentialities.'[21] Two new IP societies were formed, one consisting only of medics, but another group held fortnightly meetings in Torrington Square for lay people, and these Phyllis and her sister Mary regularly attended.[22]

Ernan felt that the most significant thing he could do for the rest of his life would be to help spread Adler's Individual Psychology. In 1936, he arranged an English lecture tour for Adler, to follow on from his Amsterdam dates. Ernan met Adler at Southampton and took him first to Plymouth, where he held a child-guidance demonstration facilitated by Lady Astor, who had always been strongly interested in the educational problems of her constituency.[23] Adler gave a lecture at Dartington Hall – though he made it clear that he was not wholly in sympathy with free-school ideas, as his theory of education was to encourage children to take responsibility and to make themselves free only to serve others; he did not approve of a situation that might allow the balance to tip in favour of freedom to exploit others. In Exeter, Adler lectured at University College of the South West and the mayor and corporation held a luncheon in his honour. In London, Adler's lectures filled the seats for three successive nights at Conway Hall in Red Lion Square, a rather appropriate venue as it had been built in 1929 to serve as a beacon for independent, intellectual, political and cultural life.[24]

Through the Torrington Square Club, a three-day conference was arranged at Liverpool in conjunction with the Home and School Council. The Catholic Archbishop Downie chaired one of the lectures and was inspired to become a staunch Adlerian supporter. Successful lectures were held at Cardiff University and at University College, London, but it proved harder to open doors at Oxford and Cambridge, 'bristling as they were with hostile Freudians'.[25] Various friends of Phyllis and Ernan were roped in: Sir Alfred Beit helped crack Oxford and Lady Isabel Margesson and her daughter Lady Cushendun had Cambridge contacts. In Cambridge, on 18 May 1936, Adler gave a lecture to the New Educational Fellowship and the Cambridge Education Society, consisting mainly of undergraduates from public schools who were interested in progressive ideas.[26] Adler was perceived as, among other things, a progressive educationist. He was also, in effect, an intellectual 'refugee', as the fascist regime had closed down Adlerian clinics attached to the state schools in Vienna. Glöckel, the sympathetic Minister of Education, had been thrown into a concentration camp, where he subsequently died. As Brian Simon wrote in his autobiography: 'Some of our speakers had an international reputation and drew large audiences. Alfred Adler, then a guru of the psycho-analytic world but having differences with Freud and Jung, drew in the crowds.'[27] Adler's talk was on 'Some Recent Developments in Individual Psychology' and was chaired by the Master of Peterhouse, Professor Ernest Barker, 'a very effective, avuncular and friendly chairman'.[28] As Adler wrote to Professor Barker afterwards, 'I have never had a more sympathetic or able chairman, or a more congenial audience.'[29]

Back in London, Adler lectured to the British Medical Association, and to the Teachers' Association in Essex Hall, a Unitarian centre. At Phyllis's request, Lilian Beit gave an 'At Home' for Adler in her beautiful Belgrave Square home, filled with Otto's remarkable collection of paintings. This was a more fashionable audience than typical, although the Minister of Education, Oliver Stanley, acted as chairman. Adler also gave a talk to members of the Anglican clergy at the invitation of Canon Percy Dearmer of Westminster Abbey, and also at a preparatory school near Dover, where he lectured to teachers.

Adler's lectures engaged large and interested audiences at every stop. There were several reasons for this. Adler's time in America meant that on this visit his English was considerably more fluent than during his visits in the 1920s. Indeed, his 1932 book, *What Life Should Mean to You,* written by him in clear English, had only needed Alan Porter to tidy it up a little before publication.[30] But, in addition, Ernan's presence and his fluent German meant that any slightly obscure nuances could be interpreted. Adler himself was a brilliant lecturer, with a ready wit and consistent good humour, which never let him down even in the face of hostile questioning. Although he personally had had years of training, both medical and psychological, he never sought to bamboozle his listeners, but rather to challenge them with humour and grace to remake their own lives. As Phyllis put it:

> Adler thought that every child forms his own life-plan unconsciously, from the examples and materials that he finds around him at birth; and since this pattern is already fixed at a time when the child is still ignorant of life and his reason is undeveloped, it is generally a faulty life-plan. Individual Psychology unmasks to a patient what he is really aiming at; and this gives him the opportunity to change a faulty life-plan for a more reasonable goal. That a man's character is formed by his goal and can be changed by substituting a more useful one is the essence of Adler's psychology. At an intellectual level, this psychology presents no difficulties, but as a method of life it makes great demands on all who try to practise it, since it includes the whole man: his intellect, his emotions and all his other powers; it is naturally the hardest, and least willingly understood, of modern psychologies.[31]

Ernan was a brilliant aide-de-camp and the tour was highly successful not only because of Adler's charm and charisma but also because of Ernan's meticulous organisation. Phyllis was very proud when Adler asked Ernan to serve formally as his European representative. Indeed, it is not pushing it too far to say that Ernan had finally discovered his own goal in this role. When Adler returned to America, Ernan set about organising another tour for 1937.

Around this time Alfred Beit was serving on a commission that was visiting mental hospitals consequent to the 1936 Lunacy Report. He asked Phyllis, because of the research she had done for *Private Worlds,* if she would speak at a Conservative Conference at Southampton. Phyllis, after having made it plain to the organiser that she was not a Conservative, and after they in their turn made her promise not to speak about politics, agreed to go. She had studied the report, and was pleased to note that:

> One of the chief changes suggested by the Report was that it should no longer allow certified patients who had improved to go before a committee chiefly composed of elderly ladies and retired admirals of over eighty in order to get their certificates cancelled.[32]

She urged the conference to support the reforms. This experience gave her useful insight into how the establishment in Britain worked; as she was about to tackle it head on, this was salutary. It also indicates that she was beginning to be recognised as a public intellectual, albeit one that the Conservative Party could not co-opt.

The world situation continued to alarm Phyllis and Ernan. At about the time that Addis Ababa in Ethiopia fell to Mussolini, a second front opened in the fascists' war. On 17 July 1936, Spain exploded with the Generals' Uprising in Morocco. General Francisco Franco crossed from North Africa to lead a military coup against the Republic. The coup turned into a civil war with the Loyalists (republicans, socialists and communists) fighting the Nationalists (monarchists, militarists, Catholic clergy and fascists). There was whole-scale killing on both sides, but the right-wing was clearly targeting progressive teachers, intellectuals, self-educated workers and 'new' women. The Republic looked for support from the Western democracies – Britain and France – but they established a non-intervention treaty in August 1936. Phyllis once again was astonished that the British seemed to think that what happened in mainland Europe would have no bearing on them. However, the most outspoken writer at this period was Stephen Spender, who sent an article on September 1936 to the *News Chronicle* exposing the fascist sympathisers among the supposedly neutral British diplomats in Spain.[33] Like Phyllis he had lived in Germany and Vienna, so he too had experience of what fascism meant on the streets. Spender was the pre-eminent British writer who reported on the war in Spain; he was at that time a Communist, and so had cooperation from and access to the International Brigade.[34] Many anti-fascists from Europe, America and Canada went to fight for the Spanish Republic, as they saw this conflict as a crucial struggle between freedom and fascism. In this view they were not mistaken: Germany and Italy signed the non-intervention treaty but supported and supplied the Nationalist cause; thus the treaty worked against the Republic throughout the war. Stalin realised that if the Republic collapsed Nazi firepower would be freed up for aggression eastwards – towards vulnerable Soviet frontiers. Risking British displeasure, Russia dispatched military assistance in the form of planes, weapons and military advisors to the Loyalists. Bizarrely, with the benefit of hindsight, hardly anyone in the British government seemed to worry that a Francoist victory might pose a threat to British interests.

Phyllis, if only a doubtful guest to the Conservatives, was welcomed with pleasure to what Ivor Novello called his 'small romps' after his theatre performances. By this stage in her life Phyllis was a well-published writer, even if better known in America than Britain, and, like Ivor, she was connected with the film world. Ivor had been especially taken with Phyllis's *Depths of Prosperity*, published in 1925, and also her *hommage* to him, her novel *The Rat*, published in 1926.[35] Ivor had returned to the London stage in 1932 after two years on Broadway and in Hollywood. He had a kind of Peter Pan quality that made his company irresistible. Phyllis found herself enjoying visits to Ivor's flat on the top floor of the Strand Theatre in the Aldwych, where he had lived since 1915. This was despite the terrifying ascent in a tiny ancient lift that jolted its way up and sometimes stopped completely for no apparent reason. Once safely inside the drawing-room, however, one found a heady maelstrom of music, laughter and gossip going on around the grand piano. Ernan and Phyllis happened to be with Ivor in his flat in December 1936 when Edward VIII made his abdication speech on the radio.[36] Edward abdicated in the face of opposition to his proposed marriage to Wallis Simpson, a twice-divorced American woman:

> His few sincere and memorable words cut straight to the heart. It was strange, just afterwards, to hear the music of *Tristan and Isolde* and to realise that what had been accepted as high romance was, now that it had happened on our doorstep, considered a crime ... There was great suspicion in the Labour Party that King Edward was pro-Nazi in his sympathies. Probably the whole Tory Party, with the redoubtable exception of Winston Churchill, were at this stage incipient Nazis, and remained so until 1939, when Hitler's evident intention of swallowing the British Isles with the rest of Europe checked them.[37]

Phyllis suspected that the real reason Edward was forced to abdicate was because of his concerns about the condition of the poor in England; she had approved of his outspoken remarks about the hardship in the South Wales mining valleys where unemployment was high.

For Adler's second English tour, Ernan wanted to improve on the previous one by shifting from single lectures to summer courses of ten lectures, each with opportunities for private discussions in between. Phyllis wrote: 'I don't know how my husband managed all the work involved, or how he overcame the innumerable obstructions from hostile Freudians and the jealous antagonism of the British Medical Authorities.'[38] With the help of a young secretary, Freda Troup, Ernan arranged courses at Aberdeen, Edinburgh, Manchester, London, Liverpool and Exeter, mostly for doctors and teachers.[39] Ernan formed a small committee, of which Alfred Beit was chair, and Ian Fleming was treasurer. Although Ian was not really an Adlerian, he adored the Forbes Dennises and never refused a request from them. Ernan often had to be persevering in his attempts to organise lectures; at Edinburgh University there was a certain amount of resistance, but fortunately, Dr Winifred Rushworth, a psychologist who had trained at the Tavistock Clinic in London, championed the visits.[40]

The summer programme began at Aberdeen University, with a course of lectures for medical students. Adler was in emotional turmoil because his eldest daughter Vali and her husband had been imprisoned in the Russian Gulag, and he did not know what her fate would be. Adler wanted doctors and medical students, as well as teachers, to think about children as whole beings, not just in terms of an apparently isolated symptom. Phyllis herself was especially impressed with Adlerian approaches to working with children:

> To see, as I have often seen, a potentially neurotic or delinquent child turn, under this treatment, into a normal child, with courage and common sense, was enough to make me long to help spread Adler's psychology in every school and family ... The test Individual Psychology used, to prove whether a child was normal or not, was to confront him with an unknown task and see how he reacted to it. If the child asked, 'Does it hurt? Is it hard? Will it take long?' you would know that this was a potentially neurotic child. But if the child asked, 'How does it work?' you would know that this was a normal child, and could probably make his own way in the world.[41]

What turned out to be Adler's last lecture was, aptly, for Aberdeen's Child Guidance Society; the mayor took the chair and most of the corporation was present.

The following morning, on 28 May 1937, disaster struck. Going for a walk before breakfast, Adler died of a sudden massive heart attack. Ernan had to break the news to Raissa, who was then in Paris, on her way to rejoin her husband in London. She flew to Croydon and arrived at Aberdeen by noon on the 29th. His daughter Nelly, with her husband, Heinz Sternberg, arrived a day later from Vienna. His son Kurt, then working at the Long Island College of Medicine, flew over from America the day after that. Telegrams expressing sympathy were sent to Phyllis and Ernan from all over the world; probably the ones they treasured most were those from Leonard Seif, and two of their old Kitzbühel boys, Lewis Way and Ian Fleming. On 1st June a funeral service was held for Adler in King's College Chapel in Aberdeen, at which Dr Lydia Sicher, who had worked with Adler in Vienna, gave one of the addresses. A cremation followed at Edinburgh, Phyllis and Ernan sorrowfully following the hearse in their car. Ernan was racked with guilt, fearing that the intensive lecturing programme he had organised had finally worn out Adler's overworked heart.

Despite being in an acute state of shock and mourning, Ernan had responsibilities as the manager of the Adler tour and had to make emergency arrangements for the business in hand. In Aberdeen, the city decided to help the university found a Chair of Psychiatry, each partner paying three hundred pounds a year so that the city might have the right to send delinquent children from Aberdeen to the university for this special treatment. That alone is a lasting testament to Adler's influence. Adler's daughter, Alexandra, now attached to the Neurological Department of the Harvard Medical School in Boston, stepped into the breach and managed to deliver the prearranged lecture courses in Edinburgh, Liverpool and London. Only Exeter College cancelled its programme when informed of Adler's death. Ernan improvised a summer school at Bishop Otter Teacher Training College to replace the Exeter venue, and Ernan's friend, the pianist and composer Desirée McEwan, entertained them in the evenings. In London, Ali Adler gave lectures at a vacation course for teachers held at Bedford College. So, to some extent, therefore, Ernan succeeded in his ambition of spreading Adler's psychology despite his premature death.[42]

On this last trip to England, Adler had asked Phyllis to write his authorised biography; he was sixty-seven and, with the book in mind, he had been telling her of his early memories. His death initially seemed to scupper the plan, and, in any case, Phyllis felt that her most pressing duty was to finish writing *The Mortal Storm*. Reluctantly shelving the Adler biography for the moment, she spent a brief but intensive period in the peaceful context of Tewin Water, invited there by Lilian Beit and her sister Marguerite Carter, who were well aware of the intensity of her bereavement. Turning from the biography of Adler to *The Mortal Storm* was not such a stretch as it might first appear. On the one hand she was applying Adler's psychology to political behaviour, and on the other she was pouring her deep love for Adler into the portrait of Professor Toller. She dedicated the novel 'To the Memory of Dr Adler'.

Arguably, *The Mortal Storm* was the most important novel Phyllis ever wrote; certainly it was her most intense and fully worked-through attempt to expose and attack Nazi ideology. She was driven to sounding alarm bells to shake Britain out of what she saw as its bystander paralysis, through efforts both personal and of a literary nature. Her observations in Munich meant that she was absolutely clear that anti-Jewish persecution had begun from the first days of Nazi rule. During 1933 the German government had enacted forty-two laws restricting the rights of German Jews; these included forbidding them from working in any branch of the civil service, including schools and universities. During 1934, the Nuremberg Laws 'for the protection of German blood and honour' prohibited marriage and extra-marital sexual intercourse between Jews and non-Jews. Shortly afterwards a new definition of German citizenship was created, which meant that no person with 'Jewish ancestry' could be a German citizen.[43] On 7 March 1936, Hitler had marched into the Rhineland. Gazing with horror at what was unfolding in Europe, Phyllis wanted her new novel to arouse Britain from its fatal slumber.

Phyllis had lived among German people whom she had loved, so she wanted to attack an ideology, not in any sense *all* Germans. Indeed, she explained that she 'wrote about the best type of Nazi to show you [how] terrible their whole creed was and how disastrous to any human character'.[44] As she commented to Upton Sinclair: 'After 1918 Germany was drenched with self-pity and self-righteousness. "Behold and see, if there is any sorrow like unto my sorrow!" Yet her sufferings never approached those of Austria, Poland or Russia; and it is even doubtful whether her grief for her many sons was as devastating as the grief for the "only sons" of France.'[45]

These thoughts are not dissimilar to those of Thomas Mann, who was to comment in 1940: 'Essentially the German spirit lacks social and political interest ... And Hitler, in all his wretchedness, is no accident. He could never have become possible but for certain psychological prerequisites that must be sought deeper down than inflation, unemployment, capitalist speculation and political intrigue.'[46]

Phyllis wanted to engage with these 'deeper down' questions. And in *The Mortal Storm*, first published in Britain in 1937, Phyllis utilised her experience of living in Munich in the early 1930s as the power of the Nazis took hold.

Her aim was to show what fascism meant, first to individual German families, then to Jews and ultimately to freedom itself. The politics of her novel are inescapable; it is an impassioned polemic against fascism and in defence of freedom, and it also contains a strong feminist line, as her protagonist, Freya Toller, is placed firmly at the centre of the novel.[47] At the start of the novel, Freya is represented as a member of a happy liberal family. Her father, Professor Johann Toller, is an esteemed Nobel Prize-winning scientist, the greatest living expert on tuberculosis;[48] her two older half- brothers, Olaf and Emil von Rohn, the sons of Freya's mother's first marriage, have joined the Nazi Party. The book is set in Munich just before the elections of March 1933, which would make Hitler Chancellor. The narrative opens with Freya Toller waking up on her twentieth birthday. She is full of joy because she is attending medical school and has just passed her first examinations 'with the brilliance her father's daughter had a natural right to possess'.[49] Getting up at five o'clock, she slips out of the house to ski alone and hug her sense of triumph to herself. As she sets out towards the Wetterstein where she is to ski, she suddenly comes across a horrifying scene:

> Eight peasants stood at intervals of a yard or two, each holding a stout stick or mallet; and in the centre of the space they had surrounded – this way and that – darted a frightened hare. It was light enough now for Freya to see everything: the heavy-clad figures of the men, with their raised sticks and the leaping, writhing, doubling hare. From side to side the little dark streak raced from their blows; there was already blood on the snow. The circle grew closer. There was less and less room for the terrified beast to escape. It was flung back upon itself – threading its agonised life upon the passive stillness of the air – a stick caught it – and it shrieked aloud like a tortured child.[50]

This image is a foretaste both of the plight of the Jews and of women's plight within the novel. Freya's intervention in saving the hare brings upon her the threat of rape. For the first time in her young life she experiences fear and shame. She is rescued from danger by another working-class man, Hans Breitner, who, despite delivering her from immediate danger, challenges her sense of being a heroine by pointing out that she has deprived hungry men of their dinner. Hans is a self-educated worker who has been 'converted' to Communism by the Russian prisoners of war who had worked on his family farm during the First World War, and who had continued to write to him about the ideals of the government in Russia. These ideals Hans sees as straightforward: that every man and woman should have a voice in government and a say in how they want their taxes spent for the good of all in each district.

Freya hero-worships her elder half-brother Olaf, so, at the beginning of the novel, she assumes that Nazis must have wise and noble aims. It is Hans who challenges her assumptions, telling her, 'It is the Nazis who attack knowledge; degrade women; persecute Jews; and drag people back into serfdom!'[51] Until this meeting with Hans, Freya had never been seriously interested in politics:

> She had accepted, as the majority of medical students accepted, the social democratic state. They were born into this new and rather stagnant republic, full of splendid privileges and no traditions, run by uneager and anxious men, who had never been trained to authority but had been brought up instead to obey the sharp short orders of their betters.
>
> The young looked for a lead out of the black cul-de-sac of poverty, defeat and unemployment that daunted their futures and ate up their strength. But they got no lead.
>
> A few of the more alert and aggressive turned Communist. Nobody liked them; startling in their doctrines, dishevelled in their appearance, they made few friends. Their fellow students jeered at their strange doctrines and the authorities weighted the dice against them. They were looked on as moral and social riff-raff.
>
> Another and larger body of students threw in their lot with the Nazis. This group was not looked down on by the authorities; its escapades were overlooked; duels by its members were leniently dealt with though against the law; even physical attacks upon their opponents in the streets were treated as playful sallies of the high spirited – 'reds' and 'Jews' were fair game ... [52]

Freya's political naïvety is shaken as events overtake her. Nazi misogyny prevents her from continuing her university training as a doctor and Nazism inevitably fractures her family.

Freya's aristocratic mother, Amelie von Maberg, had been trapped in an unhappy first marriage to a cruel husband who had eventually died of syphilis; his portrait represents the moral bankruptcy of the old feudal system. In her second marriage to a Jewish intellectual, Amelie finds herself in an impossible position, torn between the two halves of her family when the sons of her first marriage, Olaf and Emil, increasingly privilege the orders of the Nazi Party above loyalty to family. Hans's role in the novel is to challenge Freya's short-sighted assumptions, and via this method Phyllis educates her readers. Freya says to Hans, that surely

> Hitler is too just and good a man to persecute such Jews [as the Tollers]. Only wicked, corrupt Jews – usurers who suck the life-blood out of simple people – such men he will naturally seek to punish! But good German Jews cannot have anything to fear.[53]

Hitler, of course, is not interested in the finer distinctions of Jewishness. Bit by bit, her father's status is diminished. At first there are only small signals: the porter at the university ignores him, then students start to boycott his lectures; the situation becomes more serious when Amelie is asked to leave him, and his money is confiscated; the threat becomes more deadly when he is taken to a concentration camp. Professor Toller is doomed to die, because he can never practise blind obedience when it goes against his conscience.

Perhaps Phyllis's cleverest trick in this novel is to show how it could come to pass that Freya's half-brother Olaf, a young man who prides himself on his high honour, could become a Nazi murderer. And here Phyllis exposes and challenges the Wagnerian underpinnings of the Nazi movement. As Hitler himself said, 'Whoever wants to understand National Socialistic Germany must know Wagner.'[54] Wagner's thesis in *Das Judentum in der Musik*, published in 1850, starts:

> Why does the involuntary revulsion exist which is awakened by the person and character of the Jew? We deceive ourselves if we classify as bad manners all frank reference to our natural antipathy to the Jewish character ... it is our duty to bring to a state of complete intelligibility our ill-will towards him ... in the present state of things

> the Jew is more than free – he dominates; and, as long as money continues to be the power before which all our strivings are as naught, he will continue to do so.[55]

Nietzsche, among others, had spoken of the 'twin optics' of Wagner's talents, talents that enabled him to overwhelm both the finest and the coarsest. And it is here that the greatest danger of *Wagalaweia* lay. As well as appropriating the anti-Semitic ideology, Hitler also employed Wagnerian techniques of showmanship and used them in his own stage-managing of the torchlight parades, the pageants and the theatrical mass addresses, with ever-rising climaxes.[56]

It was easy for the Nazis to exploit the legend of Siegfried slaying the dragon, as they could count on their listeners – from whatever social class – responding to this oft-replayed rhetoric. Three generations of Germans had been conditioned, by Wagner's Ring Cycle in particular, to believe in a notion of the *Volk,* a fertile feeding ground for a new religion of Pan-German nationalism. The Ring Cycle implies that the German soul needed to be purged of alien elements, and must have a mystical leader or Führer. Wagner had provided Germany with the icon of Siegfried, the golden-haired Aryan hero who could only be defeated by a stab in the back, such as that administered by the dark Hagen.[57] The Nazi 'alibi', to use an Adlerian term, or excuse, for Germany's defeat in 1918 was that her 'unbeatable armies were stabbed in the back by the Jews and democrats at home'.[58] The cultural historian Peter Viereck comments that:

> During the years of the German Republic, when Versailles still kept Germany partially disarmed, opera audiences went wild with enthusiasm over the symbolic scene where Siegfried forges the German sword. When Nazi Germany finished its huge western line of forts, the German people and foreign journalists unanimously referred to it as 'the Siegfried Line'.[59]

Hitler identified himself with many Wagnerian heroes, but above all with Siegfried.

Therefore, Phyllis, in *The Mortal Storm,* uses Siegfried as a metaphor for a false kind of courage. When Olaf kills Freya's Communist lover,

Hans, he believes he is doing the right thing as a good Nazi, but according to the wise Professor Toller he was shooting a 'mythical monster'.[60] As Phyllis commented to Upton Sinclair, trying to account for a peculiarity of the German psychology, 'Siegfried has always to rush out and kill the Dragon before he has found out if it really is a Dragon or might not be on the whole rather a beneficent creature.'[61] Towards the end of the novel, after Hans has been murdered, Freya gives birth to his child at his family farm. There are strong echoes of the birth of Christ in the stable; Phyllis deliberately sets up a myth of self-sacrificing love against the Wagnerian (and fascist) mythology of false heroism.

This anti-Wagnerian schema persists throughout *The Mortal Storm*. Freya is the female 'hero' who, throughout the course of the novel, has to face tests. She has to make a series of difficult choices; her refusal to repudiate her Jewish father is the first. She then has to choose between a right-wing aristocratic lover – marriage to an aristocrat might have conveniently hidden her 'unfortunate' Jewishness – and a left-wing lover. In effect, she makes political rather than romantic choices. And this is one of Phyllis's main points. In an Adlerian moral universe, each individual must take responsibility for his or her own action. This responsibility can in no circumstances be handed over to someone else – neither to a husband, nor to a Führer. Although subsequently Freya comes to reject communism as well as fascism, the novel ends with Freya leaving her baby behind to be reared by Hans's family, while she skis out of the prison house of Germany. She is to go to a liberal democracy – America – and continue her father's work. The implication is that the baby – politically – will combine the best of Germany, namely hard-working peasant stock with that of the Jewish intellectual.

In terms of Phyllis's use of myth, at the end of the novel Freya is described as a *Wander Vogel*, which is the name of a bird, but which metaphorically conjures up the legend of the Wandering Jew.[62] Eugène Sue's left-wing novel of that name, published in 1844, had as its central conceit the figures of the Jew and the Woman, doomed to permanent exile but yearning towards each other. George Eliot had reworked this myth within the text of *Daniel Deronda,* a book Phyllis had read and admired.[63] In *The Mortal Storm,* the baby combines and represents these elements at the level of myth. At a metapolitical level, Phyllis combats dangerous Wagnerian myths with reference to new, or perhaps more accurately, specifically reworked, ones. *The Mortal Storm* is on the one hand a realist novel and on the other a parable for its time.

In the pre-Munich atmosphere, *The Mortal Storm* received very little attention, and reviews were mixed. On the whole, reviews praised or damned in line with the right-leaning or left-leaning politics of the particular publication. The right-wing press tended to dismiss it as a political tract, whereas a paper such as *The Left Review* praised the novel, regarding Phyllis's 'liberal sentiments' as being 'genuinely held'.[64] The dissemination of *The Mortal Storm* in Britain was, however, significantly increased when, in 1938, it was published as a Penguin Special. Allen Lane, the managing director of The Bodley Head, was a left-leaning liberal who had in the summer of 1935 started publishing Penguin paperbacks, determined that poor people should be able to buy good-quality writing. They sold at sixpence each, about the same price as a packet of cigarettes, whereas most hardback fiction sold at about seven or eight shillings. In 1937, Lane inaugurated the Penguin Specials, which he hoped would help to counteract the problem Phyllis had also detected – that the news as it appeared in most newspapers was terribly distorted by the interests of their proprietors. The first Special was by Phyllis's friend, the American journalist Edgar Mowrer, warning about Germany's ambitions. Thirty-seven 'Specials' were published between November 1937 and the outbreak of war, and by January 1939, the Penguin Special edition of *The Mortal Storm* had sold 100,000 copies.[65] As Phyllis commented to Upton Sinclair, 'I think English feeling must be beginning to change, although too late to save others.'[66]

Phyllis added three new chapters to her text for the American market, and presumably at the request of her American publishers, the Tollers were renamed Roth.[67] In 1938 Little, Brown & Co. in Boston published this amended version of *The Mortal Storm* and it, too, immediately became a best-seller in America.[68] She received many letters from both American and English fans. A letter from an attorney-at-law in Chicago said, 'You have managed to express, in a most concise and beautiful style, a thought which should be publicized among the

Jews.'[69] He asked her permission to print the passage that struck him so forcibly, for use at bar mitzvahs. It is the moment where Rudi, alarmed by being ostracised in school, asks his father the question, 'What is being a Jew?' Johan Roth answers him:

> 'My boy ... to be a Jew is to belong to an old harmless race that has lived in every country in the world; and that has enriched every country it has lived in.
>
> 'It is to be strong with a strength that has outlived persecutions. It has been wise against ignorance, honest against piracy, harmless against evil, industrious against idleness, kind against cruelty! It is to belong to a race that has given Europe its religion; its moral law; and much of its science – perhaps even more of its genius – in art, literature and music.
>
> 'This is to be a Jew; and you know *now* what is required of you! You have no country but the world: and you inherit nothing but wisdom and brotherhood. I do not say that there are no bad Jews – usurers; cowards; corrupt and unjust persons – but such people are also to be found among Christians. I only say to you this is to be a *good* Jew. Every Jew has this aim brought before him in his youth. He refuses it at his peril; and at his peril he accepts it.'[70]

Another touching letter to Phyllis, although much later, came from a young German-Jewish refugee, thanking her for *The Mortal Storm*:

> ... I myself am a Jewish refugee girl from Munich. I came to England in 1939. After 2 years of bitter separation from all that was dear to me I suddenly came across your book. And it was a true, deep joy and revelation to me. There I found alive once more before my mental eye all the things I had loved, but which had been silent for 2 years. The very streets of Munich, the life, the feelings of the people – but more than all these the atmosphere prevailing in Freya Roth's home – they all brought my home back to me ... I am not exaggerating when I say that the book once more brought life and light to a frozen heart, starved of love ... I have never, never met an English person who could so completely sympathise with the German psychological make-up as you have done in this book. It is

> not an outsider, making observation; it is experienced and felt as if in the German heart itself ... [71]

In June 1938 Phyllis gave her permission for *The Mortal Storm* to be transcribed into Braille. Its message was finding its way, if only slowly, into the entire world.

Having completed *The Mortal Storm*, Phyllis returned to the sacred task of the Adler biography. In 1938, Phyllis and Ernan rushed to Vienna, where they interviewed as many people as they could, gathering all the information they could glean about Adler's Viennese days.[72] Some of the people she wanted to talk to were understandably reluctant to speak to her, due to the increasingly volatile political climate. An underground Nazi movement funded from Germany had long been preparing the way for a takeover of power in the small and unstable alpine republic. Increasingly overt, it had brought terror to Austria's streets and nurtured the virulent strain of Viennese anti-Semitism. As she was to write later: 'This was a difficult time for a search. The people had already begun to be afraid of answering questions or of admitting that they had any connection with a Jewish name. Without our former knowledge of Vienna, and my husband's complete command of the language, I doubt if we would ever have been able to accomplish our task.'[73]

She had hoped that the Foreword would be written by two of Adler's distinguished colleagues, Professor Birnbaum and Dr Lydia Sicher, but as she said in her Preface, as they were both living in Austria 'for political reasons their names must not be mentioned in this book. The same political menace forces me to forgo thanking many other friends and associates of Adler's Viennese days.'[74]

Phyllis and Ernan were almost overtaken by events. In February 1938, Hitler had invited the Austrian Chancellor, Kurt von Schuschnigg, to the Berghof and told him of his resolve to absorb Austria into Germany. On 8 March, von Schuschnigg announced a plebiscite to be held five days later in order to test Hitler's assertion that the Austrian people wished to unite with Germany. Hitler, incensed by Schuschnigg's move, forced him and the President, Wilhelm Miklas, to resign. Lord Halifax, the British Foreign Secretary, told Austria that Britain could not guarantee protection, while Germany's axis partner Italy, on the other hand, offered support for the annexation. On 10 March, Phyllis and Ernan, fearing a catastrophe, left for Paris. On 11 March, the *Wehrmacht* crossed the Austrian border, with Hitler following in a triumphal procession a day later. This was known as the *Anschluss,* the forced marriage of Austria with Germany.

In 1939, Faber in England and Putnam's in America published Phyllis's biography of her mentor, under the title *Alfred Adler: Apostle of Freedom.* She dedicated the book to Ernan, and arranged for some of the royalties to go to Raissa Adler.[75] Phyllis wanted to bring out some key points of Adler's teaching, especially that of his holistic and creative view of personality. He did not, for example, believe that individuals were simply the product of circumstances, as might be assumed in Behaviourism (behaviour as the result of specific stimuli) or Psychoanalysis (problems as the result of traumatic childhood experiences). In Adler's psychology the individual acts as a whole, his or her feelings, beliefs and behaviour always responding to some goal, and each action taken creates something new. Adlerian psychologists today explain it like this: 'By influencing somebody else, I make a change not only in his or her opinions/feelings/behaviours but also in myself and in the relationship that defines both of us. In this sense, product and producer are the same, or at least cannot be told apart.' In Adler's more simple and at the same time more poetic words, 'the individual is thus both the picture and the artist'.[76]

Nothing could be more appealing to Phyllis than the emphasis on creativity, and adoring Adler as she did, her biography was somewhat hagiographic. Nor was she a trained psychologist, so it was not an academic critique of his ideas. Nevertheless, her biography was widely and favourably reviewed in broadsheets in America and the UK, and also in specialist organs, such as the *Journal of Education* and *The Woman Teacher*, and it ran to three editions.[77] A review by Leonard Carmichael is emblematic of the tone of most of the reviews and explains why the biography is eminently readable. He writes, 'It is rare that the novelist turns biographer but if this excellent book is an example the process may be widely recommended. Possibly the reason for the success of the present volume is that a psychological novelist has here become the biographer of a great psychologist.' Another reviewer remarks that 'scholarship and tenderness are creditable attributes in a biography'.[78]

How successful Phyllis and Ernan were – in their different ways – in bringing Adler's ideas into Britain is difficult to evaluate. Unsurprisingly, as two of his children became Adlerian therapists there, his work has been most influential in the USA. Rudolf Dreikurs is probably the leading Adlerian in America and his theorisation of Democratic Education arises out of a tradition that goes all the way back to the child-guidance centres established in Red Vienna.[79] In Britain, Adler's emphasis on social interactions and self-esteem seem to have had a broad, if somewhat diffuse impact. His work on siblings and sibling rivalry has become a taken-for-granted assumption. Similarly, the adoption of terms like 'inferiority complex', 'family constellation' and 'lifestyle' into common usage shows how widely Adler's ideas have spread, even though they are sometimes used in ways that might have been surprising to him. 'Lifestyle', for example, has been adopted as a concept in marketing research, albeit not in the sense that Adler intended. One explanation for this is that Adler wanted his ideas to be easily explicable to everyone, not just to specialists, so the terms he coined were drawn from everyday German language. Adlerian terms had no copyright implications, and could therefore be adopted, without reference to Adler, by other theorists. Freud's work, by contrast, uses words from Greek and Latin (for example, 'libido' and 'ego'), which are still identified with psychoanalysis, and only with psychoanalysis. The historian Ellenberger has commented: 'It would not be easy to find another author from whom so much has been borrowed from all sides *without acknowledgement* than Adler.'[80]

To sum up briefly, Adler's focus on the significance of childhood goals led him and his colleagues to pay considerable attention to educational processes. In particular, his strategies for behaviour change in schools have influenced educational psychologists and, of course, teachers themselves. One example of Adlerian principles operating in British classrooms today is the relatively new approach of conflict resolution and mediation. The trained mediator is another child (older child, peer, classmate) and not the teacher or school counsellor. Teachers today may not know that this democratic, rather than top-down, approach is inherently Adlerian, but that is no matter. Phyllis Bottome, when interviewing those who had known him, in preparation for writing her biography of Adler, was told by one of the Viennese teachers that, though the authoritative regime had closed the clinics, 'there was one thing they have not been able to do. They can rob the children of free self-development, but unless they dismiss every teacher they cannot rob the children of what the teachers have learned. What Adler and his theories made us, we remain.'[81]

But in any case, Phyllis and Ernan in the late 1930s believed that Adlerian theories were specifically pertinent in trying to understand the madness they felt overtaking the world. As mentioned elsewhere, Phyllis noted in her autobiography, 'Individual Psychology had already taught me that the real question is not, "How do people go out of their minds?" but, "What do they go out of their minds for?" '[82] She saw fascism as a form of madness, and old Europe as being turned into something akin to a prison (another common trope of 1930s literature). In Phyllis's work the asylum and the prison are often closely linked; madness in her fiction often represents a self-imposed prison for the individual, whereas the madness of power-drunk dictators makes prison houses of whole nations. Phyllis had often worried about whether she could manage to conduct a dual career of both writing and lecturing. She said that whereas Adler frequently teased her, when she asked him this question he had responded rather differently: ' "Give!" he said very gravely and urgently. "You cannot give too much! Give all!" '[83] Phyllis followed this injunction, discovering in the process the Adlerian precept that in giving yourself you most possess yourself.

Adlerian core values underpinned the way she lived the rest of her life. She was convinced that an Adlerian education was best for children and that for adults an Adlerian retraining held the key to the essential redirection of goals, away from the egotistical prestige-goals towards cooperative, socially-minded goals. This she believed was the royal road to personal and political freedom. Consequently, she lectured and wrote on Adlerian themes at every opportunity, frequently in schools. Some of her lectures, though not all, were subsequently published in *The Spectator*: they include: 'The Odenwaldschule: An Experiment in Education', 'Child Delinquency', 'The Birch and the Child', 'The Growing Child' and 'Bad Children of Britain'. One of the Kitzbühel boys, Lewis Way, became an Adlerian psychologist and translated Adler's theories into English.[84]

Immediately following the *Anschluss,* Phyllis and Ernan received lots of heartrending reports from their friends in Vienna of the savagery unleashed towards the Jews. Some Austrian Jews had already managed to get out of the country, but once the Nazis took control, a new reign of terror had commenced. Just after leaving Vienna, writing to their American journalist friend Frank Adams, and asking him to pass on what she said to Dorothy Thompson, Phyllis told him: 'I must not put into writing the wires we are trying to pull' – hinting that Ernan, as an ex-intelligence agent, had particular resources available to him. Although it is not possible to know exactly what he was doing, it can be assumed perhaps that he was in touch with diplomatic contacts. There were two related problems: the first to get Jews out of German-controlled territory and the second to get them admitted into another country. Phyllis's letter to Frank Adams was a plea for major media protest in America:

> We inadvertently escaped the avalanche in Vienna by three days. Had we known it was so near, we should have stayed to try to get our friends out; now we are sitting in Paris trying to use a corkscrew on those we can lay our hands on. We hope to get in touch with Mowrer tomorrow.
>
> We are trying to save a great psychiatrist's daughter, two doctors, one with a worldwide reputation, the only first-class Dentist that Austria possesses, and two of our dearest friends. Yesterday we saw a very quiet intelligent woman doctor who had just arrived from Vienna. She had been through the whole of two revolutions, and practised in Russia from 1918–1926 (when she gave up all hope of the revolution and managed to get out) married to a Frenchman. She told us that for sheer, avoidable, open cruelty, she considered the occupation of Vienna 'the worst thing she had ever seen'. Travelling as a French citizen, she experienced personally only rudeness and stupidity, but whatever she heard and saw, said and done to Austrian travellers, especially the few Jews that were venturing the almost impossible flight, passes belief!

The Austrian officials were still as polite as they dared to be, guarded in the execution of their duties, however, by the awful SS men. 'But officials as bullies,' she explained, 'though they are bad, are less bad than undisciplined bullies!' Nazi criminals hot from prison were allowed to search the trains at all the big stations, Linz, Salsburg, Innsbruck, and behaved as they liked! They were quite inhuman and treated Austrian travellers as if they were bugs to be flattened out against a wall.

Mothers with children were turned out in the middle of the night, upon the platforms of strange stations, roofless and foodless, allowed neither to go forward nor back.

A girl, in the same carriage as our friend, was twice stripped to the skin, by customs people looking for money, in an ice-cold room standing on a stone floor with bare feet. She spent the rest of the journey shivering and in tears. All the former concentration camps are opened and at least ten thousand innocent people have been flung there to die, or be outraged till their spirits are broken ...

One traveller, a doctor who had all his papers correct, all his money regulations fulfilled and his ticket to America, but who was not Aryan, was turned back. 'All right! I go back!' he said quietly. 'There is still the Danube!'

The suicides in Vienna have already begun, and I am afraid that some of our friends will be among them![85] As you know all the science and art of Vienna is founded on Jewish brains, ninety per cent of the doctors are Jews, and all these people have received what amounts to a sentence of death. They have no rights and all their positions under the state are taken from them. All the great Jewish shops have been requisitioned and systematically turned over to the hungry Germans. There is no permission now given for Austrians to leave Austria except signed and countersigned by the Nazis ... the French now demand an Austrian visa! The Hungarian frontier is closed. The Swiss was still open when I last heard, but the whole of Switzerland is staggering and trembling like an ox at the threshold of a slaughterhouse.

No one may enter another happier country! To our everlasting shame we too, who are responsible for this débâcle are also tightening

> up the frontiers against those people whom we have given to the wolves!
>
> ... We both do what we can, from morning till night, to try to get a few little broken winged birds out of this snare ... After the 18th April what Jews are still living will be free to leave Austria with twenty-five per cent of their fortunes. I ask you not only to find homes for all you can but to point out to England her responsibility for doing the same.
>
> Ask for doctors, both men and women! Ask for teachers, writers, journalists, painters, and musicians, and see that you get them!
>
> Try with your great wits and hearts, with your unspeakable privileges, and your unconsidered safety, to stand by the pick of the intellectual world, trodden into the mire by an empty transitory fanaticism that carries within it the seeds of its own death.[86]

Although President Roosevelt asked for an increase in the German quota for refugees and a bill was introduced on 24 March 1938 'to assure certain aliens legal admission for permanent residence in the United States', it died in committee.[87]

Shortly after the seizure of Austria by Germany, Phyllis wrote an article entitled 'I Accuse', but could not persuade anyone in Britain to publish it:

> Several liberal-minded weeklies in Great Britain refused it with regret. It was then decided to print it privately for distribution among friends and acquaintances. But this plan was never carried out. A well-known firm of British printers who had done work for me in recent years refused even to submit an estimate for it. The text was then submitted to an attorney who assured us that there was no legal objection of any kind to its being printed. However, another firm of printers with whom he had contact refused to handle it. So did a third, which had been connected with my family for three generations. In each case, an unlimited indemnity was offered to cover any possible loss that the printer might incur.[88]

It is perhaps not entirely surprising that it was refused. Phyllis accused the Archbishop of Canterbury of 'culpable credulity', when he quoted in the House of Lords a letter from an Austrian friend claiming to be 'filled with joy over the German military occupation of Austria'. Phyllis could hardly believe that the Archbishop had not realised that the Nazis censor all letters, and only letters 'supporting their crimes' are allowed out of the country. She wrote:

> Can any Christian accept lightly the fate of the 200,000 Jews in Vienna who are being systematically pillaged and tortured and the further 600,000 half-Jews who are in danger of being deprived of their livelihood if they remain, or of 75 per cent of their fortune if they leave Austria? (Note: this was subsequently increased to 92 percent – P.B.) What further proof does any sensible man need that Austria desired to keep her integrity than Hitler's refusal to allow her a free vote on it. Does the Archbishop suppose that a vote under an armed force is free?

Phyllis remained bewildered at the reluctance of Britain to face up to what Hitler's intentions meant. On 20 May 1938, Hitler moved his troops to the Czech frontier, claiming that he was defending the Germans in the Sudetenland. *The Times* recommended that Czechoslovakia should comply with Hitler's demands, a policy which, if adopted, Phyllis predicted would be catastrophic.

Further, the British government continued to regard Hitler's persecution of the Jews more in the light of an obstacle to Anglo-German relations than as a humanitarian outrage. Jews trying to enter Britain found that obtaining refuge depended on the availability of resources to maintain the applicant and thus only a fraction of the candidates were admitted.[89] From 1933, the Jewish Refugees Committee in Britain (and its associate funding bodies) had undertaken both the management of refugees and to underwrite all costs.[90] A guarantee was made by Anglo-Jewry that 'all expense, whether temporary or permanent accommodation or maintenance, will be borne by the Jewish community without ultimate charge to the state'.[91] As the danger of a European war came ever closer, Eleanor Rathbone was the most vociferous of the very few MPs who were demanding the creation of more formal policy-making machinery rather than reliance on refugee organisations.[92] In early July 1938, Roosevelt assembled an international meeting to discuss collective action on the refugee problem, which met at Evian in France.

Phyllis, who as always seized any opportunity to activate the minds of her fellow countrymen, sent a letter to the editor of the *Daily Telegraph*, printed on 12 July 1938, in which she pleaded that:

> the conscience of the civilised world should be centred on the conference for Refugees from Greater Germany now being held at Evian ... We must spur ourselves forward towards a greater generosity. Doctors could accept some of their best Viennese colleagues with immunity. There is an acknowledged shortage of good dentists in England. We have a direct lack of the right material for dental nurses. Refugees have already started businesses in depressed areas, employing more English people than the whole number of refugees yet allowed in this country.

The next day she received a letter that thanked her from one of 'the very many British Jews who will have read your letter in today's paper'.[93]

Doctors and dentists constituted the largest occupational group among German Jewish immigrants to Britain. Unlike German qualifications for doctors, however, those for dentists were recognised in Britain and indeed were often superior.[94] They could apply to be listed on a register kept by the General Medical Council. However, British dentists and their professional organisation persuaded the Home Office to close the door on further applicants, so that by May 1937 only seventy-eight dentists had been allowed to practise. Even though there was scope in the Aliens Order to admit aliens who supplied something the country lacked, it is depressing to note that the Home Office caved in to alarms about hordes of Jewish dentists flooding the profession, which their own facts and figures utterly contradicted. Arguably, the failure of the Evian Conference to take sufficiently radical steps finally convinced Hitler that the world did not care what happened to the Jews. Having begun, perhaps, only with the intent of making Germany *judenrein* (free of Jews), after Evian Hitler started to move inexorably towards his 'Final Solution' in the belief that the world would not greatly care.

Phyllis's letter pleading for generosity also garnered a letter of gratitude from Baron Fuchs; she replied:

> I do not know whether you have seen my book on Germany *The Mortal Storm*. I am glad to tell you that it is selling all over America. Unfortunately it came out here before England was roused to see what Germany was really like, so that it could not do what it is able to do in America. My husband joins me in sending you his deepest sympathy and warmest greetings. I can tell you, although I am his wife, that I do not think anyone in this world has worked or is working so hard for Austrian Jews as he is.[95]

In Vienna there were long queues of Jews outside the foreign consulates in the city, seeking exit visas. We must assume that Ernan was personally putting pressure on his diplomatic contacts to get visas issued as events in Europe continued to worsen. Captain Kendrick, the British Passport Control Officer in Vienna, was issuing visas he would not have authorised except in an acute political crisis, and in Berlin, the British Passport Officer, Captain Frank Foley, was active in expediting the escape of Jews from Germany.[96] On 18 August 1938, the Swiss authorities had closed the frontier to Austria to anyone who did not have a Swiss entry visa. Hundreds of Jewish refugees were trapped on the German-controlled side of the border.

On 12 September 1938, Hitler's pan-German ambitions led him to demand self-determination for the Germans in the Sudetenland. On 15 September the British Prime Minister, Neville Chamberlain, went to Munich to see Hitler at his mountain retreat at Berchtesgaden in the Bavarian Alps. There, Hitler threatened to invade Czechoslovakia unless Britain accepted Germany's plans to annex the Sudeten region of Czechoslovakia. Initially Chamberlain said that this was unacceptable, but from 19 September both the British and the French governments were indicating to the Czechs that they must hand over the Sudetenland if they wished to avoid war. Czechoslovakia was forced to give way to Hitler, and on 21 September he demanded that German troops be allowed to occupy the territory. At the Munich Conference of 29 September, desperate to avoid war, Chamberlain and the French Prime Minister Edouard Daladier negotiated an agreement that they would accept Germany's takeover of the Sudetenland in return for Hitler's promise that he would make no further territorial demands in Europe. President Benes resigned on 5 October and took refuge in England.

This later-to-become-infamous agreement, supposedly inaugurating 'peace in our time', was popular with most people in Britain, although Winston Churchill and Anthony Eden attacked it, pointing out that the British government had acted dishonourably in caving in on the dismembering of Czechoslovakia. After the Munich Agreement, Churchill broke decisively with Chamberlain, telling the House of Commons that, 'We have suffered a total and unmitigated defeat … What I find unendurable is the sense of our country falling … into the orbit and influence of Nazi Germany and of our existence becoming dependent on their good will or pleasure.'[97] He continued by saying that England had been offered 'a choice between war and shame. She has chosen shame – and will get war.'[98] During the winter of 1938–9, Churchill was ostracised by his own party and narrowly survived a vote of confidence in his constituency. It should be noted, however, that the Munich Agreement, however misguided we see it with the benefit of hindsight, was to some extent a delaying tactic. Britain was rearming as fast as it could.

Events continued to edge towards crisis. On 18 October 1938, more than 12,000 Polish-born Jews were taken from their homes under the guns and bayonets of the Nazis and their homes were looted. Expelled from Germany, they waited penniless at the border while the authorities in Poland hesitated to give them entry permits. One such expelled couple, the Grynszpans, and their daughter, were in exactly this predicament. The daughter sent an anguished note to her brother in Paris and on 7 November seventeen-year-old Hershel Grynszpan went to the German Embassy intending to kill the Ambassador. He was sent to the office of the Third Secretary, Ernst von Rath, at whom he fired five shots in the name of the 12,000 persecuted Jews. On 8 November, punitive revenge measures began. All Jewish newspapers were banned, Jewish children were no longer allowed to attend 'Aryan' state elementary schools and all Jewish cultural activities were suspended. On 9 November, von Rath died of his wounds and on 10 November Dr Joseph Goebbels, the Nazi propaganda chief, gave orders to the SS to commence 'spontaneous' acts of violence against the Jews. *Kristallnacht*, the 'night of broken glass' resulted in the death of a hundred Jews, hundreds were severely wounded, and more than 30,000 arrested and sent to concentration camps; 7,500 Jewish shops and businesses were destroyed and 250 synagogues set on fire. Chamberlain agreed to some easing of admission to Britain of Jewish refugees fleeing Germany.

Phyllis was desperately concerned about the situation. Writing on 19 September 1938 to the Bishop of Chichester, a friend from the Adler tour days, she says:

> My husband and I are leaving for America this week. We shall lecture from end to end of it in the hope of stemming this rising tide of anti-Semitism. Before we leave England we wanted to make our last attempt to reach people here. There is a small refugee Committee called the Austrian Self-Aid, run chiefly by three Viennese Jewish ladies [who] have been able to fit quite a good number ... into appropriate work in the permitted categories ... We should be immensely grateful if the Church of England Committee could give them a helping hand during our absence, and co-operate with them in some manner ...

The letter goes on to argue that Britain must let more Austrian Jews into the country, as 'very few other countries allow them the right of entry. We give sanctuary to a small and carefully-selected minority. Most of them are middle-class people of a useful and successful type.'[99] Clearly, they felt that sanctuary must be increased, and that it should be increased rapidly. More than anything else, Phyllis and Ernan were astonished that anyone could still to be in ignorance of Hitler's intentions concerning the Jews. Describing in *Mein Kampf* the revelatory moment when he turned from an internationalist to a nationalist, Hitler had written, 'From a feeble citizen of the world I became a fanatic anti-Semite.'[100] Speaking in Berlin towards the end of 1938, Hitler said, 'If war breaks out, the result will be not the Bolshevisation of the earth, and thus the victory of Jewry, but the annihilation of the Jewish race in Europe.'[101] Believing that 'England was going Nazi in its sleep' under Chamberlain, Phyllis and Ernan prepared American naturalisation papers, with a view to becoming American citizens.[102]

CHAPTER 9

Filming The Mortal Storm: *Phyllis as Britain's Propagandist in America*

> I do believe that humanity is going to weather the Mortal Storm of the dictatorships!
>
> PHYLLIS BOTTOME, February 1940

It is hardly surprising that Phyllis seriously considered becoming an American citizen. In America, the *New York Post* had taken out a full-page advertisement on 29 April 1938 announcing their serialisation of *The Mortal Storm.* The cover blurb on the Little, Brown edition claimed that *The Mortal Storm* 'will doubtless stand as the first significant novel torn out of the bleeding heart of modern Europe'.[1] The novel itself was reprinted thirteen times within ten months, so Phyllis herself had become a 'star' name in the States. The Colston Leigh Agency saw this as a splendid time for a high-earning tour, and arranged a somewhat gruelling programme of lectures for her from October until mid-December in 1938. She lectured in Massachusetts, Philadelphia, Michigan, Indiana, Ohio, Pittsburgh, New York, Chicago, Detroit, and Portland, speaking at universities, women's clubs, and Jewish centres. Nearly everywhere she went she was met with large and enthusiastic audiences.

In America she finally managed to get her letter 'I Accuse' published when Upton Sinclair sent it on her behalf to the *New Republic*.[2] It seems likely that Sinclair (Hal) Lewis was the initiator of this important new friendship between Phyllis and Upton. Upton was a socialist who as a young man had founded a commune and Hal had run away from Yale to join it.[3] Upton admired Hal's ability enormously, but being a teetotaller, was dismayed that Hal's drinking increasingly drowned his talent. Upton was a social idealist, wanting art to educate readers about social and economic injustice. His primary goal was, at this period, to explain in his novels the conditions that had caused industrialists to prefer fascism to democracy. He used as his protagonist Lanny Budd, a naïve although intelligent young man, whose painful political education is, in effect, shared by the reader. Upton Sinclair's 'World's End' series, fictively chronicled world history from 1911 to 1950.[4] The first of this series was published in 1940, so significantly later than Phyllis's most overtly political novels, *Old Wine* (1924) and *The Mortal Storm* (1937). Nevertheless, reading Sinclair's socialist series alongside Phyllis Bottome's political novels is a salutary experience.[5] And, just as there is renewed interest in her work, his novels have newly attracted attention following the recent Hollywood blockbuster *There Will Be Blood*, drawn from his 1927 novel, *Oil*. Upton, like Phyllis, believed that the purpose of art was to bring out the truth of history, so they had a great deal in common, although holding slightly differing political convictions.

Phyllis's article, 'I Accuse', accompanied by a letter explaining that no one in Britain would either print or publish it, finally appeared towards the end of December 1938 in the *New Republic*. Phyllis's rhetorical strategy was to make a series of ringing denunciations, each beginning with the averment 'I accuse'. The very title of the article deliberately evoked Emile Zola's famous open letter of 1894, *J'accuse*, to the president of France claiming that Alfred Dreyfus had been falsely convicted of treason because he was a Jew.[6]

> I accuse Lord Halifax of invincible ignorance, for stating in the House of Lords that he sees no reason to believe in the sinister intentions of the German government, while Spanish towns are being bombed to pieces by German airmen, whose fellow countrymen sit on the Non-Intervention Committee.
>
> I accuse the Prime Minister of being publicly cited in a German newspaper as 'Germany's man' and of having deserved this insult.
>
> I accuse the 'Cliveden set' of money-conditioned thinking, in that they are deliberately using their great wealth and the power of the press which they help to control, to hand England over to the dictators in order to save their skins and their pockets.[7]

The Cliveden set to which Phyllis referred took its name from the great country house owned by Waldorf Astor and his wife Lady Nancy Astor, the first woman to take a seat in the House of Commons. She was the Conservative MP for Plymouth, a southern American belle who had married into fabulous wealth.[8] Guests vied to be invited for the weekend to be entertained by her witty repartee. Her husband's family owned the *Observer* and *The Times*, which made her opinions more influential than if they had been simply those of one woman MP. In fact, Nancy Astor's views as arch-appeaser were very similar to those of many of her class, and it seemed that she and her set were the last people to tumble to the reality of Hitler's aims and to take heed of Churchill's warnings.[9]

One of their frequent guests at Cliveden was Princess Stephanie von Hohenlohe, whom the Forbes Dennises had first encountered in Vienna in the 1920s. Even then considered politically dangerous, she was a *femme fatale* who quickly became *persona non grata* wherever she lived; in 1932 she had been forced to leave Paris when the authorities there became convinced she was engaged in espionage. In London, she worked as a roving ambassadress for the press baron Lord Rothermere, whom she had met in a casino in Monte Carlo in 1925. As his press empire included the *Daily Mail*, *Daily Mirror*, *Evening News*, *Sunday Pictorial* and *Sunday Dispatch*, this meant that a huge section of the British press was pro-Hitler. It is notable that from 1933 onwards, Nancy Astor's comments about international matters seemed very similar to those emerging from the Nazi propaganda machine. Between 1933 and 1938 Princess Hohenlohe relayed messages between Hitler and Rothermere and for these services, and probably for others not known about, Hitler awarded her the Nazi Party's Gold Medal of Honour.[10]

The conservative appeasers – Chamberlain, Halifax, Simon and Hoare – plus Sir Oswald Mosley, leader of the British Union of Fascists, and Hitler's ambassador to Britain, Joachim von Ribbentrop, were frequent guests at Cliveden. Ernan and Phyllis were to lose some of the friends who had supported them in arranging the Adler tours as a consequence of their uncompromising stance against appeasement.[11] Phyllis always thought of winter 1938 as the darkest days of her life:

> Spain was being handed over by the rest of Europe to Fascists, while her doubtful friends, the Communists, prepared to stab her in the back if fortune went against them. Czechoslovakia and Austria were being slowly strangled, before Hitler swallowed them. On all sides the tide seemed against us. Those who had the strength to act had no wish to and those who longed to act were impotent. It was a sorry period in English history.[12]

During the spring of 1939, Phyllis undertook another leg of the Colston Leigh tour throughout California. Her talks on psychology became more overtly connected with the political as the situation in Europe darkened. One of her talks was 'Women under Fascism' and in it she made it clear, just as she had in *The Mortal Storm*, that fascism was a perverted psychopathology, embodying a false or hyper masculinity. Preferring authority to freedom – childlike obedience to a father, husband or *Führer* – was, said Phyllis, a failure to grow into responsible maturity. Women, just as much as men, she told her audiences, needed to resist the cult of leadership. Phyllis made herself ill in the gruelling tour and suffered a sharp attack of pleurisy. Cutting short the tour, much to Colston Leigh's fury, she returned to Britain in May 1939. Her last talk was to the International PEN Club about the responsibility of writers in preserving freedoms.[13] Essentially it was this renewed threat of a return of tuberculosis that brought her back to Britain at this point, although choosing Britain as her domicile was a grave error from the point of view of British taxation.[14]

In Britain, Phyllis and Ernan continued to do what little they could to uphold the ideals of liberal democracy in general and to help refugees in particular. They joined Henry Wickham Stead's Democrat Society; he had been the editor of *The Times*, and then editor of *Review of Reviews* and was the author of a large number of books on European history. His own Penguin Special was called *The Press* and drew attention to the right-wing bias of most British newspapers.[15] The MP Commander Oliver Locker-Lampson came to see them regularly and helped to organise protests. Phyllis wrote a pamphlet called 'What are Dictators?' which was distributed in Hyde Park. Ernan had been persuaded by Dr Hilda Clarke, whom they had known when she was head of the British Red Cross in Vienna, to join her on the Society of Friends' Austrian Refugee Committee, and Phyllis wrote the general appeal for Austrian refugees in England. Later both Ernan and Phyllis were to resign from this committee, as they had grave concerns that one member had Nazi leanings. As Phyllis wrote, 'As former Passport Control Officer for Austria, Hungary and Jugoslavia, Ernan had had extensive experience of the kind of people we should be wise to accept as refugees.'[16]

Ernan also, which was perhaps just as significant, had a sharp awareness of who might be undesirable. When they had moved back into their house in Lexham Gardens they had been unpleasantly surprised to find, living opposite, the son of Princess Stephanie Hohenlohe: 'The house opposite to ours had a garden gate leading directly into the passage; and through it often slipped a magnificent young man with remarkable eyes and eyebrows.'[17] As well as having connections with the Cliveden Set, they knew that the princess was then engaged in espionage in America. One of her lovers was Fritz Wiedemann, the German Consul General in San Francisco. When they realised that Phyllis's secretary, June, was conducting some kind of liaison with the princess's son, Franzi, they sacked her. They were not prepared to take any chances at this critical time.

Phyllis and Ernan increasingly felt it crucial that Churchill should be brought into the Cabinet. Trying to explain Britain's continuing efforts to mollify Hitler to an American friend, Phyllis commented: 'I believe the whole Chamberlain trouble is caused by a sort of false optimism which lies deep in the Anglo-Saxon race. They want to believe in what they like, and have not learned to tackle what they dislike.'[18] Ernan sent a telegram to the Prime Minister pleading for Churchill to be included in the Cabinet: 'Let us forget past and personal feelings until civilisation is no longer menaced.' He also sent a copy to the *Daily Telegraph*, because, following the German occupation of Prague in March 1939, it had started to campaign for Churchill's recall to office.[19] Ernan paid for the design of a round enamel badge with 'Winston Churchill' stamped on it in dark blue on a white background. He paid Harrods to make five thousand of them, which they did, but asked not to be named as the manufacturer.[20] Writing to Ernan's Aunt Chattie on 13 July 1939,

Phyllis sent her a cache of the badges for her to give to family and friends:

> I expect you all realise how important it is to get Churchill in the Cabinet. It is the only thing that we can do immediately which will convince Hitler that we shall be firm. If he knows we shall stand firm he will probably not risk bringing on a war. Therefore Churchill in the Cabinet now may prevent a war. It will make America much more sympathetic towards us because all Americans know that he is a man of courage and intelligence. It will enormously encourage all our friends and allies in France, Poland, Romania etc etc, and it will discourage our enemies including Japan, who will realise that with Churchill in the Cabinet we shall stop wobbling like a half-paralytic drunkard![21]

Ever the activist, Phyllis said, 'There is very little that people like ourselves can do, but I'm damned if we don't do it.'[22]

As she later recounted in her autobiography, Ernan organised a demonstration in Downing Street at the end of August 1939:

> Just before the elections we had large posters made with the same design as the button and, with friends and adherents, we made a procession, carrying our posters from Whitehall to Westminster. Ernan's very beautiful old aunt Chattie Forbes led the procession (at seventy) and Ernan and I followed close behind her, to be sure that she did not get knocked down. We did not get as many adherents as we had hoped, and were rather pushed about by the police.[23]

This was reported in several newspapers, including the *Manchester Guardian*, the *Star* and the *Daily Express*. The *Manchester Guardian*, in its article about 'the Churchill Sandwich Boards', referred to the presence of Phyllis Bottome, 'the novelist'.[24]

While in Britain, both Phyllis and Ernan continued to lobby anyone they felt was already in sympathy with their view, and also to speak to anyone they felt they could wake up. Phyllis had come to see herself, echoing her English/American ancestry, as someone who could to some degree translate the *zeitgeist* from one country to the other. Phyllis wrote to Sir Robert Vansittart, the Permanent Under Secretary in the Foreign

Office, to tell him: 'My friend, Mr Edgar Mowrer, suggested the other day in Paris that I should send you an account of my prolonged American visit, and the political reactions of my audiences as well as the comments of several of the American men of affairs, whom I met, and with whom I discussed events.'[25] This letter was the start of a close relationship with 'Van', as Phyllis was invited to call him.

Ultimately war with Germany became unavoidable. Poland had received an Anglo-French pledge of support and yet, in the face of this, following a series of contrived border incidents – most infamously the Gleiwitz raid, when German criminals dressed in Polish uniforms were displayed dead after a supposed attack on a German radio station – on 31 August 1939, Hitler ordered the invasion of Poland. On 1 September 1939, the German Luftwaffe bombed Polish airfields and communication centres and a German army of over a million poured across Poland's border from every direction. Chamberlain delivered an ultimatum to the German government to begin a withdrawal from Poland, which expired at 11 a.m. on 3 September. When the ultimatum was ignored, Britain declared war on Germany; France followed suit at 5 p.m. the same day. The appeasement years were over.

On the day that war was declared, Phyllis and her sister Mary happened to be visiting a relative of Ernan's, the Duchess of Atholl, who lived at Blair Castle, near Pitlochry, in Scotland.[26] Phyllis was greatly drawn to this remarkable woman, especially admiring her brilliant organisational skills. She had no interest in feminine frippery; all her adult life she appeared in a long skirt, either tweed or tartan, a long shapeless jacket and a single string of pearls. Her husband had a series of affairs during their childless marriage, and she increasingly turned her attention to public service and politics. She was Scotland's first woman MP, and although not regarding herself as a feminist, nevertheless supported a series of bills that, for example, helped unmarried mothers, and furthered the ordination of women in the Presbyterian Church. She had also joined Eleanor Rathbone in an investigation into the practice of female circumcision in various places in the Empire.

Having visited Spain to see the political situation there for herself, she had protested to Chamberlain about the government's refusal to enforce the non-intervention pact, which Germany and Italy were violating by supporting Franco against the legitimately elected government. Her Penguin Special on the Spanish Civil War caused her to be christened the 'red' Duchess by the right-wing press and resulted in her loss of the Conservative Party whip in April 1938, after which she sat as an Independent. Although Phyllis did not see eye-to-eye with the duchess on every political matter, she was encouraged by her uncompromising stance on appeasement, writing:

> She was one of the first British politicians to understand fully the Nazi menace by reading an unexpurgated translation of Hitler's *Mein Kampf.* Finally her opposition to the government's policy of appeasement, and her resultant conflict with her constituency association, prompted her in November to resign from Parliament and force a by-election on the issue ... Having already lost a recent by-election fought largely on the issue of appeasement, the government took her challenge seriously. Fifty Conservative MPs travelled north to warn that a vote for the duchess was a vote for war, and in a more sinister twist local landowners were alleged to have offered their tenants bonuses – or threats – on the understanding that they vote against her. These various factors contributed to her narrow defeat by a Conservative opponent in a two-way contest.[27]

Afterwards, instead of trying to make a political comeback, which is always difficult for a defeated MP, she served as honorary secretary of the Scottish Invasion Committee, which prepared for an attempted German invasion, and she also headed the Perthshire Red Cross. The Duchess headed an all-party national joint committee to bring refugee children to England, and, visiting her to discuss the political situation, Phyllis and Mary found themselves immediately put to work delousing the heads of refugee children.

Two days after war was declared Phyllis received a letter from the Ministry of Information asking her to refrain from engaging in any other form of national service, as her skills as a writer would be required in wartime. She replied that, given the enormous impact of her novel *The Mortal Storm* in America, the best immediate use they could make of her was to facilitate her return there to undertake covert propaganda. Phyllis sent a second letter to Van, telling him that the resumption of her Colston Leigh lectures due to take place in America that winter might be a useful cover for propaganda. Although, she wrote, her 'views about Nazism are well known since my book on the subject, *The Mortal Storm*, has sold 65,000 copies is the States', her lectures were advertised as being either about literature or about Adlerian psychology, which sounded innocent enough.[28] She also reminded him of her 'thirty-year friendship with the Roosevelt family ... [and] my own very intimate friendship with Dorothy Thompson (Mrs Sinclair Lewis), whose influence as the chief *Herald Tribune* columnist ... is of prime importance in the USA'.[29] Van set up a meeting for Phyllis and Ernan with Sir Frederick Whyte, the Director of the American Division of the Ministry of Information based at London University's Senate House. Phyllis reported back to Van that clearance had been given and that both felt that Sir Frederick 'will be easy to work with'.[30]

No doubt in this briefing, they were encouraged to tread carefully. From the eve of the German invasion of Poland to the moment of Japan's attack on Pearl Harbor, the British government used a variety of diplomatic strategies to draw the United States into the war. The conversion of American opinion from isolationism to support of entry into World War II is a story of carefully managed propaganda, which amounted, in effect, to the selling of war.[31] Although, in 1935, strict neutrality had been mandated in America by a set of Neutrality Acts, this had not prevented Vansittart, as Permanent Under Secretary of State for Foreign Affairs, from running a covert detective agency of businessmen in Europe. They had worked closely with the secret services in charting the rise of German militarism. Van had also courted prominent American journalists, such as Ed Murrow, Edgar Mowrer and Dorothy Thompson.[32] Because Americans considered that British propaganda had been a major factor in seducing the United States into the First World War on the Allied side in 1917, this time round the propaganda needed to be more discreet and oblique.

Meanwhile Phyllis's American agent Ann Watkins had been touting the screen rights of *The Mortal Storm* around various studios, trying to get the best deal for her. Initially Phyllis was puzzled by what she imagined to be a lack of courage in Hollywood. Writing to a friend in March 1939 she had commented:

> ... in Hollywood ... with perhaps the greatest opportunity in history, the very men who are going to suffer most from their cowardice are too timid to present their cause through the most perfect medium the world has ever had, and which is entirely in their own power to use. Not one of the big picture studios has yet dared to put on a straightforward anti-Nazi film.[33]

But she was perhaps unaware of the complexity of the issues. This was a period when Hitler was busy blaming Hollywood's 'gigantic Jewish capitalistic propaganda' for Germany's poor relations with the United States.[34] The Nazi Party had purged its own country's film industry of Jews, which, from March 1933, had caused the American Jewish Congress to begin demonstrating against Hitler. In April of the same year, the Nazi Party had demanded the removal of all Jews employed by American film offices based in Germany. The Hollywood studios protested – this amounted to more than half their personnel in the country – but had then complied. Meanwhile, the Nazi Party continued to attack America's movie industry, saying that it was corrupted by Jewish domination, and eventually banned all movies featuring Jewish performers from German theatres.[35]

Hollywood considered that its first duty was to make a profit, and experience had shown that political films did not make money. Walter Wanger's production of *Blockade*, an anti-Franco romance released by United Artists in 1938, and Warner's *Confessions of a Nazi Spy*, a quasi-documentary, both performed poorly at the box office. The Hays Report published in March 1938 warned that 'Entertainment is the commodity for which the public pays at the box office. Propaganda disguised as entertainment would be neither honest salesmanship nor honest showmanship.'[36] Will Hays was the president of the self-regulating body for the film industry, and although the Production Code was originally intended to enshrine middle-class, mainstream American morality, in this period it was also engaged with trying to uphold American neutrality. Indeed, this epoch, when Europe was already engaged in war, but when America was pursuing its isolationist policy, was one that film historian Colin Shindler has described as a period of 'walking on eggs' for the American film industry:

> As the territory under the jurisdiction of the dictators grew ever larger, the financial profitability of Hollywood movies lessened proportionately. After the *Anschluss*, Nazi-occupied Austria impounded the money still remaining there from the proceeds of American film rentals. Hollywood studios had learned very quickly that the masters of the New Germany found their product to be infinitely resistable ... However reluctantly, Hollywood was dragged by force of circumstances into the murky realms of American foreign policy.[37]

When war broke out in Europe, the United States was the only major power without a propaganda agency. President Roosevelt, a politician with a consummate understanding of media, tried to influence public opinion through his speeches and manipulation of the news media. But he could not openly get ahead of public opinion and in September 1939, despite the annihilation of Poland, ninety-six per cent of the population questioned by Gallup was against America entering the war. Phyllis, having been trained in the art of propaganda by John Buchan during the First World War, was keen to make the most of her opportunity, on the second leg of her Colston Leigh tour, to choreograph the occasions in Britain's interest.[38]

Phyllis and Ernan arrived on 22 October 1939 in New York. *The Times* reported: 'Six British lecturers arrived in New York on Sunday in the same liner ... One of their number said they had not been sent by the British Government, but most of them would discuss war issues. They had agreed in advance, however, not to discuss what course the United States should take in regard to the war.'[39]

Phyllis, presumably, was the lecturer who said she had not been sent by the government; another of the group was Duff Cooper, then Minister of Information and therefore chief spin-doctor.[40] On both east and west coasts Phyllis, although notionally lecturing either on literature or Adlerian psychology, always used the question-and-answer time to engage her audience on political questions. An isolationist reporter from the Shreveport, LA, *Journal* wrote an article on 6 December 1939, entitled 'Our English Cousins', which reveals the Trojan horse element of the tour:

> Here we have a good team – novelist Phyllis Bottome and her personable and handsome husband, Capt. A. E. Forbes Dennis, of the British Army. Cousin Phyllis came calling recently to convert us uncouth relatives who live the wrong side of the tracks to the 'way of light and happiness' with an engaging lecture entitled 'The New Technique of Living'. At Evansville, Ind., Cousin Phyllis unfolded her technique. Her 'new technique' consists chiefly in hoping that we heathen souls will do away with the Nazis for her and all 'Nazi-minded people'. The teamwork is simple but effective. The captain sits in the audience while Cousin Phyllis works the crowd from the platform. The captain is conveniently at hand with answers for any audience questions, such as: 'What are Britain's war aims?' The combination works smoothly and well.[41]

No doubt this reporter would have been even more concerned had he known that Phyllis and Ernan were to be the guests of Eleanor Roosevelt a few days later.[42]

This technique smacks of a British Ministry of Information (MOI) briefing either before the trip, or even on the ocean crossing, from Duff Cooper himself; the MOI's propaganda objective was – to put it at its most simple – 'to symbolise the integrity of a democratic government'. The intention was always to emphasise that the 'Nazis had a Ministry of Propaganda which told lies, the British had a Ministry of Information which told the truth'.[43] Phyllis described her successful American tour *faux*-naïvely to Admiral Reginald Plunkett as follows:

> It was an interesting fact that while I only lectured upon Psychology, our audiences (unprecedentedly large) always insisted upon a prolonged European political discussion after the lecture was over, sometimes lasting for an hour and a half, in which my husband (who has been a Government official as you may remember) took the lead greatly to the delight of our mixed audiences … Churchill's book 'Step by Step' has made a profound impression upon all thinking Americans … Our two short talks with you in St Barbara made a deep and lasting impression upon us both … [44]

Earlier in 1939, Plunkett had headed the British section of the ineffectual Anglo-French military mission to Russia in an attempt to gain agreement on opposition to German aggression, so, clearly, he was actively engaged in diplomatic missions.[45] It would be naïve to regard the meeting of the Forbes Dennises with Plunkett as a merely accidental meeting; Ernan was an ex-Military Intelligence man, and knew the ropes.

Bill Dozier, in charge of MGM's Story Department, had submitted a synopsis of *The Mortal Storm* as early as March 1938 to Louis B. Mayer. Although himself Jewish, Mayer was initially cautious about making a film that harped on the plight of Jews in Germany. Dozier knew he might have an uphill struggle to persuade the studio to make the film. In 1936 MGM had purchased the film rights of Sinclair Lewis's famous novel *It Can't Happen Here*, which described the establishment of a fascist dictatorship in America, but finally they had lacked the courage to produce it. Bolder souls at MGM, however, started to listen to the persistent Bill Dozier when he insisted a film version of *The Mortal Storm* 'fits in with today's headlines of Nazi persecutions'.[46] It seems possible that Mayer was persuaded that he could take a chance on doing it, because the central focus of the story is what happens to a *family* in a given political situation. On 27 December 1938, Phyllis had been invited to discuss a possible adaptation. In the *Hollywood Reporter* of 11 April 1939, under the heading: 'MGM Purchase "Storm" After Wild Bidding Spree', a journalist noted that, in the end, several studios had been actively bidding for the screen rights.[47] As another film-journalist in the Brockton Massachusetts *Enterprise* put it, 'MGM has bought Phyllis Bottome's *Mortal Storm* even if the Fuehrer [*sic*] doesn't like it.'[48] According to the *New York Times* of 4 July 1939, MGM paid 25,000 dollars for it, which was considered a moderate price to pay for a best-selling book.

The Mortal Storm was to be MGM's first feature film to criticise openly Germany's Nazi regime. Phyllis's novel had unflinchingly shown the effects of the rise of Nazism, and also, to some extent, helped to explain why Jews had not immediately left Germany in the face of rising Nazi persecution. Finding a way to adapt a novel for film is always a tricky business, and it seemed inevitable that there would be some watering down of the politics. Louella Parsons, the Motion Picture

Editor of International Services whose column was syndicated all over America, wrote of the novel, 'I don't believe I have ever enjoyed a book more than this one and I hope it will lose none of its interest in the filming.'[49] Here she was expressing concern that the script might be censored by the Hays Committee. MGM was between a rock and a hard place. On the one hand it was still governed by the Neutrality Act and had to avoid outraging isolationists. On the other hand it had an artistic responsibility to stay true to the essence of the novel. And the novel was emphatically political.

When MGM decided to go ahead with the project, however, it appointed the best available people to realise it. Sidney Franklin was the producer, although, later, he would be succeeded by a British producer, Victor Saville.[50] The scriptwriter, Claudine West, was also British and considered one of the finest scriptwriters in Hollywood.[51] Assisting her were two immigrants, George Froeschel and Paul Hans Rameau, a Viennese writer, to make sure that all the details were accurate for a film set in Germany. In February 1940, Phyllis and Ernan, staying in Constance Collier's flat in Hollywood, were invited to visit the studios. Phyllis was shown a screenplay that, in general terms, she applauded, realising that a Hollywood film could not stick faithfully to every detail of her novel. She accepted that it would not be able to represent Freya as an unmarried mother. Nor would it be possible to allow the hero, renamed in the film as Martin Breitner, to be a Communist, especially in the light of the recent German-Soviet pact. Nevertheless, Phyllis sent a four-page letter to Sydney Franklin, commenting on a few things that she did not like:

> I would not put in Freya's mouth the word 'Non-Aryan', instead of Jew. It was part of her character and training to keep very plainly to facts. Besides, in the early days of the Hitler regime, when the story takes place, the word 'Jew' was always used by proud and self-respecting Jews of themselves; before they could believe in the torture and humiliation prepared for them by their fellow-countrymen. They were Jews, but they were German-Jews to the core of their hearts. Freya would have flung up her head and said with pride to Fritz, 'My father is a Jew!'[52]

She also made a strong plea for them to import from her novel the scene where Professor Roth explains to his son Rudi what qualities make 'a good Jew':[53]

> All over America – on radios, in schools, and in the Jewish preparation for their coming of age, Roth's speech to his son is being used. Can you not keep the exact wording? It is a very short speech, which is the answer to Rudi's famous question: 'What is a Jew?' It would be wonderfully dramatic if during this scene of discussion you could have Olaf playing *The Moonlight Sonata*,[54] as he does in the book … Art, as well as Religion and Science, is the mortal enemy of the dictatorships.[55]

Although some of her suggestions were taken up, these two were not.[56] The film stayed with the conventional circumlocution of referring to Jewish characters as 'non-Ayran'. Claudine West did her level best to save the scene that Phyllis thought was so important, writing and rewriting it, but in the final script, it did not survive. However, the character of Professor Roth himself, as he appeared on screen, is the epitome of the Good Jew, so all was not lost.

Phyllis did win on another important point. The original screenplay ended with the murder of both Freya and Martin in the snowy defiles of the Karwendel Pass. Referring back to her novel she comments: 'There is only one more point I should very much like to see reconsidered and that is the actual end. My book ends on hope! The bird is blown in out of the storm! And I do believe that humanity is going to weather the Mortal Storm of the dictatorships! Can you not at least let Martin be saved and get Freya's body over into Austria.'[57]

This suggestion they complied with, and Phyllis wrote excitedly to a friend:

> *Mortal Storm* is being shot now and I have a most wonderful cast. MGM have been very kind to me and I have given them many suggestions with which they are strengthening their script. I think they have kept the spirit of the book, in spite of the necessary changes for screen purposes. I am extraordinarily lucky to have got James Stewart, who makes a magnificent hero, and an equally

> good Professor, Frank Morgan. We hope for the preview in six weeks and I am asked to give my opinion of it in an article in the *New York Times*.[58]

She was certainly lucky in the cast assigned to her film. The two central characters of Martin Breitner and Freya Roth were played by James Stewart and Margaret Sullavan respectively. As Victor Saville put it, 'Film stars are not just stars because the publicity department says so. They have something loosely called "star quality" and strangely enough, this quality is as distinct in each personality as fingerprints are different in ordinary mortals.'[59] Stewart was in love with Sullavan, and their chemistry on screen is palpable. Frank Morgan, born Frank Wupperman, was himself of German-Jewish origin, which meant, perhaps, that he had a special empathy for the character of Professor Roth. Martin's mother was played by Maria Ouspenskaya, who had once been a disciple of Stanislavski at the Moscow Theatre. She herself was an escapee from Communist Russia, so again, had a special investment in the role.[60] All of the actors turned in respectable performances, but these four actors were exceptional.

After much hesitation from the top ranks of MGM, filming finally started and in May Phyllis was shown the rough work print of *The Mortal Storm* in MGM's New York studio. With huge enthusiasm she wired Sydney Franklin and Claudine West in Culver City: 'Mortal Storm magnificent. Warmest congratulations. Whole cast, production and script 100 per cent of novel.'[61] More than anything else, Phyllis wrote to a friend, this film 'had been the purpose of our seven months' visit, and was our final message to the hearts and minds of America; by it we had hoped, not to drag them into war, but to awaken them in time to what must happen to humanity if the swastika took the place of the Cross.'[62]

On the boat back to Europe, Phyllis wrote *Heart of a Child* (examined in Chapter 6) in the middle of a violent storm. As she said to her friend Violet Bonham Carter, 'I wrote it coming over on the voyage when I thought [the boat] would have to break and it was a sort of last cry towards the things I most believe in ... It was a sort of swan song, when I thought we must go under.'[63]

In the spring of 1940, after six months of the so-called Phoney War, the eerie pause that had followed the conquest of Poland had been broken. Notwithstanding the storm that raged around them, Phyllis and Ernan listened obsessively to the radio news:

> Blow after hammer blow struck at our British hearts. The French gap opened at Sedan; and having opened, mysteriously, did not close. Bridges that should never have been there enabled the Germans to cross the Meuse. The Belgian and the British Armies were pressed back. Leopold suddenly surrendered – without warning either his own army or the troops of his allies of his intention. The whole British Army was – as once before – cut off from its base and divided from the main forces of the French.[64]

Allied plans for a western-front battle had been based on holding the Maginot Line, which stretched more or less from the Swiss to the Belgian border. Hitler had used about thirty divisions to prevent the main Allied armies from disengaging. But the bulk of the German army had moved through the Ardennes to cross the Meuse and then turned towards the Channel, so that the Allied Forces were cut off in the region of Pas de Calais. On 27 May, the mass evacuation of British troops from Dunkirk was made to seem, by Churchill's rhetoric, a great triumph, and indeed enormous courage was shown by the owners of the three hundred little boats from Britain that ferried the rescued troops out to the larger ships lying offshore.[65] In reality, it was a great setback.[66] France was left at Germany's mercy; on 10 June the Germans captured Rouen and the French government abandoned Paris without a fight, moving to Tours in the south-west. For months, Italy had been threatening to enter the war on Germany's side, and on 10 June it did so. It was precisely at this political moment that *The Mortal Storm* was premièred in America and this timing was crucial to its reception. It had, as Phyllis was to say to the director of the American Division of the MOI, 'Hit the Hour'.[67] Even the conservative journal of the industry, the *Motion Picture Herald*, observed after the preview: 'A few months or weeks ago this Hollywood press audience would have used the word "propaganda" to describe the film and speculated on the policy prompting its manufacture. The word was not heard in the auditorium or the foyer on June 10th.'[68]

So how did the finished film appear to its first audiences? The opening credits, with the title *The Mortal Storm* in Gothic script, appear over time-lapse photography showing increasingly threatening storm clouds. A voice-over speaks of the dark instincts of human nature, and queries, 'How soon will man find wisdom in his heart and build a lasting shelter against his ignorance and fears?' The opening establishing long shot is of a picture-postcard village surrounded by snowy mountains. A friendly postman delivers a small mountain of mail for Professor Roth on his sixtieth birthday. Roth is a professor of physiology at the university, and when he enters the lecture room his students all rise to cheer him. He receives a gift of a statuette of The Torchbearer, representing the true flame of science.

That same evening there is an intimate celebration of his birthday in his comfortable and gracious home. Present are his wife, his two stepsons, Erich and Otto, whom he regards as his own, his daughter Freya and his son Rudi. Two young men, Fritz Marberg, a young medical student, and Martin Breitner, a farmer who is training to be a vet, are part of the harmonious group around the table. The evening begins as an archetypal scene of a happy united family in the company of their close friends. But the maid suddenly announces, 'Something wonderful has happened. They have made Adolf Hitler *Reichskanzler* of Germany.' Immediately there is a schism in the family. Fritz, Otto, Erich and young Rudi become intoxicated by the repeated shouts of 'Sieg heil' coming over the radio. Martin resists their calls to join the Nazi Party, insisting, 'Peasants have no politics, they keep cows.' But Fritz threatens him, saying, 'If they want to keep their cows, they had better have the right politics.' And the young Rudi repeats what he has been taught in school, that 'the individual must be sacrificed to the welfare of the state'. This family, that the audience has already started to love, is obliterated by the fade-out mechanism.

Life becomes increasingly difficult for the 'non-Ayran' professor. He is not a man to impose his will on others, but nor can he deny the truth of science. His act of resistance is to insist that there is no difference between the blood of Aryans and non-Aryans. This contradicts Nazi ideology about race. Students, most of them now in the uniform of the Brownshirts, shout 'lies' and boycott his classes when he refuses to back down from this statement. The students make a bonfire of books by Jews, including those of Einstein, representing the loss of Jewish intellectuals to the world. Professor Roth is arrested and taken to a concentration camp. He insists that Rudi should not be told what has happened to him, as he does not want Rudi to learn to hate. He hopes that, in time, Germany will find her old virtues. However, he dies in the camp, supposedly of a heart attack, although Freya, not fooled, cries out, 'They have killed my father.' Freya, her mother and her young brother Rudi all try to leave Germany, but Freya is pulled off the train when a copy of the manuscript of her father's last book is discovered in her suitcase. She has her passport confiscated and has to turn back.

Martin has, in a sense, inherited the flame of truth from Professor Roth. Freya breaks off her engagement to Fritz because she cannot bear his adherence to Nazi ideology. Her childhood friendship with Martin ripens into love, as she comes to see him as 'the sanest man' she knows. Martin, however, is a marked man, not only because he will not become a Nazi himself, but also because he rescues a schoolteacher from being beaten up by Brownshirt thugs. At the alpine farm, Martin's mother's blesses the pair as they pledge themselves to each other in a rustic form of wedding ceremony. They attempt to escape over the border by skiing over the Karwendel Pass into Austria. Freya's erstwhile fiancé, Fritz, is ordered to hunt them down. He hesitates, but is stiffened in his resolve when the local district leader tells him that 'there are no human relationships' more important than the fascist cause. Fritz accepts the command and leads the patrol that fires on and kills Freya. As he tells her two half-brothers, 'I had no choice. It was my duty.' One of Freya's two half-brothers, Erich, accepts this, but Otto rejoices that Martin has escaped, 'free to think what he likes'. As this Aryan son comes to this anti-fascist conclusion, the shadow of The Torchbearer is distinct on the wall of the now empty family home. The family are dispersed; two of them are already dead. All that remains are footprints on the snowy path, gradually being obliterated. This last image echoes the fadeout mechanism used in the earlier scene when the family party was disrupted by the announcement that Hitler had become Chancellor.

In *The Mortal Storm* Jews were represented visually by actors with dark hair and eyes (in contrast with the blonde mother and her tall blond sons from the first marriage) and, finally, by the 'J' on Professor Roth's sleeve and those of the others in the concentration camp. This was not historically accurate, although the 'J' appeared in Jewish passports and it worked as a visual representation. Some scenes not in Phyllis's novel had been introduced into the film version to heighten the drama – for example, the book-burning scene and the lecture-room rebellion against Professor Roth – and they work well. Other areas of her novel were inevitably softened, as Phyllis knew they must be. A key change is the transmutation of Martin from a Communist into a pacifist, in order to avoid an accusation against the film of Communist sympathies (and because Hitler presented himself as the bastion against Communism). The literary scholar, Phyllis Lassner, complains that the star casting 'glamorizes and thus deheroicizes Freya. Margaret Sullavan skiing in a silk blouse marks Freya as too fragile to carry out her escape and so Jimmy Stewart, playing her bereft but stalwart lover, carries her dead body to safety.'[69] There is an element of truth in this statement: MGM was a studio that had built its system – and profits – on stars, and James Stewart was one of their biggest box-office draws.[70] But, if all politics can be described as the art of practising the possible, Phyllis's main points are sustained in the film version: the fracture of the family, the stripping away of status from a previously respected Jewish intellectual, the sense that Germany has become a prison house for anyone who resists fascism. The star casting was also key to the film's reception, because it meant that thousands of moviegoers, who might not have turned out to see a 'political' film, flocked to see a feature film, in the hope of enjoying a romance.[71]

It is a powerful film, owing its strength not only to the screenplay, but also the particular skills of the director, Frank Borzage. His name as director alongside the names of his two stars would immediately set up audience expectations of a transcendent heterosexual romance; James Stewart and Margaret Sullavan had played opposite each other in *Next Time We Love (*1936*), The Shopworn Angel* (1938) and *The Shop Around the Corner* (1940). But this is not necessarily a bad thing. As critic Robert Lightning comments, Borzage skilfully adapted elements of his usual repertoire to bear on this overtly political film:

> The union of lovers (as is usual in Borzage) operates outside of church and state law: following a peasant tradition the couple drink from the traditional wedding cup, the ritual overseen by the hero's mother. The Borzagean motif as deployed here also coincides with the generic concerns of that anti-Nazi film: the need to accommodate tradition to the urgency of the current political crisis (the ritual that is usually an adjunct to a wedding here *replaces* the wedding, the mother, in essence, conducting the ceremony); the desire to honour the mother (for whom the ritual is performed) whom the couple, pursued by Nazis, may never see again ... [72]

And as another critic, David Thomson, points out: 'The treatment of the lovers is lyrical and profuse. It is as if film itself were persuading Borzage of the justice of their cause. William Daniels did the photography, and he understood the exceptional screen chemistry between Stewart and Sullavan (at least friends in real life). Her hushed voice seems to draw him closer until he hovers over her like a guard.'[73]

This is not to argue that it is a perfect film, whatever that might be. MGM did not go in for much location shooting, but used a park that could be converted into anything 'from a football field to the gardens at Versailles', and some of the 'outdoor' scenes look stagey.[74] One unit, however, was sent out to Salt Lake City, Utah, to film the ski-runs and sequences that in the film were supposed to represent the Karwendel Pass. Olympic ski champions were used as stunt doubles for Stewart and Sullavan.

But the important point here is that genre films are not immune from radical inflection, and even if – in Hollywood style – the romance is central, fascism overshadows and threatens it. Borzage had already shot two politically-inflected films from emphatically political novels, *A Farewell to Arms* in 1932 and *Three Comrades* in 1938, so he was skilled in finding a Hollywood way of representing a transcendent love that survives – in the sense of representing the triumph of love over hate.[75] *The Mortal Storm* is Borzage's fullest anti-fascist statement; scenes of brutality, even if not the subject of lingering shots, are in no sense ambiguous. David Thomson argues that

> Borzage's political intuition is reliable, even if he treats it in conventional romantic terms. *The Mortal Storm* is a more perceptive and frightening study of fascism than, say, *The Great Dictator* or the Capra films. The shot of James Stewart and Margaret Sullavan emotionally and philosophically hemmed in by a forest of saluting arms is typical of Borzage's faith that love is a manifestation of political nature.[76]

Indeed, it could be argued that the film does not correspond to conventional romantic usage. At the beginning of the film, Fritz announces his engagement to Freya. Yet, romantic love cannot operate in a vacuum, unaffected by the politics impinging on their lives. The moment when it is announced on the radio that Hitler has become Chancellor, and half of the group round Professor Roth's birthday table rushes to listen, splinters the group. Freya will turn from her fascist fiancé towards the anti-fascist Martin; it is a political as much as a romantic choice. As film critic John Belton points out: 'Borzage's central characters, Professor Roth and his wife, his daughter Freya, the student Martin and Martin's mother, stand, like [the mountains in the opening shot] eternal and fixed in their spiritual purity and strength, within a rapidly changing, spiritually corrupt society.'[77]

And in this sense, *au fond*, whatever the necessities of adaptation from novel to film, the film honours the central tenets of Phyllis's book.

The film received rave reviews. *The Mortal Storm* made the *New York Times*' Ten Best List 1940, the Blue Ribbon Award Badge of Merit (Best Picture of the Month, June 1940), *Film Daily*'s Ten Best Pictures 1940, and the Canadian Critics Best Selection of 1939–40. Louella Parsons was not disappointed by the move from book to film. Writing in the *Los Angeles Examiner*, she said: '*The Mortal Storm* leaves you as limp as a rag and so emotionally upset you feel as if you could go and fight a one-man battle with Herr Hitler ... Of all the Nazi movies this is definitely the most potent because of the absence of all hysterics. There is unspeakable brutality and heartache so real they must affect everyone who sees this picture.'[78]

Above all, the film achieved Phyllis's goal and mobilised public opinion in America. 'What matters now,' concluded the *New York*

World Telegram, 'is not so much the national tragedy of Germany when Hitler took over, but how we can best combat such things over here.'[79]

Everywhere that Phyllis had lectured on her Colston Leigh tour had helped to create an audience for her film.[80] She had told Violet Bonham Carter, before setting out on the tour, that although her agent was 'a dreadful man', he was 'the only great agent in America ... [and could] be counted on to give you big audiences'.[81] On the second leg of her whistle-stop tour she had visited Montreal, Detroit, Louisville (Kentucky), Grand Rapids (Michigan), Chicago, Terre Haute and Evansville (Indiana), Springfield (Massachusetts), Portland (Maine), Hollywood, Washington, Los Angeles and San Francisco, effectively paving the way for the film's reception.

At MGM, Howard Dietz was in charge of film promotion, and headed the campaign for *The Mortal Storm*. He spent the bulk of his advertising budget on large-scale national campaigning in daily newspapers, but he also set up a series of local newspaper budgets centred in key cities under his team of forty 'field exploitation' men. As the *Hollywood Reporter* of 24 May 1940 put it:

> Howard Dietz and his MGM exploiteers will do something new with the advertising and exploitation of *Mortal Storm*, a Nazi yarn that is said to be a humdinger. The picture will be put into a Broadway theatre for a two- or four-week, two-a-day run, with Dietz's crowd planting important display ads in all the principal cities of the country advertising the show at the NY theatre during that run. Looks like a sweet idea that's certain to cause enough comment for the ticket buyers to chase to their own showstop when the picture is released for their town.

However, according to MGM's press book, the studio had laid out several marketing approaches to the selling of the film round the country. It warned exhibitors to 'gauge the feeling in your community at play-date time and guide yourself accordingly'. It suggested that the 'far-seeing, cautious exhibitor who does not wish to risk offending any part of his patronage will steer a middle course by omitting to state the controversial aspects' of the film.[82] In short, in some places it would be best to sell the film on the basis of its stars, rather than risking the charge of propaganda.[83]

The German ambassador in Washington was alarmed, saying: 'This film, which is now playing to all cities in the US, is one of the best anti-German pieces of propaganda created by Hollywood.'[84] On 9 July, Goebbels responded by banning all American films from occupied Europe. MGM closed its Berlin office on 14 August, and by 18 August Hollywood production was forbidden in the Reich. The head of the German Ministry's Film Propaganda Section, justified these measures with direct reference to *The Mortal Storm*, Chaplin's *The Great Dictator* and *The Beast of Berlin*.[85] Venezuela, Peru, Guatamala and Cost Rica all refused to screen *The Mortal Storm* following demands from Berlin.

Back in Britain, Phyllis had reported to the MOI on the American trip. Phyllis was anxious that her film should be released in her home country. In a letter to her friend, Israel Sieff, the managing director of Marks & Spencer, on his impending visit to America in August 1940, she said: 'If you see Louis B. Mayer soon and can get him to hasten the release of "The Mortal Storm" for England, I believe it would be a help, since it is not to appear till December 2nd.'[86] She also wrote to Sir Frederick Whyte, saying: 'I am inundated with reports of the nerving effect "The Mortal Storm" is having, not only as war propaganda in America, but also, my Canadian friends tell me, it is deepening and strengthening the war spirit in Canada ... History moves so swiftly nowadays that we cannot afford to postpone the effect of any work likely to act as a tonic.'[87] Perhaps pressure was brought to bear, because *The Mortal Storm* was shown in London in October 1940, judging from excellent reviews in the *New Statesman* and *The Spectator*.[88]

The Films Division of the MOI was actively influencing production of documentaries and feature films made in Britain during the war, because of the opportunity for propaganda.[89] Phyllis felt that the MOI did not make as much use of film as they could have done, at least in the first half or the war; writing to Jack Beddington, the director of the Films Division, she said, 'A good scriptwriter such as Claudine West of MGM – if there is such a person in our own country – could really help you from a propaganda point of view, enormously, and I know you cannot get to the American public in any other way.[90] All the young people tell me when I lecture over there, that they get all their thinking life from films.'[91]

Phyllis was determined to get her views brought to the attention of the Ministry of Information and even more directly to government. She pointed out that Sir Neville Henderson, the ex-Ambassador to Berlin, was an intimate friend of Goering's, and opined that he and Lord Brockett should be interned. She also 'enraged the whole Conservative Party by letting them have a typescript of the chief opinions I have gathered'.[92] Pointing out her almost unique opportunity of taking soundings, she had sent a letter, dated 1 July 1940, to two hundred MPs, including the following warning:

> ... American support, I gather, will not crystallise into action, until England cuts out the dead wood from the Government. Mr Chamberlain's popularity in England has never been shared by America and his late policy has been so completely discredited by events in the eyes of both prominent Republicans and throughout the Democratic Party that his retention in office causes absolute dismay, as well as frank distrust of our intentions. To put it bluntly, Americans think we are retaining Mr Chamberlain and his associates in order to make a disgraceful – because inconclusive – peace, at the expense of our democratic institutions and way of life ... Nothing can convince America that England is clenched in her resolution to fight to a finish under determined leadership except the resignation of what is looked on over there as Chamberlain's gang ... [93]

While on the US tour, the Forbes Dennises had rented out their Lexham Garden house to 'Bill' Bates and Evelyn Graham Stamper, the old friends who had served under Ernan in the Vienna Passport Office in the 1920s. Once again, they were engaged in counter-espionage work. On their return, Phyllis and Ernan took a service flat nearby for a few months. Although this was the period of the so-called Phoney War before the onset of the Blitz, there had already been some bombing and strafing; consequently, Phyllis and Ernan had returned to a country in which preparations for enemy attack from the sky were well under way. Air-raid wardens, stretcher bearers and rescue workers had been appointed, thirty-eight million gas masks had been distributed and Anderson shelters were being issued to those people who had a garden to put one in.[94] In 1937, the German bombing raid which had destroyed the town of Guernica in the Spanish Civil War had served as a terrible warning of the terror that might soon come to Britain from the skies.

On 7 June 1940, Phyllis wrote to Duff Cooper, telling him that she was back in the country, and that her services were once again available as lecturer, writer or broadcaster.[95] The enormous success of her anti-Nazi film in America was regarded as vital service, so he took up her offer with alacrity. During the war, Phyllis was to engage in all three activities for the MOI. Being placed on the Speakers' Panel of MOI meant that she travelled all round the country during the bombing, equipped with petrol coupons issued by the MOI. This was in pursuit of one of her war-jobs, keeping up morale in her home country.

However, Britain still needed to induce America to abandon its isolationist stance and to enter the war as Britain's ally. Duff Cooper recognised that *The Mortal Storm*, both the novel and now particularly the film, meant that Phyllis Bottome's name held a particular, almost iconic significance for Americans, and therefore asked her to write a book about Britain in wartime. It would be MOI-sponsored and its aim would be to arouse sympathy in America for Britain's plight. On 7 September 1940, the *blitzkrieg* began. On fifty-six of the following fifty-seven nights, with one night's reprieve due to cloudy skies, London was bombed heavily by an average of two hundred bombers.[96] Britain, albeit with support from her Empire and Commonwealth, stood alone in Europe, but, although they sent military supplies to Britain, the United States held back. Phyllis's task was to gain America's approval of Britain's courage and to convince her that Britain would never surrender.

Phyllis rushed to do the job, writing to Van in December 1940, 'I have nearly finished a book, "Britain Against Hitler", for my American publisher. It is little enough, and I wish there were more that we could do, but each must use the weapon that he has.'[97] Duff Cooper assisted her 'in every way in his power to collect material'.[98] An admiral friend helped her with introductions to naval commanders and permission to visit their ships; Violet Bonham Carter gave her the connection to the Air Ministry she needed in order to visit flying fields. The book was published in 1941 as *Mansion House of Liberty*, Phyllis taking her title from Milton's *Areopagitica:* 'Behold now this vast City; a City of refuge, the mansion-house of liberty, encompast and surrounded with his protection.' Although it was primarily designed for an American audience, Faber & Faber also bought out an edition in 1941, retitling it *Formidable to Tyrants*.[99] It was dedicated 'To all those who love human beings better than they love power'.[100]

Her American publisher advertised this book on its dust cover and in all the press releases as being by the author of *The Mortal Storm*, with a puff that said: 'From experiences more thrilling and moving than fiction, a distinguished novelist has written a book which makes one proud to share any part of the heritage of England.' In the book, made up of nineteen chapters and 264 pages, written very quickly in between lecturing all round Britain for the MOI, Phyllis sought to portray the fortitude of the British – those facing the Blitz in London, Birmingham, Coventry, Southampton, Manchester, Liverpool, Exeter, Plymouth and Belfast – and those in rural districts trying to feed the nation. Using all her skills as a novelist, she brings vividly to life ordinary women, men and children suffering in wartime. She writes of the quiet heroism of the men in the navy, the air force and the army, and those men who, either too young or too old for the forces, volunteer for the Home Guard. She felt least secure in whether she had the knowledge to give a reasonable account of the army, so asked the military historian Captain Basil Liddell Hart to look over the relevant chapter.[101]

She has words of praise too for women's efforts in the war: the ATS (Auxiliary Territorial Service), the WAAFS (Women's Auxiliary Force Service), the women who have become ambulance drivers or nursing auxiliaries. She notes that even women of the bridge-playing classes have joined the WVS (Women's Voluntary Service) to help protect homes and families against air attacks. She visited workers in the armaments factories, and noted how they had transferred their skills from domestic equipment to military equipment. She praises all those who have taken in evacuees, not underestimating the difficulties of adaptation on both sides, but blessing the fact that it all works towards the breaking down of the class system in Britain. She refers to her own experience, on the day on which war was declared, of getting roped in by the Duchess of Atholl into helping to settle in the sixty-three children and seven or eight mothers from Clydeside evacuated to Blair Castle. Phyllis and Mary had worked with her for the remaining three days of their holiday in a variety of hands-on ways, including the inevitable sorting out of nit-ridden heads. Phyllis remembered that after this necessary but unpleasant procedure the children were all released with a sweet as a reward for their patience into the grounds of the castle to let off steam:

> Their teachers had been delayed in coming to them, but I shall never forget my last sight of the children – when two of these beneficent beings loomed across the park, and like a flock of homing birds the children flew over the grass to meet them. 'Teacher! Teacher!' they shouted in joyous unison. Perhaps that cry of trust and love may have been the reward for which the teachers carry on their careers of unregarded heroism.[102]

The book is a skilled piece of propaganda, because, notwithstanding its serious message, its interest lies in the characters she depicts so vividly. As an experienced writer and propagandist, she knows how to soften the gravity of her subject with touches of humour. She quotes from a letter she has received from a previous secretary retrained as a voluntary nurse on a Red Cross mobile unit, which refers to the inconveniences of sleeping in shelters: 'Mother bewails her blankets being used downstairs on the floor, and I can't get her to take her corsets off at night – she says they give her moral support as well as physical!'[103] Throughout, Phyllis makes it clear that everyone in Britain is involved in the fight against Hitler and what Hitler stands for, and that they will never surrender. The idea of a people's war is part of the myth Phyllis is helping to create but it is also the reality that she has observed. All of her sketches imply that there is something in the British character that is unique. She suggests that a significant element of this is a largely unconscious Christian attitude:

> Another deep-seated trait in English people overlooked by Hitler, and perhaps not surprisingly overlooked by Hitler, is that they are a religious people … [there are many] who practise the fundamental

> precepts of Christianity without accepting its religious or dogmatic tenets. To this stratum belong most of the best citizens of Great Britain; they are to be found in every class, although as 'goodness' implies realism, they are to be found most often where life is hardest and where loving one's neighbour as oneself – the root of all practising religions – is as much a protection as a duty.[104]

Phyllis was careful to keep cultivating American sympathy. Describing a visit to a naval base she comments: 'If any American doubts the gratitude and love of England towards her American friends, I hope he will someday meet one of the Commanders of these Destroyers. He will not be left long in doubt of what England feels for America. I had myself a taste of it that afternoon.'[105] She ends by raising the rhetorical question, 'What then is England fighting for?'

> Americans do well to ask ... Freedom is what England is fighting for. We have not always understood it, nor always practised it; but we have always loved it ... Freedom is our Peace Aim. Those who wish us to define what we mean by freedom, for ourselves and for others, must share the struggle in order to attain it – with us.

Upton Sinclair wrote to her, 'I have been reading your last book with great interest and appreciation. You are having a terrible experience, but you have made something fine out of it. Our hearts are with you. You have rendered your country many services, and your influence over here has counted more than you perhaps realise.'[106]

At the beginning of March 1941, Phyllis made a radio broadcast to America called 'Democracy Marches'; she gave a thirteen-and-a-half minute talk from a script of 1,700 words encouraging the sense of connection between Britain and the United States:

> ... In that long famous utterance of the United States against tyranny, 'The Declaration of Independence', we are given as the 'unalienable rights of man' – 'Life, Liberty and the pursuit of Happiness'. This is still – and must always be – the true goal of Democracy. Some of us have questioned if 'the pursuit of Happiness' should be part of our aim; but if the happiness sought is for all – and in a good direction – we need not cavil at it for being happiness.[107]

Phyllis had an actress's sense of how to deliver a speech, which worked well on radio. She also invoked Hollywood films to help her make her point: 'It is the Disney films that help to keep my own spirits up ... Disney's heroic creatures slip through the mechanical jaws of disaster not only because they are small but because they are not mechanical. They do not *win* Freedom. They themselves *are* free; and Freedom is in itself a creative form of activity.'[108]

It was inevitable that there would be some kind of American isolationist counter-attack against the anti-Nazi films being made. In January 1941, US Senator Burton K. Wheeler claimed that 'the motion picture industry is carrying on a violent propaganda campaign intending to incite the American people to the point where they will become involved in war'.[109] On 1 August 1941, Senators Nye and Clark instigated a resolution ushering in a senatorial committee to investigate 'war propaganda disseminated by the motion picture industry'.[110] The odds were somewhat stacked as the committee consisted of four isolationists and only one non-isolationist, and its work was to be overseen by the afore-mentioned Senator Wheeler (in his role as chair of Interstate Commerce).[111] The films that stood accused included *The Mortal Storm*.[112] The hearings seem to have been somewhat farcical, because, as Susan L. Carruthers points out:

> It soon emerged, as the Senators wilted under questioning, that they had not actually seen the arraigned movies ... Motivated by an unappetising blend of isolationism and anti-semitism (slyly insinuating that Jewish émigré studio bosses were insufficiently American), the Senators' underlying purpose was to rally like-minded isolationist sentiment by making a sacrificial slaughter of the highest profile scapegoat to hand.[113]

Dorothy Thompson, in her *New York Post* column of 12 September 1941, rushed to attack Senator Nye as an anti-Semite. She referred to the hearings as 'Our Own Dreyfus Case', thereby picking up on Phyllis's rhetoric when, in 1938, she had attacked the leaders of the Church of England for ignoring the plight of their Jewish brothers in Europe. If Dorothy Thompson was defending Phyllis's film and other anti-Nazi films in the press, it was Will Hays who organised the legal defence of the industry. It became clear during the committee's enquiry that in 1940 surprisingly few out of five hundred and thirty pictures produced in Hollywood had dealt with anti-Nazi themes. There was an indefinite suspension of hearings in October 1941.

During that autumn, the United States had been negotiating with Japan in an attempt to bring a halt to its desires for empire in the Far East. On the morning of 7 December 1941, the Japanese air force bombed Pearl Harbor in Hawaii. Over two thousand American sailors, soldiers and civilians were killed. The United States and Britain declared war on Japan on 8 December. On 11 December, Germany and Italy declared war on the United States. America and Britain were now facing the same enemies side by side. History, as Phyllis had remarked, moves swiftly.

CHAPTER 10

Wartime in Cornwall and Therapeutic Interventions in the Colony of Artists

Writers, more than ever, must be
the world's peacemakers.

PHYLLIS BOTTOME

Upon Ernan and Phyllis's return from America, they spent a brief period of time in London, but, having let their house to their old friends in counter-intelligence, they chose to make Cornwall their own base during wartime. At the beginning of July 1940, they moved into a rented furnished house, Thymeland, in Bude, North Cornwall. Phyllis's sister Mary was with them, and they established Ernan's Aunt Chattie in the hotel next door. Freda Troup went to join them once more as secretary, typing on Phyllis's brand new Remington silent typewriter. She did not stay with them for very long, however, as she had volunteered to act as an escort taking evacuee children by ship to South Africa, and afterwards settled there with her family. In Britain, food was rationed, and fruit especially was very hard to come by during the war, so Freda sent frequent welcome boxes of apples and plums to her dearest English friends.

It was clear that Hitler intended to invade Britain, but could only do so if Germany gained supremacy in the sky. The first bombs to be dropped on mainland Britain had fallen in May 1940 in Canterbury and Middlesborough; the first fell in the London area in June, and in July there were air raids on Wick and Hull. Hitler was now able to use

France as a base and send his planes on the short flight across the Channel. In anticipation of what came to be called the Battle of Britain, evacuees began to be moved out of the targeted cities. The Forbes Dennis household had welcomed an evacuee woman from Liverpool with a little boy of two and a half, her soldier husband, and a London dressmaker.[1] They also had an extremely lively kitten called Tito as part of their ménage. Each member of their household was issued with a National Identity Card and a ration book with coupons to be exchanged for meagre amounts of butter, milk, cheese, meat, bacon and sugar. Clothing was rationed, too, so a good deal of make-do-and-mend was going on in British homes, including Thymeland.

In May 1940, the Secretary of State for War, Anthony Eden, in a broadcast to the nation, asked men between the ages of seventeen and sixty-five, who were not already on active duty, to volunteer for a new force which the government was setting up. These Local Defence Volunteers, later known as the Home Guard, were to assist in the defence of the country in the case of invasion and thereby release regular forces for more active duties at home and abroad. Many of them, like Ernan, were veterans of the First World War, and he immediately enlisted under the head of the district, who turned out to be a childhood friend.

Promises of arms and uniform were slow to be realised; indeed, the first 'uniform' was simply an armband with letters LDV inscribed in white letters. And, although the threat of invasion was real, initially weapons had to be improvised from pitchforks, truncheons, pickaxes and broom handles, a situation satirised much later by the television programme *Dad's Army*. Phyllis, ever the activist, wrote to Walter Wanger, in his role as president of the Motion Picture Academy, to ask him if he could procure all the guns he could locate on Californian ranches, and offer them to the British Ambassador, Philip Kerr.[2] She urged Wanger to continue making films to lift the spirits of the Allies: 'You are my friends and have been my work comrades. I turn to you therefore, and to the Studios of Hollywood, with which I have been proud and happy to cooperate. I ask for your courage in producing faithful, truthful, and dynamic films.'[3]

Uniforms and weapons finally began to arrive, and in another letter,

Phyllis refers to Ernan, patrolling the cliffs one night a week, 'with his mates armed and satisfied'.[4] She wrote to Wanger again, requesting field-glasses for the use of the Bude Home Guard, saying, 'I cannot tell you how proud I am to see Ernan in his new battledress, so simple and full of plain brotherhood.'[5] Once the weapons had arrived, the Home Guard needed training; Ernan had to undergo testing on handling guns. His report on shooting at a distance of two hundred yards reads: 'Not a good start, but once target found, Corporal Forbes Dennis gave first-class exhibition of gunnery, his bursts well grouped and central.'[6] Ernan also contributed his psychologist's skills by serving as welfare officer for the local forces.

Phyllis, as was usual for her generous and energetic spirit, contributed to the war effort in any way she could. Invited to give a lecture in Bude, she made a collection for a Spitfire. She ended all her British wartime lectures with a collection for something specific, such as a plane or a minesweeper. In October 1940, they bought a second-hand Austin, primarily for Ernan to drive Phyllis to her lecturing commitments. Petrol, like food and clothes, was rationed and made available according to a 'points' system, but she had a special allowance authorised by the MOI. During the war she did a massive amount of lecturing in England, Wales and Scotland – Aberdeen, Alnwick, Birmingham, Bristol, Camelford, Canterbury, Darlington, Dover, Dunblane, Edinburgh, Exeter, Hartlepool, Hexham, Kettering, Leicester, Liverpool, London, Middlesborough, Newquay, Nottingham, Paignton, Penzance, Peterborough, Plymouth, Prestwick, Rutland, Swindon, Torquay – in factories, in public libraries, in schools, in universities, in town halls, for the National Council for Women,[7] for Workers Association meetings and for Rotary Clubs.[8]

Phyllis was an inspirational lecturer; she had a phenomenal memory and needed no notes, and she had honed her skills on the Colston Leigh tours in America. The artist and writer, Allen Freer, now over eighty, recalls Phyllis's visit to Alderman Newton's Boys' School in Leicester when he was a fourteen-year-old schoolboy.

> I remember Phyllis Bottome vividly – irrepressibly lively and fluent, eager to speak up for the Free World. I seem to recall her love for

> and her enthusiasm for her 'dear friend Alfred Adler' (her words), whose teachings she endeavoured to embody in her approach to education … [9] Her personality was, in the best sense, lively and flamboyant. For schoolboys – grammar-school boys – we were subdued and provincial; Miss Bottome was a figure larger than life, with a richness of European acquaintance – at the centre of which was the psychologist, Alfred Adler. This was the first whiff I experienced of *Mitteleuropäische* culture and I've never quite forgotten it. Nobody had ever spoken to us about psychology before, nor of what had gone on in Vienna, but here was someone who had had this experience first hand and had the vivacity and eagerness to pass it on … what doesn't fade is this eager, ardent lady totally convinced of the value of her experience and hell-bent to pass it on to her young listeners.[10]

Phyllis, although she was certainly not conventionally beautiful, nevertheless cut a glamorous figure. Ever since she had been taken in hand and groomed by her aristocratic advisors in Vienna in the 1920s, she took dressing for public appearances as a necessary part of her job. Ernan spent quite a lot of his time fighting the taxman's demands, and he included such items as a green velvet dress from Harvey Nichols in Knightsbridge and Elizabeth Arden cosmetics from Bond Street in claims against earnings.[11] Her unruly hair was always a problem, but she usually tucked it under an elegant hat.

During all this era of trying to keep up morale in Britain, Phyllis was simultaneously struggling with health problems. Increasingly she was troubled by a sharp pain which ran from under her right arm up into her shoulder. In May 1941, the mysterious trouble was traced to a lump in her breast, diagnosed by her doctor as cancer. In June, she underwent an operation to remove the malignant lump, followed by a convalescent stay at the Wayside Nursing Home, in Maidenhead.[12] In August she was fitted with a radium plaque to prevent the return of the cancer and it made her feel very sick. She bore all of this with her usual stoicism, finally allowing herself to feel a bit sorry for herself when, to top everything, she suffered badly from cystitis. But by September, her surgeon confirmed that the treatment was succeeding and that she was on the road to recovery.

Nothing, of course, ever stopped Phyllis writing. She produced a short novel, *London Pride*, published in November 1941, and asked for complimentary copies to be sent to various friends: Ivor Novello, Ellen Wilkinson, Marius Goring, Storm Jameson and Phyllis Bentley. The novel was dedicated to 'The Children of Bermondsey and Bethnal Green' and its epigraph was from William Blake's 'Jerusalem':

> I will not cease from mental fight,
> Nor shall my sword sleep in my hand
> Till we have built Jerusalem
> In England's green and pleasant land.

The novel, like the polemical *Mansion House of Liberty*, invokes the notion of the people's war. It honours the spirit of working-class people in the Blitz, and is a hymn of love to London. It centres on the Barton family, the name surely a subliminal reminder of the working-class Manchester family in Elizabeth Gaskell's novel *Mary Barton*. Phyllis's story opens with Mrs Barton, a charwoman, giving birth to her fifth baby, aptly named Ben, just as Big Ben strikes midnight. Mr Barton, a docker, is a Communist, and as such is suspicious of government plans to evacuate children out of the danger areas into the country. The narrative drive finally brings Mr Barton to feel that his first loyalty is to serve Britain rather than a fantasy of a Russian-style utopia. He and his eldest son, Bert, sign on for rescue work, digging trapped people and dead bodies out of the bombed-out houses: ' "It ain't British!" Bert said darkly to his father on their way to the docks. "Thet's wot I don't 'old wiv' – we got ter do something abaht it!" To Bert's surprise, his father did not remind him that Moscow was the place to look for orders; he actually repeated his son's words as if they had reached a similar chord in his own breast.'[13]

After young Ben has been badly injured in a bombing, Mrs Barton is induced to stand up to her husband and insist that Ben should be evacuated to Bude to be kept safe. She cunningly brings her husband's own arguments to bear against him:

> 'Communists,' she said a little uncertainly, 'they 'ave a saying wot you've always told me, "Each for each, an' all for each" . . . Mr Barton

> stared with indignant astonishment at his wife. What did she mean by quoting his own wisdom against him in such an aggravating manner? And why did she put it so well, when, as a rule, she was as hopeless at putting her thoughts into words as he would have been assembling ingredients for a pudding?
>
> 'You're mixed,' he said with an angry snort, 'that's Christianity not Communism, you're torkin'. Wimmin's 'eads carn't stan' up aginst these air raids – thet's wot it is!'[14]

There are elements of social comedy, lightly drawn, throughout this small book, which shows women – working-class women, hospital nurses, upper-class women – all taking responsibility not only for their families but also for others, with an increasingly enlarged sense of 'community' in response to attack from hostile forces. City children evacuated to the country find it wild and strange, just as the country folk find the city children hard to understand. All social classes, from city and country, have a sense of what it might be to be British, and this, if not always clearly articulated by all members of society, is represented as an independent spirit that will resist fascism. The central metaphor of resistance is little Ben dancing in the air-raid shelter, which distracted the fearful people waiting out another dreadful night's bombardment, listening to the 'cruel senseless barking of the guns' overhead.[15] Phyllis knew that Britain in wartime was more a notion than a nation, and that notions were a writer's medium. And a song-writer's too, thinking of Ivor Novello's song 'We'll Gather Lilacs', which became one of the theme songs of the Second World War. It is also to be noted that in spring 1941, Noel Coward wrote a song called 'London Pride'.

However, both Phyllis and Ernan found the Methodist spirit in Bude somewhat trying and started to feel that they might find more congenial company in St Ives. Phyllis had earned 25,000 dollars from MGM for the sale of the rights to *The Mortal Storm*. Although paying tax on it of sixteen and a half per cent, it was still a tidy sum, and she had received about 6,000 dollars, too, for the screen rights of her novel *Danger Signal*. This meant that they could afford to buy, rather than rent, a house.[16] Phyllis had fallen in love with St Ives on a visit during the First World

War years, and had set a story, 'The Derelict', about a sex-worker who had become an artists' model, there. Her description then was:

> The lower part of St Ives has a strange affinity to rocks, and the houses hang and cling together, up the short uneven streets, like a heap of shells. Above it are reared the stately biscuit-boxes designed for lodgings, so readily found in all English watering places; and around the village, in a wide half-circle, stretches the murmurous blue bay ... On the left of St Ives a small green flap of land runs out into the sea. It is known as the Island, and beyond it the coast spreads, bleak and wild, free of bungalows and railway lines, a land of elfin enchantment, meagre and rock-strewn, the haunt of old secrets, a dumb, close-lipped companion of the sea ... Sometimes the Island would blaze up with all the colours under the sun: light-red table-cloths, sky-blue overalls, pink garments of singular shapes and sizes, blew and unfurled themselves on washing-day ... A catch had just come in; the bay was filled with the swooping, swirling lightning of the sea-gulls' wings, and the little fisher houses, crowding down to the brim of the bay, their roofs aslant, and silvery with rain-washed slate, seemed on the verge of joining in the flight.[17]

Ernan located a lovely house called Red Willows in the Belyars district of St Ives. It was perched high up on the hill overlooking the blue sea below, well above the strong fishy smells below where working-class people and, more recently, impoverished artists tended to live. Phyllis went ahead, reporting back to Ernan, still doing his duty in Bude:

> DEAREST LOVE – You shall have the first letter I write in the house you have given me! It is indeed enchantment ... We have Miss Jeans hurling boxes into box-room. Curtain hangers hanging curtains ... I think the little house *perfect*! I cannot imagine *ever* leaving it unless it was torn from us by enemy action![18]

The curtains being fitted were, of course, blackout curtains: the police and the ARP enforced blackout regulations strictly and fined anyone who showed a light at night ten pounds. But, more pleasurably, Phyllis enjoyed the recovery of her furniture, which had been in store while they rented in Bude and was now being tucked into the new house.

Phyllis had to learn to use the Aga, as it was almost impossible to get cooks in wartime. Phyllis's sister Mary moved into a small hotel in St Ives to be near and yet maintain her independence, and possibly to avoid Phyllis's inexpert cooking.

Neither Phyllis nor Ernan was allowed to offer jobs to refugee friends because the whole of Cornwall was a Defence Area, but, as usual, she and Ernan were working in other ways to help refugees, sending hundreds of letters to people they thought could help. Phyllis often made a point of saying in her letters: 'Ever since I wrote *The Mortal Storm* I have felt myself proud to be acknowledged as the friend and ally of the Jewish people and have loved to serve their cause.'[19] Phyllis as always needed to earn her living, but even so, she did not always accept payment for her work. Sending an article to Viscountess Margaret Rhondda, the editor of the liberal feminist weekly *Time and Tide*, Phyllis said, 'If you would like to use the enclosed for *Time and Tide*, I should be delighted for you to do so. I take no payment for what I do for the Jews, so if you wish to use the enclosed, please credit any Refugee Society with what *Time and Tide* pays for it.'[20] *Time and Tide* had an outstanding record in the fight against anti-Semitism.

In August 1940, Phyllis paid the fare for Adler's son-in-law Heinz Sternberg to go to San Francisco; it is to be noted that in America he changed his name to Harry Starr in the hopes of assimilating. In 1941, Ernan heard from Robert Pollak in California that he had received bad news from Vienna: 'They sent all the remaining Jews to Poland – i.e. to Death. Fritzi Gutterman, our cousin, and her husband sent an alarming telegram a few days ago, asking us to pay for tickets for their passage from Lisbon to N.Y. which we did immediately. Will they get permission to leave Vienna?'[21]

No doubt Ernan would have pulled what strings he could. In England they worked hard on behalf of Adler's friend, Ladislaus Zilahi ('Laci'), who had been the editor of the *International Journal of Individual Psychology*.[22] Although himself a Catholic, his wife Agnes was Jewish and therefore his daughter, Clara, was also a Jew. Ernan and Phyllis had helped to get the family into Britain in 1939, and even though they could provide evidence that Laci had been an anti-Nazi leader writer on the Vienna *Telegraf*, it took a strenuous campaign to achieve British Nationality for him.[23] Ernan introduced him to Lord Vansittart and subsequently Laci was brought into a confidential government service known as the Political Warfare Department.[24] As he was to write to Ernan, 'Without you and her I would not be alive today; nor would Agnes and Clara; nor would many, very many others.'[25] Unfortunately Laci's work was in a protected area so his wife and daughter were not allowed to join him. They were left behind in Liverpool, where Agnes was very unhappy. Phyllis and Ernan went to a great deal of trouble finding happier digs for them with a Quaker family. One of Laci's jobs was to translate suitable material for broadcasting to Austrians; for example, he translated Phyllis's *Formidable to Tyrants*, plus a script she wrote for a radio play, where a German and an English pilot discussed their politics, and an appeal she made to German mothers.[26]

They also helped Phyllis's erstwhile Viennese milliner, Irene Spierer, and her husband Julius to enter Britain, and then helped Irene to start up a hat shop at 28 South Audley Street in London. Irene's husband was interned in Liverpool as an 'enemy alien' during the war, but on his release at the end of the war, the Forbes Dennises helped them both to resettle in America with letters of introduction and money.[27] For the rest of her life, Phyllis was to be seen on public occasions in supremely stylish hats, courtesy of Irene.

One surprise during this grim time was a contact from Valerie Adler, whose soup kitchens in Vienna Phyllis had supported in the early 1920s:

> … we received a telephone message from Vienna, a mysterious anonymous message such as we were constantly receiving from those the Nazis persecuted at that time. It was Valerie' s voice. Her husband was dead. She had succeeded in saving their one child and getting him to America, but she had been robbed of every penny she possessed, and was in danger of death. She could not get a visa unless a job was found for her in England. My husband was working night and day to help refugees escaping from Hitler; and by a fortunate chance I had lately met Lady Gladstone; and through her kind help a post was found for Valerie to act as a cook to Haile Selassie, the Emperor of Ethiopia. Valerie worked for him for a

year before being [able] to join her son in America. It was a strange quirk of fortune that she, who had saved such thousands of lives in Vienna in 1920, should be hounded out of it into sudden penury, and threatened by a cruel death, in 1938.[28]

The situation for Jewish refugees was often desperate and at best deeply unpleasant. About eleven thousand Jewish refugees had been spread across Europe when war broke out. And many more were stuck awaiting immigration visas, or some other necessary piece of paper. The outbreak of war triggered the internment of 'enemy aliens'; British intelligence agents had the difficult job of distinguishing between helpless victims of persecution and Nazi secret agents. In Britain, the catastrophic defeats of spring 1940 were attributed – partly at least – to the activities of fifth columnists. Around twenty-seven thousand 'enemy aliens' found themselves interned in barbed-wire camps, the largest number being sent to the Isle of Man. Seven thousand were dispatched overseas under the re-emigration policy to Canada, Australia and the dominions.[29] Phyllis gave money to the Central British Fund for Jewish Relief and Rehabilitation and also delivered public talks on behalf of the British Association for the Jewish National Home in Palestine.[30]

However, she felt desperate to get down to working on her new novel. As she wrote to Storm Jameson in December 1941, 'I am earning my living by my work, and last year did nothing but work for the Ministry of Information and a propaganda book for America, on England ... I have only just recovered from a pretty serious operation.'[31] Storm Jameson was a novelist whose work Phyllis had greatly admired ever since reading her 1936 novel *In the Second Year*, which imagined what Britain would be like under fascist rule. Storm was in more senses than one a similar spirit. From 1938 and throughout the war, she was president of British PEN (Poets, Essayists and Novelists), which was then, as now, a forum for liberal-left writers. Like Phyllis, Storm Jameson wanted the novel 'to perform a double function, to offer a critique of society and also hold out the prospect of its renewal'.[32] Similarly, Storm was engaged with helping refugees; her husband, the socialist historian Guy Chapman, said of his wife that she was 'incapable of the saving egoism of your dedicated writer'.[33]

Phyllis was especially keen to get to work on her 'refugee novel [because] I don't think their mentality is understood by most people. My own sympathy is with men of middle age, who in full career, have been pulled up short. They feel their powers urging them on and do not know in what direction they will ever be able to use them again.'[34] In July 1943 she lectured on 'Anti-Semitism' in Penzance, and followed this up on 17 August by writing to the librarian at the Free Library in Penzance asking her to remove a poisonously anti-Semitic book from its shelves. Phyllis considered that working-class people were sympathetic to the plight of the Jews, but ' … the people I am afraid of are the middle and tradesmen class. The middle think it's 'smart' to dislike Jews – the tradesmen fear competition … you may be interested that I made my new hero in *Within the Cup*, coming out August 20th, a Jewish doctor – on purpose of course to exploit what sympathy I could, but also because the best men I have ever known were Jewish doctors.'[35] Thinking of her readership, she was well aware that people get bored with victims, and so her strategy in this novel was to acknowledge all her protagonist had lost, but to concentrate more on what he had to offer his new country.

This novel, about a Viennese doctor living as a refugee in England, was published in 1943 in Britain as *Within the Cup* and in America under the title *Survival.*[36] It was dedicated 'To those Pilgrims of Eternity whose home is Austria'. Its protagonist, Rudi von Ritterhaus, is the son of a general who fought in the First World War and a Jewish mother who died when he was ten. Rudi is represented as having been brought up as a Catholic in Vienna, his mother having given up her Jewish faith upon her marriage. He is depicted as having worked with Alfred Adler for three years until Adler, foreseeing what would happen to his beloved Austria, left for America. Rudi stayed on in Vienna with his wife Klara and son Andreas. His wife had left him when being married to a Jew struck her as unseemly and she had returned to her family, taking their son with her. Rudi found his dog hanging under his window with a note around its neck on which was written, 'Jews *are* dogs – they have no need to keep them.'[37] His good English friends, James and Eunice Wendover, arranged a permit to allow Rudi into England, where he joined their household in Oxford while they set about trying to find him a job.

The book, unusually for Phyllis, is written in the first person, as though by Rudi himself. This gives her the advantage of describing the English from the stance of an outsider, a feeling she had herself experienced when returning to England after living for twenty years in mainland Europe. Rudi, who has lost everything, describes himself as a ghost inhabiting a strange world:

> People think of Refugees as unfortunate people who have lost their homes, suffered various painful experiences, and been driven out of their country in a moneyless and embarrassing condition – embarrassing of course both for themselves and for their hosts – but we are something quite different. We are human beings changed in essence. Many people have left home before and started, penniless, new lives in foreign countries after bitter personal experiences, and yet remained much the same people that they were before these events took place. But those whom Hitler and Mussolini drove out, passed through a unique experience. The web of their lives was torn before their eyes into useless fragments. There was no security of soul, mind or body that was left to them.[38]

In the novel, as in reality, the General Medical Council refused to open its doors to Austrian doctors, so Rudi can serve his new country as a psychologist, but not a medical doctor.[39] He stays with Lord Wendover's family in this capacity, until the family house, five miles from Plymouth, is turned into an evacuation hospital for a bombed-out hospital in London. Ultimately, Rudi is recognised by all as a hero, both within the Wendover family, where he is a healing influence, and by the community at large. Overall the narrative establishes that although the British have many excellent qualities, an injection of Jewish intellectual *sprezzatura* is beneficial, not only to broken bodies and minds, but also to the body politic.

Phyllis Lassner in her critique of this novel considers that 'the analogy here between this English family system and the system that produced the death camps is neither gratuitous nor does it elide their differences'.[40] Rudi has learned his social democratism in 'Red Vienna'. Although he comes to love the daughter of the house, Gillian Wendover, he cannot tolerate her class-conscious attitudes. He says to her:

'You've got to choose today between being a person who hates – a Hitlerite, or his chief enemy, a person who loves – a lover of Life! Life is universal, it belongs equally to all of us! If you are a lover, you can't despise – if you're a hater, you can't respect – another human being. ... As I see it – we have to get rid of this top-dog world – out of which all murder springs! – Russians – Americans – Chinese – we ourselves! We must prove ourselves the spiritual enemies of the Nazis. This sense of superiority is the dead tissue of the cancer cell that must be cut away from us before victory comes, or else a new cancer will form itself.'[41]

This theme, that winning the war was only the first stage of the process, increasingly informed the talks Phyllis gave.

Then she ran into trouble. The MOI objected to one of her lectures that was called 'Our New Order or Hitler's?', and would not approve it, mistakenly believing that it had a party-political agenda. She refuted this, regarding it as liberal only in the broadest sense. Writing to protest on 24 May 1943, Phyllis said, 'I speak from the ... standpoint of Christian and democratic logic, which I take to be the exact opposite of Hitler's ... I belong to no political party and I seek to substantiate, rather than to impede British unity.'[42] Faced with this obstacle, her initial response was to publish a collection of essays, from both American and British statesmen and writers, entitled, like the banned lecture, *Our New Order or Hitler's?* In the Preface she outlined her central concerns for winning the peace:

Hitler has narrowed a human being into the least responsible and rigid type – that of a gangster gunman. Our best leaders, on both sides of the Atlantic, have done the exact opposite; they are trying to release human beings, and make more adjustable and less limited the conditions of human life ... Until we are prepared to act upon our principles with the same force and conviction with which the Nazis carry out their crimes, we cannot claim to be democrats or Christians.

Some distressing correspondence followed which resulted in her resignation on 28 March 1944: ' ... I must now publicly withdraw from my long efforts to work for the MOI. I cancelled my lecture tour in the USA in May 1940 and returned here, in order to be of service to my own country; and at the desire of Mr Duff Cooper joined the Speakers Panel of MOI. I was not asked at this time to submit my lectures to any form of censorship.'[43] She went on to give the offending lecture at her own expense at various venues, including the Wigmore Hall; the crux of its argument was that Britain must establish itself as a liberal democracy after the war, and not slip into the Scylla and Charybdis of communism or fascism itself.

Until this quarrel erupted, Phyllis had lectured tirelessly for the MOI all round the country. And, indeed, she faced the usual dangers during the course of these speaking tours. In both autumn 1942 and spring 1943 she and Ernan 'had several narrow squeaks. Once I drove through a blazing London Blitz to the BBC to speak on "Democracy" to the USA and once [I was] breakfasting in the Strand [when] a bomb dropped almost at Nelson's feet.'[44]

London and other major cities were the most brutally blitzed, but nowhere in England was immune to wartime conditions and dangers. Though Phyllis and Ernan were living in comparative comfort and safety in Cornwall, even there, on 25 January 1941, a German parachute mine had been dropped close to the potter Bernard Leach's home. Five people were injured that night, although luckily no one was killed. In April 1941, Plymouth was badly bombed; Phyllis wrote to *The Times*, telling readers that the library there had lost three-quarters of its books and asking people to send books, because, she wrote: 'in helping to rebuild and refurnish Plymouth's library your readers will defeat one of Hitler's main objects: the downfall of the mind and the spirit'.[45] During the summer of 1942, the German Luftwaffe mounted a series of 'hit and run' raids on English coastal towns; on the afternoon of 28 August, two enemy aircraft crossed St Ives Bay and attacked the gasworks just above Portmeor beach (now converted into Tate St Ives). After dropping the bombs the planes returned to machine-gun people on the beaches.[46] Phyllis described such occurrences fairly dispassionately:

> Curiously enough we were twice nearly killed in the safest spots, once through night bombing, and once through two fast planes

> coming in under cloud from the sea and bombing and machine gunning the beach on which we were bathing. Fortunately the shape of the beach gave a bad angle of fire, so that the bathers were more startled than hurt. I only grasped these were enemy machines as I watched little black oblong parcels being dropped through blue air.[47]

No one was killed on the beach itself that day, but a bomb from the second aircraft killed a woman called Kitty James, and nine other people were seriously injured, including a woman who had to have a foot amputated.

Aside from wartime battles, Phyllis was being harassed by the taxman. Ernan, who managed their business affairs, agreed at the beginning of 1942, under 'strong protest', to a compromise solution with the Commissioner of Taxes. He pointed out that, among other things, the cost of collecting material in 1938/9 for *Within the Cup* had been very expensive, and queried whether it was 'the intention of the authorities to discourage artists from taking business journeys?'[48] Largely, the tax demands were due to the exceptional income from selling the film rights to both *Danger Signal* and *The Mortal Storm* within a short space of time. In 1939, Warner had bought an option on *Danger Signal* because they saw it as a vehicle for Bette Davis in the role of a *femme fatale*.[49] Unfortunately the Hays Office considered that the story was morally objectionable, and Phyllis had fallen out – perhaps unfairly – with her American agent, Ann Watkins, over her handling of the sale. Written just before war started, it was a psychological thriller, dedicated 'To my friend Alexandra Adler, MD'. It focuses on a young, intelligent lower-middle-class woman, Hilda Fenchurch, seduced by an upper-class charmer who lodges at her parents' house. When he drops her and sets about seducing her younger sister, Annie, Hilda is moved to try to kill him. She is rescued from her acute homicidal state by a woman psychologist and restored to her previous sane self. It is tempting to speculate how much Phyllis was thinking about Ian Fleming as a type when she created the predatory male character who caused such mayhem. A line in the film version has the psychologist, Dr Siller, saying, 'An interesting study, that man, rather complicated ... He spent his adult life in pursuit of women; at the same time he had no respect for them. Men like that can be fascinating and dangerous. They prey on women and very often the women love it.'

Much changed, and re-set in America, *Danger Signal* was finally screened in 1945; in all, twenty-five writers were involved in the attempt to make the screenplay into something that would be accepted by Hays and his committee. The film, directed by Robert Florey, is not without interest to lovers of *film noir*.[50] Zachary Scott, who plays the anti-hero, rather cornered the market in handsome but sociopathic predators; he took a similar role in another example of the genre, *Mildred Pierce*, which premièred the same year. Rosemary DeCamp, an underrated but fine actress, gives a convincing performance as the woman psychologist, a type not often seen in Hollywood films. DeCamp herself said that *Danger Signal* was her favourite of 'three *film noir* appearances, citing her "smart and sophisticated" wardrobe and her enjoyment at playing the clever Viennese psychiatrist'.[51] Almost against the odds, the film turned out reasonably well; reviews were varied, but most regarded the film as both clever and interesting, and commended DeCamp's striking performance.[52]

Despite frustrations with both the taxman and the MOI, Phyllis was delighted with the move to St Ives. The first friends they made were the Arnold-Fosters, whom she strongly approved of as never-failingly wise and active citizens. Will Arnold-Foster, whose first wife, Ka Cox, had been an intimate friend of Virginia Woolf in their youth, had, after Ka's death from a heart attack in 1938, married Ka's close friend, Ruth. Will was a Labour MP and a noted garden designer who had created a magnificent garden at his house, Eagle's Nest, at Zennor, close to St Ives.[53] As soon as they moved into Red Willows, Will had asked Phyllis to serve on the West Cornwall Committee of the Ministry of Information, as they had heard of what she had done to enliven the East Cornwall Committee while in Bude.[54] Sadly, Phyllis's new friendship with Ruth Arnold-Foster came to an abrupt end when, at the beginning of June 1942, Ruth died from breast cancer.[55]

Much of the attraction of St Ives was the extraordinary density of creative people in one small town, which was largely a result of Londoners self-evacuating to Cornwall. Phyllis always enjoyed the company of artists, an experience she had first encountered when she had lived in Capri. Almost next door to Red Willows, the painter Peter Lanyon had his studio. Through Peter, Phyllis and Ernan were introduced to the Arts Club, open to artists, writers, actors and musicians. It met in an old half-boarded building in the Warren and was the centre of St Ives' vibrant culture. Plays were performed there, dances held and a reading-room kept for members.

Phyllis inevitably saw herself as something of a champion for the artists' colony; for example, she wrote to the Ministry of Labour in support of the potter Bernard Leach's request to employ two or three old men in the district who were not employed in war work.[56] To her indignation, this was refused, although Will Arnold-Foster had warned her off getting involved in this issue as one of Bernard's sons, David Leach, was in prison as a conscientious objector, and he already had another 'conchie' at work at the pottery plus several boys.[57] Inevitably, with so many local men and women away at war, feelings in some quarters ran high against the small number of conscientious objectors in the area. And local people tended to associate 'conchiness' with the artistic community. This was not entirely fair, as Bernard Leach joined the Home Guard, and Sven Berlin overcame earlier doubts and joined the Royal Artillery; but this feeling persisted.

The Forbes Dennises also met, or rather re-met, Maxwell Laurie whom, with his wife Marjorie, they had first met in Mösern. He had been a government official in Burma and she was a daughter of Sir George White, Governor of Burma.[58] She was a gifted linguist and translator for her brother-in-law, T. Werner Laurie, who was the publisher of Upton Sinclair's World's End Series. Phyllis remained in touch with Upton, thanking him for sending her his first two novels in the series that fictively chronicled the political events from the First World War through the intervening years and into the Second World War. The second of these novels was dedicated to 'My friends in England who are living under the bombs'. Just as Phyllis established her character of Freya Toller (or Roth in the American edition) to interrogate the rise of fascism in *The Mortal Storm*, Sinclair had created a 'useful' hero, Lanny Budd, whose character develops from a dilettante playboy to a brave and committed anti-Nazi secret agent during the course of the series.[59] Writing to congratulate Upton in May 1942, Phyllis commented:

> I do feel as if modern history was unrolling itself page by aching page, before my eyes. I doubt if anyone but you has ever plunged into this flood and brought out its anything but sacred mysteries to the light, in so relentless a manner. I am sure no one can contradict a single fact you have mentioned, and will see them infinitely more clearly because of the story – since only through individuals can one see the living-out of events. Events are really, if we only realised it, people outside in; and produced by those who live inside out. In a certain sense it is true to say that Nazism is Hitler, England – Churchill, America – Roosevelt, China – Chiang Kai Shek; and Lanny is certainly Europe at its very best, struggling against forces which no one in time, with sufficient power, fully understood.[60]

Some time towards the end of 1942, Phyllis met Richard Hillary, who was the author of a recently published memoir, *The Last Enemy*.[61] It graphically describes his career as a pilot and his experience of being shot down during the Battle of Britain and horribly burned on his face and hands. Subsequently he spent months in hospital having repeated operations, largely carried out by the gifted surgeon Archibald MacIndoe, and during this time wrote his book. Once out of hospital, he had persuaded the Air Ministry to send him to the Unites States on a speaking tour, but the British Embassy there thought that his scarred face might increase isolationist tendencies, and restricted him to radio broadcasts. He was, even following his injuries, enormously attractive to women; he had an affair in America with the film star Merle Oberon, which probably helped him get over his deep attachment to his best friend Peter Pease's fiancée, Denise, following Peter's death.[62] Phyllis wrote to congratulate him on the book in July 1942, offering him advice on getting it made into a Hollywood film. She told him that by a coincidence the man he hero-worshipped, Peter Pease, 'is my second cousin, which does not mean much to me as I never had time or the kind of life that went with those rich cousins, but Peter himself came to see me in Munich in 1932–3 and made an extraordinary impression on my husband and myself.'[63]

Although Phyllis had no children of her own, she had enormous empathy with the problems of the young. In particular, she seems to have had very strong relationships with young men. Richard went to see Phyllis and Ernan twice and they had two three-hour conversations with him; he was determined to fly again in order, he said, to keep faith with his dead comrades, although Phyllis attempted to dissuade him. He had by this time fallen in love with Mary Booker, a woman twenty-two years his senior with whom he seemed to find some peace of mind. In a letter to Mary, Richard commented: 'Phyllis Bottome said that it was only Nazis who forced themselves to do things and that that way was unnatural for me. I should like to believe her now, but perhaps that is just the bleat of fear.'[64]

Phyllis attempted to impart to Richard her concept of false (Wagnerian) courage, an issue she had explored in *The Mortal Storm*. However, he was not to be shaken in his decision to return to active service. Tragically he was shot down and killed in January 1943. Phyllis was exceedingly distressed and outraged that the RAF had allowed him to fly again with such damaged hands. Hillary's publisher, Rache Lovat Dickson at Macmillan, started a scheme to publish a book of essays about him that would include one by Phyllis, one by Arthur Koestler and one by Eric Linklater. However, Phyllis's essay, entitled 'Richard Hillary and the RAF', was not approved, so she contented herself with publishing an extract from it called 'Serpent-Doves' on 15 October 1943 in *The Spectator*.

Hillary's parents wished Phyllis to write a full biography of their dead son, and she certainly considered doing so, although Lovat Dickson told her that she was not the right person for the job. Phyllis wrote to him suggesting that he might be wrong, and that she might understand Hillary rather better than he thought. 'Young men show a very different side of themselves to an old woman whom they trust than to anyone else. They are off their guard: not competing: have nothing very much at stake: are in no danger of losing head or heart and have found a good audience.'[65] But by March 1945 Phyllis had decided to abandon her efforts to publish Hillary's biography because of 'the minds and nerves of his parents', who 'simply can't give a biographer a free hand'.[66] In particular, they would not consent to her including his letters to her that showed his psychological development over the period he had known Phyllis and Ernan. She had wanted to contrast letters that were full of the joys of life, with the ones when 'his days were numbered'.[67] Phyllis was devastated that Hillary had, from her Adlerian perspective, chosen a false prestige-goal of heroism that had led to his death.

Phyllis became increasingly interested in writing biography in a new way. She wrote portraits of six of her friends in the form of Adlerian case studies and, in 1944, she published them in a collection called *From the Life*.[68] Three of them – Alfred Adler, Sara Delano Roosevelt and her grandmother, Margaret Macdonald Bottome – were no longer alive. The others, Max Beerbohm, Ivor Novello and Ezra Pound, were alive and were offered the chance to object to her 'analyses' being published. One essay that was not to see the light of day was that on Dorothy Thompson, who told Phyllis in no uncertain terms that it was an invasion of privacy and a misuse of friendship. Arguably this is a problem with Adlerian psychology – at least as it was practised then – in that the private/public boundaries could become somewhat blurred. Dorothy was especially incensed because Phyllis appeared to blame her for Sinclair Lewis's alcoholism, stating that it was caused by Dorothy's withdrawal of love after the birth of their child. And indeed this was wholly unfair. Lewis was an alcoholic even during his first marriage to Grace – his publishers had paid to get him dried out on several occasions – and, although he managed to get his drinking under control for a period right at the beginning of his marriage to Dorothy, she can hardly be held responsible for his falling off the wagon. Presumably he had not been drinking heavily on the occasions when Phyllis had first met him and this may have misled her, but it seems an extraordinary failure of common sense on Phyllis's part to suggest that anyone but the person themselves can be held responsible for their own actions. What is especially odd is that it runs counter to Adlerian teaching, as Adler regarded these kinds of excuses as alibis. In the Introduction to *From the Life*, Phyllis says:

> In using my personal friendships with them as a vehicle for these studies I run a certain risk – the risk of their resentment or disapproval; and perhaps that of the public as well, but I run the risk with my eyes

> open, believing that in the present day we need as never before to study the processes of man's spirit; and that we cannot do better than to take for such a study those spirits who have made, or who are still making, a definite contribution to the times in which they live.[69]

Although Ernan sent several letters to Dorothy in his best persuasive and diplomatic style, trying to mend broken fences, the unpublished essay cost Phyllis her friendship with Dorothy. Dorothy never forgave her.

By May 1945, the Germans were facing defeat; surrender in Europe arrived at five minutes to midnight on 8 May. Throughout Europe, former prisoners of war were being flown back to Britain. Phyllis's friend, Ed Murrow, the CBS war correspondent, travelling with the Thunderbirds division of the American army, arrived with them to liberate the Buchenwald camp just outside Weimar. Broadcasting on 15 April, he described the barracks: 'When I entered men crowded around, tried to lift me to their shoulders. They were too weak. Many of them could not get out of bed. I was told that this building had once stabled eighty horses. There were twelve hundred men in it, five to a bunk. The stink was beyond all description.'[70] This broadcast was the first to try to describe the horrors of what would become known as the Holocaust. One by one, every German concentration camp came into Allied hands, but many thousands of the inmates were too sick to survive, despite the food and medical care rushed to them. Mass movements of refugees and displaced persons began.

Japan, on the other hand, refused to accept the unconditional surrender demanded of them by the Potsdam Declaration. On the night of 5 August the Americans dropped the newly developed atomic bomb on Hiroshima; on 9 August, another atomic bomb was dropped on Nagasaki. The horrors wrought by this 'new and most cruel bomb', which could do incalculable damage, persuaded Emperor Hirohito to accept on 10 August that Japan must 'bear the unbearable' shame of unconditional surrender.[71] The war, with its almost unimaginable human cost, was finally over. Now, Phyllis set out to win the peace.

During the war, as an MOI speaker, Phyllis had felt that it was important not to be identified with one particular political party. But once the war was over she felt free to become a publicly committed member of the Liberal Party, and indeed became president of the St Ives branch. She was very much a local celebrity, giving talks to young Liberals on the challenge to the young to take responsibility for the making of the new world. She opened art exhibitions and fêtes, and launched fundraising appeals for all sorts of worthy causes.[72]

Her first book to appear immediately post-war was *The Life Line*, published in 1946 by Faber & Faber in Britain and by Little, Brown in America. This was a study of the anti-Nazi underground forces in Europe, and was dedicated 'To Luischen of North Tyrol'.[73] Its focus is what happens to a decent sort of educated Englishman, Mark Chalmers, a master at Eton, when faced with extraordinary circumstances. Until 1938, when the narrative begins, Mark Chalmers had believed that this public-school code was enough to live by:

> Perhaps half of the boys went to Eton because their parents wanted them to be grand – and the other half because it was a family tradition to go there if you could. The boys that wanted to be grand – if they were like their parents, and it had to be remembered that boys very often weren't – *did* pick up all Eton's strange faults and absurdities; its isolationism; its defensive arrogance; its inconsiderate insolence; and its deep unconscious selfishness.[74]

Mark finds, after a briefing by the British Foreign Office, that he is starting to consider what Eton makes of its boys, compared with 'what Hitler had made of the Hitler Youth leaders. Hitler had airily stated that an English public school was the best training-ground for Nazi doctrines.'[75] Certainly, a sense that one's own nation was superior to any other, and an assumption that therefore it was its right to control an empire, was true of both Germany and Britain.

Mark has had little experience of thinking about the wider world. It is only as a consequence of his annual walking holidays in Austria and his being able to speak good German with an Austrian accent that he has been landed in the unexpected position of being recruited as a spy by his chum Reggie in the Foreign Office. Parachuted into Austria after the *Anschluss*, he is to pass as a manic-depressive in an asylum run by Dr Ida Eichhorn. Waiting with Father Martin, a monk who is his intermediary contact in the resistance movement, Mark watches as

> a slight, hatless figure in knee breeches, with a short blue canvas coat, scrambled over the rocks towards them. She was, Mark saw with disapproval, as she came nearer, exactly the kind of woman he didn't like. Her thick untidy ginger-coloured hair was cut close to her head, her face was inordinately white; she had not painted her lips, and she had the cold wild eyes of a sea bird. Her figure was wiry and without curves; she had no allure; no poise.[76]

Mark is thirty-six years old and his experience of women is limited; in particular, he is not used to dealing with a woman who regards herself as his intellectual equal. As Ida points out to him, his trajectory of a preparatory school, public school and Oxbridge is roughly equivalent to living in 'a cloister from ten to twenty', as a consequence of which 'he retains, in a certain portion of his brain, a one-sex world'.[77] Phyllis always expressed her distaste for any regime that kept women as second-class citizens; although it was a significant feature of Nazi Germany, she is also pointing out that educational reforms would be necessary for post-war Britain.

Initially, like many upper-class Englishmen, Mark has not regarded the regime in Germany as necessarily a bad thing, although he was upset by the occupation of his favourite country. It is Father Martin who makes him understand what to live under a Nazi regime really means:

> 'Do not think that Hitler is not prepared as well for a long war as for a short one! His whole country is permanently organised on a war footing. You do not know what that means. You who tie gas masks to your cricket bats, and still depend on horses and greyhounds to lift your untutored hearts! Remember and tell your people – the Germans are trained not only technically but spiritually for murder! Anti-Semitism is not a folly – it is an atrocious process – the Nazis manufacture cruelty – against defenceless Jews – so that a whole people may be ready to accept murder as a pastime without physical damage to themselves. The Jew is the trial rabbit on which to whet the appetite of the German nation towards destruction.[78]

The novel is among other things a *Bildungsroman* in that Mark begins the book thinking that he is 'exactly the kind of man he wanted to be', but has to reform his complacent concept of masculinity. Ida, the Adlerian psychologist, acts as the *provocateuse* who re-educates him.[79] Phyllis Lassner comments that within the novel, 'the success of Ida's experiment depends on rehabilitating those men self-consumed by Nazism by modelling them on her empathetic character, emphasizing caring principles of the feminine'.[80]

The novel exploits Gothic elements to make these points. Michael Salvatore, Ida's former lover, is an insane aristocrat whom Ida keeps in top security within the asylum, which was once his schloss. In Phyllis's novel, the mad creature locked away is not a wife, but a once glamorous and sensually attractive man. A further Gothic element, reminiscent of Oscar Wilde's *The Picture of Dorian Gray*, is the formal portrait of Salvatore who Mark perceives as being 'the handsomest man he had ever seen'.[81] What is now the cruel reality is finally revealed to him as 'a great, shaggy hair-grown figure [running] to and fro on all fours, very nimbly and tirelessly in spite of age, as if he were the wolf he now thought he was'.[82] The fierce hyper-masculinity of Salvatore as admired by Mark in his portrait is now revealed as not fully human. This theme, a critique of hyper-masculinity, arises from a clearly chartable feminist literary tradition. The nineteenth-century French writer George Sand explored it in her novel *Mauprat*, which, along with her other novels, was closely studied by both Charlotte and Emily Brontë. The representations of the wolf-like tendencies of both Rochester in *Jane Eyre* and Heathcliff in *Wuthering Heights*, before their moral education has been effected, can each be regarded as to some degree an *hommage* to their favourite woman writer.[83] Phyllis may or may not have read George Sand, but she was devoted to the work of the Brontë sisters, so is picking up on this powerful trope. Utilising this particular form of feminist Gothic, Phyllis adapts it to make a compelling psychological analysis of the connections between a perverse form of masculinity and fascism. By the end of the narrative, Mark's personal education causes him to eschew this form of masculinity and his political education means that he realises that not only have England and America their own internal problems, but also that they have been blind to their world obligations.

Throughout the novel there are examples of upper-class Austrians, such as Ida, and also peasants, such as the Planer family, who are in resistance to the Nazi spirit. But Phyllis also shows how some upper-class Austrians had bought into the deadly fascist ideology. In representing Salvatore as a fascist who believes that he is a werewolf, the psychological affinity with Hitler is clearly signalled. Phyllis creates an embodied metaphor to stand for the anti-human insanity of fascism. When interviewed about the book, she said:

> I invented the werewolf ... as part of the logic of the Nazi system. You see their logic is composed of fear, lies, force and hate. The direction is death. The werewolf is a killer going towards death. Unless we have an opposite logic of courage, truth, freedom and love which leads towards life, we are in danger of becoming Nazi. We must train ourselves.[84]

Writers, she said, more than ever, must be the world's peacemakers. *The Life Line* sold well. Phyllis was by this stage adept in combining what might seem like distinct elements of psychology, social criticism and political critique, all within a dramatic narrative that kept her readers eagerly turning the pages. When Phyllis went to America to promote her book she was repeatedly interviewed by the press. There, she was emphatically a celebrity author, fêted primarily because the force of *Private Worlds, The Mortal Storm* and *Danger Signal* had reached very large audiences, and book sales had been enhanced by the film versions.

Just after the war ended, Phyllis made a new friend who had also adopted Cornwall as her home: Daphne du Maurier. Although Daphne was twenty-five years younger, the two women had much else in common. They shared the interest of writing novels that included sharp analyses of states of mind, including the abnormal. Both had tried their hands at crime fiction, or at least had pushed at the boundaries of that genre; and they were 'old-fashioned' writers in the sense that they both saw themselves as working out of a tradition that followed that of the Brontë sisters, rather than taking a modernist turn. Daphne's best-selling novel *Rebecca* had been made into a Hollywood film in 1940, the same year that *The Mortal Storm* had taken Hollywood by storm.[85] The younger writer's novels were at that time usually regarded as romantic novels for women; she objected that hardly any of them had happy endings, and that *Rebecca* was a study in jealousy.[86] It seems clear that the two friends held a series of conversations, because in the winter of 1954 Daphne was busily studying the work of both Jung and Adler. Several of Daphne's novels after this point centred on sibling rivalry, which was one of Adler's chief contributions to psychology, and which Phyllis and Ernan had identified many years before as being one of Ian Fleming's major neurotic difficulties.[87] Daphne herself was a strikingly beautiful woman who was sexually attractive to both men and women. However, her sense of herself as having a second, partly but not completely repressed alter ego, 'the boy in the box', caused her great anxiety.[88] Daphne's husband 'Boy Browning' was a soldier turned diplomat, rather echoing Ernan's early career, so Daphne too had experienced a period of moving about the world as a result of her husband's career.[89] Nevertheless, the friendship was essentially a literary one; the two women sent each other their latest works, and compared notes about publishers. Daphne, on one occasion, commented that although she was a bit irritated with Gollancz, she could not face a change after thirty years. Publishers, wrote Daphne to Phyllis, 'are like public schools, depending on the character of the headmaster of the time'.[90]

Although the war was over, down in St Ives a localised war was going on among the artists. The official St Ives Society of Artists was dominated by old guard academics who made sure that their pictures were exhibited in pride of place. Phyllis's neighbour Peter Lanyon spearheaded a move towards getting the paintings of the younger generation (and one or two of the older generation who had 'converted' to more abstract ways of painting) some exhibition space in the crypt below the church.[91] All the 'moderns' defected to form a new group, the Penwith Society, Penwith being the name of the north side of the west Cornwall peninsula.[92] The Penwith Gallery exhibited pictures, but also pottery, sculpture, weaving, furniture and a variety of other crafts.[93] It was a time of experiment and change.

Loving the work of Cézanne and Picasso, Phyllis was excited by the abstract art she encountered at the first St Ives exhibition she attended after the end of the war. Clearly she did not agree with the strictures of

Kenneth Clark, the chair of the War Artists' Advisory Committee, who had castigated abstract art as being 'essentially German'.[94] Writing to Ernan in August 1947, she said, 'I enjoyed the Exhibition yesterday and thought it a very good one! Really interesting work by a small St Ives group – one a magnificent painter.'[95] The painter she regarded as the star of the exhibition was undoubtedly Ben Nicholson, of whom she said, 'the perfect cleanliness and precision of his work and the colour which is like light itself, give me the immensest pleasure'.[96] In June 1949, Phyllis was asked to preside over the first exhibition of the new Penwith Society, and she and Ernan became especially good friends with Ben Nicholson and Barbara Hepworth.[97] As Phyllis said, Ben, in particular, 'became one of our most intimate and valued friends'.[98] Ben Nicholson had married Barbara Hepworth in 1938, following his divorce from his first wife, and they had moved to St Ives just before the outbreak of war with their triplets, Simon, Rachel and Sarah, then aged five. If Ben and Barbara, as the outstandingly talented painter and sculptor that they were, were regarded as the king and queen of the artists' colony in St Ives, then Ernan and Phyllis seem to have adopted the role of the elder statesmen. Phyllis was always keen to champion colleagues in the face of bureaucracy. In 1950, writing to the *St Ives Times*, Phyllis expressed her 'shock' and 'grief' when the town council evicted the painter Sven Berlin in order to turn his studio into a public convenience.[99] Her letter, published under the title 'Superfluous Convenience', accused the council of being in effect dictatorial, refusing artists 'freedom to create'.[100] On another occasion, Phyllis wrote a furious letter to the editor of the *News Chronicle*, complaining that a reviewer had ridiculed Michael Tippett's opera *The Midsummer Marriage,* with a set designed by Barbara Hepworth, before he had either seen or heard it.[101]

Ernan, too, contributed to the cultural life of St Ives. He took on the role of impresario for the pianist and composer Desirée McEwan, organising concerts in the Guildhall for her in 1947, 1948, 1950 and 1955. He seems to have underwritten the costs of this enterprise, and did not come out of it with any profit. Through Barbara Hepworth they also became close friends with the avant-garde composer Priaulx Rainier, a fellow of the Royal Academy of Music, who came to live in St

Ives in the early 1950s.[102] In 1953 she helped established the St Ives Festival of Music and the Arts and persuaded Phyllis to be on the council. Ernan, again, made a donation to costs.[103]

A glimpse of the Forbes Dennises at this period is captured in a memoir by one of their neighbours. In 1948, Frank Halliday, his wife Nancie and their son Sebastian came to live next door to Red Willows. Following a career as a headmaster, culminating as head of English at Cheltenham College, he took early retirement, hoping to write on Shakespeare.[104] Phyllis and Ernan immediately introduced the Hallidays to the key players in the artists' colony. Frank describes a tea party at Red Willows as:

> just a little formal, Phyllis, all sails set and driven on the great gale of her vitality, impetuously leading the conversation, Ernan, as became a retired diplomat, more warily tacking, and courteously manoeuvring his guests into appropriate formations.[105]

Ernan carefully seated Frank next to Barbara so that they could talk about her triplets who were then attending Dartington Hall. What Frank may not have immediately realised was that many of the friends they met through the Forbes Dennises were also 'pupils' of Ernan's in his profession as psychologist.[106] Like Adler, Ernan saw no difficulties in his pupils becoming friends, or friends becoming pupils, something that, today, would be regarded as wholly inappropriate. It seems likely that Barbara was the first to receive counselling from Ernan, but in spring 1951, Ben also started having an Adlerian treatment with Ernan, and it may well be that he paid for his sessions in paintings rather than in cash; certainly he gave them two oil-wash-and-pencil drawings – *San Bartolomo, Tuscany, May 23 1950* and *Villa Bonda Tuscany, May 23 1950*.[107]

The embargo that remains on Ernan's case notes, which is quite correct from a professional point of view, means that information can only be picked up from stray indiscretions in Phyllis's letters, which were written to people far removed from the scene of the crimes. Ernan saw Ben and Barbara's turbulent marriage as fitting the Adlerian description of the 'neck-and-neckers', meaning the kind of couple who vie with each other, even taking lovers more to compete with one another than out of real desire.[108] 'Neck-and-neckers', in Ernan's view, are often much admired by other people, but simultaneously find it difficult to 'succeed' in their main relationship. Ernan thought that Ben and Barbara were in deadly competition with each other, and, unless they could reform this aspect of their life together, it would be almost impossible to make their marriage work.[109] Ben and Barbara's marriage came under severe strain when Ben embarked on a relationship with Rhoda Littler, a thirty-five-year-old married woman, who, with her husband, cultivated flowers for sale at Covent Garden.[110] Ben, aged fifty-six, felt reinvigorated by this relationship and wanted Rhoda to leave her husband, even though he continued to slip in and out of bed with Barbara.

In 1952, Phyllis wrote to her nephew, Philip Bottome, 'Uncle Ernan has quite a lot of patients here now, and it is quite extraordinary how successfully he works on their problems – I have never seen one of them that has not benefited by their work.'[111] And again, writing to her Uncle Harry Bottome in the USA, she said:

> Ernan is very busy and happy over some interesting patients and it is quite extraordinary how devoted they are to him in so short a time and how quickly improvement in their whole life plan is noticeable. People who do not even know that they are working with him say to me: 'I wonder why so-and-so is so much nicer?' I think Ernan is settling down much more to Red Willows, but he suffers very much from rheumatism, and the whole climate of England in winter is obnoxious to him ... [112]

This somewhat glosses over two things. Ernan had a restless streak; much more than Phyllis, he needed the stimulation of the London Library, the Reading Room at the British Museum, French cinema, theatres and concerts, and he could not get enough of that in St Ives. But after his Aunt Chattie died, Ernan inherited her war stock, and so was able to buy a house in London. As Phyllis told a friend in February 1946, 'We have a lovely home in Cornwall but he was not happy there as there was not enough for him to do and he now has bought a house on Campden Hill.'[113]

Phyllis's letter also glosses over the violent explosion of Ben and

Barbara's marriage break-up, despite Ernan's best efforts. Although the Forbes Dennises took care to stay friends with both of them, it was often hard to keep on an even keel. From May 1953, Ernan was also counselling one of the Hepworth-Nicholsons' triplets, Sarah, who was described by Phyllis as 'being cruelly pecked by the other two'; her symptoms, according to her mother, were tiredness, overweight and a tendency to be rude.[114] Ernan believed that her primary problem was the burden of expectations of artistic genius from both her parents, and tried to rescue her from that. Phyllis herself, although she recognised Barbara's genius, eventually came to be 'secretly convinced that she has a heart of stone'.[115] As Phyllis wrote in January 1953: 'Ernan works on with his psychological misfits and we keep a full house. It is wonderful to see that when a child understands its situation, it can recover so speedily from its bad habits, including physical symptoms which have been looked on for so long as organic illnesses.'[116] Ben found his Adlerian sessions with Ernan highly productive to his imaginative world, and recommended both Adler in general, and Ernan in particular, to all his friends. One effect of this was that Ben's mistress Rhoda, as well as his wife, Barbara, were being treated by Ernan; Ben fondly believed that Ernan would persuade Rhoda to leave her husband so as to be available when Ben needed her as his muse. However, this was not Ernan's agenda; he actively disliked Ben's attempts to coerce Rhoda. Ernan instead suggested to Rhoda that Ben's intense competitive spirit inclined him to 'steal love from men & give it to [him]self'.[117] Ernan told Ben that he should either give Rhoda sufficient money so that she could make her decision from a position of financial independence, or give her up altogether. And he also told him firmly that playing with the feelings of both women amounted to emotional cruelty.

Another of Ernan's many St Ives patients was David Nevill Lewis, the son of an artist who had studied under Stanhope Forbes in Newlyn in 1914 and then emigrated to South Africa. When David came back to England, he moved to Zennor in 1947, and scraped a living working in the broccoli fields in summer and as a Workers' Education Association lecturer in literature. Through Peter Lanyon, he got to know everyone in the St Ives art colony, working his way to the centre, first as honorary secretary of the Penwith Society, and then as its curator. He ended up as the leading authority on the St Ives artists, writing, for example, a marvellous book on the artist Terry Frost who lived at Newlyn. In 1949, David married an exceptionally fine Scottish painter, Willie Barns-Graham, who had been part of the St Ives colony since 1940. Although ten years older than him, Willie was an exceptionally attractive woman, beloved by all in her community.[118] For whatever reason, according to Phyllis, Lewis was 'always putting people's backs up and boasting', so Ernan started to work with him on a treatment that rendered him, again according to Phyllis, 'quite modest and not aggressive'.[119]

Lewis's marriage to the artist Willie Barns-Graham began to run into trouble and Ernan started counselling her, too. But in January 1953 Willie left David, and wrote to Ernan from Hampstead to ask him whether she was doing the right thing. Ernan encouraged her to make a go of her marriage, if she could. It seems that at least for a time he had helped them though a sticky patch, since, in 1955, Phyllis dedicated a collection of her essays, *Not in Our Stars*, 'to our beloved friends David Lewis and Wilhemina Barns-Graham'.

But, according to Phyllis, the responsibility of treating all these star-crossed lovers meant that Ernan ended up collapsing that spring as a result of overwork, as he had been involved in some 'very hard cases' with 'marriage difficulties', among some of 'the best artists in England, who seem among them to have the most problems'.[120] The fact that they had problems is hardly surprising. The most significant early patron of the St Ives group, Margaret Gardiner, commented on the bohemian culture in the art colony:

> They *thought* they were freeing themselves from [the constraints of bourgeois marriage] and they *thought* there was no such thing as jealousy and that you should follow your fancy, and your partner, or ex-partner, would be only too pleased since anything that made you happy would make them happy too. But it didn't seem to work out that way![121]

Clearly, the fact that ex-lovers could never wholly get away from each other in the then tiny town of St Ives, but would always be bumping into each other in the bread queue, meant that wounds did not get a chance to heal. It was all very intense, and it is hardly surprising that Ben Nicholson's biographer, Sarah Jane Checkland, makes her subtitle *The Vicious Circles of his Life and Art*.

Ben's serial love affairs continued apace. His next love was 'Feli' (Felicitas Vogler), a thirty-five-year-old German journalist who came to report on the Cornish art colony for Munich radio.[122] He made one last attempt to win Rhoda, by telling her that if she did not come with him, he would leave for the Ticino with his new girlfriend. Rhoda heeded Ernan's advice that this was emotional blackmail and resisted. Ben married Feli six weeks after meeting her in July 1957, and she, too, became part of the Forbes Dennis friendship group – Ernan's good German was no doubt useful in this new friendship – but wisely, in March 1958, and possibly on Ernan's advice, Ben and Feli left the overheated little town to live in Switzerland.[123]

The local jealousies were not only sexual; just as fierce were the professional rivalries and resentments. Their neighbour and friend Peter Lanyon was a native of St Ives, a landscape painter, who had been strongly influenced by Ben Nicholson to move towards abstract drawings and constructions. In 1940, Peter had joined the Royal Air Force, and was extremely disappointed when his tendency to migraines excluded him from pilot training, However, his training as a flight mechanic proved a godsend in his desires to make abstract metal constructions.[124] Extremely ambitious, he was sometimes disabled by bouts of severe depression. Having a private income, he could devote himself entirely to painting, and he liked to act as the link between the incomers to St Ives and the artist community. But Peter felt that Barbara and Ben were manipulating the Penwith Society for their own purposes, and resigned after a particularly acrimonious row. He turned against his former friends in a manner so bitter that Ernan regarded him as suffering from paranoia.[125] Friends with all three, Phyllis wrote to Ernan in London that they had all said 'injurious, intimate things to each other – which it will be hard to get right'.[126]

Nevertheless, although the artists seemed to be always falling out with each other, they all trusted Phyllis and Ernan, as the warmth of all their letters testifies. Even though the difficulties of his patients' complicated love lives and professional rivalries sometimes exhausted him, Ernan did not feel a difficulty or conflict between counselling

12 The poet and femme fatale, *Edna St Vincent Millay, caused quarrels in Vienna*

13 Phyllis met the intrepid reporter, Dorothy Thompson, in Vienna

14 Robert Pollak, the Viennese virtuoso violinist, became a lifelong friend

15 Albertina Rasch, the Viennese dancer and choreographer, who performed at Ernan and Phyllis's soirées in Vienna

16 Phyllis, and her beloved dog, Luchs, lonely without Ernan at a tricky stage in their marriage

17 Phyllis's renewed bout of tuberculosis resulted in a retreat to the mountain village of Kitzbühel

18 Ian Fleming attended Ernan's school in Kitzbühel, where he was frequently involved in scrapes with girls

19 Alfred Adler and his psychology had a profound effect on the lives of both Phyllis and Ernan

20 Max Beerbohm, whom Phyllis and Ernan visited in Rapallo

21 Phyllis was a celebrated author and lecturer in America by the late 1930s

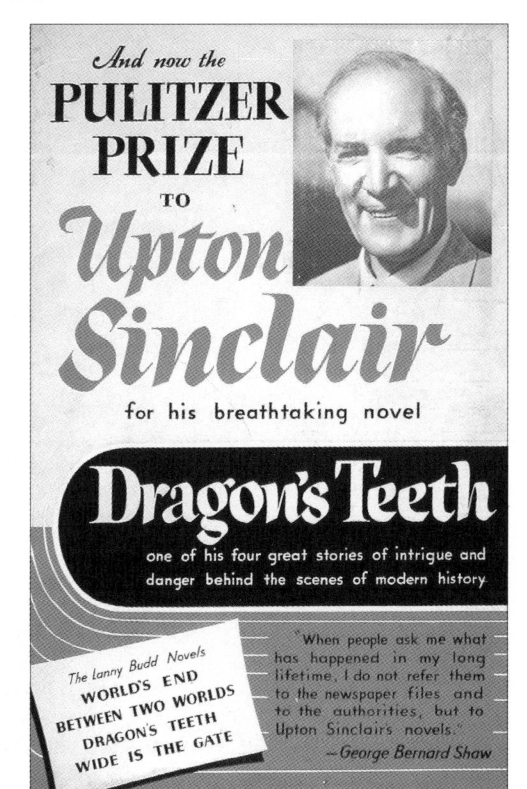

And now the
PULITZER
PRIZE
TO
Upton
Sinclair
for his breathtaking novel
Dragon's Teeth
one of his four great stories of intrigue and danger behind the scenes of modern history
The Lanny Budd Novels
WORLD'S END
BETWEEN TWO WORLDS
DRAGON'S TEETH
WIDE IS THE GATE
"When people ask me what has happened in my long lifetime, I do not refer them to the newspaper files and to the authorities, but to Upton Sinclair's novels."
—George Bernard Shaw

22 Upton Sinclair shared many of Phyllis's views of the world, and was, like her, a best-selling author

23 Phyllis's anti-Nazi novel, The Mortal Storm, *was adapted into a blockbuster film in 1940, starring James Stewart*

24 Phyllis and Ernan moved to Cornwall in 1940, living at Red Willows above St Ives

25 Daphne du Maurier, Phyllis's friend and fellow-writer in Cornwall

26 Phyllis's friend, the political activist Freda Troup, with Nelson Mandela

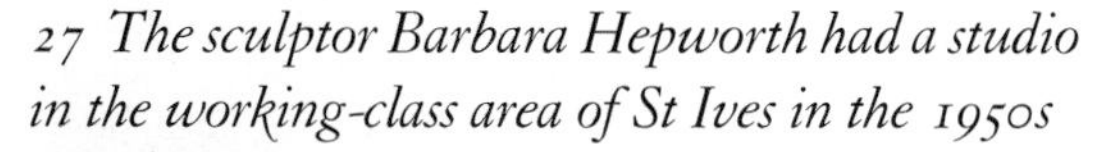

27 The sculptor Barbara Hepworth had a studio in the working-class area of St Ives in the 1950s

28 Ben Nicholson was another friend, but the break-up of his marriage to Barbara Hepworth strained Ernan's skills as an Adlerian therapist

29 Phyllis and Ernan adoring their young charges at Knox College, Jamaica

30 Phyllis and Ernan, in their seventies, still devoted to each other

someone and maintaining a friendship with them. And it seems that everyone Ernan treated felt helped by him, and the warmth of Phyllis's sparkling personality, too, seemed part of the healing process. As David Lewis wrote to them: '... We all came to you in some way broken, and we have returned to the world with a deep sense of obligation to people and wonder at the creativity and sense of moral progress in us that both of you have unlocked ... '[127]

CHAPTER 11

Post-Colonial Jamaica and the End of Empire

Their arrival at Kingston was almost as startlingly beautiful as they had been told to expect.

Phyllis Bottome, 'Convenient Food'

Phyllis's experience of witnessing the rise of fascism in Germany in the 1930s continued to shape her major political concerns even after the war had ended.

Her horror at the anti-Semitism revealed during the Second World War made her acutely aware of what she called the 'silliest and most arrogant of all human delusions – race superiority'.[1] In Phyllis's frequent visits to America she had noted: 'There *is* a negro problem for adults: but there is no such problem for a child. Almost every dark face shines with good-fellowship and laughter. Negroes play – sing – guard – protect and love every child white or black; and are loved in return by them.'[2] She thought that Martin Luther King, the leader of the civil rights movement for people of colour in the United States, was 'one of the greatest heroes in the world'.[3]

Throughout her long and politically active life, Phyllis's attitude and understanding underwent a natural development. During the First World War, Ernan had felt that he was fighting for and with the British Empire, and his career in pageant-making meant that he was psychologically and symbolically involved. Until World War I, neither Ernan nor Phyllis had seriously queried whether the British Empire was a good thing. But their experience in Vienna, where the vanquished starved in the streets, had brought about the first stage of a readjustment to a wholly new political world view. The nineteenth-century adulation of the Empire was challenged, and this was the era when the Forbes Dennises first inescapably encountered modernity. Virginia Woolf famously asserted that 'in or about December, 1910, human character changed'.[4] But for Phyllis and Ernan, the challenge of modernity struck them not in the form of a new aesthetic, but in the encounters in the Passport Office in Vienna, where Ernan was trying to deal with misplaced persons, and in the soup kitchens, where Phyllis tried to help the starving.

Both Phyllis and Ernan believed that the Second World War had arisen, at least partly, out of unresolved conflicts from the imperial clash of the First World War. They had lived among Germans and Austrians for too long to assume that all of them were Nazis, but they could see how Nazism was – among other things – a desire for empire. As Noël Coward remarked in his diary as war ended, 'Now we are starting again with officially declared peace and the world in physical and spiritual chaos. History in the making can be most exhausting.'[5]

Following World War II, Phyllis felt compelled to combat racist oppression both in her fiction and in her personal/political action. As literary critic Phyllis Lassner expresses it, Phyllis Bottome was one of several British women writers who recognised:

> That those principles of freedom and self-determination which Britain carried in its fight to survive and defeat Nazism had to be extended to their colonized subjects. And so even as they supported and endured the war against Nazi domination, these writers represented two other struggles – that of the colonized to become their own political agents and their own conflicts about the place of British subjects in colonial and postcolonial worlds.[6]

Europe's retreat from world leadership in the years after 1945 was marked by the success of anti-colonial movements throughout Asia and Africa. Phyllis had been thinking a great deal about the colonial world; she reflected on the 'ill-conceived and unprepared for [Boer] War', when Britain had been 'exposed to the just and fierce criticisms of the civilised world'.[7] She engaged in a continuing discussion by letter with her erstwhile secretary, Freda Troup, first taken on to help with the preparation for Adler's tours.[8] Freda had been born in South Africa and then educated in England at St Hugh's College, Oxford. At the outbreak of war she volunteered as an escort on a ship taking evacuee children to South Africa. There, in 1944, she married a Russian émigré photographer, Leon Levson. His politics matched hers, and they became involved in the liberation movement in Johannesburg.

Towards the end of the Second World War, there was a brief moment of hope that a more tolerant government might emerge in South Africa. The Prime Minister, Jan Smuts, had interned large numbers of Nazis and German supporters of Hitler in South West Africa during the war. Thanks largely to the work of the enlightened Army Education Units, men of all races met and mixed on equal terms. There was – briefly during the war – a 'liberal gust of change'.[9] When Smuts, along with Winston Churchill and Franklin Roosevelt, signed the Atlantic Charter, advocating freedom, democracy and the right of the people to self-determination, the African National Congress (ANC) old guard had assumed that this charter promised them universal suffrage. In August 1946, however, a miners' strike for better conditions and more pay was ruthlessly put down on Smuts's orders, resulting in nine dead and hundreds wounded.[10] A new generation of young African intellectuals, products of mission-school education and the only black university in South Africa (Fort Hare), formed the Youth League, in which Nelson Mandela began to emerge as a leading figure.

Freda's letters about what she called the Nazi tendency of the whites in South Africa worried Phyllis enormously, and she was deeply disappointed in Smuts. At Freda's suggestion, Phyllis read *Cry, the Beloved Country* by Alan Paton, and considered it 'the most impressive novel of its kind I have ever read'.[11] She was somewhat disappointed later at the gloss of the Hollywood film version on Paton's book, although conceding that it would do some good, because at least 'it did not make dark people funny ... and if we want to raise our respect of dark people, we must do so by taking the best members of their race, presenting them as a contribution to human values'.[12] Freda's direct involvement with liberation politics began when she assisted Michael Scott, an Anglican missionary, in his international campaign against South Africa's racism. She turned his dossier on the plight of the

Herero people, driven out of their lands, into a book called *In Face of Fear,* which Phyllis persuaded Faber to publish in 1950.[13] From 1952 onwards, Freda became actively involved with the launch of the ANC, suffering imprisonment on several occasions. The ANC drew up a Freedom Charter for the democratic future of South Africa, to represent everyone in the country regardless of race and colour. When Nelson Mandela and others were accused of treason, Freda was one of the administrators of the Treason Trial Defence Fund. Nelson Mandela referred to her as one of his supporters in his autobiography.[14]

Phyllis took inspiration from Freda's activism and wrote a story set in South Africa, published as 'The Prize' in *Good Housekeeping* in December 1952. In the story she shows how a careless act of unkindness from a white farmer towards a young black boy on his way to school undermines his courage, but also how the situation is remedied by the sympathetic intervention of a white South African priest.[15] The editor received a string of complaints about it from South African readers, and sent two of them on to Phyllis as examples, written by a Miss Pretorius and a Miss Mary Vaughn Edwards.[16] On 2 January 1953, Phyllis replied to them saying, 'I hope you will realise that because the story criticises the dangers of colour bar, it nevertheless upholds very strongly, in the person of the priest, the Christian form of cooperation which is, I believe, the only solution for this difficult problem.'[17] Although Phyllis had long-since lost her dogmatic faith, she continued to admire the kind of Christian activists whom she observed doing practical social work in difficult situations. Through Freda she sent money to a nursery school for children of colour that Father George Norton had set up.[18]

Phyllis always puzzled about what on earth happened to ex-pats when they left for the colonies, in particular how it was that many of them got trapped in a time-warp fantasy of an England that never was. As she wrote to Freda, 'If only people who lived out of England were half as nice as those who lived in it! The worst of our "Colonials" is that something happens to them when they step off the cliffs of Dover and their sense of humility and fair play seems to stiffen into something less attractive.'[19]

During the war, travel abroad was largely impossible. However,

Ernan was keen to travel again as soon as it was possible to move freely, especially towards the sun. Their first post-war trip was to America, and was intended initially for the purposes of a book launch; but they also included a visit to their beloved 'Dormouse', Robert Pollak, who was still teaching at the Music Conservatory in San Francisco. But Phyllis's attention was turning towards issues of Empire and race, and they decided to take a boat from New Orleans to Jamaica, and stay there long enough for her to study the situation first hand. Freda's letters about South Africa continued to float in Phyllis's mind: 'Of course,' she wrote to Freda, 'Jamaica and all the West Indies are *very very* different from S.A. but nevertheless they are part ... of the same central problem – how to get rid of hate!'[20] Her trip to Jamaica, at the age of sixty-four, was to furnish the material for her next major novel.

Although self-government was the British policy for post-war Jamaica, the wind of change was already blowing. During the war, Jamaicans had been exhorted to donate metal to help build planes for Britain and had given enormous amounts of spare 'kettles, colanders, zinc baths and clothes hangers for the mother country'.[21] Thousands of black Jamaicans had served in the British forces during the war. Black soldiers had fought alongside white soldiers, and when, after the war, they returned to Jamaica, they had new expectations of self-determination.

Jamaica had been repeatedly colonised, first by the Spaniards, who decimated the indigenous Arawaks and brought over the first enslaved Africans in 1517. In 1655, a British fleet had sailed into Kingston harbour and captured Jamaica. The Spanish escaped to Cuba, releasing their slaves as they went, and these people, the Maroons, fled to the hills. Phyllis observed that 'the British Empire [was] not at all behindhand in barbarity', because the slave trade had been conducted by the British 'in a manner that for sheer insensate cruelty outrivalled Belsen under the Nazis'.[22] By 1670 Jamaica had been formally ceded to Britain by the Treaty of Madrid. The white plutocracy developed the island as a sugar economy, bringing in thousands of Africans to work the plantations until the slave trade was abolished in 1834. Thus the majority of the inhabitants of Jamaica were descendants of African slaves, or their unions – forced or otherwise – with members of the white plantocracy. The Jamaicans they encountered on this first visit were compounded of an extraordinary mix of ethnicities: Sephardic Jews from Spain, Brazil, Holland, Guyana and Surinam had arrived. Ashkenazi Jews from Poland, Germany, the Baltic and parts of north-west Russia had arrived too, and from 1888 had shared a synagogue with Sephardic Jews in Kingston. Other significant minorities came from Syria, India and China.

From February to April 1947, Phyllis and Ernan stayed in the Myrtle Bank Hotel in Kingston, a run-down city of fading colonial splendour, with Phyllis busily taking notes on everything she could find out about the social and political scene. They soon made friends with the Colonial Secretary, Hugh Foot, and his wife Sylvia, who could introduce them to many of the people they were keen to meet.[23] Foot was an experienced and enlightened colonial administrator, who appreciated that Jamaica must soon cast off an out-of-date colonial system, though not, he hoped, all of its English traditions. Every adult Jamaican citizen had been able to vote since 1944, so Jamaica was among the first of the British colonies to achieve full adult suffrage. Foot believed that Jamaica offered an excellent opportunity to 'prove that the brotherhood of man is not an empty phrase or an idealist's delusion but an exciting, immediate possibility – a practical adventure which can and will and must succeed'.[24] Then – as now – there were two main political parties: the People's National Party, formed in 1938 by the Rhodes scholar and barrister Norman Manley, and the Jamaica Labour Party, formed in 1943 by Alexander Bustamente.[25] These two men were cousins, and their political activities must have at least given rise to speculation in Ernan's mind about the 'sibling' rivalry between these two near relations. Phyllis, in her notes, commented: 'Manley and his cousin Bustamente are the exact opposites – Bustamente is almost illiterate ... and so full of bounce he becomes almost insane with his own fluency.'[26] This was something of an exaggeration, although it is true that Hugh Foot regarded him as 'unpredictable but brilliant', and probably this is largely what Phyllis based her impression on.[27] Certainly Manley was a man of measure and reason, but Bustamente's crowd-pleasing rhetoric, swigging from a bottle of rum, won him the 1944 election decisively.

In Jamaica, over sixty per cent of the most fertile land was the private property of some few hundred white families. This unjust historical distribution of land ownership was nevertheless juxtaposed with the problem that the white farmers tended to be skilled agriculturalists, while, on the other hand, the Jamaican smallholders did not always know how to make the most of their land, and in the hill districts, particularly, were beset with problems of erosion. Phyllis wrote that the smallholders

> unfortunately do not understand how to prevent erosion, so destroying crops for the future. I do not see how [agricultural education] can be achieved except by people like Anselm Hart – who lives among them cultivating his land beautifully with alternating crops – and being so good a friend they take all their troubles to him. He is a wise Jew of the best type, and from him, they can and do learn.[28]

She could see that, despite its fertile land, many of Jamaica's inhabitants were suffering from malnutrition.

Phyllis and Ernan also met, at Kingston Public Hospital, Dr Aub, whom Phyllis described in her notes as 'a refugee German Jew… the best all round doctor in the Island, separated for 7½ years from Aryan wife and children'.[29] The hospital had been established in 1776 for white patients; ill slaves used to be treated in the sugar plantations' 'hothouses' until the Emancipation.[30] Dr Aub told the Forbes Dennises that hospitals in Jamaica were now crammed to the brim, forcing patients to share beds. He also told them that before he could start curing a patient of what he had come to the hospital for, 'I have to cure him of three other diseases – syphilis, malaria and hookworm.'[31] Always interested in education, they had visited 'Boys Town', an initiative undertaken to rescue some of the children who lived in the slums.[32] It was run by the Reverend Hugh Sherlock, a Methodist minister and man of colour, who was trying to supply some education and job-training to boys there; Phyllis learnt from him that only one child in four received any education in Jamaica.

They were delighted when Ian Fleming offered them a few days holiday in his home Goldeneye above the old banana port of Oracabessa on the north coast of Jamaica.[33] It had a sparsely furnished large sitting-room, no hot-water plumbing and no glass in the jalousied windows. Phyllis thought staying there a magical experience, the house itself 'fantastically beautiful, open only to stars and sea, sharks and pelican'.[34] Ian's friend, the playwright and composer Noël Coward, was not quite so ecstatic on his first visit and rechristened the house 'Golden Eye, Nose and Throat', considering that it possessed all the discomforts of a bad hospital.[35] But Phyllis and Ernan loved it; they could go down to the small private beach with its lint-white sand accompanied only by Ian's fox terrier, Charles, and float in the warm clear water threading through the forests of coral, observing the sea creatures. Jamaican food such as calah soup, goat fish, black crab, pork curry, sweet potatoes, salt fish, ackee fruit, stewed guavas with coconut cream were provided courtesy of Violet, Ian's cook and housekeeper.[36]

Their stay at Ian Fleming's house, however delightful, could not blind them to the extremes of wealth and poverty on the island. Remembering, by contrast, the squalor and dirt of the docklands in Kingston, Phyllis wrote:

> ... it does not seem a solution to Jamaica's problems to turn the Island into a Paradise for white tourists, set in a Hell of dark people's poverty and unemployment. Visitors from distant Continents may be most valuable if they bring with them any value of their own, in fair exchange for their blissful holidays; but a few carefully run Palaces dotted about the beauty spots of the Island, filled with rich denizens from another Planet, do nothing to raise the living conditions of thousands of starving and unemployed people. They merely madden them by fantastic contrasts.[37]

This first visit was during the epoch when Jamaica was being 'discovered' as a fashionable resort for the rich and famous, emblematised by the film star Errol Flynn who was busily establishing himself at Port Antonio. [38] Phyllis promptly wrote to him, asking him to contribute a film projector to Boys Town.

They stayed in Jamaica on this visit until September 1947. Phyllis was thinking about how to explore the issues of colonialism, independence and racism through fiction. Being Phyllis, she empathised with the reluctant colonial agents as well as the colonised subjects. Looking at the old graves of the mostly young men who had died in

Jamaica in the early days of colonisation from malaria and yellow fever, she spoke of them as 'poor, long-exiled, homesick boys! What a price such boys paid for an Empire that was as empty to them as a broken shell.'[39] Phyllis thought that colonial government should regard itself as a trust, exercising power for the benefit of a subject people for a limited time until they achieved what she regarded as their birthright of freedom. The British Empire should, in her view, be moving towards an ideal of becoming what *The Times* in 1942 had suggested it should be, 'a self-liquidating concern'.[40]

On her return to St Ives, Phyllis settled down to writing her novel, combining the experience of the stay in Jamaica with her musings about the end of empire. From 1946 onwards, Ernan divided his time between London, where he could always count on Ivor Novello getting him a box for his latest show, and St Ives, practising Adlerian psychotherapy in both places. In April 1948, a restless Ernan had visited Kitzbühel, and gone on from there to Casa Forbes in Italy. He was irritated that Phyllis would not go with him, but she needed to stay put for a few months to finish her book. Writing daily to him, as was her habit when they were apart, she told him domestic details such as the sad fact that she had had to have their dear old cat Tito put down, as he had a horrid abscess in his ear. But she had also said rather wistfully, 'so there you are alone in Europe – our Europe – on which and for which – we have spent together the greater part of our lives! … Last night I had to act as chairman for a United Nations meeting.'[41] But Phyllis was, as ever, the major breadwinner and needed to work steadily on a new novel to be called *Under the Skin.*

It may be that on the Jamaican trip Phyllis had met some of the British women teachers who had found teaching posts throughout the Empire after the end of the war: Sheila Duncker, for example, the mother of the novelist Patricia Duncker, taught English at Wolmers Girls' School at this period; another, Mary Turner, taught at Wolmers Boys' School.[42] Whether or not she had met these particular women, Phyllis chose someone with a similar occupation as the protagonist for her new novel. The character she created was a young woman called Lucy who had served in the war as a WAAF wireless controller when she was already a widow. At nineteen, Lucy had married a pilot,

Michael, and had subsequently taken a new lover; neither of them had survived the war. One set of certainties had died with her husband: 'They were a perfect match. Both were well-born and well-bred, yet an innate austerity prevented either of them from using these privileges in a self-indulgent manner. Just what Michael thought about cricket, food, the Royal Family, and how to treat those beneath you, Lucy herself thought.'[43]

When her parents are killed in the war, Lucy, aged twenty-eight, makes a fresh start in a Caribbean British colony – which although not named as Jamaica, is clearly based on Phyllis's Jamaican sojourn – as headmistress of Everslade, a boarding school for girls, mostly of mixed-race:

> A hundred girls sat before Lucy, their eyes popping out of their heads. Most of them were dark. But among the African faces there were a few spectacular white ones. A heavy-looking girl, half Chinese and half African, stared at Lucy, her mouth open, her brows meeting in a concentrated frown ... There were half a dozen very dark faces with delicate, chiselled features and straight black hair. Perhaps Indian, Lucy thought, or perhaps from far back Spanish blood had mingled with African and had produced these delicate Aryan features.[44]

Lucy Armstrong wants to be a good head teacher; 'she felt warmly and kindly towards those whom she believed to be her inferiors. She wanted to do right by them, more scrupulously and with greater effort than if she had thought them her equals.'[45]

Lucy has to undergo an uncomfortable political re-education in a new world. Phyllis Lassner comments that:

> Phyllis Bottome ... recognised how the priorities of World War II created a definition of a just war that also disguised and concealed the colonial injustices of those democratic nations fighting for their right to live. What catches the eye of [Phyllis Bottome] and other women writers is that racism and oppression are not just the obvious and sole provenance of Nazi evil run amok. They are the hidden agenda of any imperial plot, however benign its articulated mission.

Lucy's journey of political understanding mirrors that of Phyllis Bottome's as she considered the situation in Jamaica in 1947.

For Lucy, it is rendered as a question of how she can forge a new identity; when she received her award from Buckingham Palace, she 'hardly felt as if she had a self to be decorated'.[46] She has become a kind of ghost; and she has to make a choice between being a ghost of the past or achieve agency in a future post-colonial world. *Under the Skin* is an Adlerian text in the sense that Lucy needs to find happiness through love and work and by finding an integrated role in the community. Ultimately she is able to make that journey, but Phyllis also shows how post-colonial subjects may find those three aspects exceptionally difficult to achieve. The novel is a *Bildungsroman*, taking a pretty decent young woman, with many good human qualities, but also with some blind spots, who is tested in complex social and political colonial circumstances.[47]

Lucy's first encounter with the inbuilt racism of the island takes place as soon as she comes ashore. Greeted by Mabel Gosse, on behalf of the management committee of the school, she sees the friendly greeting suddenly dry up:

> Mabel Gosse suddenly stopped speaking. It was more than a pause in speech, it was a pause in the flow of something friendly and warm, which had encircled the whole group. The friendliness, the ease of hospitality, withdrew like a wave, as if a law of its being forced it back into the deep; yet nothing had happened, only a tall, well-dressed woman, slightly swinging on her high heels, had stopped in front of Lucy. She had liquid, dark-brown eyes, thick black eyebrows and very carefully reddened lips.[48]

The sudden appearance of Elvira Loring, who has been the acting head for two years, but has not been appointed head because she is a woman of colour, is telling. Mabel is thunderstruck because she had intended to take Lucy home to lunch, but she knows that her husband 'would never have a coloured person eat at his table'.[49] Lucy is at a loss in this initial encounter; because of Elvira's pale skin Lucy has not yet realised that she is a woman of colour. Her mixed race signifies a whole history of white men's sexual associations with female slaves; since there is more than a hint of alluring sexiness even in Elvira's walk, she makes white women feel obscurely anxious.

Elvira has reasons to be bitter; she describes herself as passionately pro-British, Anglo-Catholic and Conservative, yet she is discriminated against as a non-white. In aligning herself with the British, ironically, she too adopts racist prejudices. ('Personally I've no use for Asiatics.')[50] In a sense it is Elvira's nearly-whiteness – she is seven-eighths white – that poisons her life; to the casual eye she can pass for a white woman, but socially and politically she can never be one. She is 'colourist' because she believes herself better than darker-skinned Jamaicans, and her envy of Lucy – whom she wants to be – renders her poisonous. Philip Calgary, the doctor who attends the school is also mixed race, and Elvira is infuriated because, although darker than her, he is more acceptable to the British because he has had an English education.

Lucy is puzzled by the post-war situation in Jamaica: 'Was this Island wavering toward bankruptcy, or a civilisation crumbling into decay. Whose responsibility was it? Whose interests were guiding it?'[51] In discussions with the Chinese communist teacher, Whiteleaf Ho Sung, Lucy becomes frustrated with the constant reference to the history of slavery on the island as an explanation of current problems.

> 'But they can't *remember* being slaves,' Lucy replied a little impatiently. 'It's over a hundred years since they were all freed.'
>
> 'Yes, in 1838,' Miss Ho Sung said softly, 'and even now what are they freed for? To be destitute? To be uneducated? To be sick? They have so little life of their own on their Island – these dark ones – only what belongs to other people. No language, no tradition, no religion, even as a rule, though they cultivate them, no bananas! All the rich Island produce goes away on ships ... forgive me, but Anglo-Saxons do not often think of Asiatics or Africans very thoroughly ... '[52]

Initially Lucy is somewhat offended; she feels that, as the British Empire had led the way in abolishing slavery, it should have full credit for its generosity. This comment is allied to her blindness to some of the things that she sees in front of her. On her first morning at the school, she feels as though she has woken in paradise, although: 'A mocking bird with slate-blue wings rocketed its swift body across Lucy's balcony, shouting an urgent, unintelligible warning. A dark man in blue cotton, with a huge umbrella-shaped hat, and practically no nose, sauntered soundlessly across the terrace, drawing a thin, reluctant cow after him.'[53] Lucy does not recognise the evidence of advanced syphilis in the man's eaten-away nose, though venereal disease is endemic on the island.[54]

Phyllis Lassner tackles what is perhaps the key question about Phyllis Bottome's brave foray into this subject. She asks whether ' … the collective experience of racial subjection be addressed through the narrative of individual development, that is, of a white Englishwoman whose sense of self has been built on fulfilment and agency as the pathway to social and political responsibility.'[55]

The answer to this legitimate question is – yes – if only imperfectly. As the narrative proceeds, Lucy increasingly queries the views of the white plantocracy with whom she socialises at weekends. She is courted by Bob Anstruther, who argues that 'the British *are* the Island … we conquered it – we've held it for three hundred years', but Lucy challenges him by asking whether conquering something 'makes a thing ours'.[56] For the white settlers the question of identity is not so much 'Who am I?' but 'Where is here?' Instead of becoming 'Jamaican', the British try to reproduce – by means of their clubs, dances and social arrangements – that other island, a fake Britain. A whites-only dance in the Grand Hotel is a pivotal moment for Lucy, since it is here that she makes the actively political as well as romantic choice. She tells Bob that she is love with the black Jamaican doctor, Philip Calgary. In effect, Lucy chooses Jamaica, rather than little-England in Jamaica.

The account of Elvira's recourse to *obeah* (Caribbean sorcery) is arguably less satisfactory, and a tad melodramatic, although in the novel it is represented as the action of a powerless person, tempted to seek power by illegitimate means.[57] It echoes, too, Elvira's misuse of sexual power over men, and also – arguably more dangerously – over the inexperienced adolescent girls in her care. Elvira's hybridity causes her a psychic wound; if she cannot be Lucy, then she will try to destroy her. As ever, in any novel by Phyllis, the personal is the political. People are often willing to give up individual responsibility in order to obtain power, and, as she shows, this can be at a personal level or at the level of a whole system, when people align themselves with a false ideology.

In Phyllis's world view, both fascism and communism are false ideologies because both systems are prepared to overwhelm the dissenting individual by force, though one notes that her representation of the communist teacher is much more sympathetic than her representation of the racist whites.

If Elvira represents a despairing hybridity, Philip Calgary represents a more positive form. On the one hand, he has Western science as the backbone of his knowledge and professional status, yet, on the other, he does not despise his mother's knowledge of the healing uses of native herbs. If not entirely free of bitterness, he is – unlike Elvira – self-identified as Jamaican, not would-be-British, and therefore has the potential to achieve the undivided wholeness that Adler advocated. Philip and Lucy's union signifies a union between Jamaica and the kind of white persons who become not tourists but inhabitants, to use Phyllis's own formulation. As she writes in 'The Pirate's Isle', despite its problems she felt that:

> Jamaica has been extraordinarily blessed by its small band of helpers. They are the pick of both white and dark people working together with equal courage and intelligence, teachers, doctors, nurses, welfare and research workers; doing their jobs beyond all praise against insuperable difficulties, and except for a few individuals here and there, not generously supported by those who profit most from the Island's resources.[58]

Philip Calgary is not only highly educated, but also extremely handsome. Bob Anstruther, who had enjoyed a love affair with Philip's sister, Jenny, had never considered marrying a woman of colour. He says to Lucy 'in a savage undertone' that the black Jamaicans had no right ' "to be so damned good-looking" '.[59] It is to be noted that the word 'savage' has here become attached to the white man; Bob's rejection of Jenny, whom he loved, has destroyed his own integrity.

When the hurricane – a recurring natural phenomenon in Jamaica – comes, it tests them all. Elvira only wants to save her own skin, whereas Philip and Lucy are heroic in their attempts to save others. On the other hand, neither of them can save one of Lucy's pupils, Marjorie Fielding, whose suicide represents a different kind of hurricane. Marjorie has no love for Jamaica; she feels herself superior because she is the daughter of an English brigadier, and therefore part of the ruling elite. Elvira finds it only too easy to exploit the discontented fifteen-year-old; Marjorie's intense adolescent crush on Elvira means that she will do anything that Elvira merely hints at in terms of sly plots against Lucy Armstrong that might cause her to lose her job. Marjorie even accompanies Elvira when she seeks to bring about Lucy's death by means of a visit to the old man on the island who is the king of *obeah*, though he warns them both, ' "If you don't use death – death will use you." '[60] Indeed the first 'death' is that of Marjorie's identity as a worshipper of Elvira; Marjorie is bereft when she sees Elvira's cowardice in the face of the hurricane:

> Marjorie stood before Elvira silently, and with dread, awaiting perhaps a fresh enchantment, or, instead, a fresh bewildering pang of disillusionment. How could she tell what to say to this new Elvira, who had deserted her in danger, and lied to cover her desertion, but who had the same exquisite, soft, deep voice, whose long slender hands were outstretched to greet her, with the old terrible tenderness?[61]

Although no longer seduced and hypnotised by Elvira, in a sense *obeah* has destroyed Marjorie; she has leaned on an external power instead of learning to trust in her own self-realisation.

The blindness of Philip's mother is symbolic – she cannot see colour – she can only sense the essence of people, what is 'under the skin'. Lucy reiterates this point to Bob, claiming that what matters is 'beneath our colour – it's our real selves', and she links this observation about race with the feminist point – 'People used to think women weren't real selves either.'[62]

Phyllis's view was that miscegenation had produced in Jamaica remarkable human beings:

> Unless the observer is a victim to Goebbels' philosophy, he is bound to admit that they are amongst the most outstanding and successful human beings to be found on the Island. In the old slave days, marriage was not permitted between white men and their slaves, but

> as few white women were available, many of the planters chose (and often had specially educated) as their life companions, slave women. The result of these common-law marriages are a remarkably fine set of descendants.[63]

This glosses over a whole history of rape and coercion; nevertheless, in *Under the Skin*, in alliances like that of Lucy and Philip, and perhaps even more, in the children they will have, are the hopes for a decolonised future.

Back in England, Phyllis, not surprisingly, was horrified when Sir Geoffrey Faber regretfully insisted that she must make significant changes to *Under the Skin* before he could publish it, for a variety of reasons, including its similarity in plot to a novel by a writer called Richard Mason.[64] As she wrote to Freda Troup in December 1948:

> You will laugh when you hear that the whole of my book *Under the Skin* must be rewritten, to preserve us from six major libel suits. This, in spite of the fact that every character in the book was invented, except two public characters to whom I was sending the manuscript before publication for their approval. This is the English law of libel, which, as it stands, amounts to a censorship.[65]

The rewriting proved exhausting, and Geoffrey Faber suggested that she might find it easier to write another novel altogether. Although agreeing with him that it would indeed be much easier, she could not let the novel go. As she said to him: 'I must write about this particular race problem as it is in my heart, so that I could not do anything else until I worked it out.'[66] Phyllis always felt that the revisions insisted on resulted in a loss of the spontaneity and originality that had existed in the first version. Nevertheless, there were also some initial negotiations towards turning the book into a film, and indeed Phyllis wrote a script for it, but its financial backer so emasculated its Adlerian teaching that Phyllis lost faith in the project, and was rather relieved when it came to nothing in the end.[67] And, despite her misgivings about the rewrites, when *Under the Skin* was finally published in 1950 she received good reviews in a wide range of papers. The *Sunday Times* commented that the novel was: 'Entertaining, civilised and wise. The scene is the West

Indies, the problem those complex race relations ... The chief distinction of Miss Bottome's work is a fairness and delicacy of perception on top of a heart that is steadily warm.' The *Glasgow Herald* commented on its 'unprejudiced frankness and sympathy' and nearly every review considered that the analysis of race relations was timely.[68]

Phyllis also received uniformly good reviews for a collection of short stories, *Fortune's Finger,* also published in 1950, and dedicated, in celebration of their long friendship, to the Maxwell Lauries. It contained eighteen short stories, of which seven were set in Jamaica ('Habits', 'The Shark's Fin', 'The Lesson', 'Among Thieves', 'First-Degree Murder', 'Convenient Food' and 'Adoption by Grace'). These tales reworked some of the themes of *Under the Skin,* or extended them. In 'First-Degree Murder', for instance, Bottome explores the marriage of the son of a white planter, Andrew, who, following his return to Jamaica after serving in the RAF during the war, marries a black woman, Miranda. The marriage ends disastrously; her family see the marriage as an opportunity to get money and his see the whole thing as a social disgrace. Ultimately, Miranda kills herself and her baby, and Andrew shoots himself. This is much less sanguine than the ending of *Under the Skin*, which is tentatively hopeful. A central conversation occurs when, after Andrew has explained how his beloved has been educated at a convent school and is as clever as she is beautiful, Andrew's father accuses him of naïvety:

> 'An African *is* an African – he's a person of an inferior race. He's, in a sense, sub-human!' Andrew shook his head obstinately, 'I don't see that a different pigmentation – nature's protection against a hot sun – is either an inferiority or a superiority,' he said quietly. 'It's just a convenience. Even different habits are mostly a geographical accident. Our differences are bound to work out, now that we have conquered space – and thinned out time. It's no use calling Jews or Africans bad names, or trying to hold on to our fancied superiorities in order to boost ourselves. This colour question – is not a class distinction – it is simply a recognisable difference.'[69]

Andrew's idealism cannot overturn his parents' prejudice and this breaks his wife's heart – that is the murder – and then his own. Phyllis's short stories achieved very good reviews across the board. Many of them drew particular attention to the Jamaican stories. The reviewer for the *Daily Worker* of 14 December 1950 approved of 'her belief in human brotherhood which has no room for colour bars, which insists on the equal right of all children to food, sunlight and fresh air'.[70] And the *Manchester Daily Dispatch* of 8 December 1950 commented that Phyllis had been 'bold enough to take sides on the colour question, coming down in favour of the Negroes ... '

Like all liberals Phyllis and Ernan saw education in its broadest sense as the key to transforming society. As Phyllis wrote in her essay, 'The Pirate's Isle': 'eighty per cent of Jamaicans are still illiterate. Even today only one child in four can achieve any education, lack of transport and malnutrition proving insuperable obstacles.'[71] On their first visit to Jamaica, they had visited all the schools on the island and had not been overly impressed. They felt that Wolmers Girls' School in Kingston, with its emphasis on posture, elocution and lawn tennis, was offering an already outdated imperial education. But at Wolmers Boys' School in Kingston they discovered an educationist whose vision they both applauded. This was Lewis Davidson, who in 1939 had been appointed headmaster; aged only twenty-three, he was the youngest headmaster of any school in the Empire.[72] Wolmers was the oldest secondary school in the Caribbean, having been founded in 1729, and Lewis was rather too radical for the school board's taste. He wanted as much emphasis on the creative arts as on intellectual skills, and he set up a college department to offer further education to students who did not gain scholarships to foreign universities. The sugar industry had always been central to the Jamaican economy, but he started a summer course geared towards diversifying agricultural study. In short, he thought that the school should provide the education that Jamaicans needed, rather than offer a carbon copy of what was taught in Britain.

However, he was too advanced and idealistic for his board. He committed a few 'crimes' that were not forgiven. He tried to change the uniform for something more fitting to Jamaica than Britain. When he arrived the boys were all made to wear jackets and ties, looking more like London clerks than schoolboys. He banned the caning of boys in his school. He appointed a German-Jewish doctor, who had arrived as a refugee in 1933, as the school doctor. The board insisted on this appointment being terminated. They also forbade Lewis's wife Jean from teaching in the school after a talk she gave was reported as revolutionary in the *Daily Gleaner*; she had been quoted as saying, 'Here in Jamaica we find race distinction rampant.' This was in the context of Jean's comment that banks on the island refused to employ well-educated boys of colour.[73] In 1942, at the end of his three-year contract, the board dispensed with Davidson's services, despite protests from the Parent-Teacher Association and the fact that a hundred boys sent a letter of protest to the *Daily Gleaner*.

Lewis and Jean might easily have returned to their native Scotland, but they stayed in Jamaica, continuing to work in the field of education; he was a member of the committee to found a University College in the West Indies, he served as the acting head of the Quaker Education Service and he was acting headmaster for a term at Manchester High School in Mandeville, the fifth largest town in Jamaica, about sixty miles west of Kingston.[74] Phyllis regarded him as 'a real educator [he] ... was given the most noted school (not I think the best) on the Island – to run at twenty-three. It was a mistake – for he was too young for such a wholly independent job.'[75] In 1944, he offered his services to the Overseas Department of the Church of Scotland and was appointed to serve the Presbyterian Church of Jamaica. The Presbyterian Church was doing a variety of caring work in its scattered congregations, but post-war it was looking to do an increasing amount of social reconstruction. Lewis visited all the Presbyterian churches round the island, reporting on progress and recommending improvements. Having discovered that the people in the rural areas were keen to have their own education centre, he recommended to the Synod that a school be built in the highlands of central Jamaica, above the little town of Spaldings, three thousand feet above sea level, which had superb views. The choice was apt socially as well as geographically, as Spaldings was situated on the borders of four Jamaican parishes, with roads intersecting from every part of the island, with electricity and a new hospital, and with five elementary schools within a radius of six miles. The climate was cool and refreshing, and its distance from the distractions of the city was seen as advantageous too.

Getting this new school built was a test of faith; Davidson went back to Britain to raise funds – he came back with the first thousand pounds – and to visit co-educational boarding schools, including Frensham Heights, where Ernan had so nearly become headmaster many years before. He visited the Cambridge Examinations Syndicate to discuss changes in the curriculum to make the examinations more suitable for Jamaica. He wrote of this visit, 'They are keen to give us quite a lot of scope, and will definitely offer the examinations in Handcraft, General Science, Domestic Science and Art. They are also prepared to offer a Syllabus in West Indian History.'[76]

The name 'Knox' was chosen because, notwithstanding his harsh treatment of Mary Queen of Scots, John Knox had promoted universal education. Construction on the new school began in June 1946, under the expert guidance of David Bent, a man of colour, who was an elder at the Webster Memorial Church. He had had a good job in Machado's Tobacco Factory in Kingston, but had relinquished financial security to serve the new project.[77] Although Lewis Davidson is usually regarded as the founder of Knox, he himself said that he could never have done it without David's practical support, and regarded him as the co-founder. They had first to build a road to the site on the bare hilltop above Spaldings, and, as there was no piped water, it all had to be brought up from the river below, first on donkeys and then, when the road was built, on trucks. Using a kind of Spanish adobe method, they had built an all-purpose school building, which was comprised of two classrooms and boys' and girls' dormitories. They also built two identical bungalows to house the Davidson and Bent families. On 3 September 1947, following two years of fund-raising by Presbyterian churches from all over the island, Knox College was opened in a ceremony attended by Sylvia Foot, wife of the Colonial Secretary. The aim of Knox, according to the souvenir programme, was 'to equip boys and girls and men and women with the training, knowledge, techniques and character that will fit them to live well themselves and to contribute to the development of the country'.[78]

The college opened with just fourteen pupils, including the Davidsons' two children and the Bents' three. It was called a 'college' from the start because although at this stage it had no secondary-aged children, the aim was to have an infant school for children from four to eight years old, a junior school for children aged eight to eleven, and a secondary school for children of eleven years and older. There were also plans for a rural technical school for young people over fifteen years, and summer schools for adults. In short, it was to be a community college.

It was not surprising that Ernan and Phyllis admired Lewis Davidson. He had taken an honours degree at Glasgow in philosophy and psychology and had been ordained in the Presbyterian Church in July 1946. Jean Lewis had an MA from Edinburgh and a bachelor's degree in divinity from New College. As Phyllis commented in the notes from the 1947 visit, 'If anything can pull this island together in a favourable direction it is the work begun together in school and hospital by the Davidsons and the Harts.' Dr Kenneth Hart was in charge of the hospital in Spaldings and his wife, Gwenllian, a trained teacher, was engaged in voluntary welfare work for children. She was also the secretary of the committee for founding a University College of the West Indies.[79] These people were just the kind of intellectual and practical visionaries that the Forbes Dennises admired.

An added dimension to the friendship between them was that Lewis, during his study of psychology, had come to think that Adler's work, with its strong social dimension, was the best underpinning for his educational practice. One of Lewis's favourite Adlerian quotes was: 'You must have courage to fail; for if you don't have that, you won't have the courage to begin anything even slightly adventurous.'[80] Lewis had certainly lived up to this adage in founding Knox.

Every four years, Lewis was required by the Presbyterian authorities to take a sabbatical, so at the end of 1949 he and his family went back to Britain on leave. Lewis asked Ernan to become acting headmaster at Knox while he was away. On 28 November 1949, Phyllis and Ernan returned to Jamaica, and stayed at Knox College for eight months. Back in Britain, Lewis took the opportunity to attend meetings of the Adlerian Society and observe the work at some of the children's clinics. He reported back to Jamaica that at one of the play-therapy sessions he watched children working out their problems. 'One vital youngster (David) – a terror – had a great fight with me and then plumped down on my knee. He needed affection desperately. His case record showed a runaway father and a philandering mother, resentful of the boy who hates her – and all women.'[81]

So, while Lewis was learning more about Adlerian theory in England, Ernan was practising it in Jamaica. By the time Ernan and Phyllis arrived to take charge of the college, there were about thirty pupils between the ages of five and seventeen. Some were boarders and some day students; a bus went round and picked children up from as far away as Colyville. The girl boarders were in a separate hostel from the boys, where the school nurse acted as matron, but they were taught together.

There was a family spirit at Knox, so each evening Ernan and Phyllis took coffee with the staff, and engaged with all the problems and successes of their school day. They were both impressed by Mae Grant, a trained Froebel teacher, who had thrown in her lot with Knox, having given up a secure job at an infant school in Falmouth to join the venture.[82] Leo Jones, young and enthusiastic, taught Latin, mathematics and religious knowledge, and was hostel master for the boys. He was not a Presbyterian, and his religious teaching was always more along the lines of teaching students to think rather than to swallow dogma. Leo was extremely good looking and just a little naïve; the adolescent girls at the school were highly creative in finding ways to catch his eye.[83] Similarly, pretty Elizabeth Hutchins, the nurse in charge of the sanatorium attracted the attention of the adolescent boys and they were endlessly inventing illness and injuries in order to get over to the sanatorium. All of these situations needed to be delicately 'managed'. Another member of the early Knox staff was George Scott who, although newly out of school, promised to be an excellent teacher. Much later he would become principal of the school.[84] David Bent himself taught bookkeeping to some of the older students, and his wife, Thelma, helped out with the younger children in a variety of ways. The children themselves 'were of all colours, from blackest black to whitest white, with all shades in between, and mixtures of ancestry from China and India and the Middle East as well as from Europe and – above all – Africa. The many beautiful children of mixed ancestry Lewis called "the golden people".'[85]

There were children from French- and Spanish-speaking countries around the Caribbean, from Venezuela and Cuba, and also from Bermuda where schools were not racially integrated. There was a scattering of children whose parents from abroad were on contract to various industrial firms like the bauxite and sugar companies. The college was mixed in every way possible – mixed races, mixed genders, mixed social classes, and it was both parochial, in the best sense of serving the local community, and international, in its 'league of nations' ethos. This was exactly the ideal that Phyllis and Ernan had striven for in their school in Kitzbühel back in the late twenties, but they had hardly experienced such a mixed catchment of pupils there.

Phyllis regarded this epoch of close involvement with a progressive college as one of the most exciting and profitable experiences of her life; as she pointed out, although she was anti-racist by instinct, she had 'never before lived and worked wholly with dark people. The staff was most companionate and, with one exception (a white one), very helpful to us and we could not have enjoyed better company on our mountain-top. Nor was there a single exception to our delight in the children! My husband helped those with special psychological difficulties, while I acted as extramural speaker in the University.'[86]

Phyllis is referring here to what would become the University of the West Indies, but at this time had been recently founded as an External University College of London University.[87] Phyllis was an experienced lecturer and happy to oblige. She also gave talks to the Spaldings Social and Literary Club, when the hall was always 'filled to overflowing for the talks on literature by the outstanding speaker with the dark flashing eyes and vivid personality'.[88] Phyllis also threw herself into the Spaldings Drama Festival, helping the English teacher, Trixie Grant.

Phyllis wrote regularly to the Davidsons to assure them that their school was thriving and giving them bits of news, such as: 'The children are going to do the first three scenes from *As You Like It*, ending on "We go to freedom, not to banishment", which Miss Grant and I thought specially suited for the Knox children.'[89] No doubt Phyllis was in her element; it was all very reminiscent of helping Luischen in Kitzbühel with the Shakespeare festivals. Other letters relate to sports days, and one especially lively letter recounts an adventure:

> The Naturalist Club, the other day, had quite an adventure. Overtaken on a bad road by a terrific rainstorm, only Mr Bent's consummate driving and the splendid help of Leo and George saved the bus from overturning. Not a single child showed a flicker of fear and all acted with triumphant goodwill. When he had to turn all the bigger ones out into solid sheets of rain, to run a mile before reaching the main road and being picked up, each a spectacular fountain, not a complaint and no harm came to anyone. I invited them into the bungalow where we made a huge fire and ate whatever was in the house, reinforced by relays of hot tea, ginger ale and lemonade and melted ice cream used as milk.[90]

Both Phyllis and Ernan were hugely impressed with Knox College, but overall could not shake off their central concern about Jamaica. They could not see how the critical economic problem of the enormous gap between rich and poor could ever be resolved. As Phyllis wrote to Van: 'We are afraid of Jamaica being too much used by playboys and income-tax dodgers. They encourage, by giving excuse for, Communist propaganda on an island so terribly over-populated and under-employed. There is no bridge between abject semi-starvation and those who pay thirteen and a half guineas a day to enjoy themselves.'[91]

Once the Davidsons returned to Jamaica at the end of their leave, Phyllis and Ernan went back to England. But they missed the lively Knox children enormously; writing to Jean Davidson, Phyllis said, 'We shall never forget them.'[92]

As the century wore on, Phyllis and Ernan increasingly fell out of love with the idea of empire, seeing that its protectionism was part of an international economic system that was incompatible with fair trade, and ultimately with peace. Phyllis wrote in 1952 ' ... this dreadful business in Kenya is being put down, or rather, stirred up, by Nazi methods. People that could save the situation are checked or exiled.'[93] In June 1956, Colonel Nasser was elected President of Egypt and promptly nationalised the Suez Canal. The Suez Canal was the line of supply to and from Australia, New Zealand, India and other Asian countries, and, significantly, was the conduit for three-quarters of Western Europe's oil.[94] The Suez Crisis proved to be 'the psychological watershed, the moment when it became apparent that Britain was no longer capable of being a great imperial power'.[95] The humiliating pull-back of the British troops was in effect the death-knell of the British Empire. Writing to Upton Sinclair, Phyllis indicated that Anthony Eden, with his decision to send gunboats, had attempted to cling on to an outdated version of the world. He had been unable to accept the fact that at this particular point in history, ' "Great Britain" is a small island off the coast of Europe! Greatness has nothing to do with size or strength fortunately – as we can develop it if we try!'[96] The end of the Empire proceeded inexorably, but this was not seen as a tragedy by the Forbes Dennises, rather as a necessary adjustment to modernity.

CHAPTER 12

Final Years in London

In some ways, though we were in late middle-age when Adler died, the next quarter century seems to have been the fullest and most fruitful of our lives.

PHYLLIS BOTTOME, *The Goal*

In 1950, Phyllis and Ernan had been delighted when their nephew, Nigel Dennis, came back to England. He was their 'almost-son', and they both adored him. He had spent fifteen years earning his living in New York, primarily by reviewing books and films, but in 1949 his novel *A Sea Change* won the Anglo-American Novel Award for that year. Ever since the Kitzbühel days, Phyllis had envisaged a career for him as a writer, and so felt vindicated and gratified by his success.[1]

They were now at an age to turn first to the obituaries when the newspapers arrived. They were saddened to hear of the death of Edna St Vincent Millay, who on 19 October 1950 fell down a flight of stairs at her home in the Berkshires, Massachusetts.[2] Officially she had died of a heart attack, though she had long been ravaged by alcoholism and addiction to morphine. Despite Phyllis's siding with Dorothy Thompson against Edna back in the days of 1920s' Vienna, she had approved of Edna's stand against American isolationism in the 1940s ('there are no islands any more'). And Phyllis, notwithstanding any personal quarrel, always thought that Edna was a genius, although after her death her star faded. Edna, too, could be described as a victim of the academic privileging of modernism over work that is passionately and politically engaged.

They were more deeply saddened, in February 1951, by the news that Ivor Novello had died of a heart attack, shortly after completing his evening performance in *King's Rhapsody*. The committal at Golders Green Crematorium was held on 12 March 1951, with the interment of his ashes two months later at the foot of a lilac tree planted in honour of one of his most popular songs, 'We'll Gather Lilacs' from his musical *Perchance to Dream* (1945). A memorial service at St Martin-in-the-Fields on 28 May 1951 was relayed outside on loudspeakers to a crowd of thousands. His will included various legacies to theatrical charities and his country home, Redroofs, was left as a convalescent home for actors.[3] Ernan received a letter from Fred Allen, Ivor's business manager for thirty years, deploring a biography of Ivor by Peter Noble.

> No story of Ivor's wonderful achievement can be complete without a considerable reference to your part in it, for apart from Mam no one did as much as you to start him on the right road by taking him in his adolescence to Canada and the States and awaking him from that period of inertia which at the time he was passing through.[4]

Although Ivor's possessive love had caused terrible strain between Phyllis and Ernan in the early years of their relationship, Ivor had long since become the beloved friend of both.

King George VI died on 6 February 1952, and his daughter, Elizabeth II, succeeded him. Her coronation was the first to be televised. Phyllis had been born in the reign of Victoria, had lived through the reign of George V, the brief reign of Edward VIII before he abdicated, and now had experienced the end of another era, that of George VI. Whereas in 1935 she had felt ignored in her native land, by the last decade of her life Phyllis had become something of a public intellectual in Britain. She was frequently asked to speak on the BBC Home Service, whether it was to give a talk on Adler or to speak on programmes such as *Writers' Choice of Music*, *Books and Authors* and *Woman's Hour*.[5] Well known for her best-selling novels, she was also receiving new critical acclaim for her short stories.

For some of the post-war years, Phyllis and Ernan divided their time between St Ives and London. In London, Ernan had bought a rather grand house at the corner of Bedford Gardens on the top of Campden Hill. It had once been the home of the composer, Hayden Coffin, who was the Ivor Novello of the 1890s. Coffin had converted the stables into a separate cottage that they were able to offer to their friend, the pianist Desirée MacEwan. The house had fine oak panelling throughout, which served to set off their growing collection of old china. On 7 April 1954, the *Daily Sketch* celebrated what they took to be Phyllis's seventieth birthday, although she was actually seventy-two, with lots of photographs.[6] And on 4 June, *John O' London's Weekly*, also labouring under the misapprehension that she was seventy, published a front-page article entitled 'Fifty Years of Success', with a large photograph of a smiling Phyllis seated at her writing desk. When in London, they particularly enjoyed the company of Geoffrey Faber and his daughter Ann, and also that of the writer Rose Macaulay and Margery Fry (Roger Fry's sister).

Following the critical success of Phyllis's collected stories *Fortune's Finger* in 1950, in 1953 Faber published another collection of short stories entitled *Man and Beast*.[7] Phyllis asked Faber to send copies to various friends as Christmas presents. One of the names on her list was that of Ezra Pound; he was at this time incarcerated in the criminal lunatic ward of St Elizabeth's Hospital, Washington DC's asylum for the insane. In 1945 he had been charged with 'accepting employment from the Kingdom of Italy in the capacity of a radio propagandist ... to persuade citizens and residents of the United States to decline to support the United States in the conduct of war'.[8] In order to avoid the possibility of execution, his lawyer had made a plea of insanity, which would at least be certain to save him from a death sentence.[9] Phyllis believed that Ezra's narcissism and devotion to social-credit economics amounted to a form of monomania.[10] She did not abandon friends in trouble, and was persistent when she championed someone; in 1945 she had written to a variety of people, hoping that they would sign a letter she had drafted:

> We the undersigned ask in the name of English Literature for special clemency to be shown to Ezra Pound, now under sentence of death as a war traitor.
>
> We beg the American authorities concerned with the punishment of war criminals to take into consideration the great contribution Ezra Pound formerly made to our common heritage of intellectual life, both as a poet and as a critic ... His political convictions were

> largely due to the intellectual isolation of his life in a Dictatorship country. His opinions were always more of a danger to himself than to others; and were united to a personal character of rare integrity; and to a courage which exposed him to risks never run by less sincere and disinterested persons.
>
> We believe that an act of clemency granted to Ezra Pound by the United States, at this time, would signalise the victory of intellectual freedom throughout the civilised world.[11]

This she had sent to a range of her writer friends, including Max Beerbohm. Upton Sinclair, unsurprisingly, sent a dusty answer, although Phyllis tried to explain to him that Upton's own views about the centrality of money and the stranglehold of big business were *au fond* similar to those of Ezra. The fundamental difference, however, was that Ezra had come to believe that only a strong leader could force through change and had veered to the right, whereas Upton's commitment to democracy meant that he tended to socialism. Phyllis had anticipated that Sinclair Lewis, although 'one of my pals, might be even less sympathetic' to a campaign in support of Ezra.[12] In 1946, Phyllis had visited Ezra in St Elizabeth's Hospital and subsequently wrote to his lawyer and to his wife Dorothy advising a slow and careful campaign of rehabilitation. She sent him long and cheering letters (signed with 'unalterable affection'), without ever once agreeing with his politics. He still believed in force, rather than democracy, and she, as ever, patiently disagreed, responding that liberalism should surely be the 'natural creed of every creative mind'.[13] She regretted, she wrote, that the Liberal Party in Britain seemed a spent force, but even so considered that 'they see what should be done to make the world a fair and decent place'.[14] In one letter to Ezra, she outlined her fundamental conviction:

> Freedom to me is the responsibility of doing what I think right – and I don't feel as if I were a human being at all unless I have this choice – any Dictatorship from the Left or from the Right takes this power of choice away from me by force. Democracy merely hampers me, because it is imperfect – but in a Democracy the obstacles to freedom are not insuperable, and I believe with good-will and tolerance can be overcome.[15]

The five stories in *Man and Beast* that she sent to Ezra have an intense quality that is born of a close observation of animals and how they relate to humans.[16] They could be described as fables for adults and it is interesting to conjecture what Ezra Pound made of the tale of a bull that became so consumed with hate that it destroyed itself. There seems an irresistible connection between this tale and her description of the man who had come to be regarded as traitor. Writing about Ezra more in sorrow than in anger, Phyllis said, 'there is a shade of moral perspicacity which depends upon considering the wills of others as of equal importance to our own, which I feel that even the later Ezra wholly lacked'.[17] The most successful of the *Man and Beast* stories describes the relationship between horse and man, working as partners in the Spanish Riding School in Vienna, in a tale so stripped and formal that the deep harmony and schooled rhythm of their dual performance is utterly convincing. Reviewers all noted the maturity and economy with which she wrote, so that, while no extra words are needed, none could be eliminated.[18]

As usual, Phyllis and Ernan took great interest in the well-being of all their friends and worried about the ones who they felt had not found their way to the light. In December 1951, they were horrified to hear that Walter Wanger had been arrested after twice shooting his wife's lover, her agent Jennings Lang, in what the papers euphemistically called his groin. Phyllis and Ernan had visited Walter and his second wife, the actress Joan Bennett, while in Hollywood during the making of *The Mortal Storm*, and liked them both very much.[19] Fortunately Lang recovered, and Wanger served only four months in prison.

Their love and concern for Ian Fleming similarly remained unabated following his stay with them as a troubled adolescent in 1920s' Kitzbühel. Ever since they had first known him they had regarded him as having sex on the brain, and an unstoppable desire to make conquests of women. Generally he neither liked nor respected women; Phyllis was a rare exception in being a woman he revered. The intense sibling rivalry he experienced with his brother Peter seemed to be replayed in his endless cuckolding of men he regarded as his friends. Alongside a variety of other sexual liaisons, Ian had conducted a longstanding affair with a married woman, Lady Anne Rothermere, and, when she became pregnant with his child, he felt that he would have to marry her. Phyllis wrote to her nephew in 1952:

> Perhaps you will have seen that our poor Ian, who must now be forty-five and has never stopped having love affairs which were all catastrophic, has now at last got himself – in the direction to which they all pointed – well into the Divorce Court. He is cited as co-respondent in the Rothermere case. He introduced us to Lady Rothermere once, and I thought her as hard as nails; so I very much doubt – even if he wanted to marry her – whether such a marriage would not be the end of him.[20]

Ironically, it was because there were no guests at Goldeneye that year, while Ian waited for Anne's divorce to become final, that he settled down to write and produced the first draft of the thriller *Casino Royale* that was to make both his name and his fortune. Ian married his mistress in Jamaica in March 1952.

In April 1954, Faber held a party to launch Phyllis's latest novel, *Against Whom*; its American title was *The Secret Stair,* taken from a William Watson poem that she had first referred to in her 1904 novel, *The Master Hope*.[21] This quotation is:

> Ah, if indeed there be
> Beyond one darksome door, a secret stair
> Which winding to pure light, free air,
> This is the master hope, or the supreme despair.[22]

Tautly written and set in the hothouse of a Swiss sanatorium, it is an anatomy of neurosis that examines the character of a young woman called Caroline who is suffering from tuberculosis. As one perspicacious reviewer noted, Caroline 'had been "spoiled" in the literal sense that she had been rendered unfit for functioning normally and was beyond repair'.[23] As Phyllis once commented in another context, 'there is something highly pleasurable about voluntary martyrdom. Cutting oneself with knives, and crying aloud until the evening, is far more exciting than an ordinary day's work – and more noticeable.'[24] Following her own analysis with Adler, Phyllis was never sentimental, even though she was compassionate. *Against Whom* is novella-length and has some of the economy and bite of her short stories; it came out to generally good reviews and some excellent ones in both England and America, although not every reviewer enjoyed this Adlerian case-study form of fiction.[25]

Phyllis was somewhat unwell in 1954, so Nigel Dennis and Lewis Way took them on a six-week motoring trip through France and Switzerland to Casa Forbes in Italy. In this favourite company, both Phyllis and Ernan thoroughly enjoyed making their way southward while the climate and vegetation slowly changed from Alpine to Mediterranean. Their eighteenth-century villa, with a loggia overlooking Lake Orta, was exquisitely situated, though still somewhat primitive in its facilities. Now in their early seventies, they thought themselves unlikely to go there very often, and on this visit made a present of it to their delighted nephew.

In 1955, the success of *Against Whom* encouraged Faber & Faber to reprint in one book three of her early 'long-short' stories which had gone out of print; these were 'Belated Reckoning', 'The Victim' and 'Rose'. Phyllis had in Britain a loyal fan base that meant a secure market for anything written by her. Reviewers noted her ease with the long-short, a length of writing which had largely gone out of fashion by the 1950s, and commented that she had a 'style which is pleasantly and deceptively easy to read; it glides along so easily that the reader – unless he pauses, or goes back on the occasional phrase – may not notice how much acuteness of observation and how much shrewdness of expression have gone into the finished article'.[26] *Woman's Hour*, on the BBC's Light Programme, followed up by broadcasting 'The Belated Reckoning' in ten instalments, beginning on 24 January 1956.[27]

In May 1956, they were sad to hear of the death of Max Beerbohm in Rapallo. His wife, Florence, had died a few years ealier, and on his deathbed he married his secretary and close companion, Elizabeth Jungmann, to ensure that she would inherit his possessions under Italian law. Although he had lived in Rapallo since 1910, and was cremated in Italy, his ashes were interred in St Paul's Cathedral in June 1956.

As always, Phyllis worried about the state of the world. Around 1956 she became friends with the radical cleric John Collins, a canon of St Paul's Cathedral,[28] their having almost certainly been put in contact with each other by Freda Troup. Like Phyllis, Collins had read Alan Paton's *Cry, the Beloved Country*, and then a visit to South Africa in 1948 had convinced him that he needed to do more than the conventional Christian Aid remit allowed him to do. In 1956, when a hundred and fifty-six activists had been arrested and charged with high treason, Collins set up the International Defence and Aid Fund for Southern Africa. Among other things, it raised money and funnelled it illegally for defence trials of ANC members and to help their families and dependents. This 'laundering' of money through a variety of unlikely conduits sounds as though someone like Ernan, with knowledge of spycraft, might have been advising him. A series of letters signed by Phyllis and other writers protested about cruelty in South Africa and pleaded for racial equality in general.[29] She was, for example, a co-signee of a letter to *The Times* on 24 December 1959; other signees included W. H. Auden, Pamela Hansford Johnson, Storm Jameson, Doris Lessing, Daphne du Maurier, John Osborne and Colin Wilson.

It was also the era of the Cold War, and of the arms race, with both sides building stocks of nuclear weapons. Fear of global annihilation was rife, and Canon Collins became the first chairman of the Campaign for Nuclear Disarmament (CND). Although supportive of CND, Phyllis felt that it was only education, in its broadest Adlerian sense, that could cure social ills and avert international danger. Following the Second World War, she had hoped for a radical reform of the educational system, but in this hope she was largely disappointed; there seemed to exist something of an atmosphere of moral panic about delinquency among the young, especially adolescents, whose marginal status between child and adult made them objects of anxiety and alarm. The Crown Film Unit (as a section of the Films Division of the Ministry of Information) made a series of films in a drama-documentary style, of which *Children on Trial* (1946), on the subject of the reform-school system, is the most telling.[30] Phyllis was dismayed when the Conservative Government decided to close down the Crown Film Unit in 1952. As she wrote that same year, 'The world situation seems to be growing worse and worse, and even here in England we try to go back to the birch for young criminals – I suppose to harden them in their crimes.'[31]

Phyllis's next novel, tackling similar themes to those of *Children on Trial*, was published in 1956. Called *Eldorado Jane* in the British edition and simply *Jane* in the American edition, it focused on the subject of the delinquent child. Like Adler, Phyllis believed that the use of force was always wrong, and that corporal punishment could never reform a child, so her book was a fictive exploration of how an adolescent might be re-educated and re-formed. The book is set largely in a remand home, and follows the adventures, moral and otherwise, of a young criminal called Jane, just after the Second World War.

Typical of Phyllis's style, the novel has an arresting start. Jane, aged fifteen, expertly relieves a middle-class woman of her gold wristwatch on a bus journey – so skilfully that no one on the bus realises. Jane, at this young age, is already a consummate professional thief. She lives with a burglar called George, who is old enough to be her father, in the household of a woman who is on the surface a pawnbroker and antiques dealer, but more significantly, is a fence. Jane knows nothing about love, except for a dim memory of her mother: 'Nobody had kept Jane's birthdays since her mother died, when she was seven years old; but she could quite well remember a strawberry-coloured cake with seven pink candles on it. It seemed to sum up the whole of her life with her real mother before her stepmother came.'[32] George is the father-figure in her life, and he is a professional criminal who has 'educated' her in thief-craft. She depends on him to survive; George is simply the climate in which she lives. Although Jane does not think of him in these terms, George is an abusive 'father', in that she is scared to cross him and accepts his assumption that he should have sex with her. Phyllis's brief mention of Beatrice Cenci, subliminally suggesting Shelley's version of the daughter who murders her abusive father, economically makes this point.

Jane is apprehended taking part in a burglary, and sent to a remand home. She has now been labelled: 'A delinquent child! What was a delinquent child? What did the Law think it was? And what would the Law do about it – after it had thought?'[33] Corporal punishment was commonly used in remand homes, although it is clear that the enlightened principal of this particular one, Miss Bartlett, will herself never use it or endorse it because she 'would not rob even a delinquent child of its dignity'.[34] Miss Bartlett is an Adlerian in that she endeavours to educate, train and crucially to *encourage* her charges to have the self-respect that will give them a real chance of a productive life when they return to society. The remand home Miss Bartlett runs has the added responsibility of a group who are there not so much because they have committed a crime, although they may have been selling sex on the streets, but because they are suffering from venereal disease. Although the other girls call this group 'the lepers', Miss Bartlett sees them simply as girls needing medical help and health education. Her second in command, Emily Potter, is more judgemental, on this and on other matters. She is, for example, very perturbed by the lesbianism she perceives in the adolescent crushes that some of the girls have on one another. Jane herself falls in love with Elsie, a young girl who, suffering at the hands of her drunken mother, has taken comfort and presents from various predatory men, and is now infected with venereal disease. Miss Potter admonishes Miss Bartlett about what she perceives as Miss Bartlett's lax moral views about the matter. Miss Bartlett responds:

> 'I'm very sorry, Emily, I know some things seem as clear as day to you, while I'm lost in a fog. I've seen what you've seen; but I can't help remembering that I have to deal with two girls – one who has been physically degraded almost below the reach of affection, and one who is in grave danger of knowing no affection at all, going from violence to violence which may end in murder, through *lack* of affection. Here – perhaps for a few weeks, or even days, for they may be separated any day – they have a chance to learn a little of this most perplexing but surely *creditable* instinct of human love. If this feeling, mixed or not with sex stimulation, can make Jane gentler and give Elsie some self-respect, why should I check it? I simply cannot bring myself to do it.'[35]

Miss Bartlett in all cases sees the need for love as the first stage of a moral education, rather than as an aberration.

The novel was in many ways a bold one: it dealt with such issues as sexual abuse, infanticide and illegal abortions in a matter-of-fact rather than a scandalised fashion. It also objected to capital punishment, even for a criminal as vividly dangerous as George.[36] When he is tried for murder, Jane is called to court as a reluctant, even hostile witness:

> Jane had never seen a Judge before and wondered what he would look like. Suppose he had a grudge against Jews – or suppose he didn't like a prisoner who was dark instead of white? Perhaps he had – as some men had – a prejudice against women? Could the law save that prisoner whom the Judge – for no real reason – didn't like? What was the law anyhow? Something a lot of men had made up hundreds of years ago, when they weren't any radios – or motor cars – or aeroplanes – and nobody was in a hurry, or could get anywhere quickly if they were? Hadn't anybody ever learned anything more about each other since – or about themselves – so that they could really see why people like George did things and stop them doing them, without having to kill them when they hadn't been able to stop them?[37]

The novel was a bit too bold for some reviewers, who were concerned by the casual violence portrayed, where Jane, as a twelve-year-old girl brought up in America, is involved with some boys in a situation where her stepmother and father are murdered. However, only two years later, Charles Starkweather and his fifteen-year-old girlfriend Carol Fugate went on a murder spree which seemed to have little motive other than boredom, an episode later to be cinematically represented in Terrence Malick's film *Badlands*. Phyllis was an avid reader of newspapers, including American ones, and, as usual, she had her finger on the pulse of what was happening in the times she lived. *Time and Tide*, although it approved of Phyllis's narrative style as 'crisp and authoritative', felt that the dialogue was somewhat stilted. This is a fair criticism, as Phyllis did not have first-hand knowledge of – and was therefore not in possession of an ear tuned to – the argot of London criminals. Its subject matter, however, is not unrealistic. The psychology of the young criminal, Jane, is convincing, and Phyllis's key concern, represented by Miss Bartlett in the novel, that the psychological handling of delinquent children should be improved, is compelling. Jane, although only sixteen at the end of the novel, has witnessed and been actively involved in a great deal of criminal behaviour.

Nevertheless Miss Bartlett does not consider her irredeemable; nor does the reader, given Phyllis's skills as a novelist. On the whole reviewers recognised and acknowledged what she was trying to do in this book. Pamela Hansford Johnson commented: 'How many people are going to realise that *Eldorado Jane* is the absolute truth, by a writer who has not 'read up' her subject, but knows it through the experience of a lifetime? These are the facts as they are. This is what the innumerable Janes of the world are like.'[38]

And, similarly, Phyllis received a good review from Daphne du Maurier, who said that:

> *Jane* is not only an extremely important social document but a rattling good story, and I followed the fortunes of this lovable, but never sentimentalised delinquent girl, with the deepest interest. The whole work is beautifully done and ought to be made into a film while the problem of child delinquency is at the peak. There are too many Janes on both sides of the Atlantic who, through neglect and indifference on our part, never pull out of trouble.[39]

From her earliest work Phyllis had the knack of making her novels page-turners, and *Eldorado Jane* was no exception. It was broadcast on the Light Programme on 6 November 1956, when the BBC referred to it as 'the best novel to buy for Christmas'. Faber & Faber were pleased to note that sales increased after the broadcast and were at about 8,000 copies.[40] Columbia Pictures expressed an interest in adapting the novel for the screen, although in the end this came to nothing. This was followed by interest from Elstree Studios; indeed Phyllis signed a contract with Paul Soskin, who on leaving the orbit of the Rank Organisation, had become an independent producer, and sent her a script in August 1957. This, too, however, came to nothing.[41]

Nevertheless, it is worth noting that Phyllis, aged seventy-four, was still writing novels dealing with concerns of the moment that she had no trouble getting published. This is not something to be taken for granted, notwithstanding her long association with Faber. Other writers at this period, even if they had long track records with their publishers, found that they were dismissed perfunctorily if their publishers decided that they could not make any profit out of their work. One very fine writer,

Barbara Pym, suffered exactly this fate when her publisher, Cape, baldly announced that they could not sell her books in sufficient numbers, and refused to publish any more of her novels. As Pym's biographer explains, this was partly because of a sea change in the publishing world: 'The closing of many of the circulating libraries did incalculable harm to books [like Pym's]. A large market of middle-class, middlebrow readers – the backbone of the novel-reading public at that time – was gone and, although they took books from their public libraries, that did not greatly help sales, since they were, by and large, book borrowers and not book buyers.'[42]

Phyllis, on the other hand, if no longer producing best-sellers like *The Mortal Storm*, continued to relate strongly to the social and political *zeitgeist* and thus her books continued to sell in sufficient numbers for Faber to keep faith with her. She never had a finished book unpublished, which, given her long publishing life and shifting patterns of fashion, is in itself remarkable.

A continuing area of concern for her was how to eradicate the anti-Semitism that she thought still existed in British society. She believed that laws should be passed creating penalties for anti-Semitism and indeed any kind of racism, but as usual, she thought that education was the best key to change and that every teacher should be encouraged to work with their pupils in a way that challenged the cloud of unreason and neurotic disease that racism implied. In terms of anti-Semitism in particular, she commented that teachers:

> need not show pictures of Belsen Camp or acts of passion or hatred. But they could explain that we can discourage people – as the Germans were discouraged after their first beating in the 1914/18 war – into taking readily to tyrants who promise them greater privileges than other still weaker people whom they have in their midst and can persecute at will. This desire to punish scapegoats lies deeper even than the anti-Semitism prejudice, and I think it must be tackled psychologically if at all ... [43]

She continued to protest in every way possible against discrimination on the grounds of race, writing numerous letters to the papers, and organising a petition signed by writers. Her reward for these efforts was to be 'deluged with insulting, offensive and even obscene communications. (Filthy postcards, no less!) It is troubling to think that such people as the writers exist in England.'[44]

Her enthusiasm for anything that helped to disseminate Adler's ideas remained ever-present. Lewis Way, by this time a practising Adlerian counsellor, published a book on Adler's psychology in 1956, and, in 1961, translated and to some degree rewrote a book by Oskar Spiel, the headmaster of an experimental school (Individualpsychologische Versuchsschule) which had been founded in Vienna in September 1931.[45] It had been closed when the Dollfuss regime came to power in 1934, but had reopened at the end of the Second World War. Phyllis wrote to her nephew Phillip that '*Discipline without Punishment* [was] about a Vienna school of slum children brought up on Adlerian psychology. They have had more than 25 years of it now, and the Chief of Police told Ernan that it had cleared delinquency out of the whole quarter.'[46] By this stage, Lewis had become – alongside their beloved nephew, Nigel – an almost-son.

Phyllis was especially delighted when a young British director, Clive Donner, wanted to film *Heart of a Child*, first published in 1940.[47] On the Forbes Dennises' suggestion, Donner went to visit their old friend Luischen in Kitzbühel in May 1957, to take her advice on suitable locations. A letter from Sydney Box to Phyllis in August tells her that they have cast Donald Pleasance and Maureen Pryor in key roles, and have also found 'a charming St Bernard' dog.[48] As a J. Arthur Rank production, it did not, of course, produce as much income for Phyllis as a Hollywood movie would have done, but, nevertheless, this film gave her enormous satisfaction. It is a modest black-and-white film, made on a low budget with a small crew, and it was only the second film that Clive Donner had directed. Although the film undoubtedly has a certain charm in its depiction of the close relationship between a young boy, Karl, and his dog, it also has a more serious underlying message. The bullying father is a dictator in his own family, and the boy's courage in defying him comes at a high cost. Nevertheless, as a result of the boy's stand against his father, the rest of the village community start to gather round the vulnerable victim and the dictator is defeated. The political parallel is clear. Both the bullying father and the boy, played by the young actor Richard Williams, are convincingly portrayed. It retains, too, a certain authenticity: the character of Karl was based on the young boy Phyllis had watched daily from her balcony in Mösern, as he competently managed the livestock of his father's farm, assisted only by his dog. During the austerity years in Britain, there seems to have been a particular fascination with children; on the one hand so many had been lost in the war, and on the other, they represent the future. Recently, film critics have started to take an interest in this aspect of 1950s films, and it is into this genre that *Heart of a Child* fits. In June 1958, Phyllis and Ernan attended the première of the film at the Odeon in Leicester Square and Faber & Faber quickly reissued the novel.

Phyllis was good at keeping up with old friends, many of whom were fellow writers, such as Storm Jameson, Pamela Hansford Johnson and Daphne du Maurier. After dining with the Forbes Dennises in 1957, Pamela wrote in her diary, 'They are two beautiful and good old people having the most serene of Lapland night sunsets, listening to Beethoven Quartets.'[49] But Phyllis also continued to make new friends among younger writers. She was that clichéd thing, 'young at heart', but also, and perhaps more accurately, she was young in mind. In 1957 she met one of the so-called Angry Young Men, Colin Wilson, at a cocktail party, following the success of his best-selling book, *The Outsider*. After a prickly start, when he thought that she was patronising him, they became fast friends. Their letters, including a discussion on the representation of women in novels, are interesting: Phyllis wrote to him: 'Meredith was fair to us for all his flummery; and Henry James quite remarkably fair. Never Wells; he wanted women like pieces of cake and of course bolted them down too quickly so that they gave him indigestion from which he never recovered. I feel John Osborne might suffer in the same way.'[50]

In particular, Colin admired Phyllis's short stories, admittedly rather to his own surprise, as becomes clear from the following letter:

> I suppose that, being of a younger generation, I get used to making allowances for an older generation – especially for your own type of liberal-humanistic thinking. Therefore it's a refreshing and very

> salutary surprise for me to find myself listening to you with an interest that has to make no 'adjustments' for the difference in generations ... I mean that if you were seventeen now and just about to write your first novel, your 'sense of our own age' would certainly cause you to be hailed as the most penetrating of the 'Angry Young Women' (or whatever label the critics decided on). I felt the same astonishment on reading your *Walls of Glass* [collection of short stories]: having been brought up on Hemingway, Sartre and Camus, I was practically certain that I would find both the style and content alien to me (thinking, I suppose, of my mother's admiration for your work). I was amazed to find not only that the style was so tough and economical but that I was moved to excitement again and again by the quality of your intuitions. In this sense, you are far closer to reality than the Angus Wilsons and Stephen Spenders, who still have far too much that is sentimental and wishy-washy about them.[51]

By October 1957, Phyllis and Ernan were finding English winters increasingly trying. Following the death of their dog, Willow, and their little Siamese cat, Tito, they decided to move wholesale to London, leaving themselves enough money to escape to Gibraltar and North Africa for the winter months.[52] For Phyllis, Red Willows had been the perfect writer's home, with peace for the most part, but with a circle of creative artists near at hand when she wanted stimulating company. As she wrote to the editor of the *St Ives Times*, elegiacally describing her first sighting of her home seventeen years before: 'I walked up the path to Red Willows between the man-high fuchsia hedges and I thought "this is the most beautiful home anyone could possibly possess".'[53] In truth though, Ernan had always preferred living in London, with easy access to concerts and theatre. By the time they were in their late-seventies, they could not cope with running two homes. Phyllis's farewell to her beloved adopted town continues:

> We leave St Ives reluctantly because old age now limits our working life to London. We leave Cornwall even stronger and more convinced Liberals then when we came to it, more sure of the need for individual freedom and more anxious to see those who believe in it, practise it.[54]

Phyllis, however, never really liked the house that Ernan had bought in Bedford Gardens. Its wood panelling perhaps reminded Phyllis of the false grandeur of Frank Lascelles' house, and as such served as a reminder of less happy days. In any case, she thought it was 'much too large and old-fashioned for modern life'.[55] Red Willows was at first rented out, but finally they agreed to sell both houses in order to buy another, more modest one.

In the first two weeks of September 1959, Ernan dismantled Red Willows and they moved to Hampstead, which, with its connections to both the literary and the psychoanalytic world, seems a singularly appropriate place for Phyllis and Ernan's last home. Little Greenly, at 95 South End Road, close to Keats's house, was much more to Phyllis's taste; it echoed, in some sense, her beloved St Ives house.[56] Like Red Willows, its gaze was outwards, though in this case towards the Heath, rather than towards the sea.[57] As she wrote to Basil Liddell Hart, 'Although we have only a mouthful of garden, it fills up in a beautiful way and is neighboured very satisfactorily by other gardens. A real nightingale sings next door.'[58] Phyllis was still indefatigable in spirit; she exuberantly helped launch the Hampstead Literary Circle on 28 September 1959 and gave one of the first talks.

However, from 1960 on, her body was letting her down: her legs were very shaky, and she suffered from chronic intestinal troubles. Her last years were punctuated by visits to hospital for a series of minor operations.[59] And she worried, too, about Ernan, whom she described to Robert Pollak as 'suffering from rheumatism and low blood pressure, & is somewhat frail'.[60] Robert responded by sending them some delicate Japanese teacups for their china collection, collected when he had been the chief violin teacher at the Tokyo Conservatoire. In the summer of 1961, the two of them went to visit some of Ernan's Scottish relatives, following which Ernan underwent an operation on his prostate. Phyllis waited six weeks for him to recover, before going in for yet another minor operation on that writer's curse, painful haemorrhoids. Nigel Dennis, writing to commiserate, said that they were a typical 'author's disease – we sit and sit and think and think'.[61] Although the indignities of old age were overtaking them both they were always comforted by devoted and loving visitors. Nigel took Ernan 'fresh eggs, and an old friend from Cornwall [brought him] wonderful mountain gentians ... they were just like our old home in the Tyrol, a burning blue going out and in with the sun'.[62]

In 1961, in shaky health, Phyllis was delighted by good reviews of the third and final instalment of her autobiography, *The Goal*. Respectful reviews abounded in a wide range of national and local publications; John Lehman's in the *Sunday Telegraph* commented that 'as a general rule the autobiographies of prolific novelists are not among the most absorbing. It seems to me almost inevitable that the juice goes into the fiction.'[63] He went on to say that nevertheless there was much of interest. It is fair to say that one might get a more vivid sense of life in Vienna shortly after the First World War by reading *Old Wine*; however, reading the fiction and the autobiography side by side, a multi-faceted vision of personal and international events emerges. Daphne du Maurier rated it as 'one of the best autobiographies I have ever read'.[64] Vera Brittain immediately recognised the book's Adlerian title, indicating that the goal in question is self-knowledge and human understanding.[65] As the epigraph to *The Goal,* Phyllis had quoted the first two lines of Chaucer's *The Parliament of Fowles,* chosen, appropriately enough, as a dedication both to love and to the craft of writing:

> That lyf so short, the craft so long to lerne
> Th'assay so hard, so sharp the conquerynge.[66]

Although admiring this 'distinguished and well-adjusted writer', Vera Brittain could not resist an element of rerunning their battle over whether or not going to war against Hitler was the correct response to fascism. But she was deeply moved by Phyllis's account of the death of her closest friend Lislie, finally defeated by the tuberculosis that had long threatened them both. Brittain, too, had grieved over the loss of her close friend Winifred Holtby, who, like Lislie, had died aged thirty-seven.

Phyllis's three volumes of autobiography claim to tell the truth about her life, although – inevitably – there are various lacunae. She is discreet about why she failed to get on with Ernan's bachelor friends, for example, and why this group cold-shouldered her. She does not make plain the homosocial and even homosexual underpinnings of this set, and some knowing reviewers felt tantalised at what they suspected was being unsaid. The *Daily Telegraph* reviewer of *The Goal* for example, comments that 'we are left sadly guessing at why her husband's set cold-shouldered her'.[67] Ivor Novello's homosexuality was by this time a fairly open secret in the literary and film world. Film reviewers, in particular, while commending his brooding beauty, had been inclined to complain about his hysterical acting style, which was a pretty transparent code for homosexuality. But male homosexuality was illegal in Britain until some years after Phyllis' death, so perforce she needed to be discreet.

In any case, autobiography is never simply 'a naked and transparent presentation of existence' removed from the social world, and Phyllis was, of all people, engaged with the social and political world.[68] Today, in the academy, there is an increasing interest in life writing (as Virginia Woolf called it), by feminist scholars in particular, as they contemplate the opportunities seized by women writers to insert their voices into 'history'. Individual autobiographies are, almost every day, being retrieved to punctuate gaps in history.[69] Phyllis's own autobiography charts a remarkable life and, as many reviewers comment, it is as fascinating as reading fiction. The long historical sweep and the turbulent political period form a major part of its attraction, but also, the acute psychological attention to character, including her self-analysis.

Phyllis's three-volume autobiography had in fact experienced a hard birthing. The first volume, published by Faber & Faber as *Search for a Soul* in 1947, had originally been entitled by Phyllis 'The Education of a Child'.[70] Her American agent, at that time Ann Watkins, could not place it, and indicated that as it dealt with an epoch long past, she was unsure whether an account of the Edwardian era in which Phyllis grew up would really attract readers. Phyllis had answered rather spiritedly on 15 February 1947:

> what the world is suffering from today is not atomic bombs, but spoilt children, of which I was certainly one: I don't know whether you remember a book which roused terrific controversy in its day – and has now become a classic – called 'Father and Son' by the late Edmund Gosse? Gosse was a most pleasing and popular writer, but

> this book met with great disapproval, and indeed, I believe his own publisher refused it, but in a very short time it outsold most novels of its day. Here was truth – and nobody ever likes truth when it is first told, and never quite forgets it once it has been told. The same thing might happen with my own book. I do not say 'The Education of a Child' is a great book – as I believe 'Father and Son' to be – but I know it is a truthful book, from the inside out. It is not a novel: its drama – if it has any – is of quite another kind; the drama of a cactus growing on the little water it can get – in a desert of emotional ignorance.[71]

It is not surprising that Phyllis made reference to Gosse's *Father and Son*. Its publication in 1907 marked the transition from Victorian to modern life writing. Its subtitle, 'A Study of Two Temperaments', indicates a psychological approach to the autobiographical form, and a commitment to what Gosse called a 'faithful portrait of a soul in its adventures through life' (surely this phrase had an impact on Phyllis's eventual choice of title).[72] Phyllis wished to emulate Gosse's form, placing herself as an individual in the context of the family, and, in revealing her struggle to break from the patterns of the previous generation, also attempting to do justice to both generations.

As Phyllis had explained to the sceptical Watkins, who thought that a mere fragment of autobiography, ending when the protagonist reached eighteen, had limited value:

> The reason why I stopped when my childhood was over at 18 was because it is an Adlerian book, and is meant to show how every human being's life is formed and can be influenced, for or against, by family, education and friends during the malleable years. Later on I could not write with the same complete directness because I should require the privacy due to every adult. In our Adlerian Clinics we always stopped public sessions at 15 or 16; after this the Psychologist saw the young person alone. If I write any further memoirs ... it will have to be in quite a different way.[73]

In 1948 Phyllis had fired Watkins as her American agent, and had instead persuaded Reynall & Hitchcock to publish *Search for a Soul* in

America; it was also serialised in the *Ladies' Home Journal* for a fee of 6,000 dollars. Although the unfortunate Watkins had not cared for this odd hybrid of case history and memoir, she had perhaps underestimated the deep and widespread interest in psychological matters in America following the Second World War. *Search for a Soul* had received very good reviews almost everywhere; one astute American reviewer commented that Phyllis's writing here was 'more delicate than surgery' in unmasking her childhood choices.[74] Phyllis had pulled off the trick of writing as *both* analyst and patient, while holding the form in balance. It is hardly surprising that this first volume was well received; Phyllis was not only a very experienced writer, but also, by this time, an experienced life writer, having written biographical case studies of Alfred Adler, Max Beerbohm, Ivor Novello, Ezra Pound, Stella Benson and others.

The following two volumes of autobiography were more significantly engaged with the social and political world than the first almost wholly Adlerian volume. Nevertheless, as chronicles of a very unusual woman's life in unusual times, they also attracted critical interest. In 1952, the second volume, *The Challenge*, was published by Faber & Faber in Britain and by Harcourt Brace in America. According to Phyllis, at first it 'fell very silently on the book market, but since then has had very good reviews'; these included ones in the influential *Times Literary Supplement* and the *Observer*.[75] The second volume dealt with the death of her sister Wilmett, and it is useful to read *The Challenge* (1952) and her novel *Against Whom* (1954) together as attempts to deal with some of the same difficulties, albeit in two different genres. Phyllis recognises that in her childhood she had operated in intense sibling rivalry with Wilmett, but also acknowledges her mother's tyranny, which had functioned almost secretly via a distracting, disarming and essentially dishonest charm. Her mother is exposed as a *malade imaginaire* and self-elected family martyr. As Phyllis had observed elsewhere, 'martyrdoms often pay better than any other form of self-expression, but not always. They do not noticeably affect the Laws of the Universe. Canutes get wet.'[76] It is interesting to note that she does not mention her mother's death in the autobiography, as though Phyllis's escape in 1919 to join her husband in Marseilles was the 'death' of her mother's hold over her, and in that sense more significant than Daisy's actual death in 1926. The memoir deals, albeit admirably lightly, with her own sufferings from tuberculosis, the long stormy engagement to Ernan and, in conclusion, with their marriage during the First World War. Many reviewers noted that she showed no traces of self-pity when writing about a period of her life cruelly constrained by ill-health, and felt that this was both rare and honourable. Pamela Hansford Johnson had commented that *The Challenge* had: 'the flow and interest of a work of fiction, with all the human truth of unsensational autobiographical writing; I thought she had made something admirable, and in human terms, profoundly instructive, out of a theme very hard to tackle at length and in this way.'[77]

Given her commitment to the autobiography, although the first volumes had not attracted a great deal of critical attention, Phyllis felt vindicated by the almost universal good reviews of the third instalment, *The Goal.* And of course, she treasured the letters from those writer friends whose views she respected. After reading *The Goal*, Storm Jameson commented that: 'I do not know any two people who can have given – out of their own resources of mind and spirit and strength – so much to so many people, as you and Ernan. Forgive me if this is a presumptuous thing to say to you. It is said humbly, with love. Many, many people have warmed their hands at that fire.'[78] Phyllis was especially pleased to receive a letter from Ian Fleming:

> Looking back I am sure that your influence had a great deal to do with the fact that, at any rate, three of us [from the Kitzbühel school] later became successful authors, and I remember clearly writing a rather bizarre short story for you which you criticised kindly and which was in fact the first thing I ever wrote … Anyway, I loved the book, and above all I was delighted to be reminded of what really beautiful English you write. It is quite brilliantly good and clear and true.[79]

During the course of her career, Phyllis had engaged with all forms of life writing, but her 'voice' – unsurprisingly – is more immediate in the three volumes of autobiography than anywhere else.

Overall, however, the winter of 1961/2 was difficult. Phyllis was confined to the house for four and a half months, at first recuperating from her latest operation; but then, just as she seemed to be getting better, she suffered a heart attack and was confined to bed for nine more weeks. After the heart attack, Phyllis was very unsteady on her legs and Ernan had a chrome bar put in the bath to help her to get in and out safely. Ernan doted on her, as ever, and their cook-housekeeper Molly was indefatigable in her care for her. Increasingly, Phyllis had trouble with swollen feet and knees, which made getting about something of a trial. However, whenever he could spare the time, Nigel, their loving nephew, chauffeured them in his splendid Jaguar to see their old friends.[80]

On Easter Sunday 1962, the Forbes Dennises received the news that Raissa Adler had died. Although they had not experienced the intimate relationship with her that they had enjoyed with her husband, nevertheless it was another sorrow that marked the end of a generation.[81] Phyllis always regarded meeting Alfred Adler as 'the greatest event in my life'.[82]

Phyllis's mind remained keen. One review of *The Goal* commented that although still writing at eighty years old, Phyllis never lapses into 'that archness or faded sweetness which marks some elderly "lady" writers'.[83] Indeed not. Phyllis remained a woman angry at injustice and full of passionate integrity to the end. It was an interview with Phyllis in *The Bookseller* on the occasion of her eightieth birthday in May 1962 that alerted Daphne du Maurier to her friend's advanced years.[84] Sending her 'fondest love', Daphne wrote:

> It's a silly question, like a press reporter, to ask what it feels like to be 80. I think, as one grows older, one simply sheds a skin or two – consisting of prejudices or desires – and that is the only change that comes upon one.
>
> Big things can be taken in one's stride, but sometimes the trivial loom larger, like the sudden disappearance of a comb, or having run out of toothpaste on early-closing day ... Where is the ultimate security? I suppose when there is no more fear, but then we would be without adrenalin in the blood and would have turned into turnips.[85]

Daphne, well-aware that Phyllis's life was drawing to a close, was busily choosing what she thought were the best twenty-five of Phyllis's short stories for a collection. Faber had published *Walls of Glass* in 1958, and once again reviewers had praised the maturity and economy of her work in the rarely perfected short-story form.[86] As du Maurier put it, 'When she chose this particular form she did so deliberately, knowing that her thought could be transmuted in no other way, for only in this sudden brief exposure to the light could the essence of her idea be captured.'[87] It is certainly the case that in this genre, the opening sentence has to hook the reader; there can be nothing extraneous; a short story should be 'a small, highly polished jewel'.[88] Daphne wrote in the Preface to *Best Short Stories of Phyllis Bottome* that:

> The writer, more than any other artist, stands self-betrayed. The painter can catch a living scene on canvas, or a sitter's mood, and still stay hidden from his or her contemporaries, and from posterity too: but the writer, in the very choice of words and subjects, admits and indeed confesses, the problem within. Compelled by some driving instinct to spill words upon paper transmitting belief or interrogation, the writer reveals, sometimes in all unconsciousness, the spiritual battle of a lifetime.[89]

Daphne noted accurately that Phyllis, although a writer with huge sympathy for erring human beings, was in no way sentimental; she never let her subjects get off the hook. As du Maurier expressed it, in Phyllis's work 'neither God nor our neighbour can be blamed for our mistakes or our misfortunes. We are ourselves responsible.'[90]

Phyllis and Daphne, however, did not see eye to eye on which stories were the best; Daphne especially favoured those with an ironic twist and subtle humour. Phyllis was keen that 'Mountain Lover' and 'The Point of Vantage' should be included, but Daphne thought that they were 'rather too subtle for the ordinary reader'.[91] Nevertheless, Daphne bowed to pressure and allowed 'Vantage' into the selection, as the last essay. And it is a good choice, not because it is the best of her stories – Daphne's literary judgement is right about that – but because it sums up Phyllis's whole stance on the responsibilities of an artist, a subject on which she had frequently lectured, and which was the reason for her membership of PEN. Loosely based on an experience of her beloved friend, Robert Pollak, it serves, in a certain sense, as her epitaph. Set shortly after the political upheavals of World War I, it features an opera singer faced with a decision that brings about a crisis. Teobaldo Dubrik represents all Europe: 'His mother had been an Italian; and on his passport it stated that his father had been a Hungarian. Teobaldo himself had been born and bred in a Baltic province under German rule.'[92] As an artist he feels himself to be a citizen of the world, but now, finding himself under Soviet rule, he needs a visa to leave and perform. He risks his own security and freedom by appealing to the head of the Cheka to release an elderly songwriter, Wolnikoff, from gaol. Teobaldo claims: 'one bar of Wolnikoff's music will outlast any form of government! One rule of harmony is stronger than any dictatorship.'

By the beginning of August 1963, Phyllis was so poorly that Ernan reluctantly started to look for a nursing home. He tried to reassure Phyllis that there was a life in the world to come, but this had long ceased to be part of her faith. Although she took the basic tenets of Christianity as a good model for a life well lived, part of the urgency of her writing was that, to Phyllis, there was only one life to live, and making a good job of that was what counted. All in all, her last two years were pretty tough, although nothing could stop her writing. She was working on a new novel called *Home without Angels* when she succumbed to a second, and this time fatal, heart attack. After weary weeks of suffering her always-supposedly-weak heart had finally ceased to beat. It had lasted her through an extremely active life until the age of eighty-one. She was a brave-heart, rather than weak-hearted.

Phyllis died on 22 August 1963. The following morning, her death was reported on the BBC Radio News at 8 a.m. and in *The Times*; she had indeed become a public institution. The radio obituary described her as 'the champion of the underprivileged and the misunderstood', a description that would have pleased her.[93] Her death was reported in the major American papers too.[94] An obituary in the *Jewish News* on 8 November 1963 reprinted 'I Accuse' and referred to *The Mortal Storm*. A letter that Phyllis wrote to another author may perhaps be used as her own obituary for herself: 'I have written more or less successfully with a long apprenticeship of failure, and with interludes of illness for over fifty years. I do not suppose much of what I have written will have any lasting significance, but *The Mortal Storm* helped the Jews in the 1930s and I have been told that *Under the Skin* has also been useful in removing racial prejudice.'[95]

She did not lay claims to writing a literature that would last the ages; instead she wrote with passionate urgency, out of the pressures of the day. On 26 August, Phyllis was cremated at Golders Green and her ashes scattered there.[96] Appropriately enough, given her support of the Jewish cause, this crematorium is adjacent to the Jewish cemetery on the other side of Hoop Lane; Phyllis could be described as a righteous Gentile.

Nigel Dennis and his second wife Beatrice rushed to Ernan's side at the Hampstead house, where endless telegrams and letters of condolence poured in.[97] These letters are evidence not only of the huge affection in which she was held, but also of the eclectic range of their friends. Among them were letters from Alexandra Adler, the Countess of Athlone, Frank Halliday, Storm Jameson, Baroness Malahide, Ben Nicholson, Barbara Hepworth, Willie Barns-Graham, Bernard Leach, Daphne du Maurier, PEN, Priaulx Rainier, Irene Spierer, Lord Vansittart, the Davidsons from Knox College in Jamaica and from all the old Kitzbühel boys.[98] Ian Fleming's letter to Ernan said:

> She was such a *dear* person and between you, you spread an extraordinary warmth and light and sympathy wherever you went. You were father and mother to me when I needed them most and I have always treasured the memory of those days at Kitzbühel. By chance I am going back there tomorrow and I will say a prayer for Phyllis and for you, dear Ernan.[99]

A letter from Sylvia Foot, a friend from their sojourns in Jamaica, commented aptly that, 'Phyllis spent a lifetime keeping the flame of Liberty burning.'[100] At Knox College in Jamaica, a mahogany reading desk was commissioned in memory of Phyllis, with her name and the inscription, *Homo sum: humani nil a me alienum pute* – a quote from Terence, which translates: 'I am a man: I count nothing human alien from me.' The themes most often touched upon in the hundreds of letters Ernan received were Phyllis's energy, her courage, her interest in people, especially in young people, her great intelligence, her delight in ideas, her quick wit, the champagne of her conversation, her smiling beautiful eyes, her boundless exuberance.

Probate was granted on 2 October 1963 of £23,995 5*s*. 2*d*., not a huge amount of money for a best-selling author, especially considering that four of her books had been made into films, but she and Ernan had given a great deal of money away over the years, both to private and public charities. In November, Ernan sold the Hampstead house because he needed money to settle Mollie and Jack Baker, their Irish cook and her husband, who had been their live-in staff since the end of the war, in a house in County Kildare.[101] The Bakers were now over seventy and ready to retire, and in any case Ernan could not afford to keep them on simply to look after him.

Ernan spent some weeks in a London hotel before boarding a cargo boat to Malta, a place that he had never visited with Phyllis.[102] At first he could not face visiting anywhere he had shared with her as he felt that Phyllis's absence would be too intense to be borne. But this psychological manoeuvre did not help him much, especially since he found that his own faith in an afterlife of the soul shattered after her death. Writing to Ruth Aspinall in January 1964, Ernan said, 'I find that all beauty stabs as well as comforts. Perhaps this is because of Phyllis's full and instant response to beauty of every kind, which doubled its intensity. One tends to say: "How she would have loved that": and of course the pain returns as one says it.'[103] He went on:

> Much depends on the length of the partnership, the depth of the habit of sharing. In our case it was sixty years overall. There were breaks after the five years in the Swiss mountains and we were not married until 1917. The sharing, however, with its enhancement of life, was there from the very start and nothing really shook it. During the absences, the joy of life faded ... [but] ... there are also things to be thankful for: that Phyllis should not have known of Kennedy's assassination and all the outbreak of hatred and intolerance on Cyprus, in Kashmir, in Indonesia, in Panama, in Ghana would, I think have killed her ... [104]

Ernan knew so clearly all the things that Phyllis cared deeply about;

echoing a phrase she herself had coined about a pair of fictional lovers, 'their deep courtesy of loving' had survived the long years of their marriage.[105]

Poor Ernan, very lonely, lived in a kind of vacuum. He missed not only Phyllis but also Jack and Mollie, who had been not merely housekeeper-cook and gardener-chauffeur, their 'official' roles, but also close companions for over twenty years. His immediate major occupation was writing thank-you letters to the hundreds of condolence letters he had received. Phyllis and Ernan's marriage was remarkable; he had been her best friend, her support, her business manager and impresario. Perhaps he had lived a little too much in her shadow for his own best good, following the surrender of his diplomatic career in the mid-1920s, when she had been diagnosed with a resurgence of tuberculosis. A letter from Ernan to Phyllis early in their marriage said, 'I feel sometimes that you and I are like an eagle and a mole – you try to teach me to see & I try to teach you to burrow. The danger is we may both turn into a bat, which flies like the eagle and is blind like the mole.'[106] However, nothing could stop Phyllis from being an eagle, whereas the first thing to be mentioned in Ernan's obituary in *The Times*, when he died some nine years later, was that he had been 'the devoted husband of the novelist Phyllis Bottome'.[107]

He was lost without her, and wandered from place to place, staying with old friends; he spent nine months with Luischen in Kitzbühel, four months at Knox College in Jamaica, and six months at a time with Nigel and Beatrice Dennis in Malta, and a month with them every summer at Lake Orta.[108] But his undiminishing sense of loss was testimony to the deep roots of the long partnership with Phyllis. A biography of Phyllis must include a portrait of their marriage; she was, rightly, as proud of her marriage as she was of all her other endeavours.

However, to pay tribute to Ernan's own qualities, as Phyllis would have wished, many of his 'pupils' had benefited from his wise counsel, just as Phyllis herself had massively benefited from his intellectual companionship and emotional support over all the years.[109] Ernan received many invitations to visit old pupils; he enjoyed especially a visit to Ben Nicholson, at that time living in the Ticino.[110] When Ernan died, his obituary justly commented, 'Friends all over the world will mourn the loss of this distinguished and generous man.' The fond love of Nigel – whom Ernan regarded as 'the best possible son' – of Beatrice, and of Nigel's two daughters, helped him through his last decade. He died in July 1972, and, like Phyllis, was cremated at Golders Green, his ashes scattered on the crocus lawn. Although, at the end of their lives, neither Phyllis nor Ernan had any secure religious faith to uphold them, they were both able to find consolation in small things. As Phyllis herself wrote, even in the darkest times, 'There is still sun on the wall.'[111]

Conclusion

> All writers have different conditions which help with their writing. I write as I live. The more intensely I am preoccupied by life itself, the clearer is my perception of what I can do with the subject of my work.
>
> PHYLLIS BOTTOME, *The Goal*

Phyllis began life in a relatively conventional middle-class home towards the end of the nineteenth century, when women of her social standing were expected to do a little philanthropic work rather than be breadwinners. Yet her work with the poor in her father's parishes alerted her to social and political circumstances at a fairly young age. In a bizarre way, her life-threatening illness, which removed her from the family, rescued her. It meant that she no longer simply accepted her mother's views of a respectable woman's role in society. Her father's financial fecklessness meant that at an early stage she needed to earn her own living; so she, in effect, lived as a feminist before formally acknowledging the justice of the feminist cause. Since she didn't have a private income, like some middle-class women writers of her generation, she was always a working writer, whose output was necessarily prolific. Her lifestyle was unusual for a woman of her class and circumstances, and departed from the path set out for her by society.

Her marriage too was unusual. She did not simply marry a man of the professional classes and become a mother and figurehead of a middle-class household. She had become aware that women in her class, although often put on a pedestal by men, were not really accepted as equals by them, and also that women's dependence on men, rather than helping them forge significant roles for themselves, could sometimes make monsters of them. These things formed the basis of her feminist impulses. Equal rights for women, albeit possibly with different duties, but certainly with equal humanity, was her first political understanding. In choosing to marry Ernan Forbes Dennis, she chose a partner who shared her social and political ideals, and, notwithstanding the difficulties in their marriage, it was also a long love affair. It is not by coincidence that when Phyllis was invited on to the BBC programme *Writers' Choice of Music* she selected Schubert's Unfinished Symphony as the symbol of their long romance.[1]

She very early recognised the misogyny that lay at the heart of fascist regimes. In 1934, she wrote in New York's *Herald Tribune* praising the young women of the day who were physically and intellectually as free as young men:

> No wonder [that] Hitler and Mussolini pit themselves against the Zeitgeist, as King Canute did against the waves of the Atlantic, to drive these threatening Amazons back into their homes. No wonder! But have these masterminds, in the pauses of their dynamic labours, read what happened? The waves went on advancing; and after getting thoroughly wet, King Canute moved back.[2]

First in Vienna in the 1920s, and then in Munich in the 1930s, Phyllis was the reluctant witness of both subtle and gross forms of anti-Semitism. She recognised that the psychological 'alibi' for behaving disgracefully towards the Jews as an oppressed group was to find a mechanism for considering them as not fully human.[3] She exposed this kind of false thinking in several of her books. *The Mortal Storm*, first published in 1937, and made into an anti-Nazi film by MGM in 1940, remains a powerful exposure of how even seemingly-decent people can descend into madness. The reluctance of Britain to allow Jewish refugees into the country, long after Britain had understood the peril that faced them, struck her as shameful. If Britain itself was a 'bystander' nation, Phyllis herself was never a bystander. She actively aided refugees and supported a Jewish homeland (although she did not foresee at the time how this would bring the Israelis into deadly conflict with the Palestinians). The Russian poet Yevgeny Yevtushenko said, 'In the presence of anti-Semites, I am a Jew'; likewise Phyllis could be described as a righteous Gentile.[4] After the Second World

War, she became sharply aware of the wrongs of colonialism, 'excused' once again by racist ideology. This, at its briefest, is the trajectory of her political awareness.

Phyllis was always liberal by instinct (and after World War II a Liberal, too, in the party-political sense). The liberal tradition contains strong ideals of freedom that, however, always need to be balanced against issues of decency and order. The philosophical roots of her own liberalism went back to John Stuart Mill's 'On Liberty', and she endorsed his 'harm principle' – that the individual must be free to follow his own course unless this interfered with the liberty of others. Phyllis's own model of what she regarded as the liberal stance was to be 'open-handed, generous, open-minded, unprejudiced'.[5] She lived her life that way, and the last of the four adjectives is crucial to understanding much of her activism. In her view it was impossible to be liberal and simultaneously anti-Semitic or racist, as this would overturn notions of tolerance and equality. She wrote out of this fervent personal and political conviction.

She did not subscribe to any concept of class war but she felt that 'no country was a Democracy where the education of one class ends at fourteen and that of another at twenty-three'.[6] This must always, in her view, exacerbate social class divisions. She was against corporal punishment in any school or remand home. Free choice, so long as it did not offend the harm principle, was part of her liberal credo; she supported the Voluntary Euthanasia Legislation Society.[7] She was utterly opposed to capital punishment, and was, for example, particularly incensed over the Bentley case, when a man with learning difficulties, and not even the man who pulled the trigger, was hanged.[8] She supported Cannon Collins's campaign for nuclear disarmament.

As a left-leaning liberal, Phyllis was more sympathetic to the *ideals* of communism than to any right-wing ideology, but as she said, 'I could not be a Communist because I could not agree in my mind to any form of dictatorship.'[9] Indeed she rejected all absolutist politics. She believed that any new order in Britain must consider social and economic democracy as part of political democracy. Phyllis regretted the inexorable decline of the Liberal Party in Britain following the First World War, and, following the Second World War, put some effort into trying to build it up again.[10] A letter to *The Times* on 14 December 1951 sums up her dismay at its decline:

> In the world today the lamentable absence of the essential liberal virtues of tolerance, freedom and equality is patent. For that reason and believing now, as in the past, this country can do much by its own example to spread these virtues, we deplore the eclipse of organised British Liberalism and we should welcome its reappearance as an effective force in the House of Commons.[11]

Phyllis Bottome's writing was always highly responsive to politically charged situations, which is unsurprising given that she regarded liberalism 'as the natural creed of every creative mind'.[12] Her best books are emphatically the ones most closely aligned to her political experiences. Whereas modernists believed that to mix politics and art was to 'adulterate' art, Phyllis would, if necessary, sacrifice perfection of form for urgent politics.[13] For her, modernism represented a kind of aesthetic absolutism; and, in a crunch, she privileged ethics over aesthetics. In her best work, though, as for example in *Old Wine* and *The Mortal Storm*, her writing maintained the balance between substance and style. She herself made no claims to be a great writer in the formal sense, although she felt that she had done one or two things that she was proud of. Writing to a fan, she said that *The Mortal Storm* 'had been translated into Yiddish and ran through the chief American paper. The definition of a good Jew which I make the old professor give his son is also used now as part of the confirmation service for young Jews.'[14] She was especially proud of this.

By the end of her life she had become a public intellectual, often asked to lecture, broadcast or be interviewed about her opinions on a wide range of subjects. But whereas many such 'celebrities' are willing to pontificate, what made Phyllis Bottome remarkable is that she lived – more than almost anyone – what she believed. Even at eighty she was a rebel. Daphne du Maurier described her as 'a tilter at windmills, a champion of brave causes, a warrior for the misunderstood and the underprivileged, whether they be refugees from European prison camps, or rootless Jamaicans, or maladjusted boys from broken homes'.[15]

Many of the reviews of her work and the letters of condolence after her death emphasise that Phyllis had both impressive intellectual gifts *and* a warm loving heart. There is a certain irony here in the fact that Phyllis all her life suffered from a weak heart, yet she was lion-hearted in her support of the oppressed. Ezra Pound had told Phyllis that he could not figure out whether, as a writer, she was a Realist or a Romantic. Phyllis did not see why these should be considered binary opposites; her Romanticism produced her vital response to beauty and evocation of place, but her political acuity meant that there was always the gravel of the real in the mix of her narratives. And this was partly why she could reach out to such a wide readership: different kinds of readers found a broad palette of colours to savour in her work.

Phyllis accurately described herself as 'not a great traveller but a thorough inhabitant'.[16] Unjustly forgotten by the literary world of the present, she is a unique twentieth-century writer in that she was a witness in several countries other than Britain for substantial periods of her life. She was more European in sensibility than most British people, and she was international in spirit. Alongside her alert sense of politics, she wrote out of an unquenchable fascination with people. She did not begin with a structure or shape for a book, as a modernist might; instead she began with a person and their problems. 'If a writer is true to his characters they will give him his plot,' she said, and this dictum, though sometimes causing a weakness in her writing, was more often the source of strength in her best work.

Virginia Woolf, in a 1932 letter to the *New Statesman*, condemned 'middlebrows' and what she called the 'betwixt and between'. This view, now increasingly challenged by feminist critics in particular, has meant that many good women writers have been left out of the canon. The neglect of Phyllis Bottome is emblematic of the neglect of other once popular writers.[17] Recently, there has been a concerted effort to change this, and there have been some lively conferences deliberately asserting the title 'Middlebrow' and wishing to recuperate the term, rather as some academics have recuperated the term 'queer'.[18] It is probably a useful initial strategy, but it may run the risk of the casual observer assuming that these writers were not intellectuals, but were merely capable of producing amusing tales of domestic life or romantic novels. This is not to deny that domestic life or love and its representation is important, and figures in their work, but it hardly takes stock of the intense political commitment, the depth of knowledge and the international range of some of these writers. Many of them serve as vital cultural barometers of their times; new terms probably need to be invented, and this remains a work-in-progress.[19]

Unlike most people, Phyllis Bottome became more tolerant – not less – with age. Her training – and that of her husband – with Alfred Adler in the 1930s, was crucial to this. Writing at the time of the publication of her collection of short stories called *Fortune's Finger*, a reviewer commented: 'Miss Bottome sees human nature with the tolerant, but searching eye of a psycho-analyst.'[20] This is correct up to a point, but she was not allied to Freudian psychoanalysis, notwithstanding her admiration for Freud *as a writer*. From her point of view, she objected that for Freudians the 'unconscious' was presented without any grain of criticism as an explanation for any sort of behaviour. Adler, on the other hand, laid more stress on the development of a highly responsible consciousness. Over time, some earlier prejudices, such as the homophobic tendency of her early years, were discarded, and arguably all Phyllis's post-Adlerian writings show enlarged empathy. But it is also the case that she did not let anyone in her fiction off the hook from her or his human responsibilities. She never allowed emotion as a substitute for conduct. And this moral positioning is glimpsed in its most concentrated form in her short stories. Even though many of them displayed an ironic twist and a subtle humour, and often appeared to be fables of modern life, they were possessed of a peculiar lucidity and grace that attracted reviewers on all sides. A *Guardian* reviewer concluded: 'Miss Bottome's stories are ... small moments ... biting on a nerve of mental or moral truth.'[21]

Whereas modernists upheld a stance of anonymity for the writer and insisted that the arts should be free of teaching, Phyllis laid a different stress on what she considered the responsibilities of an artist. They were, she said, threefold: an artist 'has a responsibility to himself, to his brother man and to truth ... ' and it was 'not necessary to put morals in fiction, but the morals must be in the artist'.[22] In that sense, Phyllis was her own Adlerian experiment, one that she tracked in three volumes of autobiography.

The American journalist Alice Dixon Wood, interviewing her in 1946, wrote:

> Talking with Phyllis Bottome is comparable to the experience of looking into the heart of a fire when the logs are all aflame and the shifting embers glow with darting life. There are warmth and color, incendiary sparks of exciting ideas, a sense of power and the radiance which emanates from something beautiful and very lovely. Vividly and eloquently alive, Miss Bottome reflects the multiple experiences of her own generous and dauntless life: the pity and tenderness, laughter and anguish, compassion and courage, just as trees, when burned, they say, show every color they have known when alive – the rose of dawn; the varied greens of the forest; the deep blue of cloudless skies and the bright gold of sunlight.[23]

It is noticeable that many reviewers of her work over many years were drawn to images of light and fire. Phyllis was never cool in her responses, either to life or to literature; she was always full of passionate integrity. Her kind of writing may have gone out of fashion, as it would not have been considered 'cool' in the 1960s. Literary canons are largely defined by fashion and politics, although this is not always acknowledged. Regarding Phyllis Bottome's work in terms of literary history, we note that, although she generally employed realist narrative traditions, she simultaneously charted both a feminist and a political engagement with her turbulent times. Today, we are moving into a period of global recession following unchecked capitalist speculation. Unemployment brings with it attendant dangers, such as a resurgence of racism. It might prove salutary to reread *The Mortal Storm*. As concern mounts today that society is becoming increasingly fractured, many of Phyllis Bottome's insights into broken lives, and broken societies, might seem startlingly in touch with modernity after all.

Notes to the Text

Notes to the Introduction

1 See Marilyn Hoder-Salmon's biographical essay on Phyllis Bottome, which is to be found in *Late-Victorian and Edwardian British Novelists*, Second Series, Volume 197 of *Dictionary of Literary Biography*, edited by George M. Johnson (Detroit, Washington DC, London, Bruccoli Clark Layman, Gale Research, 1998). I am greatly indebted to this essay, which was an enormous help in starting my own research. See also, *The Oxford Companion to Edwardian Fiction*, eds Sandra Kemp, Charlotte Mitchell and David Trotter (Oxford University Press, 1997).

2 See Virginia Woolf, 'Mr Bennett and Mrs Brown', *Nation and Athenaeum*, 34 (1 December 1923).

3 Introduction to *The Oxford Companion to Edwardian Fiction*, op. cit., which inevitably does not chart any of Phyllis Bottome's later work.

4 Phyllis Lassner, *Colonial Strangers: Women Writing the End of Empire* (Rutgers University Press, 2004), p. 177

5 One significant attempt to undertake a re-evaluation of the canon appears in a collection of essays called *Outside Modernism*. In particular, an attempt is made to 'reconceptualize the relationship between modernism and its early twentieth-century *doppelgänger*, realism'. Lynne Hapgood and Nancy Preston suggest that we should regard 'realism and modernism as terms which describe literary techniques rather than define conflictual literary movements'; they demonstrate 'how these two techniques interacted, complemented and coexisted with each other, often within the same text'. They argue that 'the interplay between realist and modernist approaches calls into question not only exclusive definitions but also dismissive or period-bound definitions of realism'. This is a useful formulation, but I want to be more argumentative still, and contest modernism's claim to be the dissident voice of the twentieth century, pushing open the gate of conventional literary culture. In particular, I want to claim that modernism is a literary form that, however fascinating, has had a disproportionate share of attention, and that there are other versions of, and responses to, modernity.

6 'The middlebrow is the man, or woman, of middlebred intelligence who

ambles and saunters now on this side of the hedge, now on that, in pursuit of no single object, neither art itself or life itself, but both mixed rather indistinguishably, and rather nastily, with money, fame, power, or prestige.' Virginia Woolf, 'Middlebrow', collected in *The Death of the Moth and Other Essays* (London: Hogarth Press, 1942)

7 See *Encyclopedia of British Women's Writing, 1900–1950*, eds Faye Hammill, Esme Miskimmin, Ashlie Sponenberg (Palgrave Macmillan, 2006), which includes my essay on Phyllis Bottome.

8 Nicola Beauman, *A Very Great Profession: The Woman's Novel 1914–1939* (London, Virago, 1983); see also Nicola Humble, *The Feminine Middlebrow Novel: 1920s to 1950s: Class, Domesticity, and Bohemianism* (Oxford University Press, 2004), and Alison Light, *Forever England: Femininity, Literature and Conservatism Between the Wars* (London, Routledge, 1991).

9 See Barbara Brothers' essay 'British Women Write the Story of the Nazis: A Conspiracy of Silence', in *Rediscovering Forgotten Radicals: British Women Writers 1889–1930*, eds Angela Ingram and Daphne Patia (University of Carolina Press, 1993).

10 *1001 Movies You Must See Before You Die*, ed. Steve Jay Schneider (Quintet Publishing Ltd, 2004)

11 Phyllis Bottome, *The Goal* (New York, Vanguard Press, 1962), p. 40

12 Henry Louis Gates Junior, 'A Liberalism of Heart and Spine', *New York Times* (27 March 1944), p. 22

13 *St Ives Times and Echo*, Friday, 6 September 1963

14 See letter from Baroness Malahide, 23.8.1963, to Ernan Forbes Dennis: 'I was very sad when I heard about Phyllis this morning on the BBC 8 o'clock news. Not for her, because she must have suffered much and for so long, but for you and all those who loved her.' See Bottome Papers, ADD 78862 BL.

15 Frank Swinnerton (1884–1982), writer and publisher's reader from 1907 at Chatto & Windus, quoted by Vera Brittain, *Testament of Experience* (London, Virago, 1979), p. 96

16 ibid., pp. 96–7

Notes to Chapter 1 – Childhood of a Writer

1 This is the opening line of Tolstoy's *Anna Karenina*.

2 Phyllis Bottome, *From the Life* (London, Faber & Faber, 1944), p. 84. As a biographer, I have used Bottome's three volumes of autobiography to help with the time frame, though my study of the Bottome Papers in the British Library shows that Phyllis skimmed over difficult areas, even

though she says, quoting De Quincey, that 'candour must be the chief aim of all autobiography', in the Preface to *Search for a Soul*, the first volume of autobiography.

3 It was founded at a meeting in Margaret Bottome's house at 18 Washington Place, New York, at which she was elected president, an office she retained until her death in 1906. Beginning as a women-only venture, largely run by women who were used to helping in their husbands' parishes and by women head-teachers, it proved very successful, and, as a consequence, men became eager to join the organisation. In 1887, the organisation duly changed its name to include 'Sons', and in 1891, such was its wide-reaching appeal, its name was formally changed to the 'International Order of the King's Daughters and Sons'.

4 Phyllis Bottome, *Search for a Soul* (London, Faber & Faber, 1947), p. 12; I note that on Daisy Bottome's death certificate her maiden name is spelled as 'Leatham', rather than 'Leathem', as it appears in Phyllis's autobiography.

5 *From the Life*, op. cit., p. 88

6 *Search for a Soul*, op. cit., p. 262

7 ibid., p. 38

8 ibid., p. 32

9 ibid., p. 21; see Marilyn Hoder-Salmon's essay on Phyllis Bottome in *Late-Victorian and Edwardian British Novelists*, op. cit., which makes this point.

10 *Search for a Soul,* op. cit., p. 13

11 ibid., p. 42; p. 98

12 ibid., p. 95

13 ibid., p. 56

14 ibid., p. 31

15 ibid., p. 30

16 ibid., p. 55

17 ibid., p. 59

18 ibid., p. 23

19 ibid., p. 72

20 Phyllis Bottome, 'Kingdom of The Young', photocopy of article in Bottome Papers, Add 78858 BL

21 *Search for a Soul*, op. cit., p. 102

22 Letter from Anne Dunn from Bellevue Palace, Berne, 14 March 1925, saying that Miss Burnett had died, but had been reading Phyllis's novel *The Kingfisher* shortly before. Bottome Papers, Add 78865 BL

23 *Search for a Soul*, op. cit., p. 108

24 ibid., p. 108

25 ibid., p. 171

26 George Herbert McCord (1848–1909) was a pupil of Samuel F. B. Morse

and James Firman in 1866, and had exhibited at the National Academy of Design by 1870. He made frequent trips to sketch in New England, Canada, Florida and the Upper Mississippi. His Romantic landscapes revealed a highly developed sense of colour. See *300 Years of American Art*, compiled by Michael David Zellman (Wellfleet Press, 1987).

27 *Search for a Soul,* op. cit., pp. 171–2
28 ibid., p. 180
29 ibid., p. 191
30 ibid., p. 181
31 ibid., p. 181
32 ibid., p. 224
33 Grandma Bottome felt that Wilmett, at seventeen, should not be spending her days as the nurse-cum-drudge of her mother. She hoped that the climate in Egypt might help restore her health. She then accompanied Wilmett back to England, handing her over to Grandma Fowler, released from cares. Wilmett was to stay in the Grosvenor Square House until she was twenty, with her doting maternal grandmother and step-grandfather.
34 *Search for a Soul*, op, cit., p. 228
35 ibid., p. 235
36 ibid., p. 241
37 ibid., p. 235
38 ibid., p. 242
39 ibid., p. 262
40 Bottome Papers, Add 78898 BL
41 This winter, too, she enjoyed a deep friendship with a boy called Gerard Coleridge, who was a year older than Phyllis (and the son of friends of her parents). Although this was not a romance, it seems to have acted as a kind of model for the relationships she wanted with a man. First and foremost it was a deep intellectual sharing. See *Search for a Soul*, op. cit., pp. 265–6.
42 ibid., p. 265
43 ibid., p. 268
44 ibid., p. 276
45 ibid., pp. 270–1
46 Phyllis Bottome, *Raw Material* (John Murray, 1905)
47 *Dictionary of Literary Biography,* Volume 197, op. cit.
48 'It was thought to be the result of the bacillus gaining entry through the tonsil and being carried by lymph to the nearest lymph nodes.' Thomas Dormandy, *The White Death: A History of Tuberculosis* (London and New York, Hambledon, 1999), p. 3
49 In *Etudes sur la Tuberculose*, in 1868, Villemin noted that 'tuberculosis was

more frequent among the medical personnel and soldiers stationed for long times in barracks than among troops in the field' and that 'prisoners, industrial workers and members of religious cloistered orders were more apt to contract the disease than were ordinary citizens'; quoted by Selman A. Waksman, *The Conquest of Tuberculosis* (Robert Hale, 1964), p. 83

50 Pam Hirsch, *Barbara Leigh Smith Bodichon: Feminist, Artist and Rebel* (Chatto & Windus, 1998), p. 218; p. 223

51 *Search for a Soul*, op. cit., pp. 281–2

52 ibid., p. 282

53 ibid., p. 286

54 ibid., p. 290

55 See Mary Ann Gillies, *The Professional Literary Agent in Britain 1880–1920* (University of Toronto Press, 2007).

56 *Search for a Soul*, op. cit., p. 302

57 Phyllis Bottome, *Life, the Interpreter* (Longmans, Green, 1902), p. 137

58 ibid., p. 188

59 Huber, quoted by Selman A. Waksman, op. cit., p. 14

60 Bottome Papers, Add 78869 BL

61 Within the family structure, boys did not seem to have to bear the same expectations of them. Phyllis's brother George went to preparatory school, then public school and finally Cambridge, so he was never in the claustrophobic situation of his sisters.

62 According to Dormandy, op. cit., p. 211, the bacillus enters by 'inspired air inside liquid droplets or particles of dust to the microscopic air-sacs of the lungs'.

63 Sir Richard Douglas Powell, 1st baronet (1842–1925). His chief published work was *On the Principal Varieties of Pulmonary Tuberculosis with Practical Comments* (1872). He was physician in ordinary to Queen Victoria, whom he attended in her last illness (1901), Edward VII and George V.

64 Phyllis Bottome, *The Challenge* (London, Faber & Faber, 1953), p. 24

65 ibid., p. 38

66 Wilmett had been almost engaged to a young officer she had met in Egypt, and then had a romance with the son of one of her father's oldest friends, but there was no encouragement on the side of the young man's family, because the Bottomes had no money. See *Search for a Soul*, op. cit., p. 244.

67 Phyllis Bottome, *The Master Hope* (Hurst and Blackett, 1904), p. 228

68 ibid., p. 16

Notes to Chapter 2 – St Moritz and the White Death

1 Dormandy, op. cit., p. 4
2 Phyllis Bottome, *The Challenge* (Harcourt, Brace and Co., 1954), p. 63
3 Dormandy, op. cit., p. 170
4 Margaret Macdonald Bottome to Rachel Fowler, Bottome Papers, Add 78869 BL
5 *The Challenge*, op. cit., p. 108
6 ibid., p. 100
7 ibid., p. 102
8 ibid., p. 101
9 ibid., p. 109
10 ibid., p. 110
11 Phyllis Bottome and H. de Lisle Brock, *Crooked Answers* (London, John Murray, 1911)
12 *The Challenge*, op. cit., p. 114
13 ibid., p. 116
14 ibid., p. 118
15 Letter from Phyllis Bottome to Geoffrey Faber, Bottome Papers, Add 10308 BL
16 *The Challenge*, op. cit., p. 131
17 ibid., p. 140
18 Suzanne Raitt suggests that Lucy Gwatkin did not share her husband's intellectual interests and that he especially enjoyed the role of mentor to intellectual young women. See Suzanne Raitt, *May Sinclair: A Modern Victorian* (Oxford University Press, 2000), which has many references to Gwatkin's role in May Sinclair's young life.
19 Cambridge University did not award degrees to women until 1948.
20 See *Newnham College Roll Letter*, 1917. Professor H. M. Gwatkin died in the early months of the First World War; his daughter, Esther Ruth Gwatkin, a mathematician, left a large bequest to Newnham on her death in 1952. The money was to be used for Maths and History.
21 *The Challenge*, op. cit., p. 171
22 ibid.
23 In 1899 the habitual hostility in South Africa between the Dutch Boers, in their independent states of the South African Republic (later Transvaal) and the Orange Free State, and the British Cape Colony and Natal flared into war. At issue was the claim of 'Uitlanders' (foreigners, mainly British), who had been attracted in large numbers to prospecting for gold in the Transvaal, to equal rights of citizenship with the Boers. The Boers

surrendered in 1902. By the Treaty of Vereeniging, the Transvaal and the Orange Free State were incorporated into the British Empire, paid £3m in indemnity and promised future self-government.

24 *The Challenge*, op. cit., p. 180
25 ibid., p. 218
26 ibid., p. 223
27 ibid., p. 226
28 ibid., p. 221
29 ibid., p. 220
30 ibid., p. 221
31 ibid., p. 234
32 ibid., p. 235
33 Bottome Papers, Add 78859 BL
34 ibid.
35 *The Challenge*, op. cit., pp. 244–5
36 Pollak had been taught by the distinguished teacher Henri Marteau, who had early recognised his genius.
37 Phyllis to Ernan, Bottome Papers, Add 78881 BL
38 It was reprinted twice by E. P. Dutton in America.
39 Phyllis Bottome, *The Imperfect Gift*, published in England by John Murray in 1906
40 *The Imperfect Gift* (E. P. Dutton, 1907), pp. 135–6
41 ibid., p. 1
42 Phyllis sent it on 14 October 1906, with an inscription from *All's Well That Ends Well* (1, 1, 180–5). Helena, in these lines, is thinking of an absent male beloved:

> 'Tis pity . . .
> That wishing well had not a body in't,
> Which might be felt; that we, the poorer born,
> Whose baser stars do shut us up in wishes,
> Might with effects of them follow our friends . . .

43 *The Challenge*, op. cit., p. 254
44 Bottome Papers, Add 78882 BL
45 A form still exists in France in the *son et lumière* shows staged at the Loire châteaux and other locations.
46 Phyllis Bottome to Geoffrey Faber, 1956, Bottome Papers, Add 10308 BL
47 Phyllis Bottome to Ernan Forbes Dennis, Bottome Papers, Add 78895 BL
48 ibid.

Notes to Chapter 3 – Unfinished Symphony: The Years without Ernan

1 *The Challenge*, op. cit., p. 269
2 Bottome Papers, Add 78884 BL
3 ibid.
4 ibid.
5 ibid.
6 ibid.
7 *The Challenge*, op. cit., p. 277
8 ibid., p, 295
9 ibid., p. 297
10 ibid.
11 ibid., p. 333
12 ibid., p. 338
13 ibid., p. 343
14 Bottome Papers, Add 78866 BL
15 *The Challenge*, op. cit., p. 306
16 ibid., p. 368
17 Phyllis Bottome to Mr Collis, 19 March 1953: 'His mother wrote to me when he shot himself. He did not die; but was for a year or two in a *maison de santé* and then revived enough to live for years at Tarascon, with a horrible American sissy called Mr Bishop. I never saw him again, although I wrote to him once at Marseilles after my marriage. He had always said he never would see me again if I married; but I had hoped the years might have made it possible for us to meet, and I was quite sure that my husband would have enjoyed him! He could play at one time most beautifully on the piano, and should, of course, been an executive musician. Do let me know if you recognise him from my description in "Challenge". I only did not give his second name because I did not want to wound any of his possible relations.' Bottome Papers, Add 78866 BL
18 *The Challenge*, op. cit., p. 340
19 ibid., p. 344
20 Preface to Phyllis Bottome and Charles Paul Frèrejean, *Broken Music* (Boston and New York, Houghton Mifflin Company, 1914)
21 Phyllis Bottome, *The Common Chord* (London, Martin Secker, 1913), p. 172
22 Nicola Humble, *The Feminine Middlebrow Novel*, op. cit., p. 5
23 *The Challenge*, op. cit., p. 349
24 *Broken Music*, op. cit., p. 144

25 'Brother Leo', *Best Stories of Phyllis Bottome*, edited and with a Preface by Daphne du Maurier (London, Faber & Faber, 1963), p. 86
26 ibid., p. 100
27 James Pinker (1863–1922)
28 *The Challenge*, op. cit., p. 356
29 This is an archaic term for malaria.
30 *The Challenge*, op. cit., p. 362
31 Alice Meynell (1847–1922) was a poet and a journalist.
32 Mary Amelia St Clair (May) Sinclair (1863–1946); see Suzanne Raitt, *May Sinclair: A Modern Victorian* (Oxford University Press, 2000), for an insightful biography.
33 After about 1925, May Sinclair began to suffer from Parkinson's disease and started to withdraw from the literary scene; when she died, in 1946, she left a present to Lucy Gwatkin.
34 Phyllis Bottome, *From the Life*, op. cit., p. 71
35 Helen Carr, *The Verse Revolutionaries: Ezra Pound, H. D. and the Imagists* (Jonathan Cape, 2009), p. 1
36 *From the Life*, op. cit., p. 72
37 ibid., pp. 73–4
38 *The Smart Set* was founded by William D'Alton Mann in 1900. It published a mixture of society news, gossip and literary criticism. It also published some fiction. Work by Jack London, Ambrose Bierce, Theodore Dreiser, Floyd Dell and D. H. Lawrence appeared there before the journal ceased publication in May 1929.
39 published as a two-story volume, *Helen of Troy and Rose* (New York, Century Co., 1918), and dedicated to her brother George and his wife Marjorie
40 *Best Stories of Phyllis Bottome*, op. cit.
41 Preface by Daphne du Maurier to *Best Stories of Phyllis Bottome*, op. cit., p. 10
42 *The Challenge*, op. cit., p. 383
43 Phyllis Bottome, *The Captive* (Chapman and Hall, 1915), p. 39
44 ibid., p. 226
45 ibid., p. 294
46 Phyllis Bottome, *The Goal*, op. cit., p. 40
47 *The Challenge*, op. cit., p. 377
48 ibid., p. 380
49 ibid., p. 381
50 ibid., p. 383
51 ibid.

52 ibid., p. 260
53 H. V. Nelles, *The Art of Nation-Building: Pageantry and Spectacle at Quebec's Tercentenary* (University of Toronto Press, 2000), p. 67
54 ibid., p. 149
55 ibid., p. 166
56 ibid., p. 313
57 Bottome Papers, Add 78883 BL
58 23 May 1905, Bottome Papers, Add 78800 BL
59 Arthur Mee, quoted by Deborah S. Ryan in 'Staging the Imperial City: The Pageant of London, 1911', in *Imperial Cities*, eds. Felix Driver and David Gilbert (Manchester University Press, 1999)
60 *The Challenge*, op. cit., p. 390
61 Ivor Novello (1893–1951), composer, stage and film actor and playwright, was born David Ivor Davies in Cardiff.
62 David Slattery-Christy, *In Search of Ruritania* (AuthorHouse, 2008)
63 Information kindly supplied by Dr Robin Darwall-Smith, Archivist, Magdalen College, Oxford.
64 James Harding, *Ivor Novello: A Biography* (Welsh Academic Press, 1997), p. 17
65 Although later he told people that his scholarship lasted only until his voice broke, this was a rewriting of history. Choristers were not discarded when their voices broke. All of Ivor's contemporaries received a bursary to complete their education.
66 Phyllis wrote a biographical sketch called 'The Secret of Ivor Novello', in *From the Life*, op. cit., p. 49.
67 Lascelles staged the Union Parliament of South Africa celebrations at Cape Town in 1909 and the Coronation Durbar in Calcutta with over 300,000 participants. He also staged the Pageant of Empire at the British Empire Exhibition at Wembley in 1924.
68 *The Challenge*, op. cit., p. 387
69 Deborah S. Ryan, 'The Man Who Staged the Empire: Remembering Frank Lascelles in Sibford Gower, 1875–2000', in *Material Memories: Design and Evocation* (Oxford and New York, Berg, 1999), p. 171
70 Richard Dyer, *The Culture of Queers* (London, Routledge, 2002), p. 3
71 See my argument on this point in *Teacher Training at Cambridge: The Initiatives of Oscar Browning and Elizabeth Hughes* (Woburn Press, 2004), p. 175
72 *The Challenge*, op. cit., p. 389
73 David Cecil, *Max* (Constable, 1964), p. 74. Cecil, for example, in his biography of Max Beerbohm, argues that although part of the social crowd of Oscar Wilde and Alfred Douglas in the 1890s, Max was not himself

homosexual. Although not judgemental of his individual friends, he regarded homosexuality as a misfortune to be avoided if possible.

74 Once Germany had invaded Belgium, the two European camps, the Triple Alliance (German, Austria–Hungary and Italy) and the Triple Entente (England, France and Russia), were in conflict.

Notes to Chapter 4 – World War I

1 *The Challenge*, op. cit., pp. 393–4
2 Bottome Papers, Add 78884 BL
3 ibid.
4 Phyllis Bottome to G. Faber, 23 February 1953, re *Man and Beast*, Bottome Papers, Add 10308 BL
5 George Bottome and Marjorie had a home of their own and were expecting their first child. See *The Goal*, op. cit., p. 43
6 Phyllis's friend May Sinclair, for example, had in 1914 gone out to Belgium to join the women driving ambulances to retrieve the wounded.
7 *The Goal*, op. cit., p. 42
8 Bottome Papers, Add 78859 BL
9 *The Challenge*, op. cit., p. 395
10 Andrew Lownie, *John Buchan: The Presbyterian Cavalier* (Pimlico, 2002), pp. 127–33
11 *Dictionary of National Biography*, Oxford University Press on-line
12 ibid.
13 Bottome Papers, Add 78885 BL
14 ibid.
15 ibid.
16 *The Dark Tower* (New York and London, D. Appleton-Century Company, 1939), p. 375
17 Phyllis Bottome, *The Second Fiddle* (New York, Century Co., 1917), p. 211. It was dedicated 'To Marguerite and Lilian [Carter], two sisters who, alike in joy and sorrow, are a light to their friends'.
18 *The Second Fiddle,* op. cit., p. 272
19 Bottome Papers, Add 78885 BL
20 ibid.
21 ibid.
22 ibid.
23 Ernan to Phyllis, 12 October 1917, ibid.
24 Ernan to Phyllis, 23 October 1917, ibid.

25 James Harding, *Ivor Novello: A Biography*, op. cit., p. 30
26 See Michael Williams, *Ivor Novello: Screen Idol*, pp. 68–9: 'Just as Germany's downfall seemed to be on the horizon, the British government decided that the neutrality of Sweden was endangered by the invidious influence of German propaganda, which spread in the form of entertainment in its clubs and cabaret. To counter this the epitome of British fortitude, Ivor Novello, was dispatched … to undertake a three-month tour of Sweden to counteract a similar tour by the German conductor Nikisch.'
27 When Ivor died suddenly of a heart attack in 1951, Bobbie immediately made a bonfire of any incriminating letters, photographs or films. This, in an era when homosexual practice was illegal, was to make sure nothing escaped that might have led to blackmail attempts on his erstwhile friends and lovers.
28 Bottome Papers, Add 78885 BL
29 *The Challenge*, op. cit., p. 402
30 Bottome Papers, Add 78885 BL
31 *The Challenge*, op. cit., p. 404
32 This was a battle when British tank power proved decisive.
33 See Christina Rossetti, *The Prince's Progress and Other Poems* (1866).
34 *The Goal*, op. cit., pp. 404–5
35 *The Challenge*, op. cit., p. 405
36 letter from Ernan to Phyllis, 26 September 1917, Bottome Papers, Add 78885 BL
37 *The Goal*, op. cit., p. 406
38 *The Challenge*, op. cit., p. 257
39 *The Goal*, op. cit., p. 13
40 Other examples are Rebecca West's *The Return of the Soldier* (1918) and May Sinclair's *The Tree of Heaven* (1918).
41 See Rosa Maria Bracco, *Merchants of Hope: British Middlebrow Writers and the First World War, 1919–1939* (Berg, 1993), who comments, 'But even though he learns of cruelty and pain he has a newly-found vision, born of his searing contact with reality, to help him make sense of what he has learnt' (p. 90).
42 Phyllis Bottome, *A Servant of Reality* (London, Hodder & Stoughton, 1919), p. 82. She dedicated the book to Betty and Maida McCord.
43 ibid., pp. 135–6
44 Charles Carrington, *Soldier from the Wars Returning* (Hutchinson, 1965), p. 160
45 Bottome Papers, Add 78886 BL
46 ibid.
47 Phyllis Bottome, *The Goal*, op. cit., pp. 16–17

48 ibid., p. 26
49 Fred Dennis to Phyllis Bottome, 28 March 1918, Bottome Papers, Add 78870 BL
50 *The Goal*, op. cit., p. 24
51 information from War Office Records, National Archives
52 Phyllis to Ernan, Bottome Papers, Add 78886
53 ibid.
54 James Harding, *Ivor Novello: A Biography*, op. cit., p. 143
55 *The Goal*, op. cit., p. 30
56 In his will Ivor left Ora two hundred pounds a year for life.
57 *The Goal*, op. cit., p. 32
58 ibid.
59 Fred had married Louise Bosanquet, the daughter of a city banker who lived near Holsworthy, and near the Dennis family. The Dennis and Bosanquet families were friends. Information from Frederica Freer.
60 information on Captain A. E. Forbes Dennis in War Office Records, National Archives
61 *The Goal*, op. cit., p. 36
62 Phyllis Bottome, *The Kingfisher* (George H. Doran, 1922), pp. 48–9
63 *The Goal,* op. cit., p. 36
64 Bottome Papers, Add 78887 BL
65 ibid.
66 *The Goal*, op. cit., p. 37
67 ibid.
68 Bottome Papers, Add 78888 BL
69 *The Goal*, op. cit., p. 38
70 Phyllis Bottome, *Innocence and Experience* (John Lane, 1935), p. 46
71 'The Victim', *The Victim and The Worm* (George H. Doran, 1923), p. 20
72 Bottome Papers, Add 78887 BL
73 Much later, Phyllis wrote to Geoffrey Faber that 'The Victim [was written] out of deep affection for the special kind of American I had been partly brought up with and by.' Bottome Papers, Add 10308 BL
74 Bottome Papers, Add 78888 BL
75 ibid.
76 ibid.
77 Bottome Papers, Add 78887 BL
78 ibid.
79 ibid.
80 *The Goal*, op. cit., p. 35
81 Bottome Papers, Add 78887 BL
82 Bottome Papers, Add 78885 BL

83 *The Goal*, op. cit., p. 24
84 ibid., p. 41
85 ibid., p. 44
86 Bottome Papers, Add 78859 BL
87 *The Goal*, op. cit., p. 45
88 ibid., p. 47
89 ibid.
90 Phyllis Bottome, *Strange Fruit: Stories* (London, Collins, 1928), p. 129
91 *The Goal*, op. cit., p. 56
92 For example, 'The Little Red Band', 'The Tug of War', 'The Residue', 'A Lost Leader' (this last one was included in Daphne du Maurier's selection, *Best Stories of Phyllis Bottome*, op. cit.)
93 Phyllis Bottome, *The Derelict and Other Stories* (London, Collins, 1923)
94 ibid.

Notes to Chapter 5 – Vienna and *Old Wine*

1 *The Goal*, op. cit., p. 54
2 ibid., p. 60
3 An excellent book for understanding the history of this period is by Andrew Wheatcroft, *The Habsburgs: Embodying Empire* (London, Penguin Books, 1996).
4 See entry on Arthur James Balfour in the *Dictionary of National Biography*.
5 A. J. P. Taylor, *English History 1914–1945* (Oxford, Clarendon Press, 1965), p. 98, n. 1
6 Phyllis Bottome, *The Crystal Heart* (New York, Century Co., 1921), p. 214
7 *The Goal*, op. cit., p. 66
8 See Martha Schad, *Hitler's Spy Princess: The Extraordinary Life of Stephanie von Hohenlohe*, translated and annotated by Angus McGeoch (Sutton Publishing, 2004).
9 *The Goal*, op. cit., pp. 72–3
10 Nancy Milford, *Savage Beauty: The Life of Edna St Vincent Millay* (New York, Random House, 2002)
11 *Strange Fruit*, op. cit., pp. 96–7. See letter from Phyllis in Kitzbühel to Dorothy Thompson, 25 July 1928: ' "Blue Clay" is of course Edna, but that you knew before.' Dorothy Thompson Papers, Special Collections, University of Syracuse
12 *The Goal*, op. cit., p. 99
13 ibid., p. 70

14 ibid., p. 87

15 Albertina Rasch (1891–1967), born in Vienna. In 1923 she left Vienna and established her own New York dance studio, where Bill 'Bojangles' Robinson later taught tap. She supplied dancers, called 'The Albertina Rasch Girls', for shows and films that needed 'terped' (ballet) numbers within them. She adapted her classical training and technique for the Broadway theatre and served as a choreographer for a number of musical films in 1930s Hollywood, the most famous of which might be her choreography for 'Begin the Beguine' in the Cole Porter show *Jubilee*. When Rasch arrived in the United States, dance numbers tended to be inserted into musicals with no consideration for moving the narrative along. As a choreographer, it is considered that her work 'nudged the public towards readiness for more artful integration of dance in musicals'. Mark N. Grant, *The Rise and Fall of the Broadway Musical* ((Northeastern University Press, 2004), p. 253

16 Phyllis Bottome, 'The Cup of Alteration', *Masks and Faces* (Faber & Faber, 1940)

17 A letter to Ernan from Irene Spierer, of Spierer Furs, Madison Avenue, New York, after Phyllis's death, refers to a photo of Ernan 'in an 18th century costume and wig ... Xmas Party in Vienna'. Bottome Papers, Add 78868 BL

18 'Professor Robert Pollak was caught by the Russians in the First World War, interned but immediately released when his capability as a violinist was discovered, and made head of the Moscow Conservatoire violin department. When he returned to Vienna he had a short European career before joining his friend, Bloch, in San Francisco, to start a Conservatoire there. From San Francisco he was invited to become chief violin teacher at the Tokyo Conservatoire, a post which he held with great distinction for seven years.' Phyllis Bottome to Miss Anne Munro-Kerr, Society of Authors, Bottome Papers, Add 10308 BL

19 *Masks and Faces*, op. cit. This collection was dedicated 'To Robert Pollak, violinist, the source of unforgettable enchanted hours of music and of friendship'.

20 information from the San Francisco Conservatory of Music

21 *The Goal*, op. cit., p. 90

22 Nor did they thrive without it. Baron Höfflinger married Gräfin Berchtold, and stuck with Vienna throughout the rise of Hitler and the Second World War. Schumpeter became a professor of political economy in the USA, but was not especially happy there.

23 *The Goal*, op. cit., p. 77

24 ibid.

25 letter from Ernan to Phyllis, dated 25.1.1918, Bottome Papers, Add 78886 BL
26 *The Goal*, op. cit., p. 80
27 Phyllis Bottome, 'Would You Have Children Again', *Boston Herald,* 8 April 1934
28 *The Goal*, op. cit., p. 79
29 *The White Death*, op. cit., p. 251
30 The phrenic nerve 'crush' deliberately interfered with the diaphragm, causing the lung to collapse. Similarly the injections of air into the pleural cavity caused the lung to collapse.
31 *The Goal*, op. cit., p. 93
32 ibid., p. 99
33 ibid., p. 95
34 Max Beerbohm's essay 'Going Out for a Walk' was published in 1918. See Phyllis Bottome to Max Beerbohm, 15 October 1933, Beerbohm Papers, Merton College, Oxford.
35 *The Goal*, op. cit., p. 105–6
36 Bottome Papers, Add 78859 BL
37 Phyllis Bottome and Dorothy Thompson, *The Depths of Prosperity* (London, Collins, 1924; New York, Doran, 1925)
38 *The Goal*, op. cit., p. 108
39 ibid., p. 110
40 *Old Wine* was first published in 1925 by Frederick A. Stokes and Company in New York.
41 *The Goal*, op. cit., p. 128
42 Phyllis Bottome, *Old Wine* (Northwestern University Press, 1998), p. 81. This modern edition is equipped with an excellent Introduction by Phyllis Lassner and Marilyn Hoder-Salmon.
43 *Old Wine*, ibid., p. 9
44 Phyllis Lassner, in a brilliant essay called 'Objects to Possess or Discard', raises a series of difficulties with Bottome's portrait. I quote, 'How do we sort out the rhetorical and ideological moves of texts that express outrage against the oppression of women and the tragic fate of Jews, that point the finger of blame at a fallen European civilization, when they also represent the Jew either as a despicable woman or a noble healer who resembles a Christian more than a Jew.' See *Borderlines: Genders and Identities in War and Peace 1870–1930*, ed. Billie Melman (Routledge, 1998), p. 255. Certainly Dr Jeiletes seems saintly, but I think Bottome's portrait of Elisabeth Bleileben, though a risky strategy, does not depict her as utterly despicable.
45 My argument is that Bottome was doing something similar to what George Eliot attempted in her portrait of Gwendolen in *Daniel Deronda*, that is to

take a somewhat despicable character and then persuade her readers to have sympathy for her; in *Deronda* too, there is an unrealistically idealised figure of a male Jew in Deronda himself, and another in Mordecai.

46 *Old Wine*, op. cit., p. 85
47 ibid.
48 ibid., p. 348
49 ibid., p. 334
50 ibid., p. 140
51 ibid., p. 156
52 ibid., p. 186
53 ibid., p. 365
54 Bottome Papers, Add 78862 BL

Notes to Chapter 6 – Mösern, Kitzbühel and Meeting Alfred Adler

1 *The Goal*, op. cit., p. 112
2 ibid., p. 117
3 ibid., p. 122
4 Phyllis Bottome, *Heart of a Child* (London, Faber & Faber, 1941; New York, Putnam, 1940). After the Second World War this novel was made into a film. See Chapter 12.
5 ibid., p. 15
6 ibid., p. 89
7 '*Wissenheit*' translates as 'wisdom'; I thank Arabella Finyves for pointing this out to me.
8 *Heart of a Child*, op. cit., p. 109
9 ibid., p. 154
10 Phyllis had good luck with her agents, except that they tended to die on her. Her first agent, A. P. Watt, had died in 1914 and her second, J. B. Pinker, died in 1922.
11 *The Goal*, op. cit., p. 125
12 ibid., p. 129
13 Phyllis Bottome, *The Messenger of the Gods* (George H. Doran, 1927), p. 27
14 Caroline Dow 'discovered' Edna St Vincent Millay when she heard her recite her own poetry when working at a tourist hotel and financed her to go to Vassar. Edna increasingly pulled away from her patroness as she achieved success.
15 *The Messenger of the Gods*, op. cit., p. 85
16 ibid., pp. 82–3
17 ibid., p. 266

18 Bottome Papers, Add 78867 BL

19 Today, much extended, it is a luxurious five-star hotel.

20 *The Goal*, op. cit., p. 130

21 See Andrew Lycett, *Ian Fleming* (London, Phoenix, 2002), for an account of Kitzbühel days (*c.*p. 34).

22 *The Goal*, op. cit., p. 133

23 ibid., p. 136

24 Alfred Adler, *Superiority and Social Interest*, eds Heinz L. Ansbacher and Rowena R. Ansbacher (Routledge & Kegan Paul, 1965), p. 378

25 John Pearson, *The Life of Ian Fleming*, op. cit., p. 35

26 There are countless books about the individual psychoanalysts and psychologists in Vienna but most of them are partisan to one theorist or another. A useful book for a balanced view is George Makari, *Revolution in Mind: The Creation of Psychoanalysis* (HarperCollins, 2008): Makari writes: 'Adler's dismissal revealed a troubling problem for the Freudian community. In an attempt to resolve the differences between Adler and Freud, it had not been possible to demonstrate that one system of thought had more truth value than the other. Adler's theory of inferiority and aggression constituted an alternative to Freudian psychosexuality. Freud's theory itself was based on an interdisciplinary synthesis that, at its heart, defined the empirically unknowable unconscious by a series of deductions and analogies. When his academic enemies attacked his libido theory, they attacked Freud's Achilles heel, not just because it was personally offensive to some, but also because it seemed to flout the rules of empiricism and scientific epistemology. When Adler presented an alternative model based on different unconscious contents, he forced those within the movement to consider how they might possibly adjudicate between Freud and Adler. In the end, Freud did not prove that Adler was wrong; rather he declared Adler was not a psychoanalyst' (p. 263).

27 Adler's split from Freud was as a direct consequence of his publication of 'Zur Kritik der Freudschen Sexualtheorie des Seelenlebens'. In this paper, Adler declared that the pillars of Freudian psychoanalysis (the so-called oral, anal and genital stages of psychosexual development) were mere artefacts of education and not innate natural development. And Adler refuted Freud's Oedipus Complex, saying that family dynamics had more to do with power and authority in the family than with sexuality. In particular, Adler suggested that sexual disorders, which often existed in neurotic individuals, might be the consequences or metaphoric expressions of neurosis, but not its cause. Adler essentially accused Freud of making circular arguments to 'prove' his hypotheses. Clearly, he could not remain in Freud's group when he disagreed so fundamentally.

28 I interviewed John Pearson, who had himself interviewed Ernan Forbes Dennis.
29 John Pearson, *The Life of Ian Fleming*, op. cit., p. 34. John Pearson was able to interview Ernan, so these quotes are verbatim.
30 See death certificate from the General Register Office.
31 In her autobiography she does not mention the death of her mother. It is as though when she left England to join Ernan in Marseilles it was for her the 'death' of any significant relationship between them.
32 *The Goal*, op. cit., p. 138
33 Phyllis Bottome, *Alfred Adler* (Vanguard Press, 1957), p. 242
34 *The Goal*, op. cit., p. 139
35 John Pearson, *The Life of Ian Fleming*, op. cit., pp. 35–6
36 ibid., p. 36 and p. 41
37 ibid., p. 38
38 ibid., p. 40
39 See Fergus Fleming, *Amaryllis Fleming* (Sinclair-Stevenson, 1993), for an account of this strange deception.
40 Undated letter from Ian Fleming to Ernan Forbes Dennis, Bottome Papers, Add 78868 BL. I have been told privately that Ian had got one of the maids at the Tennerhof pregnant. Although this seems not unlikely, I have no way of finding out whether it is true.
41 John Pearson, *The Life of Ian Fleming*, op. cit., p. 43
42 ibid., p. 41
43 ibid., pp. 39 and 40
44 Bottome Papers, Add 78867 BL
45 *The Goal*, op. cit., p. 148
46 ibid., p. 150
47 Phyllis Bottome, *Windlestraws* (Houghton Mifflin, 1929), pp. 130 and 140
48 ibid., p. 36
49 Bottome Papers, Add 78891 BL
50 See Isaac Stern, *My First 79 Years* (Alfred A. Knopf, 1999), pp. 11–12, where he writes, 'The first decent music teacher I had was a man named Robert Pollak … I have another photograph of Mr Pollak, this one of him alone, dated 1930, on which these words appear above his signature: "To my beloved pupil Isaac Stern – May he watch every day over the treasure nature has given him." '
51 See Phyllis Bottome to Dorothy Thompson, 25 July 1928, Dorothy Thompson Papers, Special Collections, University of Syracuse.
52 Phyllis Bottome to Dorothy Thompson, 3 October 1928, Dorothy Thompson Papers, Special Collections, University of Syracuse
53 *The Goal*, op. cit., p. 158

54 Written under the pen-name of Richard Vaughan, it was published by John Miles in London.

55 Kenton Bamford, *Distorted Images: British National Identity and Film in the 1920s* (I.B. Tauris, 1999), p. 152. Novello had previously starred in *The Call of the Blood, Miarka: Daughter of the Bear, Carnival, The Bohemian Girl, The White Rose, The Man Without Desire, Bonnie Prince Charlie, The Rat, The Triumph of the Rat, The Lodger, Downhill* and *The Vortex.*

56 Phyllis Bottome to Dorothy Thompson, 3 October 1928, Dorothy Thompson Papers, Special Collections, University of Syracuse

57 ibid.

58 Phyllis Bottome, *Tatter'd Loving* (Houghton Mifflin, 1930), p. 76

59 Robert Pollak was to remain at the San Francisco Conservatory until 1930. He then took up a post as head of the violin department of the Imperial Academy of Music in Tokyo. In 1937 he returned to the San Francisco Conservatory.

60 Phyllis Bottome to Dorothy Thomson, 12 December 1928, Dorothy Thompson Papers, Special Collections, University of Syracuse

61 Phyllis Bottome to Dorothy Thompson, 25 July 1928, Dorothy Thompson Papers, Special Collections, University of Syracuse

62 Phyllis Bottome, *Wind in His Fists* (London, Collins, 1931); published in America as *Devil's Due* (Boston & New York, Houghton Mifflin, 1931); republished by Faber & Faber in 1948

63 *The Goal*, op. cit., p. 182

64 ibid., p. 134

65 ibid., p. 163

Notes to Chapter 7 – The Gathering Storm in Munich and the Study of Adlerian Psychology

1 Seif had been trained as a Protestant pastor, but had broken off his training to become a doctor instead. He had then practised as a Freudian analyst but had found its theoretical base unhelpful when counselling patients. Attending a conference held by Adler he had felt that the idea of teleological retraining was likely to do more good for more people than Freud's theories.
2 *The Goal*, op. cit., p. 189
3 ibid., p. 165
4 ibid., p. 166
5 Phyllis Bottome, 'Alfred Adler', transmission on BBC Home Service, 20 March 1945. The two alternative services, the National Programme and the Regional Programme, were merged into a single all-day service from two days before the official declaration of war; in 1967 it was renamed Radio 4.
6 Adlerian counsellors call what a Freudian analyst would call a patient a 'pupil', in order to indicate that a re-education process is what is, or should be, taking place.
7 *The Goal*, op. cit., p. 167
8 Bottome Papers, Add 78891 BL
9 Ernan to Phyllis, 26.11.1931, Bottome Papers, Add 78891 BL
10 'Love and Marriage', in Phyllis Bottome, *Not in Our Stars* (Faber & Faber, 1955)
11 *The Goal*, op. cit., p. 177
12 First published in 1933 in both the UK and America it was dedicated to Harry and Marion [Bottome]'.
13 *The Goal*, op. cit., p. 176
14 *The Advances of Harriet* (John Lane at The Bodley Head, 1948), p. 274
15 Elisabeth Marbury (1856–1933)
16 Ansel Adams, *An Autobiography* (Little, Brown & Co., 1985), p. 132. It appears Adams photographed her again in 1938, and this photograph is the centre spread.
17 Tobias Matthay (1858–1945); Dame Myra Hess (1890–1965) was an English concert pianist who was awarded the DBE in 1941 in recognition of her wartime concerts at the National Gallery.
18 Michael Williams, *Ivor Novello: Screen Idol* (bfi publishing, 2003), p. 4; sequel films *Triumph of the Rat* (1925); *Return of the* Rat (1928)

19 Phyllis Bottome, *The Rat: A Novel Based on the Play by Ivor Novello and Constance Collier* (London, Philip Allan, 1926; reprinted in 1934)

20 On this visit she asked Harry to take charge of her American earnings.

21 See James M. Hutchisson, *The Rise of Sinclair Lewis 1920–1930* (The Pennsylvania State University Press, 1997), for a useful account of Lewis's early literary career. Mark Schorer's biography, *Sinclair Lewis: An American Life* (McGraw-Hill, 1961), is also useful. Josef left Dorothy for Eileen Agar, British painter (1899–1991); she lived with Hungarian writer Josef Bard from 1926 and married him in 1940; he died in 1975. See entry on Agar by Katy Deepwell in *Dictionary of Women Artists*, Volume 1, edited by Delia Gaze (London & Chicago, Fitzroy Dearburn Publishers, 1997)

22 *Main Street* (1920), *Babbitt* (1922), *Arrowsmith* (1925) and *Elmer Gantry* (1927) are probably his best books.

23 Letter from Dorothy Thompson to Letitia Irwin, quoted by Marion K. Sanders in *Dorothy Thompson: A Legend in Her Time* (Houghton Mifflin, 1973), p. 157; see also Peter Kurth, *American Cassandra: The Life of Dorothy Thompson* (Little, Brown & Co., 1990), for other glimpses of Phyllis's relationship with Dorothy.

24 Phyllis Bottome was to write of her later: 'Sara Delano was one of the three beautiful Delano sisters … she had great compassion for those less well off than herself.' *From the Life*, op. cit.

25 *The Goal*, op. cit., p. 185. Franklin Delano Roosevelt was elected Democratic President of America in November 1932, in the depths of the Great Depression, to the first of four terms of office. He possessed the kind of courage that Phyllis most admired. Aged thirty-nine he had been stricken with poliomyelitis, yet had fought to regain the strength in his legs. He famously asserted in his Inaugural Address, 'The only thing we have to fear is fear itself.'

26 Bottome Papers, Add 77892 BL

27 'Alibis' are what Adler called excuse-makings or safeguarding activities, which are typically employed in a situation which allows the neurotic person to claim: 'If only I didn't suffer from insomnia/depression/migraines, etc., I would be able to … ' This 'alibi' then allows the person to avoid meeting the challenges of work, relationship and community.

28 A useful account of how Individual Psychology works in practice is to be found in Ursula E. Oberst and Alan E. Stewart, *Adlerian Psychotherapy: An Advanced Approach to Individual Psychology* (Hove & New York, Brunner-Routledge, 2003).

29 Bottome Papers, Add 78891 BL

30 It is not certain who 'Cyril' was, although it has been suggested by a family member that it might have been 'Cyril Hare', the pen-name of Judge Gordon Clark who wrote a number of detective stories, published, like Phyllis's work, by Faber & Faber. She might have known him through her publishers, but there is no reliable source.
31 Bottome Papers, Add 78891 BL
32 *The Goal*, op. cit., p. 192
33 Hitler was Austrian, but had come to Munich in 1913 and volunteered for the German army in 1914.
34 Quoted in Marion K. Sanders, *Dorothy Thompson: A Legend in Her Time*, op. cit., p. 167
35 *The Goal*, op. cit., p. 193
36 The swastika, or hooked cross, has an exceedingly long history. In the late nineteenth century, the German archaeologist Heinrich Schliemann connected the discovery of the hooked cross on the site of ancient Troy with similar shapes found on pottery in Germany, and speculated that it was a significant religious symbol of their remote ancestors. This suggestion was taken up by the Völkische Movement, for whom the swastika became a symbol of Aryan identity and German nationalism.
37 Lewis's description, quoted in *Dorothy Thompson: A Legend in Her Time*, op. cit., p. 177
38 Published in October 1935, *It Can't Happen Here* was a best-seller.
39 *The Goal*, op. cit., p. 205
40 Bavaria Film Ltd in Munich was formed in September 1932 in order to produce Nazi propaganda films.
41 See Maik Kopleck, *Munich 1933–1945*, translated by Adelheid Korpp (Links, 2006). Of the 19,000 Jewish residents of Munich in 1933, only 84 were left at the end of the war.
42 *The Goal*, op. cit., p. 207
43 ibid.
44 By 1955 there was general medical consensus that the best chemotherapeutic combination was streptomycin, PAS and isoniazid. See *The White Death*, op. cit., p. 368.
45 *The Goal*, op. cit., p. 263
46 ibid., p. 190
47 ibid., p. 191
48 Phyllis Bottome, *Private Worlds* (London, John Lane, 1934), p. 97
49 ibid., p. 54
50 ibid., p. 352
51 ibid.

52 There were 12,500 advance orders in America before publication day.
53 Phyllis Lassner, ' "On the Point of a Journey": Storm Jameson, Phyllis Bottome and the Novel of Women's Political Psychology', in *And in Our Time: Vision, Revision, and British Writing of the 1930s*, edited by Antony Shuttleworth (Bucknell University Press, 2003), p. 117
54 *Monthly Film Bulletin*, vol. 2, no. 18, July 1935, pp. 89–90; *Film Weekly*, vol. 14, no. 354, 26 July 1935, p. 32
55 Walter Wanger to Phyllis Bottome, 18 April 1935, Bottome Papers, Add 10308 BL
56 Louella Parsons, *Los Angeles Examiner*, 26 April 1935
57 Walter Wanger to Phyllis Bottome, 8 March 1935, Bottome Papers, Add 10308 BL
58 Walter Wanger to Phyllis Bottome, 30 July 1935, Bottome Papers, Add 10308 BL
59 See Marilyn Hoder-Salmon's entry on Phyllis Bottome in *Dictionary of Literary Biography*, Volume 197, op. cit., p. 37.
60 In Vienna, Albertina Rasch had talked to Phyllis about Sarah Bernhardt.
61 Phyllis Bottome, *Masks and Faces*, op. cit., pp. 7–19
62 *The Goal*, op. cit., p. 220
63 The time has still not come, apparently, given Hillary Clinton's failure to be elected to represent her party as presidential candidate in 2008. See Emily Wortis Leider, *California's Daughter: Gertrude Atherton and Her Times* (Stanford University Press, 1991), for a full account of her life.
64 PEN's commitment to free speech is the *sine qua non* of democracy. PEN was founded to bring the writers of the world together after World War I. The rise of fascism in Germany, the burning of books and the exile of Thomas Mann and many other writers set PEN on the path of protest. This is a role it continues today.
65 Bottome Papers, Add 10308 BL
66 *The Goal*, op. cit., p. 236
67 ibid., p. 158
68 Letter from Nigel Dennis to Ernan and Phyllis, thanking them for sending him money, Bottome Papers, Add 78861 BL. In 1936, Nigel married a Frenchwoman, Marie-Madeleine Massias, with whom he had two daughters. He stayed in New York until 1949, and became a highly successful writer.
69 Dorothy Shakespear (1886–1973); see an account in Penny Dunford, *A Biographical Dictionary of Women Artists in Europe and America since 1850* (Harvester, 1990). Ezra had married Dorothy Shakespear in 1914. She was she daughter of Olivia Shakespear, a great friend of Yeats. In marrying Dorothy, Ezra thought he was joining a kind of literary aristocracy.

70 Phyllis Bottome, *From the Life*, op. cit., p. 80
71 See Louis Dudek, *Some Letters of Ezra Pound* (Montreal, DC Books, 1974), p. 32
72 *The Goal*, op. cit., p. 240
73 Olga Rudge bore him a daughter in 1925; the baby was handed over to a peasant couple to be reared in the Austrian Tyrol. See Humphrey Carpenter, *A Serious Character: The Life of Ezra Pound* (Faber & Faber, 1988), pp. 455–6.
74 Ezra spent late summer and early autumn wholly with Olga in Venice, while Dorothy visited her mother in England. See Anne Conover, *Olga Rudge and Ezra Pound* (Yale University Press, 2001). Even the concerts were an excuse to get Olga into Rapallo.
75 Italy retained control of Abyssinia until Egyptian and British forces liberated the country in 1941.
76 Ezra Pound to Phyllis Bottome, Bottome/Ezra Pound Correspondence, Beinecke Rare Book and Manuscript Library, Yale University
77 Phyllis Bottome to Ezra Pound, 28 September 1935, ibid.
78 Quoted by C. David Heymann, *Ezra Pound: The Last Rower* (Faber & Faber, 1976), p. 87
79 *From the Life*, op. cit., p. 79
80 Subsequently he was instead imprisoned in a lunatic asylum in Washington DC for many years.
81 Phyllis Bottome to Ezra Pound, 17 November 1936, Bottome/Ezra Pound Correspondence, op. cit.
82 Phyllis Bottome, *Level Crossing* (John Lane, 1936), p. 279
83 ibid., p. 275
84 *From the Life*, op. cit., p. 34
85 N. J. Hall, *Max Beerbohm: A Kind of Life* (Yale University Press, 2002), p. 126
86 Phyllis Bottome, *From the Life*, op. cit., p. 35
87 In 1900, Max had written a one-act version of *The Happy Hypocrite*, which Mrs Patrick Campbell used as a curtain raiser. Thirty-six years later Clemence Dane turned it into a three-act play.
88 Collected in *Masks and Faces*, op. cit. The collection included a short story called 'The Point of Vantage' which was inspired by a story of Robert Pollak's (see Note 19, p. 375 above).
89 The only published novel written by Oscar Wilde; it first appeared in *Lippincott's Monthly* in June 1890.
90 Ivor Novello starred as Sir George Hell, Marius Goring played Cupid and Vivien Leigh played the innocent little heroine. Other actors included

Isabel Jeans, Viola Tree (Max Beerbohm's niece), Charles Lefaus and Carl Harbord. It was produced by Maurice Colbourne. The reviewers remarked, for the first time, that Ivor was an actor of significance. Prior to that they had largely harped on about his matinée-idol looks.

91 Mary Costelloe had left her family when her daughters were small to live with Berenson. One of her daughters, Ray (who married Oliver Strachey), wrote *The Cause: A Short History of the Women's Movement in Great Britain*, published in 1928.

92 *The Goal*, op. cit., p. 245

93 However, he left the Villa I Tatti and its vast collection to Harvard University, and it is now the Harvard University Center for Italian Renaissance Studies.

94 *The Goal*, op. cit., pp. 249–50

95 Letter from Phyllis to Mr Mairet, the editor of *New English Weekly*, shows that their address in September 1935 was Cobenzglasse 2, Wien XIX.

96 *The Goal*, op. cit., pp. 251–5

97 A. A. Joffe was a friend and a patient of Adler's. After the Russian Revolution, Joffe headed the first Soviet peace delegation at Brest-Litovsk and later was Soviet ambassador to Japan. For a good account of Adler's life in Vienna, see Carl Furtmüller's biographical essay, in *Superiority and Social Interest: Alfred Adler*, edited by Heinz L. Ansbacher and Rowena R. Ansbacher, op. cit.

98 Letter from Alexandra Adler to Phyllis Bottome, 27 June 1963, Bottome Papers, Add 78835 BL

99 *The Goal*, op. cit., p. 256

Notes to Chapter 8 – The Battle against Appeasement in Britain: the Writing of *The Mortal Storm* and the Adler Tours

1 *The Goal*, op. cit., pp. 236–7

2 ibid., p. 257

3 ibid.

4 Phyllis Bottome wrote, 'When my husband and I returned in pre-Munich days from shadowed Austria, I can well remember the stunned sickness of heart we felt when we saw placards up all over London, "What Hitler thinks of the World". Never "What does the world think of this diseased tramp Hitler!" ' From her essay 'Our New Order – or Hitler's?', in *Our New Order or Hitler's?*, edited by Phyllis Bottome (Penguin Books, 1943)

5 *The Goal*, op. cit., p. 258

6 Sir Alfred Lane Beit, 2nd baronet (1903–94), was the son of Sir Otto Beit

and Lilian Carter. The Beits were of Sephardic Jewish descent. Alfred was MP for South-East St Pancras from 1931 to 1945.

7 This clause read: The Allied and Associated Governments affirm and Germany accepts the responsibility of Germany and her allies for causing all the loss and damage to which the Allied and Associated Governments and their nationals have been subjected as a consequence of the war imposed upon them by the aggression of Germany and her allies.

8 quoted by Martin Gilbert, *The Roots of Appeasement* (New York, Toronto & London, Plume, 1970), pp. 126–7

9 Ian Colvin, *Vansittart in Office* (Victor Gollancz, 1965), p. 19

10 The League of Nations branded Italy an aggressor and imposed economic sanctions. Oil, however, was left off the list of sanctioned items, and only an oil embargo might have forced Mussolini to withdraw. Italy retained control of Abyssinia until Egyptian and British forces liberated the country in 1941.

11 Later when Austria was taken over by Hitler, Furtmüller and his wife were forced to emigrate. They went first to France, and then to Spain, where they were imprisoned for three months. They finally reached the US in January 1941.

12 See Andrew Sharf, *The British Press & Jews under Nazi Rule* (Oxford University Press, 1964), for a comprehensive account of the British press during this epoch

13 Ezra Pound to Phyllis Bottome, undated but *circa* December 1936, Bottome/Pound Correspondence, op. cit.

14 *The Goal*, op. cit., p. 261

15 George V (1910–1936)

16 See Phyllis Bottome, 'An Appreciation of Sir Geoffrey Faber by one of His Authors', Bottome Papers, Add 78858 BL

17 letter dated 1 June 1936, Bottome Papers, Add 77892 BL

18 *The New Age* was 'perhaps the quintessence of Edwardian radical culture – heterogeneous, eclectic, contradictory, sometimes brilliant; often cranky; above all, always open to something new'. Helen Carr, *The Verse Revolutionaries: Ezra Pound, H. D. and the Imagists*, op. cit., p. 152; the *New English Weekly* had the same open-door policy.

19 See Jennifer Birkett, *Margaret Storm Jameson: A Life* (Oxford University Press, 2009), p. 127, where she lists such eclectic contributions in 1935 as C. H. Douglas on 'The Use of Money', Ezra Pound on 'Social Credit: An Impact' and Herbert Read on 'Essential Communism'.

20 In particular, Adler did not wish to have his name connected with that of a rather wild Serbian philosopher called Mitrinovic. Just as Freud's original group had experienced fractures, so too had the Adlerians. For example, Manes Sperber studied with Adler in Vienna from 1921 onward. He

remained an Adlerian psychologist, but his commitment to Marxism, among other things, led to rupture in 1932. See Manes Sperber, *The Unheeded Warning 1918–1933*, translated by Harry Zohn (New York & London, Homes & Meier, 1991).

21 *The Goal*, op. cit., p. 233

22 A Dr O. H. Woodcock was appointed chairman and Dr James Moore was vice-chair, with Dr Redfern as secretary.

23 Lady Astor, and many others of the friends who had helped willingly with the Adler programmes, were, by 1938, to become estranged because of Phyllis and Ernan's anti-appeasement stance.

24 It was named in honour of Moncure Daniel Conway (1832–1907), anti-slavery campaigner, supporter of free thought and biographer of Thomas Paine.

25 *The Goal*, op. cit., p. 264

26 Held in the Mill Lane lecture theatre. See Bottome Papers, Add 10308 British Library. Some of the most idealistic, such as Brian Simon, had visited progressive schools abroad. Simon, for example, had spent two terms at Kurt Hahn's school in Salem, in southern Germany. In March 1933, after the election of the Nazi Party, Hahn had been thrown into jail. As a Jew his position had been precarious, although pressure from Ramsay MacDonald meant that he had been released, albeit ousted from Salem. In 1934 he had emigrated to Britain and set up Gordonstoun, a progressive school on the coast of Moray, in Scotland.

27 Brian Simon, *A Life in Education* (London, Lawrence and Wishart, 1998), p. 8

28 ibid., p. 10

29 Alfred Adler, Grand Hôtel du Louvre, Paris, letter to Professor Barker at Peterhouse College, Cambridge, 10 June 1936, Bottome Papers, Add 10308 BL

30 Alfred Adler, *What Life Should Mean to You*, edited by Alan Porter (George Allen & Unwin, 1932)

31 *The Goal*, op. cit., p. 226

32 ibid., p. 271

33 John Sutherland, *Stephen Spender: The Authorized Biography* (Penguin, 2005), p. 196

34 Spender's book, *Forward from Liberalism* (1937), is interesting politically, as it did not follow the approved Communist line, but rather seemed to suggest that Russia should move to Liberalism. Ernest Hemingway was, similarly, the most influential American writer. His novel *For Whom the Bell Tolls* was published in 1940. It tells the story of a young American attached to an anti-fascist guerrilla unit during the Spanish Civil War.

35 In an undated letter to Phyllis, *circa* 1925, Ernan wrote: 'Ivor offers us the flat (we I imagine paying for whatever food we order) from Tuesday 28th till Friday 31st. – and I have provisionally accepted thinking it may suit you. Constance Collier, who is here, asks you and me to a theatre on Wed & Thursday nights, and we give her food in the flat after – if you care to – so that she can tell you her experience of stagecraft – she adapted "Peter Ibbetson" and is supposed to know a lot about stage technique ... Much love from Ivor – He was crazy about "Depths".' Bottome Papers, Add 78897 BL

36 *The Goal*, op. cit., p. 276

37 ibid., p. 277

38 ibid.

39 Bottome Papers, Add 10308 BL, letter dated 20 May 1937 from Phyllis Bottome to Sir Squire Spriggs:

> My old friend and physician, Dr Des Voeux, tells me I may use his name freely in writing to you about Professor Adler's projected Summer Course. My husband and I have arranged the enclosed programme for him. [There was a] ... phenomenal decrease of delinquency in Vienna, when Glöckel (the Minister of Education) attached Adler cliniques to the State Schools, and [there has been an] equally spectacular relapse since Nazi pressure put a stop to the cliniques and, incidentally, killed Glöckel by two years of concentration camp.
>
> A Chair of Medical Psychology was founded by Professor Adler at the Long Island College of Medicine, in USA, and one of the States (New Jersey) has already adopted his treatment for delinquent children with marked success.
>
> Up till now there has been no one in England, who had learned enough of Individual Psychology by watching its effects in the cliniques of Vienna and Munich at first hand, to press it sufficiently upon the English public. Unfortunately, one of its most brilliant and enthusiastic adherents over here, Dr Crookshanks, had never accepted its fundamental character-training implication and his suicide was a great set-back to the movement. Adler has been very badly served in England, since his books are wretchedly translated, as a rule, and have been far too-hurriedly flung together by adoring pupils from lectures and expanded notes.

(The letter also speaks of Munich where Dr Leonard Seif ran an Adlerian clinique and lectures on IP at the university.)

40 Winifred Rushforth, *Ten Decades of Happenings* (London, Gateway Books, 1984), p. 82

41 *The Goal*, op. cit., p. 228 and p. 225

42 See Pam Hirsch, 'Alfred Adler and his British Disciples', in Special Issue 'Insiders and Outsiders in the History of Education', *History of Education*, volume 34, number 5, September 2005.
43 See details in Martin Gilbert, *Kristallnacht: Prelude to Disaster* (HarperCollins, 2006), pp. 120–3.
44 Bottome Papers, Add 78836 BL
45 Phyllis Bottome to Upton Sinclair, 2 May 1940, Sinclair Manuscripts, Lilly Library, Indiana University, Bloomington, Indiana
46 letter from Thomas Mann to the editor of *Common Sense* in 1940, reprinted in Peter Viereck's *Metapolitics: From Wagner and the German Romantics to Hitler* (Transaction Publishers, 2007), p. lix
47 See Barbara Brothers' essay 'British Women Writers: The Story of the Nazis: A Conspiracy of Silence', in *Rediscovering Forgotten Radicals: British Women Writers 1889–1930*, op. cit. Brothers raises important questions about why Bottome's books (along with those of other women writers of the period) have not been taken seriously by academics. She points out that much radical fiction by women gets dismissed as romance, when its protagonist is a woman. I am sure this is correct, even though marriage does not provide the conventional resolution in *The Mortal Storm*.
48 It seems likely that Phyllis chose the name 'Toller' in honour of Ernst Toller, the German-Jewish poet and playwright who had been detained by the Nazis in 1933 because he had denounced heroism as a stupid ideal. Although tortured in a concentration camp, he was released and exiled. In 1938, he published a play called *Pastor Hall* which in turn honoured the Protestant pastor, Martin Niemöller, whose opposition to Hitler in Germany resulted in his arrest and trial for high treason. In May 1939, when news reached him in New York that his sister and brother had been arrested and sent to concentration camps, Toller committed suicide. In 1940 the Boulting Brothers in Britain produced a film version of *Pastor Hall*.
49 Phyllis Bottome, *The Mortal Storm* (Faber & Faber, 1937), p. 8
50 ibid., p. 10
51 ibid., p. 22
52 ibid., p. 63
53 ibid., p. 27
54 quoted by Peter Viereck, *Metapolitics*, op.cit., p. 126. Wagner's essay, 'Das Judenthum in der Musik' (Jewishness in Music), attacked Jewish composers, saying that Mendelssohn's music 'has shown us that a Jew can possess the richest measure of specific talents ... without even once being able to bring forth in us that profound, heart-and-soul-searching effect

we expect from music'. In effect, Wagner condemned Jewish composers as effeminate, when, in Wagner's view, German music should be strong and ambitious and serve emerging German nationalism. In *Deutsche Kunst and Deutsche Politik*, Wagner spoke of the harmful influence of Jews on the morality of the nation. These ideas, as well as the Aryan mythology of the *Ring* cycle in particular, proved a fertile feeding ground for Nazi ideology and cultural conception.

55 quoted by John Chancellor, *Wagner* (Little, Brown & Co., 1978), p. 116

56 Wagnerian music was often played at book-burning ceremonies, and when concentration-camp prisoners were about to be put to death.

57 See Elmer Davis, *Not to Mention the War* (New York, 1939), pp. 205–6.

58 Peter Viereck, *Metapolitics*, op. cit., p. 139

59 ibid.

60 *The Mortal Storm* (1937), op. cit., p. 380

61 Phyllis Bottome to Upton Sinclair, 2 May 1940, Sinclair Manuscripts, Lilly Library, Indiana University, Bloomington, Indiana.

62 Wandervogel was also the name of a German youth group, young men and women who went out walking with knapsacks on their backs. However, I think Bottome is using the term figuratively as well as literally.

63 See Pam Hirsch, 'Women and Jews in *Daniel Deronda*', in *The George Eliot Review*, 1994.

64 See review by Eric Duthie, *The Left Review* (4 December 1937), p. 695

65 Ernan's relative, the Duchess of Atholl, was a passionate partisan of the republican cause in the Spanish Civil War. After this she was known as the 'Red' Duchess. See Jeremy Lewis, Penguin Special: *The Life and Times of Allen Lane* (Penguin, 2006), p. 137

66 Phyllis Bottome to Upton Sinclair, 3 January 1939, Sinclair Manuscripts, Lilly Library, Indiana University, Bloomington, Indiana

67 See Introduction by Phyllis Lassner and Marilyn Hoder-Salmon to Northwestern University edition of *The Mortal Storm*; they comment that the three new chapters 'significantly deepened the feminist and anti-Nazi themes'. They also comment: 'The initial lackluster British reception of the novel disappointed Bottome, but once the public understood the reality of its warning, the book reached a wide audience.'

68 See also Phyllis Lassner, ' "A Cry for Life": Storm Jameson, Stevie Smith, and the Fate of Europe's Jews', in M. Paul Holsinger and Mary Anne Schofield (eds), *Visions of War: World War II in Popular Literature and Culture* (Bowling Green, 1992), pp. 181–90.

69 undated letter from Carl Sigal to Phyllis Bottome, but likely to be 1938 when Little, Brown & Co., Boston, published the book in America

70 Phyllis Bottome, *The Mortal Storm* (Little, Brown & Co., 1938), p. 72

71 Eva Nathan to Phyllis Bottome, 23. 12. 47, Bottome Papers, Add 78866 BL
72 Preface to *Alfred Adler: Apostle of Freedom* (Faber & Faber, 1939). Phyllis could only list by name those people who were safely out of harm's way: 'Dr Alexander Neuer gave us the fullest possible information upon Adler's later Freudian and pre-War period in Vienna. Neuer was one of the members of Freud's circle who left with Adler – a most brilliant younger colleague – whose knowledge of the forming and building up of Individual Psychology in its early days throws a light on the whole subject of this biography. Dr Franz Plewa, Adler's former assistant in the Psychiatric section of the Franz-Joseph Ambulatorium Hospital in Vienna, and the late President of the Viennese School of Individual Psychology. Dr Lydia Sicher, also one of Adler's best-known Viennese colleagues of post-War days, to whom he transferred his appointment when he finally left Vienna. Both these colleagues gave me information covering their own exhaustive knowledge of Adler's post-War year in Vienna. Dr Greta Simpson, a well-known New York psychologist, who worked with Adler for eight years in Vienna, and continued her friendship through the American period of Adler's life. Dr Babbott, the President of the Long Island College of Medicine, where Adler occupied the first Chair of Medical Psychology to be founded in the world during the last five years of his life, who put at my disposal a most interesting dossier of Adler's work while at the College. Charles Davis, Adler's most devoted and intimate friend during the American period of his life, who kept a valuable diary of all Adler's public engagements in America, which was placed at the author's disposal. Philip Mairet, the Editor of the *New English Weekly*, one of the original members of the first London group of Individual Psychologists; and Dr James Moore, also one of the most constant members of the Medical Society of Individual Psychology, which arose out of the earlier group.'
73 *The Goal*, op. cit., p. 287
74 Phyllis Bottome, *Alfred Adler: Apostle of Freedom*, op. cit., Preface, p. 13
75 Letters from Alexandra Adler to Phyllis Bottome, 3 January 1938 and 18 October 1938, Bottome Papers, Add 78835 BL
76 Ursula E. Oberst and Alan E. Stewart, *Adlerian Psychotherapy: An Advanced Approach to Individual Psychology*, op. cit., p. 13
77 *The Woman Teacher*, 19 April 1940, p. 156
78 review by Leonard Carmichael, president of Tufts College and president of the American Psychological Association in Boston, Mass., *Transcript*, 7 December 1939; *Los Angeles Times*, 3 December 1939
79 See Rudolf Dreikurs, *Fundamentals of Adlerian Psychology* (Alfred Adler Institute of Chicago, 1989), and 'Democratic and Autocratic Child Rearing'

in *The Children's Culture Reader*, edited by Henry Jenkins (New York University Press, 1998).

80 Ursula E. Oberst and Alan E. Stewart, op. cit., pp. vi–vii. There is also a renewed interest in birth order, although here Adler is acknowledged as the founding father of this theorisation. See, for example, Frank J. Sulloway, *Born to Rebel: Birth Order, Family Dynamics and Creative Lives* (Pantheon Books, 2007).

81 T. Raymont, *The Journal of Education,* May 1940, p. 246. There are today Adlerian institutions in Chicago, San Francisco, Washington, New York, West Texas, Quebec, Dusseldorf, Zurich, Genoa and Tel Aviv; there are Adlerian psychologists in various universities and Adlerian societies all around the world. Many school counsellors have undertaken Adlerian training and accreditation, and there are many private therapists.

82 *The Goal*, op. cit., p. 191

83 ibid., p. 257

84 Lewis Way's *Alfred Adler: An Introduction to Psychology* was published in 1956 but is now out of print. There is a typescript in the Bottome Papers in the British Library.

85 For example, Heinz Sternberg's (Adler's son-in-law, married to his youngest daughter, Nelly) father, mother and grandmother all committed suicide when Hitler occupied Vienna. Nelly left her husband at this point, but it is not known what happened to her. Ernan and Phyllis helped Heinz get to the USA, and used their contacts to get him a job. He also lived with them in the United States for a period of four or five months. They also managed to help Irene Spierer (Phyllis's favourite Viennese milliner) and her husband to come to England in 1938, and helped them financially to start up a hatshop. Later they helped Irene get to the USA. See Bottome Papers, Add 10308 BL

86 Phyllis Bottome to Frank and Esther Adams, 19 March 1938, Bottome Papers, Add 10308 BL

87 Martin Gilbert, *Kristallnacht: Prelude to Disaster* (HarperCollins, 2006), p. 126

88 It was eventually printed in the *New Republic* in America in December 1938.

89 See Louise London, *Whitehall and the Jews 1933–1948: British Immigration Policy and the Holocaust* (Cambridge University Press, 2000).

90 Otto Schiff was the chairman; the JRC's activities were limited to helping refugees in the United Kingdom. Its funds came from the Central British Fund for German Jewry (CBF), founded in 1933. CBF supported JRC, but also funded emigration to Palestine. The banker, Anthony de Rothschild, was heavily involved with refugee work; he

became chair of the CBF and the Central Council for Jewish Refugees in 1939.

91 quoted by Louise London, op. cit., p. 28, from 'Proposals of the Jewish Community as regards Jewish Refugees from Germany', signed by Neville Laski KC, president of the London Committee of Deputies of British Jews, Lionel L. Cohen KC, chairman of the board's Law, Parliamentary and General Purposes Association, and Otto Schiff.

92 She published 'A Personal View of the Refugee Problem' (1939) and 'Falsehoods and Facts about the Jews' (1944); see Chapter 7 of Johanna Alberti, *Eleanor Rathbone* (Sage, 1996).

93 Bottome Papers, Add 78847 BL

94 According to Louise London, op. cit., pp. 51–2, 'Insufficient British students were entering the profession. About half of the 15,000 British registered dentists were unqualified and the majority were, according to one Home Office official, "thoroughly bad dentists".'

95 Bottome Papers, Add 78847 BL

96 Martin Gilbert, *Kristallnacht: Prelude to Disaster*, op. cit., pp. 128 and 130; see also George Weidenfeld, *Remembering My Good Friends* (HarperCollins, 1995), pp. 76–8.

97 *Dictionary of National Biography*, Oxford University Press

98 Philip M. Taylor, *Britain and the Cinema in the Second World War* (Basingstoke, Macmillan, 1988), p. 11

99 Bottome Papers, Add 10308 BL

100 Hitler, *Mein Kampf*, thirteenth German edition (Munich 1932, p. 69), quoted by Peter Viereck, *Metapolitics*, op. cit., p. 134

101 quoted by Martin Gilbert, *Second World War* (London, Phoenix, 2000), p. 6

102 *The Goal*, op. cit., p. 236

Notes to Chapter 9 – Filming *The Mortal Storm*: Phyllis as Britain's Propagandist in America

1 Phyllis Bottome, *The Mortal Storm* (Boston, Little, Brown & Co., 1938)

2 Phyllis Bottome, 'I Accuse', *New Republic*, 1938, pp. 232–3

3 It was called the Helican Home Colony; see *The Autobiography of Upton Sinclair* (W. H. Allen, 1963).

4 The 'World's End' series was published in the UK by T. Werner Laurie, who was a friend of Phyllis's.

5 See essay by Sally E. Parry, 'Learning to Fight the Nazis: The Education of Upton Sinclair's Lanny Budd', in *Visions of War: World War II in Popular Literature and Culture*, op. cit.

6 See Stuart T. Miller, *Mastering Modern European History* (Basingstoke, Palgrave, 1997), pp. 240–2

7 *Time and Tide* (summer 1936) had warned that dangerous views were held by a number of upper-class Britons, including Lady Astor; in November 1937, Claud Cockburn wrote in the left-wing journal *The Week* that the Astors and their newspapers were fomenting pro-Nazi goals and making rearmament impossible.

8 See Chapter 4 of John Halperin, *Eminent Georgians* (Basingstoke, Macmillan, 1998), for a concise account of Nancy Astor. He notes, however, that once war had begun she admitted publicly that she had been wrong. Phyllis Bottome acknowledged this too.

9 Phyllis Bottome to Upton Sinclair, 29 March 1939, Bottome Papers, Add 78861 BL: ' … Nancy Astor has always been a curse to England. She has behaved continuously as a spoiled and forward child, snatching the privileges and over-looking the duties, while always expecting to be made a pet of.'

10 There seems to have been some kind of rivalry between her and Unity Mitford. Unity Mitford was an upper-class British woman who became obsessed with Hitler, and attempted suicide once Germany and Britain were at war. Unity's sister, Diana Mitford, married Oswald Mosley, the head of the British Union of Fascists.

11 Nancy Astor had supported the Adler tours, but at a dinner party with some of the Cliveden set, the Forbes Dennises had realised how dangerous they were and had subsequently parted with them as friends.

12 *The Goal*, op. cit., pp. 272–3

13 Bottome Papers, Add 10308 BL

14 Ernan, as Phyllis's ADC, was engaged in a running battle with the tax authorities from this point onwards.

15 Jeremy Lewis, *The Life and Times of Allen Lane*, op. cit., p. 134

16 *The Goal*, op. cit., p. 273

17 ibid., p. 260

18 Phyllis Bottome to Professor Potter, 9 March 1939, Bottome Papers, Add 10308 BL

19 Bottome Papers, Add 78846 BL

20 ibid.

21 Phyllis Bottome to 'Aunt Chattie', 13 July 1939, Bottome Papers, Add 78846 BL

22 Bottome Papers, Add 78846 BL

23 *The Goal*, op. cit., p. 274

24 *Manchester Guardian*, Friday, 25 August 1939, p. 10

25 Phyllis Bottome to Robert Vansittart, 18 July 1939, Bottome Papers, Add 78848 BL

26 Katharine Marjory Stewart-Murray (1874–1960) became Duchess of Atholl when her husband succeeded to the title in 1917. Her public work began with organising district-nursing associations in Perthshire. In 1918 she was created one of the first dames of the British Empire.
27 *Dictionary of National Biography*, Oxford University Press on-line
28 Phyllis Bottome to Robert Vansittart, 9 September 1939, Bottome Papers, Add 78848 BL
29 ibid.
30 Phyllis Bottome to Robert Vansittart, Bottome Papers, Add 78848 BL
31 A good account of this is to be found in Nicholas John Cull, *Selling War: The British Propaganda Campaign Against American Neutrality in World War II* (New York and Oxford, Oxford University Press, 1995).
32 Dorothy Thompson had formed a close friendship with Phyllis Bottome when they had both lived in Vienna in the 1920s. Edgar Mowrer had been head of the Berlin-based press correspondents and was well informed on Nazi Party activities.
33 Phyllis Bottome to Professor Potter, 9 March 1939, Bottome Papers, Add 10308 BL
34 J. Hoberman and Jeffrey Shandler, *Entertaining America: Jews, Movies and Broadcasting* (Princeton and Oxford, Princeton University Press, 2003), p. 63
35 In 1934, in America, a new and stringently enforced Production Code had been enacted. Partly in order to combat its strictures, the Hollywood Anti-Nazi League (HANL) had been formed in 1936 to campaign again fascism, through its newsletter, by sponsoring radio broadcasts and by organising meetings. Within a few months it had enrolled several thousand members, mostly Jewish, but not exclusively so. In the spring of 1938 the newly established House Committee on Un-American Activities (HCUAA) was convened. It postulated that HANL was a Communist front, and, though its hearings were not held until late 1947, it was this period which opened up the political opportunity, as it were, for the subsequent inquisition in Hollywood. J. Hoberman and Jeffrey Shandler, op. cit., p. 59
36 In March 1922, studios had responded to the threat of government censorship by establishing the Motion Pictures Producers and Distributors of America (MPPDA) and recruiting United States Postmaster General Will Hays, a prominent Indiana Republican and Presbyterian elder, to be its president. Colin Shindler, *Hollywood Goes to War: Films and American Society 1939–52* (Routledge & Kegan Paul, 1979), p. 5
37 See Chapter 3, 'Walking on Eggs', in Colin Shindler, op. cit., and p. 2 for the quotation.
38 In lectures scheduled to last from October 1939 until August 1940. On the

east coast she gave lectures in New York and in Boston, including Columbia and Harvard Universities and Wellesley College for Women.

39 *The Times*, Wednesday, 25 October 1939

40 Duff Cooper was a diplomatist and politician, married to Lady Diana Manners, one of the great beauties of the age. In September 1944, he was sent to Paris as British Ambassador, where Lady Diana's glittering gatherings helped his popularity.

41 Article by Boake Carpenter, December 1939, Bottome Papers, Add 78858 BL

42 Boston, Mass., *American*, 13 December 1939, Mrs Eleanor Roosevelt's column 'My Day': ' ... Monday night ... among our guests were Mr and Mrs Ernan Forbes Dennis, who are English friends of my mother-in-law', Bottome Papers, Add 78858 BL

43 *Britain and the Cinema in the Second World War*, ed. Philip M. Taylor (Basingstoke, Macmillan Press, 1988), p. 3

44 Phyllis Bottome to Admiral Reginald Plunkett, Bottome Papers, Add 10308 BL

45 Stalin had signed a mutual non-aggression pact with Hitler on 23 August 1939. Its secret clauses included the sharing out of Poland. Averting the possibility of a war on two fronts strengthened Hitler's hand enormously, so the failure of this mission was critical.

46 Bernard F. Dick, *The Star-Spangled Screen: The American World War II Film* (Kentucky, University Press of Kentucky, 1996), p. 70. Dick's quotes are taken directly from the production files at MGM/USA.

47 Bill Dozier at Berg-Allenberg was sub-contracted to do the deal for Ann Watkins Inc.; Watkins was Phyllis Bottome's American agent at this point, but she was based in New York.

48 Bottome Papers, Add 10308 BL

49 *Hollywood Reporter*, 11 April 1939

50 Victor Saville (1897–1979) was later to claim that he had directed most of the film. This seems highly unlikely as the film shows all the hallmarks of Borzage's direction. However, his presence, even as a producer, would have needed to be downplayed, as the association of a flagrant anti-Nazi film with a British citizen might have stirred up accusations of propaganda.

51 West had been a code breaker for British Intelligence in World War I; later she won an Academy award for her adaptation of *Mrs Miniver*. She was assisted by Hans Rameau, who usually wrote under the pseudonym of Ellis Anderson, presumably because he still had family remaining in Germany.

52 letter from Phyllis Bottome to Sidney Franklin, dated 7 February 1940, MGM Collection, USC Cinematic Arts Library

53 Phyllis Bottome, 'Speaking as one who should know. A Novelist talks about the screen version of her book', in *New York Times*, 16 June 1940. She said this was her only regret about the film.

54 This piece of music by the German composer would have been an apt choice. Phyllis was also bound to have been familiar with Beethoven's only opera, *Fidelio*, which centres on resistance to a tyrant and is famous for the scene in which the prisoners and townsfolk sing to the day and hour of justice that has come ('Heil sei dem Tag!' ['Hail to the day!']).

55 letter from Phyllis Bottome to Sidney Franklin, dated 7 February 1940, MGM Collection, USC Cinematic Arts Library

56 Chaplin's *The Great Dictator* represented the Jews fairly and squarely as the Nazis' chosen victims. 'Chaplin's adorable everyman is no longer just anybody; he is a persecuted Jew.' This point is made by Thomas Doherty in *Projections of War* (Columbia University Press, 1999), p. 130. However, Chaplin's film was released on 15 October 1940 *after* Hitler's entry into Paris.

57 letter from Phyllis Bottome to Sidney Franklin, 7 February 1940, MGM Collection, USC Cinematic Arts Library

58 Bottome Papers, Add 10308 (War Letters from 1938) BL; she mentions in the same letter that Duff Cooper's lectures in the US were doing good work for England's cause.

59 Roy Mosley, *Evergreen: Victor Saville in His Own Words* (South Illinois University Press, 2000), p. 141

60 After a tour with the Moscow Art Theatre in 1924, she stayed on in New York. She founded the Maria Ouspenskaya School of Dramatic Art in 1929. She had her first Hollywood role in 1936, as the German countess in William Wyler's *Dodsworth*.

61 wire from Western Union, dated 21 May 1940

62 Phyllis Bottome, *Mansion House of Liberty* (Boston, Little, Brown & Co., 1941), p. 5

63 Phyllis Bottome to Violet Bonham Carter, 25 November 1940, Bottome Papers, Add 78849 BL. Like Phyllis, Violet denounced appeasement. In 1936, Churchill gave her a central role in his anti-fascist Freedom Focus. This cross-party pressure group acted under the auspices of the League of Nations Union, of which Violet remained a patron until 1941.

64 *Mansion House of Liberty*, op. cit., p. 8

65 Churchill's view was that although Britain should recognise that 'whereas the present battle was of great importance, it would not be decisive one way or the other for Great Britain ... If this country were defeated, the war would be lost for France no less than for ourselves.' Clive Ponting, *Churchill* (London, Sinclair-Stevenson, 1994), p. 448

66 The British Expeditionary Force left behind its artillery, tanks and other equipment. Six destroyers were sunk and nineteen damaged. The Air Force lost 177 aeroplanes.
67 Charles Chaplin's *The Great Dictator*, a comic propaganda film that, ironically, warned against the dangers of propaganda, was released by United Artists, also in 1940.
68 *Motion Picture Herald*, 15 June 1940; *The Mortal Storm* opened at the Capitol in New York on 30 June 1940.
69 Phyllis Lassner, *British Women Writers of World War II: Battlegrounds of Their Own* (Macmillan, 1998), p. 275, n. 6
70 See Douglas Gomery, *The Hollywood Studio System: A History* (bfi publishing, 2005), for a good account.
71 One might consider for comparison some more recent political films. The casting of stars such as George Clooney in *Syriana*, Angelina Jolie in *A Mighty Heart*, Jake Gyllenghall in *Rendition*, Daniel Craig in *Defiance*, etc. will attract an audience for a political film that other, no doubt equally good, actors might not.
72 Robert K. Lightning, ' "We have secrets": Borzage, romance and the bourgeois state', in *Cineaction*, June 1988, p. 67
73 David Thomson, *Have You Seen? A Personal Introduction to 1,000 Films* (Allen Lane, 2008)
74 Douglas Gomery, *The Hollywood Studio System*, op. cit., p. 104
75 *A Farewell to Arms* (1932) was adapted from a novel by Ernest Hemingway, and starred Gary Cooper; *Three Comrades* (1938) starred Robert Taylor and Margaret Sullavan and was adapted from a novel by Erich Maria Remarque.
76 David Thomson, *The New Biographical Dictionary of Film*, fourth edition (Little, Brown & Co., 2003), p. 97
77 John Belton, *The Hollywood Professionals, Volume 3: Howard Hawks, Frank Borzage and Edgar G. Ulmer* (Tantivity, 1974), p. 104
78 Louella Parsons, *Los Angeles Examiner*, 18 July 1940
79 William Boehnel in *The New York World Telegram*, 21 June 1940
80 The film's success in turn created a new audience for her book. A paperback version of *The Mortal Storm*, a Popular Library edition for 'Books of Proven Merit', was published in New York by arrangement with Little, Brown & Co. The blurb comments: 'She first gained prominence in America with the publication of *The Dark Tower*. Later came *The Mortal Storm*, a best-seller which was made into an unforgettable movie starring James Stewart and Margaret Sullavan.'
81 Phyllis Bottome to Violet Bonham Carter, 18 July 1939, Bottome Papers, Add 78849 BL
82 *Journal of Popular Film and Television*, vol. 30, no. 2 (Summer 2002), p. 92

83 Notwithstanding the two-pronged campaign, Middle America to some extent shunned the film, so that *The Mortal Storm* took only 4,000,000 dollars. Although this sounds a lot, it is only a fifth of what *Gone with the Wind* took in 1939.
84 Botschaft, Washington, to 'AA', 9 March 1941, Bundesarchiv, Berlin, R901, Nr. 600449, p 3, quoted by Hervé Dumont, *Frank Borzage: The Life and Films of a Hollywood Romantic*, translated by Jonathan Kaplansky (McFarland, 2006), p. 300
85 Charles Chaplin directed himself in *The Great Dictator* (1940) in two roles: one as a little Jewish barber, and the other as a caricature of Hitler. During the First World War, films such as *The Beast of Berlin* started off riots in some American cities.
86 Phyllis Bottome to Israel Sieff, 28 August 1940, Bottome Papers, Add 10308 BL
87 Phyllis Bottome to Sir Frederick Whyte, 28 August 1940, Bottome Papers, Add 10308 BL
88 Review by Colin Whitebait in *New Statesman*, 19 October 1940; and by Basil Wright, *The Spectator*, 4 October 1940
89 Jack Beddington took over the Films Division at around the time of the fall of Chamberlain and the formation of the Churchill coalition. See James Chapman, *The British at War: Cinema, State and Propaganda, 1939–1945* (I. B. Tauris, 1998).
90 Claudine West wrote the screenplay for *Mrs Miniver* (1942), which was MGM's highest grossing film in the 1940s, and the one most often taught on film courses, but by then America was already in the war, and the studio was taking no risks in producing the film at that stage.
91 Phyllis Bottome to Jack Beddington, Films Division of MOI, 16 June 1942, Bottome Papers, Add 10308 BL
92 Bottome Papers, Add 78836 BL
93 Phyllis Bottome to MPs, 1 July 1940, Liddell Hart Centre for Military Archives, King's College, London
94 See Peter Stansky, *The First Day of the Blitz* (Yale University Press, 2007), for a good account of the preparations.
95 7 June 1940, Bottome Papers, Add 10308 BL
96 Peter Stansky, *The First Day of the Blitz*, op. cit., p. 28
97 Phyllis Bottome to Sir Robert Vansittart, 15 December 1940, Bottome Papers, Add 78848 BL
98 Phyllis Bottome to Lady Violet Bonham Carter, 2 November 1940, Bottome Papers, Add 78849 BL. However, the Ministry of Information did not always back her. For example, she later wrote an article on Charles Lindbergh called 'The American Hitler', which Edgar Mowrer

would have placed for her, but the Ministry of Information blocked it. Given that Lindbergh preached total isolation because he thought that the German armed forces were invincible and that Germany would inevitability dominate Europe, it is hard to know what risk the MOI thought they would be running.

99 *The Goal*, op. cit., p. 230
100 *Mansion House of Liberty*, op. cit.
101 Their correspondence is in King's College, London.
102 *Mansion House of Liberty*, op. cit., p. 159
103 ibid., p. 184
104 ibid., p. 252–3
105 ibid., p. 256–7
106 Bottome Papers, Add 78872 BL
107 script of 'Democracy Marches' by Phyllis Bottome, Overseas North American Transmission: Saturday/Sunday, 8th/9th March 1941, in Sinclair Manuscripts, Lilly Library, Indiana University, Bloomington, Indiana
108 Phyllis Bottome, 'Democracy Marches', for Overseas North American Transmission: Saturday/Sunday, 8/9th March 1941, 0300 GMT, Bottome Papers, Add 78854 BL
109 See John Trumpbour, *Selling Hollywood to the World: US and European Struggles for Mastery of the Global Film Industry, 1920–1950* (Cambridge University Press, 2002), p. 76.
110 ibid., pp. 75–6
111 The isolationists were Senators D. Worth Clark of Idaho, Homer T. Bone of Washington, Charles W. Tobey of New Hampshire and C. Wayland Brooks of Illinois; the non-isolationist was Senator Ernest W. McFarland of Arizona.
112 Others were Anatole Litvak's *Confessions of a Nazi Spy* (1939), Charlie Chaplin's *The Great Dictator* (1940) and Howard Hawks's *Sergeant York* (1941).
113 Susan L. Carruthers, *The Media at War* (Palgrave Macmillan, 2000), p. 38

Notes to Chapter 10 – Wartime in Cornwall and Therapeutic Interventions in the Colony of Artists

1 This may have been Sisi Berman, who lived at Thymeland with the Forbes Dennises. She wanted to join her brother, a jeweller in New York. Phyllis wrote trying to hasten the processing of her papers. Bottome Papers, Add 10308 BL
2 Philip Henry Kerr, Lord Lothian (1882–1940), writer and politician. Initially he was part of the Cliveden set, and an appeaser, but he arrived as the British Ambassador in Washington four days before Britain joined the war. He was a good choice, as throughout the inter-war years he had been a fervent advocate of closer cooperation between Britain and America. Behind the scenes he was negotiating the destroyers-for-bases deal of September 1940.
3 Phyllis Bottome to Walter and Joan Wanger, 20 June 1940, Bottome Papers, Add 10308 BL. 'Joan' was Walter's second wife, the actress Joan Bennett.
4 Phyllis Bottome to 'Winnie', 19 September 1940, Bottome Papers, Add 10308 BL. The Home Guard volunteers worked as normal during the days, taking up Home Guard duties in the evenings and at weekends.
5 Phyllis Bottome to Walter Wanger, 1 February 1941, Bottome Papers, Add 10308 BL
6 Cornwall Home Guard, training report, 20 July 1941, Bottome Papers, Add 78903 BL
7 Nottingham Branch of the National Council of Women on 30 April 1942. Her talk is reported in the *Nottingham Guardian*, 1 May 1942, Bottome Papers, Add 78854 BL.
8 Bottome Papers, Add 10308 BL. A letter dated 17 February 1941, from Phyllis to Helen Raymond, now Mrs John Eugene Lambert, who had acted as Phyllis's secretary on her most recent visit to America, lists some of her visits prior to that date. Itinerary for 1942 also detailed and comprehensive. See also newspaper reports: *The Scotsman*, April 1942, and the *Evening Express*, Aberdeen, Saturday, 25 April 1942. This petrol allowance was both vital and strictly controlled; in 1944 they were to hear that Ivor Novello had been arrested, charged with unlawful conspiracy to commit offences against the Motor Vehicles (Restriction of Use) Order 1942, and jailed for a month. As Ivor Novello had done a huge amount to keep up British spirits in wartime, through the ENSA organisation for entertaining troops in France, this seems especially unreasonable and ludicrous. His song, 'We'll Gather Lilacs', became one of the theme songs of the Second World War, just as 'Keep the Home Fires Burning' had been the theme song of the First World War.

9 letter to the author from Allen Freer, dated 17 April 2006
10 letter to the author from Allen Freer, dated 22 July 2006
11 Bottome Papers, Add 78872 BL
12 Ernan Forbes Dennis to Stella Isaacs, Lady Reading, dated 18 June 1941, telling her that Phyllis 'lately had to have an operation. You will be glad to hear she is making a good recovery.' Bottome Papers, Add 78862 BL
13 Phyllis Bottome, *London Pride* (Faber & Faber, 1941), p. 67
14 ibid., p. 181
15 ibid., p. 108
16 Bottome Papers, Add 78872 BL
17 Phyllis Bottome, *The Derelict and Other Stories* (London, W. Collins Sons & Co. Ltd, 1923), p. 42
18 Phyllis to Ernan, 28 October 1941, Bottome Papers, Add 78893 BL
19 Bottome Papers, Add 10308 BL
20 ibid. Founded in the 1920s, *Time and Tide* gave an opportunity for women in particular to express their views in an independent press. By the 1930s it was offering serious weekly competition to the *New Statesman* as the leading weekly review in Britain.
21 Robert Pollak to Ernan Forbes Dennis, 2 March 1941, Bottome Papers, Add 78863 BL
22 See Phyllis Bottome, *Alfred Adler, Apostle of Freedom*, op. cit., p. 217: 'In 1934 [Laci] had been offered the permanent editorship, and complete immunity from future persecution, if he would undertake to carry the *Journal* on in Germany under another name; he had only to repudiate Adler as the Founder of Individual Psychology for one of his now Nazi-minded German adherents. No one who has not had such an offer made to him can know what it cost Zilahi to refuse it. For it did not only mean personal security for his wife and child; it meant the continuation of his life … '
23 Bottome Papers, Add 10308 BL
24 14 March 1941, Bottome Papers, Add 78835 BL
25 Laci to Ernan Forbes Dennis, 23 August 1963, Bottome Papers, Add 78835 BL
26 Laci to Phyllis Bottome, 15 May 1941: 'It is an unparalleled presentation of the British cause, of Freedom's cause, of the soul of this country.' Bottome Papers, Add 78835 BL. Ernst Gombrich, Martin Esslin and George Weidenfeld were other émigrés recruited by the BBC Monitoring Service to help keep British authorities up to date with the latest Axis pronouncements.
27 One element of the British wartime policy of emigration, or rather re-emigration, was that refugees were allowed into this country for a limited period and then sent on to America or to British colonies.

28 *The Goal*, op. cit., p. 84. The passage continues: ' … when I last heard of her she was approaching seventy, unwilling to be a burden on her son, who had a family, and still earning her living as a mental nurse in New York City; and I am perfectly sure that she was a good one.'
29 See Michael R. Marrus, *The Unwanted: European Refugees in the Twentieth Century* (Oxford University Press, 1985), for a detailed account.
30 For details, see Bottome Papers, Add 78847 BL; she gave one such talk, called 'A Solution of the Jewish Problem', at Wigmore Hall in February 1944.
31 Phyllis Bottome to Storm Jameson, 18 December 1941, Bottome Papers, Add 78861 BL
32 Jennifer Birkett, *Margaret Storm Jameson: A Life*, op. cit., p. 148
33 ibid., p. 118. Phyllis wrote offering Storm a two-month stay at Red Willows when Storm became particularly run down in December 1941.
34 letter from Phyllis Bottome to Mr Stalleybrass, Bottome Papers, Add 10308 BL
35 Phyllis Bottome to Miss Sibthorpe, 17 August 1943, Bottome Papers, Add 10308 BL
36 Phyllis Bottome, *Within the Cup* (Faber & Faber, 1943); in US as *Survival* (Sundial, 1943)
37 ibid., p. 12
38 ibid., pp. 11–12
39 To be precise, Austrian and German qualifications were not recognised in the United Kingdom.
40 Phyllis Lassner, *British Women Writers of World War II: Battlegrounds of Their Own*, op. cit., p. 227
41 *Within the Cup*, op. cit., p. 281
42 Bottome Papers, Add 10308 BL
43 ibid.
44 ibid.
45 letter to the Editor, *The Times*, 18 September 1941
46 See Ted Lever and Nigel Jeyes, *Memories of Wartime St Ives* (A St Ives Trust Archive Study Centre Publication, 2005), for details.
47 Bottome Papers, Add 10308 BL
48 Bottome Papers, Add 78873 BL
49 'Hollywood Reel', in *Philadelphia Bulletin*, 24 May 1940, commented: '*Danger Signal*, adapted from the Phyllis Bottome novel, is expected to be placed next on the list for Bette Davis.' Bottome Papers, Add 78858 BL
50 Robert Florey (1900–79), a French director who mainly worked in Hollywood
51 Karen Burroughs Hannsberry, *Femme Noir: Bad Girls of Film* (McFarland, 1998), p. 92

52 Rosemary DeCamp (1910–2001). See the obituary in the *Independent*, 28 February 2001, where she is quoted as saying, 'I would love to have had glamour-girl roles, but my deplorable nose wouldn't photograph.' The obituary also says: 'Her distinctive performances include a canny psychoanalyst in the noir thriller *Danger Signal*.'
53 later to be owned by the artist Patrick Heron
54 Will Arnold-Foster to Phyllis Bottome, 8 November 1941, Bottome Papers, Add 78849 BL
55 Bottome Papers, Add 78849 BL
56 draft letter to Ministry of Labour, Bottome Papers, Add 78849 BL
57 Will Arnold Foster to Phyllis Bottome, Bottome Papers, Add 78849 BL
58 See Phyllis Bottome's obituary of Maxwell Laurie in Bottome Papers, Add 78858 BL. Laurie retired from his job as Deputy Commissioner in Burma in 1915 and moved to St Ives where between the wars he wrote a number of novels, *The Black Blanket* and *A Young Man at Sea* being the most well known in his day. In October 1943, Phyllis, always keen to help her friends, tried to get Faber to publish Maxwell Laurie's poems. They said no at first but later published them as *Young Wheat*, for children.
59 The first two novels are called *World's End* (1940) and *Between Two Worlds* (1941); the series of eleven novels came to be known as the World's End Series. The third of the series, *Dragon's Teeth*, was awarded the Pulitzer Prize in 1942.
60 Phyllis Bottome to Upton Sinclair, 28 May 1942, Sinclair Manuscripts; quoted courtesy of the Lilly Library, Indiana University, Bloomington, Indiana.
61 Richard Hillary, *The Last Enemy* (Macmillan, 1942); the epigraph quotes I Corinthians 15:26: 'The last enemy that shall be destroyed is death.'
62 Merle Oberon was the star of *The Lion Has Wings* (1939), the first propaganda feature film of the war. Although there was no direct subsidy from the newly established MOI, nevertheless it had offered help and encouragement. A RAF liaison officer was provided and he arranged for location shooting at the Mildenhall base in Suffolk.
63 Bottome Papers, Add 10308 BL
64 David Ross, *Richard Hillary: The Definitive Biography of a Battle of Britain Fighter Pilot and Author of 'The Last Enemy'* (London, Grub Street, 2003), p. 304
65 Bottome Papers, Add 10308 BL
66 Quoted by Ross, op. cit., p. 359
67 ibid.
68 Phyllis Bottome, *From the Life* (Faber & Faber, 1944)
69 ibid., p. 8

70 CBS radio broadcast, 15 April 1945, quoted by Christopher Robbins, *The Test of Courage: A Biography of Michel Thomas* (Century, 1999), p. 201
71 Martin Gilbert, *Second World War*, op. cit., pp. 716–17
72 Bottome Papers, Add 10308 BL
73 Phyllis Bottome, *The Life Line* (Faber & Faber, 1946)
74 ibid., p. 42
75 ibid., p. 41
76 ibid., p. 24
77 ibid., p. 99
78 ibid., pp. 114–15
79 ibid., p. 5
80 Phyllis Lassner, *British Women Writers of World War II: Battlegrounds of Their Own*, op. cit., p. 231; see also Judy Suh's reading of the novel, in *Fascism and Anti-Fascism in Twentieth-Century British Fiction* (Palgrave Macmillan, 2009).
81 *The Life Line* , op. cit., p. 76
82 ibid., p. 282
83 See Pam Hirsch, 'Charlotte Brontë and George Sand: The Influence of Female Romanticism', in *Brontë Society Transactions* (1996) for this argument.
84 Interview with Alice Dixon Bond, the *Boston Herald*'s Bookstore Edition for July 1946, p. 5. It is perhaps no coincidence that Nazi guerrilla fighters who continued to wage war against the Allied occupation armies called themselves 'the Werewolves'.
85 Both of these films are included in a collection called *1001 Films You Must See Before You Die*, edited by Steven Jay Schneider, op. cit.
86 Phyllis Bottome and Daphne du Maurier are both popular novelists, whose work, until recently, has been given little appropriate critical attention. See Alison Light, *Forever England: Femininity, Literature and Conservatism Between the Wars*, op. cit., Chapter 4, for a rich reading of du Maurier's work.
87 See Daphne du Maurier's *The Flight of the Falcon* (1965) and *The House on the Strand* (1969) as examples of novels in which Adler's notion of the *gegenspieler* is a key feature.
88 See Margaret Forster, *Daphne du Maurier* (Chatto & Windus, 1993), for an insightful biography of Daphne du Maurier, although it does not include the friendship with Phyllis Bottome.
89 Like Ernan, too, Boy Browning seemed to conduct a somewhat separate London life, dining with Noël Coward at the Ivy and the Café Royal, for example.

90 Daphne du Maurier to Phyllis Bottome, 26 June 1962, Bottome Papers, Add 78861 BL; for Phyllis Bottome's correspondence with Victor Gollancz, see Warwick University Archives.
91 Peter Lanyon (1918–64), painter. See Margaret Garlake's entry in the Oxford *DNB*.
92 The founding members are recorded as Shearer Armstrong, Wilhemina Barns-Graham, Sven Berlin, David Cox, Agnes Drey, Leonard Fuller, Isobel Heath, Barbara Hepworth, Marion Grace Hocken, Peter Lanyon, Bernard Leach, Denis Mitchell, Guido Morris, Marjorie Mostyn, Dicon Nance, Robin Nance, Ben Nicholson, Hyam Segal and John Wells.
93 In the new society, to ensure fair jurying of works submitted for group exhibitions, the Society created three categories, A for figurative, B for non-figurative and C for crafts.
94 quoted by Brian Foss in *War Paint: Art, War, State and Identity in Britain 1939–1945* (Yale University Press, 2007), p. 186
95 Phyllis to Ernan, 2 August 1947, Bottome Papers, Add 78894 BL: 'I also bought a £10 picture of Peter's [Lanyon's] boats.'
96 Phyllis Bottome to Freda Troup, 12 April 1954, Bottome Papers, Add 78860 BL
97 Penwith Society of Arts' first exhibition, in summer 1949, was held at St Ives Public Hall, Fore Street. Phyllis bought a painting by Peter Lanyon for £50. It may have been his painting of West Penwith.
98 Sarah Jane Checkland, *Ben Nicholson: The Vicious Circles of His Life and Art* (John Murray, 2000), p. 278
99 ibid., p. 272
100 Phyllis Bottome's letter was in the *St Ives Times*, 3 November 1950. St Ives Trust Archive Centre includes a letter from Sven Berlin thanking her:

> Dear Phyllis Bottome – I've just read your letter in defence of my workshop. Bless you for it. That such reinforcement should come unbidden – and with such force – at a time when I thought the battle was lost, really makes me feel the gods are with us. I intend to fight steadily until the official minds are changed and I'm sure the things you've said will do much to help this come about. Many thanks for real sympathy. With best wishes, Sven Berlin

101 letter from Phyllis Bottome, dated 27 January 1955, Bottome Papers, Add 10308 BL
102 Priaulx Rainier (1903–86); see entry by Raymond Holden in the Oxford *DNB*; born in South Africa, she divided her life between lodgings in St Ives and Notting Hill. In London, she extended hospitality to a trail of political refugees.

103 See programme of St Ives Festival, Cornwall, 6–14 June 1953.
104 Phyllis, ever keen to help friends, had tried to interest Faber in Halliday's work on Shakespeare, but without success.
105 Frank Halliday, *Indifferent Honest* (London, Gerald Duckworth, 1960), p. 122. The tone suggests that the Forbes Dennises, though much-loved, were also just a little bit of a joke, too.
106 Adlerians called the people they analysed 'pupils' because the implication was that Adlerian counselling was effectively a re-education of the individual. While irrespective of age, it indicates a condition or relationship; a pupil is one who is taught by another (see *Shorter Oxford English Dictionary*).
107 They lent them to various exhibitions. See *Ben Nicholson: A Retrospective Exhibition, Tate Gallery, June–July 1955*, and also the British Council borrowed them for Ben Nicholson Exhibition Europe 1954–5.
108 See an article by Phyllis Bottome, 'How to Keep a Heart', in *Modern Woman*, September 1937, in which she defines four common types of relationship, of which the 'neck-and-neckers' is one.
109 Phyllis gave a lecture on 'Human Relationships' in St Ives in the winter of 1950/1, in which she described the various categories into which married couples tend to fall. It is interesting to conjecture whether Ben Nicholson or Barbara Hepworth happened to be in the audience.
110 Checkland, op. cit., p. 267
111 letter from Phyllis to her nephew, Phillip Bottome, 19 February 1952, Bottome Papers, Add 10308 BL
112 letter from Phyllis to Harry Bottome, 18 February 1952, Bottome Papers, Add 10308 BL
113 Bottome Papers, Add 10308 BL
114 Checkland, op. cit., p. 441, n. 42, and p. 272
115 Phyllis Bottome to Freda Troup, 12 April 1954, Bottome Papers, Add 78860 BL
116 Phyllis Bottome to Ezra Pound, 9 January 1953. Pound Manuscripts II, Lilly Library, Indiana University, Bloomington, Indiana
117 quoted in Checkland, op. cit., p. 285
118 See Lynn Green, *W. Barns-Graham: As Studio Life* (Lund Humphries, 2001), for an account of this marvellous artist.
119 letter written in June 1951, Checkland, op. cit., p. 279
120 Checkland, op. cit., p. 28
121 Margaret Gardiner, *A Scatter of Memories* (London, Free Association Books), p. 14
122 Checkland, op. cit., p. 316. Sally Festing, in *Barbara Hepworth: A Life of*

Forms (London, Viking, 1995), says she was a photographer working for *Time and Life* (p. 227).

123 See, for interest's sake, 'The Roundhouse of International Spirits', a catalogue edited by Sebastiano Barassi, about artists in the Ticino, produced to accompany the exhibition in Kettle's Yard, Cambridge, in January 2009. See especially the essay by Peter Khoroche, 'Ben Nicholson the European'. Typically, Ben became bored with her, and divorced her in 1977.

124 Oxford *DNB*; see entry by Margaret Garlake on Peter Lanyon.

125 Checkland, op. cit., p. 272. Checkland has quoted from Ernan's notes, which she saw in a family house, but which were not intended by the family to be published. They are now held in the British Library with an embargo until 2022. As they are already in the public domain as a consequence of Checkland's biography, they have been requoted here. Her description of Ernan as a gentleman amateur is certainly inaccurate as by this stage he was a trained Adlerian psychologist, so whereas he was not a medical doctor, he was trained in this therapeutic psychology. He was at this time running a successful practice in both Cornwall and London.

126 Sarah Jane Checkland, op. cit., p. 264.

127 David Lewis to Ernan, 23 August 1963, Bottome Papers, Add 78861 BL

Notes to Chapter 11 – Post-Colonial Jamaica and the End of Empire

1 Phyllis Bottome, 'The Pirate's Isle', in *Not in Our Stars* (London, Faber & Faber, 1955), p. 195

2 Phyllis Bottome, 'Kingdom of the Young', a photocopy of an article in Bottome Papers, Add 78858 BL

3 Bottome Papers, Add 78866 BL

4 Virginia Woolf, 'Mr Bennett and Mrs Brown' (1924), in *A Modernist Reader: Modernism in England 1910–1930* (Batsford, 1986). This is the essay in which Woolf attacks the aesthetic of Edwardian writers.

5 *The Noël Coward Diaries*, edited by Graham Payn and Sheridan Morley (Macmillan, 1982), p. 39

6 Phyllis Lassner, *Colonial Strangers: Women Writing the End of the British Empire*, op. cit., p. 7

7 *Search for a Soul*, op. cit., p. 277

8 Phyllis's nephew Philip Bottome went out to South Africa after the war; See letter from Phyllis to Freda Troup, '[He] has married a charming Dutch girl from South Africa and is most anxious to get a job there. He is a

very good book-keeper and business manager, having worked for years for that horrible NAAFI.' In 1948, he succeeded in getting a job as a manager of a Radio Company in the Cape. Bottome Papers, Add 78860 BL

9 Freda Troup, *South Africa: An Historical Introduction* (History Book Club by arrangement with Eyre Methuen, 1972), p. 273

10 *Mandela: The Authorized Portrait*, editorial consultants Mac Maharaj and Ahmed Kathreda (Bloomsbury, 2006)

11 Phyllis Bottome to Freda Troup Levson, 12 December 1948, Bottome Papers, Add 78860 BL

12 Phyllis Bottome to Freda Troup Levson, 17 June 1953, Bottome Papers, Add 78860 BL

13 Phyllis Bottome, 'An Appreciation of Sir Geoffrey Faber by one of His Authors', typescript, op. cit., in Bottome Papers, Add 78858 BL

14 Nelson Mandela, *Long Walk to Freedom* (Abacus, 2001)

15 Probably these figures were based on the real-life Mr Scott and Father Norton, both referred to in a letter to Upton Sinclair on 17 December 1953: 'I am a friend of Michael Scott's, and my best friend, Father George Norton, who was drowned last week, by a curious accident, had just returned to South Africa … ' Sinclair Manuscripts, Lilly Library, Indiana University, Bloomington, Indiana

16 See letter from Oliver Robinson to Phyllis, Bottome Papers, Add 78850 BL; the story appeared as 'The Prize Basket' in the collection of her short stories entitled *Walls of Glass* (Faber & Faber, 1958).

17 Bottome Papers, Add 78850 BL

18 Phyllis Bottome to Freda Troup Levson: 'Here is our first small donation to George's coloured school – how I wish I could send more – but until we have sold our house R. W. [Red Willows] we have to "back delicately" ' Bottome Papers, Add 78860 BL

19 Phyllis Bottome to Freda Troup Levson, 4 February 1946, Bottome Papers, Add 78860 BL

20 Phyllis Bottome to Freda Troup Levson, 29 May 1950, Bottome Papers, Add 78860 BL

21 Ian Thomson, *The Dead Yard: Tales of Modern Jamaica* (Faber, 2009), p. 65. At Barclays Bank in Kingston the imperial administration set up an account under the name 'Jamaica Plane Fund'.

22 Phyllis Bottome, 'The Pirate's Isle', op. cit., p. 189. Bottome's title refers to the colourful history of buccaneers who sallied out of Port Royal in Jamaica from the mid-1600s.

23 See correspondence between the Forbes Dennises and Sir Hugh and Lady Foot 1947–63, in Bottome Papers, Add 78862 BL.

24 Hugh Foot, *A Start in Freedom* (Hodder & Stoughton, 1964), p. 122

25 Bustamente's Labour Party had swept the board in the 1944 elections.
26 Phyllis Bottome's notes on Jamaica, taken on her first trip, Bottome Papers, Add 10308 BL
27 Hugh Foot, *A Start in Freedom*, op. cit., p. 136
28 Bottome Papers, Add 10308 BL
29 Phyllis Bottome's notes on Jamaica, Bottome Papers, Add 10308 BL. Dr Aub's address was 25 Phoenix Avenue, Kingston 10, Jamaica.
30 See article in the *Jamaica Gleaner*, 18 August 2004.
31 Phyllis Bottome, 'The Pirate's Isle', op. cit.
32 There was also a Roman Catholic orphanage, founded in 1880, for wayward youth. Roman Catholics had lived in Jamaica since the Spanish period, and had established some of the best secondary schools.
33 Goldeneye is now owned by Chris Blackwell (who set up Island Records) and his mother, Blanche, and is part of an expensive hotel complex. Blanche had affairs with Errol Flynn and Ian Fleming.
34 letter from Phyllis Bottome to her nephew Philip, 9 February 1952, Bottome Papers, Add 10308 BL; letter from Phyllis Bottome to Countess of Athlone, 21 June 1960, referring to the countess's visit to Jamaica, Bottome Papers, Add 78862 BL
35 Nevertheless, in the late 1940s Coward settled in Jamaica, in Ocho Rios, ten miles up the coastal road from Ian Fleming's house. He built two homes, the beachside 'Blue Harbour' and 'Firefly', a hilltop retreat where he lived with Graham Philip Payn, a South African-born actor.
36 Phyllis Bottome's notes on Jamaica, taken on her first trip. Bottome Papers, Add 10308 BL
37 Phyllis Bottome, 'The Pirate's Isle', op. cit. Unfortunately, this still seems an accurate comment. Travellers' guides to Jamaica, *circa* 2007, all warn about petty thieves, muggings at gunpoint on the streets and in hotel bedrooms. Parts of Kingston are sometimes subject to curfew and tourists are advised to avoid ghetto area at all times.
38 In 1947, Errol Flynn's yacht *Zacca* was blown ashore by a storm. He thought it an earthly paradise and bought Navy Island, the Titchfield Hotel (Rudyard Kipling's favourite hotel) and a cattle ranch on Priestman's River. Bottome Papers, Add 10308 BL. Max Beaverbook had a house at Montego Bay.
39 Bottome Papers, Add 10308 BL
40 *The Times*, 21 November 1942, quoted by Piers Brendon, *The Decline and Fall of the British Empire 1781–1997* (Jonathan Cape, 2007), p. viii
41 Phyllis Bottome to Ernan Forbes Dennis, 3 April 1948; she promises to arrange her deadlines better in the future so that they can be together 'at all times'. Bottome Papers, Add 78894 and Add 10308 BL

42 The Overseas Settlement of British Women found and filled teaching and other posts abroad for 'surplus' women.
43 Phyllis Bottome, *Under the Skin* (London, Faber & Faber, 1950; New York, Harcourt Brace, 1950), p. 10
44 ibid., p. 41
45 ibid., p. 54
46 ibid., p. 13
47 Phyllis Lassner argues: 'Bottome combines two genres in this novel – romance and political thriller – as the heroine struggles with, first, her romantic attraction to the school's doctor and, second, with those who are threatened by her romantic agenda to build harmonious race relations within the school community.' 'A Bridge Too Close: Narrative Wars to End Fascism and Imperialism', in *Journal of Narrative Theory*, 31 (Summer 2001), p. 139
48 *Under the Skin*, op. cit., p. 21
49 ibid., p. 22
50 ibid., p. 29; p. 32
51 ibid., p. 25
52 ibid., p. 53
53 ibid., p. 43
54 There is a debate among medical historians about the origins of syphilis. It first appeared in Europe in 1493–4, during the war between France and Spain waged in Italy. Most countries ascribed the disease to the voyages of Columbus, which suggested an American origin. See Roy Porter, *The Greatest Benefit to Mankind: A Medical History of Humanity from Antiquity to the Present* (HarperCollins, 1997)
55 Phyllis Lassner, *Colonial Strangers: Women Writing the End of the British Empire*, op. cit., pp. 180–1
56 *Under the Skin*, op. cit., p. 121
57 A form of witchcraft or sorcery practised in Africa and the Caribbean.
58 Phyllis Bottome, 'The Pirate's Isle', op. cit., p. 194
59 *Under the Skin*, op. cit., p. 302
60 ibid., p. 260
61 ibid., p. 283
62 ibid., p. 307
63 Phyllis Bottome, *The Pirate's Isle*, op. cit., p. 195
64 Geoffrey Faber to Phyllis Bottome, 9 November 1948, ' … The coincidences between *Under the Skin* and Richard Mason's book certainly appear extraordinary.' This is a novel called *The Shadow and the Peak* (first edition published by Hodder & Stoughton in 1949) which is based on a young man's trials as a teacher in a progressive school. Faber encloses the libel

report, which lists several features: 'the real coloured Dr is Dr Overton; Ransome in the book is obviously Manley; schools are recognisable – cd lead to suit by the schools; allegations of obeah … ' Bottome Papers, Add 10308 BL

65 letter from Phyllis Bottome to Frieda Troup Levson, 12 December 1948, Bottome Papers, Add 10308 BL

66 Phyllis Bottome, 'An Appreciation of Sir Geoffrey Faber by one of His Authors', op. cit.

67 Richard Masion's novel, however, was turned into a film called *The Passionate Summer*.

68 See reviews for *Under the Skin*, in Bottome Papers, Add 78858 BL, e.g. *Glasgow Herald*, 13 July 1950; *Press and Journal* (Aberdeen), 24 June 1950, ' … the theme is not new but with the spur of democracy at work among the coloured races it is assuming bigger proportions'; *Birmingham Post*, 20 June 1950, listing *Under the Skin* as one of the books of the week.

69 Phyllis Bottome, *Fortune's Finger* (Faber, 1950), p. 235

70 other reviews in Bottome Papers, Add 78858 BL, e.g. *Belfast Telegraph*, 12 December 1950, refers to her 'sensitive, understanding mind'; *Sketch*, 3 January 1951, comments: 'I particularly liked a re-telling of the parable of the Good Samaritan against a Jamaican background, called "Among Thieves"!'

71 Phyllis Bottome, 'The Pirate's Isle', op. cit.

72 Lewis Davidson (1915–81) had been appointed when his predecessor, Philip Sherlock, had become Secretary of the Institute of Jamaica.

73 Jean Davidson, *Lewis Davidson: Man of Vision and Action* (William Culross, 1992), p. 36

74 'A Brief History of the Founding of Knox College', in the *Jamaica Weekly Gleaner*, North American edition, 21 August 1997

75 Phyllis Bottome, Notes on Jamaica, Bottome Papers, Add 10308 BL

76 *Lewis Davidson*, op. cit., p. 58

77 David Bent was one of the eleven children of the headmaster of Carron Hall School in rural St Mary.

78 *Lewis Davidson*, op. cit., p. 73

79 She became vice-chair of the governing body of Knox, as she was a trained teacher.

80 *Lewis Davidson*, op. cit., p. 116

81 ibid., p. 112

82 Friedrich Froebel (1782–1852), the German educationist credited with devising a system of principles and practices for an interactive learning process. In 1892, the Froebel Educational Institute was established in

England and following this there was a diaspora of committed Froebelian teachers all over the world.

83 Leo Jones had been head boy at Wolmers School, and had won the island's agricultural scholarship. After a year at McGill University and a year's postgraduate work in Trinidad, he returned in summer 1947.

84 George Scott's father was labour adviser to the government. In 1953, George left for St Andrews University, Scotland, where he took an honours degree. He returned to Knox as head of the junior school. He left after a few years to be guidance officer in the Ministry of Education, but returned to Knox in 1963 as vice-principal. He took over from Lewis Davidson as principal in 1970.

85 *Lewis Davidson*, op. cit., p. 79

86 Bottome Papers, Add 10803 BL; see letter dated 8 February 1950 from Knox College, Spaldings. Phyllis says that she and Ernan 'are doing IP for all we are worth'.

87 See the Charter and Statutes of the University College of the West Indies held in Senate House, University of London. It is now the University of the West Indies.

88 *Lewis Davidson*, op. cit., p. 110

89 ibid., p. 111

90 ibid., p. 110

91 Phyllis Bottome to Lord Vansittart, 17 August 1950, Bottome Papers, Add 78848 BL

92 Phyllis Bottome to Jean Davidson, quoted in *Lewis Davidson*, op. cit., p. 111

93 Bottome Papers, Add 78835 BL

94 See Peter Wilby, *Eden* (Haus Publishing, 2006).

95 Piers Brendon, op. cit., p. 498

96 Phyllis Bottome to Upton Sinclair, 4 March 1957, Sinclair Manuscripts, Lilly Library, Indiana University, Bloomington, Indiana

Notes to Chapter 12 – Final Years in London

1 Nigel Dennis's work, riding high in the 1950s, fell out of fashion, but recently there has been renewed interest here, too, with new editions of three of his novels being planned. *Cards of Identity* (1955) made his name; at the request of George Devine of the English Stage Company, Dennis turned it into a play, which was produced in London in 1956. He wrote a second play, *The Making of Moo*, in 1957, and his last play, *August for the People*, in 1961.

2 Obituary of Edna St Vincent Millay, in *The New York Times*, 20 October 1950

3 In 1964, Redroofs was purchased by the Keston-Bloom family, who seem to be a singularly appropriate family to be there. June Keston Bloom (née Rose) was already running the Gladstone School of Speech and Drama in London NW1 and is a passionate drama teacher. Ludo Keston, her eldest son, was chief executive at York Theatre Royal from September 2001 until he became general manager at the Royal Shakespeare Company. Carolyn and Samantha Keston now run the house as Redroofs Theatre School with their mother.

4 Fred Allen to Ernan Forbes Dennis, 14 April 1951

5 Phyllis Bottome's talk on Adler was broadcast on 20 March 1945 (transcript in Bottome Papers, Add 78838 BL). See also Bottome Papers, Add 78854 BL. She also made radio appeals for a whole range of charities.

6 Bottome Papers, Add 78856 BL

7 Harcourt Brace published them in America in 1954. Phyllis asked for free copies of *Man and Beast* to be sent to – among others – Pamela Hansford Johnson, Mark Arnold-Forster, Daphne du Maurier, Storm Jameson, Ezra Pound and Lord Vansittart

8 Humphrey Carpenter, *A Serious Character: The Life of Ezra Pound* (Houghton Mifflin, 1988), p. 700

9 See C. David Heymann, *Ezra Pound: The Last Rower: A Political Profile*, op. cit. There are two references to Phyllis Bottome in the biography, but not this point. Pound was released in 1958 and died in Venice in 1972.

10 See Chapter 7 of Philip Mairet, *A. R. Orage: A Memoir* (University Books, 1966), for an account of how Douglas's social-credit economics influenced the circle around Orage's *New Age*, including Ezra Pound.

11 draft sent in a letter to Max Beerbohm, 12 November 1945, Beerbohm Papers, Merton College, Oxford

12 Phyllis Bottome to D. D. Paige, 24 July 1947, Pound Manuscripts II, Lilly Library, Indiana University, Bloomington, Indiana

13 Phyllis Bottome to Ezra Pound, 25 August 1947, Lilly Library, Indiana University, Bloomington, Indiana

14 Phyllis Bottome to Ezra Pound, 25 August 1947 and 18 February 1952, ibid.

15 Phyllis Bottome to Ezra Pound, 8 November 1948, ibid.

16 This is also one of the themes of *The Life Line* (London, Faber & Faber, 1946).

17 *From the Life*, op. cit., p. 81

18 Daphne du Maurier especially loved Phyllis's stories featuring animals or children.

19 They had first met Wanger when he was producing *Private Worlds*; the trial for attempted murder was a celebrated court battle, and proved an indirect inspiration for the Billy Wilder-directed film *The Apartment* (1960),
20 letter from Phyllis to her nephew, Phil Bottome, 19 February 1952, Bottome Papers, Add 10308 BL
21 'It must have been more than twenty-five years later that I wrote *Against Whom?* But it was in Montana, and with its mountains for a background, that this novel sank into my heart.' Phyllis Bottome, *The Goal*, op. cit., p. 208
22 See epigraph to *The Master Hope* (London, Hurst & Blackett, 1904).
23 review in the *Providence Journal*, 6 June 1954
24 Phyllis Bottome, 'Idols: Ancient and Modern', in *New English Weekly*, 28 November 1938, p. 131, Bottome Papers, Add 10308 BL
25 See Charles Lee in *New York Times Book Review*, Edmund Fuller in *The Saturday Review* and David Tilden in the *New York Herald Tribune Book Reviews*, printed on the dust jacket of the Harcourt Brace edition of *The Secret Stair*.
26 *Express & Star*, 3 October 1955, Bottome Papers, deposit 10308, 3 October 1955
27 The story involved an unsophisticated middle-aged woman who spends her life savings on a trip to Italy.
28 John Collins (1905–1982), educated at Cambridge, became Dean and Fellow of Oriel College, Oxford, and served as an RAF chaplain in World War II. He founded Christian Action to help the starving people of post-war Europe. In 1948 he was appointed a canon of St Paul's Cathedral.
29 For example, an earlier letter to *The Times*, 'Sentence on an African', 8 April 1953, had protested about a South African man who had been sentenced to eight strokes of the lash and one year's imprisonment with hard labour, because he had challenged South Africa's race laws
30 directed by Jack Less and produced by Basil Wright
31 Bottome Papers, Add 78835 BL
32 Phyllis Bottome, *Eldorado Jane* (Faber & Faber, 1956), p. 26
33 ibid., p. 63
34 ibid., p. 88
35 ibid., p. 144
36 Phyllis supported the National Campaign for the Abolition of Capital Punishment; see letter to the editor of the *St Ives Times*, 11 November 1955, urging others to protest.
37 *Eldorado Jane*, op. cit., p. 281
38 Bottome Papers, Add 10308 BL
39 ibid.

40 Phyllis Bottome to Freda Troup Levson, Bottome Papers, Add 78860 and Add 10308 BL
41 Bottome Papers, Add 10308 BL
42 Hazel Holt, *A Lot to Ask: A Life of Barbara Pym* (Macmillan, 1990), p. 194. After some years of being out of print, Pym was rediscovered in the 1970s. It is worth noting that Nicola Beauman of Persephone Books is doing a fine job of reprinting many of the 'lost' women writers of the twentieth century.
43 Phyllis Bottome to Mrs Franks, 8 July 1961, Bottome Papers, Add 78866 BL
44 letter from Phyllis Bottome to Victor Gollancz, 27 November 1956, MSS.157/3/MI/308 Du Maurier Correspondence, Warwick University
45 Oskar Spiel, Ferdinand Birnbaum and Franz Sharmschool had written this book in 1947. Adler did not have any personal connection with it, but the school was founded in accordance with his educational principles
46 Phyllis Bottome to her nephew Phillip Bottome, 12 June 1961, Bottome Papers, Add 78866 BL
47 Clive Donner was born in London in 1926. See David Thomson, *The New Biographical Dictionary of Film* (Little, Brown & Co., 2002), p. 243
48 Bottome Papers, Add 10308 BL. The very good cast also included Jean Anderson as Maria.
49 Pamela Hansford Johnson, unpublished diary entry of 4 December 1957
50 Phyllis Bottome to Colin Wilson, 29 October 1957, Bottome Papers, Add 78861 BL
51 Colin Wilson to Phyllis Bottome, 3 May 1959, Bottome Papers, Add 78861 BL
52 Bottome Papers, Add 78866 BL
53 Phyllis Bottome to the editor of *St Ives Times*, 29 October 1957, Bottome Papers, Add 78858 BL
54 ibid.
55 Phyllis Bottome to Freda Troup Levson, 29 May 1959, Bottome Papers, Add 78860 BL
56 The house is currently the home of Deborah Moggach. There seems a certain synergy in this. Moggach is a popular writer (this is meant as a compliment) who is possessed of an acute psychological sense. She is also very much politically engaged, like Phyllis Bottome, with PEN.
57 Having been to visit it, at the kind invitation of Deborah Moggach, it seems clear to me why Phyllis liked it, although their relatives felt at the time that a tall, narrow house was a singularly unsuitable shape for two elderly people.

58 Phyllis Bottome to Basil Liddell Hart, 11 February 1960, Kings College Archives LH/1/93/23
59 Phyllis Bottome to Sister Anne, 28 April 1960, Bottome Papers, Add 78866 BL: ' … I expect to go into [Westminster] hospital tomorrow, and it gives me great comfort that you will think of me, although I don't imagine this time I shall have a very bad time. It is more to prevent one coming than to deal with what is there … '
60 Ernan and Phyllis to Robert Pollak, 17 June 1960, Bottome Papers, Add 78863 BL
61 Bottome Papers, Add 78861 BL
62 12 October 1961, Bottome Papers, Add 78866 BL
63 *Sunday Telegraph*, 7 January 1962; *Times Educational Supplement*, 19 January 1962; *Kentish Observer and the Canterbury Times*, 20 March 1962; *The Scotsman*, 20 January 1962
64 puff on dust jacket of first edition of *The Goal*, op. cit.
65 Vera Brittain, 'The World of Phyllis Bottome', in *John O'London's*, 18 January 1962, Bottome Papers, Add 78856 BL
66 I thank my colleague, David Whitley, for this gloss.
67 *Daily Telegraph*, 23 February 1962
68 Introduction to *The Uses of Autobiography*, ed. Julia Swindells (Taylor and Francis, 1995), p. 1
69 See *Encyclopedia of Life Writing: Autobiographical and Biographical Forms*, ed. Margaretta Jolly (Fitzroy Dearborn Publishers, 2001); Leigh Gilmore, *Autobiographics: A Feminist Theory of Women's Self-Representation* (Cornell University, 1994).
70 Her agent, Ann Watkins, was not keen on the book, and at this point Phyllis removed her full-length books from the agency. She had already done so in terms of films. She therefore left only short stories with this agent; and finished with them altogether in May 1951, when she transferred to A. D. Peters, who had a London and a New York office.
71 Bottome Papers, Add 10308 BL
72 Edmund Gosse (1849–1928), English biographer and autobiographer. In a 1902 essay for the *Dictionary of National Biography*, he laid out this claim for what a biography should be. See Hermione Lee's essay, 'Father & Son, Philip and Edmond Gosse', in *Body Parts: Essays on Life-Writing* (Chatto & Windus, 2005)
73 Bottome Papers, Add 10308 BL
74 ibid.
75 Bottome Papers, Add 78835 BL
76 Phyllis Bottome, 'Idols: Ancient and Modern', op. cit., Bottome Papers, Add 10308 BL

77 See reviews in Bottome Papers, Add 78856 BL.
78 Storm Jameson to Phyllis Bottome, 2 January 1961, Bottome Papers, Add 78861 BL
79 Ian Fleming to Phyllis Bottome 11 January 1962, Bottome Papers, Add 78866 BL
80 See letters 9 February 1962 and 22 March 1962, Bottome Papers, Add 78866 BL.
81 telegram from Alexander Adler to the Forbes Dennises, April 22 (Easter Sunday) 1962, Bottome Papers, Add 78835 BL: 'Dearest Phyllis and Ernan. Yesterday mother died. Ali.' Phyllis and Ernan had given Raissa some financial support after Adler's death.
82 Bottome Papers, Add 78866 BL
83 Moray McLaren writing in *The Scotsman*, 20 January 1962
84 *The Bookseller*, 26 May 1962, pp. 2059–60
85 Daphne du Maurier to Phyllis Bottome, 30 May 1962, Bottome Papers, Add 78861 BL
86 See, for example, *The Daily Post*, 27 August 1958.
87 Daphne du Maurier, Preface to *Best Stories of Phyllis Bottome*, op. cit.
88 *Saturday Guardian*, Review Section, p. 5, 12 July 2008
89 Daphne du Maurier, Preface to *Best Stories of Phyllis Bottome*, op. cit.
90 ibid.
91 Daphne to Phyllis, 10 September 1962, Bottome Papers, Add 78861 BL
92 *Best Stories of Phyllis Bottome*, op. cit., p. 309
93 See Note 14 to Introduction on page 362 above.
94 For example, there were long obituary articles in the *New York Times* and the *New York Herald Tribune*, both on 24 August 1963.
95 Letter from Phyllis Bottome to a Mr Potts, author of *Dante Called her Beatrice*, 13 July 1960, Bottome Papers, Add 78866 BL
96 See index card from Golders Green Crematorium, and personal information from Frederica Freer, daughter of Nigel Dennis, who writes: 'Laci Zilahi told Freda Levson how many hundreds of people Ernan and Phyllis had rescued during the war.'
97 Nigel Dennis's marriage to Marie-Madeleine Massias had been dissolved in 1956. In 1959 he married Beatrice Matthew.
98 See these in Bottome Papers, Add 78862 BL.
99 Bottome Papers, Add 78867 BL
100 Sylvia Foot to Ernan Forbes Dennis, 5 December 1963; the letter went on: '... her own flame has flickered out and must have left darkness and cold for you ... ' Bottome Papers, Add 78862 BL
101 See Bottome Papers, Add 78867 BL; Mr and Mrs John Baker were installed at 921 The Crescent, Moorfield, Newbridge, County Kildare, Eire.

102 I note that Nigel Dennis and his wife Beatrice visited him there. In 1967, Dennis and Beatrice moved to Malta.

103 Ernan to Ruth Aspinall, dated 20 January 1964, Hotel Phoenicia, Valletta, Malta, Bottome Papers, Add 78862 BL

104 ibid. She would undoubtedly have despaired too at the murder in May 1964 of two black teenagers by the Ku Klux Klan. The KKK tied an engine block to their feet and threw them alive into the Mississippi River.

105 Bottome used the phrase to describe the relationship of Whiteleaf and Philip in *Under the Skin*, p. 184.

106 Ernan to Phyllis, 9 February 1920, Bottome Papers, Add 78890 BL

107 *The Times*, 5 August 1972. The obituary for Ernan Forbes Dennis was written by Frank Halliday, their friend from St Ives days. It is not quite accurate factually, though certainly correct in spirit:

> Ernan Forbes Dennis, whose death was reported in your issue of July 8, was the devoted husband of the novelist Phyllis Bottome, whom he married while serving in the First World War, in which he was badly gassed and wounded.
>
> He spent the next 18 years abroad, mainly in Switzerland and Austria, for the sake of his wife's health; and it was in Vienna, where he was British Consul, that he met Alfred Adler and became a practising psychiatrist.
>
> Sickened by what they saw of early Nazism, the couple returned to England, and for 16 years lived in St Ives, but in 1957 went back to London, partly to be near their nephew Nigel Dennis. Phyllis Bottome died in 1963, but her husband survived her for nine years and died in Brighton on July 6.

108 Bottome Papers, Add 58867 BL

109 Adlerian psychologists refer to their patients as 'pupils' because the idea is a re-education of the whole human being.

110 See letters from Ernan Forbes Dennis to Ben Nicholson and Feli, which refer to two visits to their house and thanks them for their 'great bounties', Ben Nicholson Collection, reference TGA 8717/1/2/1133–1138, Tate Gallery Archive.

111 A letter from Ruth Aspinall, of Warren Cottage, Cranleigh, Surrey, to Ernan Forbes Dennis, 19 August 1963, Bottome Papers, Add 78862 BL, was followed by a second letter of condolence in October 1963 to Ernan, which copies out a line about finding consolation in small things from a book by Rumer Godden called *China Court*, and a line from Phyllis's *The Life Line*, op. cit., p. 111.

Notes to Conclusion

1 Bottome Papers, Add 78554 BL

2 Phyllis Bottome, 'Woman – In Reverse', *New York Herald Tribune*, Sunday, 15 April 1934. This was a theme Virginia Wolf explored in *Three Guineas* in 1938, but Phyllis had said it first.

3 'Alibi' is a term used by Alfred Adler to describe an excuse for not acting with integrity.

4 quoted by Christopher Robbins, *The Test of Courage: A Biography of Michel Thomas*, op. cit., p. xii

5 letter from Phyllis Bottome to the editor of the *News Chronicle*, 27 January 1955

6 Phyllis Bottome, 'What Democracy Means to Me', in *Home*, 14 March 1942, pp. 414–15

7 The honorary secretary of the Voluntary Euthanasia Legislation Society, C. Kilick Millard, wrote to Phyllis on 13 August 1947 thanking her for allowing them to use her name in their list of well-known literary honorary members. Bottome Papers, Add 78850 BL

8 Phyllis Bottome to Freda Troup Levson, 16 February 1953, Bottome Papers, Add 78860 BL

9 Bottome Papers, Add 78866 BL

10 See George Dangerfield, *The Strange Death of Liberal England* (Serif, 1997), for an interesting account.

11 Other signatories include E. M. Forster, Gilbert Harding and Rose Macaulay.

12 Phyllis Bottome to Ezra Pound, 25 August 1947, Pound Manuscripts II, Lilly Library, Indiana University, Bloomington, Indiana

13 See Virginia Woolf, 'Why Art Today Follows Politics', in *Communist Daily Worker*, December 1936.

14 Phyllis Bottome to Mrs Franks, 8 July 1961, Bottome Papers, Add 78866 BL

15 quoted on the dust jacket of *The Goal*, published in 1962, when Phyllis was eighty

16 See 'Notes for Talks for American Lecture Tours in 1939 and 1940', Bottome Papers, Add 10308 BL.

17 I would cite as examples of twentieth-century women writers in whom there is renewed interest: Elizabeth Von Arnim, Stella Benson, Rumer Godden, Winifred Holtby, Storm Jameson, Pamela Hansford Johnson, Rose Macaulay, Naomi Jacob, Dorothy L. Sayers, Elizabeth Taylor and Dorothy Whipple.

18 For example, an excellent and wide-ranging conference called 'Investigating the Middlebrow' was held at Sheffield Hallam University on 23 June 2007, where I gave a paper on Phyllis Bottome's *The Mortal Storm*.

19 The best approximation I have heard yet is the 'politicised middlebrow' novel, but even that term seems not wholly satisfactory.

20 *Birmingham Post*, Bottome Papers, Add 78858 BL

21 *Best Stories of Phyllis Bottome* (op. cit.), reviewed in the *Guardian*, 13 September 1963

22 Phyllis Bottome, 'The Responsibility of the Artist', in *Not in Our Stars*, op. cit.

23 Alice Dixon Bond, *Boston Herald's Book Store Edition* for July 1946, p. 5

Phyllis Bottome Timeline

Phyllis is born in Kent	1882		
Family moves to New York	1890		
Family settles back in England	1896		
Phyllis's sister Wilmett dies. Phyllis diagnosed with TB	1901		Death of Queen Victoria; succeeded by Edward VII
	1902	*Life, the Interpreter*, her first novel, published	
Phyllis travels to Italy and Switzerland and meets Lislie (Hope de Lisle Brock) in St Moritz	1903	*The Master Hope* published	
Phyllis spends her second winter in St Moritz. She meets Ernan Forbes Dennis.	1904		France and Britain sign Entente Cordiale
Ernan proposes marriage and Phyllis accepts	1905	*Raw Material*, a series of sketches, published	
Phyllis spends winter in Davos, and summer in Southwold	1906	*The Imperfect Gift* published	
Ernan's Mamma dies and he goes to Canada with Frank Lascelles	1907		

Phyllis stays with Lislie over the winter in Bournemouth. In spring she suffers from serious bout of TB	1908		
In winter, Phyllis is nursed by Julia Farrer in Italy; Ernan breaks off the engagement	1909		
Phyllis meets Charles Paul Frèrejean; during the winter she lives in Capri. Ernan begins friendship with Ivor Novello	1910		Death of Edward VII; succeeded by George V
Meets Lilian Beit at Nauheim	1911		
In London, Phyllis meets Alice Meynell which leads to her meeting May Sinclair and Ezra Pound	1912		
Phyllis's father dies	1913	*Broken Music* published with its sequel, *The Common Chord*	
Phyllis and Ernan start to see each other again. He leaves for the front. Phyllis works at Hammersmith looking after Belgian refugees.	1914		Archduke Franz Ferdinand assassinated; the Great War begins
	1915	*The Captive* published	
	1916	*Secretly Armed* published in England, and, under the title *The Dark Tower*, is successful in the USA	United States enters the war
Phyllis works for John Buchan in the Department of Information. Phyllis and Ernan marry in Paris	1917	*Second Fiddle* published	

Ernan is badly wounded and transported back to London. Ernan's brother Fred is killed and his son, Nigel Dennis, comes into their lives	1918	*Helen of Troy and Rose*, two long-shorts, published as one volume	The Great War ends in November 1918
Ernan is working in Military Intelligence in Marseilles. Phyllis joins him	1919	*A Servant of Reality* is a best-seller in the USA. Hollywood releases a film which steals her plot	Germany forced to sign the Treaty of Versailles; League of Nations established
Ernan and Phyllis move to Vienna where he is Passport Control Officer; they meet Dorothy Thompson, Edna St Vincent Millay and Albertina Rasch. Ernan's friend Robert Pollak is also in Vienna	1920		
	1921	*The Crystal Heart* published	
	1922	*The Kingfisher* published	Mussolini assumes dictatorial powers in Italy
Lislie dies in February after operations trying to cure her of TB; Phyllis suffers from TB again, and in October they move to the Austrian mountain village of Mösern	1923	*The Derelict and Other Stories* and *The Victim and the Worm* – all long-shorts – published	Hitler makes his first bid for power with the 'Beer Hall Putsch'
	1924	*The Perfect Wife* and *The Depths of Prosperity* published	
Ernan and Phyllis set up a school for boys in Kitzbühel	1925	*Old Wine*, referring back to Phyllis's time in Vienna, published	

Phyllis's mother dies; Ian Fleming is sent out to be 'reformed'	1926	*The Rat* and *Belated Reckoning* published	
Phyllis meets Alfred Adler when he visits them in Kitzbühel. Nigel Dennis comes to join them	1927	*Messenger of the Gods* published	
Phyllis has a bout of TB but stays in Kitzbühel looked after by Luischen, the district nurse; Ernan goes to America with Robert Pollak	1928	*Strange Fruit*, a collection of short stories, published	
	1929	*Windlestraws* a best-seller in America; *Tatter'd Loving* published	Wall Street Crash
Phyllis and Ernan move to Munich to study Individual Psychology with Dr Leonard Seif	1930		
Phyllis travels to the USA on her own to meet her new publisher Houghton Mifflin	1931	*Wind in His Fists* (*Devil's Due* in America) published. MGM decide not to film it due to its 'shocking nature'	
Phyllis observes Hitler at Café Heck in Munich	1932		
	1933	*The Advances of Harriet* published	Hitler become Chancellor of Germany
Phyllis goes to USA on a Colston Leigh lecture tour and then to Rapallo in Italy to meet Max Beerbohm and Ezra Pound	1934	*Private Worlds* is a best-seller. *Stella Benson*, a biographical essay, published	Hitler takes Germany out of the League of Nations
In Vienna they meet Adler's family	1935	*Innocence and Experience* published; the film of *Private Worlds* made in Hollywood, starring Claudette Colbert	Italy invades Abyssinia

England: Ernan organising Adler tour	1936	*Level Crossing* published	Death of George V; succeeded by Edward VIII, who abdicates; King George VI succeeds him. Hitler marches into the Rhineland; Civil War breaks out in Spain
On his second British tour, Adler dies of a heart attack	1937	*The Mortal Storm*, her anti-Nazi novel set in Munich, published in England, but Phyllis unable to get 'I Accuse' published because it named and shamed arch-appeasers	Japanese invasion of Nationalist China
Phyllis and Ernan rush to Vienna to get information for Adler's biography. They leave Vienna only three days before Hitler enters	1938	'I Accuse' is published in America; and *The Mortal Storm* is published in America and is a best-seller	*Anschluss*, or union of Germany and Austria
Phyllis in America using cover of Colston Leigh lecture tour for covert propaganda	1939	Biography of Alfred Adler and *Danger Signal* published	Britain and France declare war on Germany
Move to Bude in Cornwall; Ernan in Home Guard	1940	The film of *The Mortal Storm*, starring James Stewart and made in Hollywood, is a block-buster; *Masks and Faces* published	France falls
Ernan buys Red Willows in St Ives	1941	*Heart of a Child* and *London Pride* published *Formidable to Tyrants* (renamed for America *Mansion House of Liberty*) published	Japan bombs Pearl Harbor; America and Great Britain declare war on Japan

Phyllis lecturing for the Ministry of Information all over Great Britain	1942		
	1943	*Within the Cup* published (renamed *Survival* for the American edition)	
	1944	*From the Life*, a collection of biographical essays, is published	Paris liberated. Jamaica grants universal adult suffrage
	1945	Film of *Danger Signal* made in Hollywood, starring Rosemary DeCamp	Germany surrenders to the Allies; atomic bombs dropped on Hiroshima and Nagasaki: end of WWII
	1946	*The Life Line* published	
Phyllis and Ernan visit Jamaica	1947	*Search for a Soul* (first volume of her autobiography) published	India and Pakistan celebrate national independence
	1948	The film of *Heart of a Child* made by Rank, starring Donald Pleasance	In South Africa the Nationalists win election on apartheid programme
Ernan is practising as an Adlerian psychologist; 'pupils' include Ben Nicholson and Barbara Hepworth	1949		
Ernan temporarily acting head of Knox College in Jamaica	1950	*Under the Skin* published and *Fortune's Finger* (a collection of short stories) published	
Phyllis and Ernan saddened by sudden death of Ivor Novello	1951		

	1952		Death of George VI; succeeded by Elizabeth II
	1953	*The Challenge* (second volume of her autobiography) published and *Man and Beast* (a collection of short stories) published	
Phyllis becomes friends with Daphne du Maurier	1954	*Against Whom* (American title *The Secret Stair*) published	
	1955	*Not in Our Stars* (a collection of lectures) published	
	1956	*Eldorado Jane* (American title *Jane*) published	Nasser nationalises the Suez Canal
	1957	*Alfred Adler: A Portrait from the Life* published	Treaty of Rome establishes the EEC, usually called the Common Market
	1958	*Walls of Glass* published	
	1960		Massacre in the black township of Sharpeville in South Africa
	1962	*The Goal* (third volume of her autobiography) published	Cuban Missile Crisis; Jamaica granted independence, with Bustamante as its first Prime Minister.
Phyllis dies	1963	*Best Stories of Phyllis Bottome* published	
Ernan dies	1972		

Bibliography

PRIMARY SOURCES

Manuscripts

Bottome Papers in Manuscript Department of the British Library
Bottome/Max Beerbohm correspondence at Merton College Library, Oxford
Dorothy Thompson Papers, Special Collections, University of Syracuse
Bottome Correspondence, Stanford University Library, Stanford, California
Bottome Correspondence with Bodley Head/John Lane, Special Collections, University of Reading
Bottome/Victor Gollancz Correspondence at the Modern Records Centre, University of Warwick
Bottome/Upton Sinclair Correspondence and Bottome/Ezra Pound Correspondence, Lilly Library, Indiana University, Bloomington, Indiana
Bottome/ Basil Liddell Hart Correspondence at Liddell Hart Centre for Military Archives, King's College London
Ben Nicholson Collection, Tate Gallery Archive, London
Bottome/Ezra Pound Correspondence, Beinecke Rare Book and Manuscript Library, Yale University
First World War, War Office Records, National Archives
MGM Collection (USC Cinematic Arts Library)
San Francisco Conservatory of Music Archives

WORKS BY PHYLLIS BOTTOME

Novels

Life, the Interpreter (New York and London, Longmans, Green and Co., 1902)

The Master Hope (Hurst and Blackett, 1904)
The Imperfect Gift (London, Murray, 1907; New York, E. P. Dutton & Co., 1907)
Crooked Answers, written with Hope de Lisle Brock (London, John Murray, 1911)
The Common Chord (London, Martin Secker, 1913)
Broken Music (Boston and New York, Houghton Mifflin Company, 1914)
The Captive (London, Chapman & Hall, 1915)
Secretly Armed (London, Chapman & Hall, 1916); as *The Dark Tower* (New York, Century, 1916)
A Certain Star (London, Hodder & Stoughton, 1917); as *The Second Fiddle* (New York, Century, 1917)
A Servant of Reality (London, Hodder & Stoughton, 1919; New York, Century, 1919)
The Crystal Heart (New York; Century, 1921)
The Kingfisher (London, Collins, 1922; New York, George H. Doran, 1921)
The Perfect Wife (New York, George H. Doran, 1924)
The Depths of Prosperity, written with Dorothy Thompson (London, Collins, 1924; New York, George H. Doran, 1925)
Old Wine (New York, Frederick A. Stokes, 1925; London, Collins, 1926)
The Rat: A Novel Based on the Play by Ivor Novello and Constance Collier (London, Philip Allan, 1926)
Wild Grapes (London, Collins, 1927); as *The Messenger of the Gods* (New York, George H. Doran, 1927)
Windlestraws (London, Collins, 1929; Boston & New York, Houghton Mifflin, 1929)
Tatter'd Loving (London, Collins, 1929; Boston & New York, Houghton Mifflin, 1930)
Wind in His Fists (London, Collins, 1931); as *Devil's Due* (Boston & New York, Houghton Mifflin, 1931); republished (London, Faber & Faber, 1948)
The Advances of Harriet (London & Edinburgh, John Lane, 1933; Boston & New York, Houghton Mifflin, 1933)

Private Worlds (London, John Lane, 1934; Boston & New York, Houghton & Mifflin, 1934)

Level Crossing (London, Bodley Head, 1936; New York, Stokes, 1936)

The Mortal Storm (London, Faber & Faber, 1937; Harmondsworth, Penguin Special, 1938; Boston, Little, Brown & Co., 1938; New York, Popular Library, *circa* 1940)

Murder in the Bud (London, Faber & Faber, 1939); as *Danger Signal* (Boston, Little, Brown & Co., 1939)

Heart of a Child (London, Faber & Faber; New York, Putnam, 1940)

London Pride (London, Faber & Faber, 1941; Boston, Little, Brown & Co., 1941)

Within the Cup (London, Faber & Faber, 1943; Boston: Little, Brown & Co., 1943)

The Life Line (London, Faber & Faber, 1946; Boston, Little, Brown & Co., 1946)

Under the Skin (London, Faber & Faber, 1950; New York, Harcourt, Brace, 1950)

Against Whom (London, Faber & Faber, 1954); as *The Secret Stair* (New York, Harcourt, Brace, 1954)

Eldorado Jane (London, Faber & Faber, 1956); as *Jane* (New York, Vanguard, 1956)

Fictional sketches

Raw Material: Some Characters and Episodes among Working Lads (London, John Murray, 1905)

Long shorts

Helen of Troy and Rose (New York, Century, 1918)

The Victim and The Worm (New York, George H. Doran, 1923)

The Belated Reckoning (London, Collins, 1927; New York, George H. Doran & Company, 1927); republished as *Belated Reckoning* (Faber & Faber, 1955), a collection including 'Belated Reckoning', 'The Victim' and 'Rose'.

Short-story collections

The Derelict and Other Stories (Collins, 1923)

Strange Fruit: Stories (London, Collins, 1928; Boston and New York, Houghton Mifflin, 1928)

Innocence and Experience (London, John Lane, 1935)

Masks and Faces (London, Faber & Faber, 1940; Boston, Little, Brown & Co., 1940)

Fortune's Finger (London, Faber & Faber, 1950)

Man & Beast (London, Faber & Faber, 1953; New York, Harcourt, Brace, 1954)

Walls of Glass (London, Faber & Faber, 1958; New York, Vanguard, 1958)

Best Stories of Phyllis Bottome, chosen and with a Preface by Daphne du Maurier (London, Faber & Faber, 1963)

Non-fiction

Formidable to Tyrants (London, Faber & Faber, 1941); as *Mansion House of Liberty* (Boston, Little, Brown & Co., 1941)

Our New Order or Hitler's? (London, Hunt, Barnard & Co., 1943), edited by Phyllis Bottome: Part One is called 'Voices of Britain' and includes sections of speeches by Winston Churchill, Anthony Eden, Sir Stafford Cripps, Sir Richard Gregory, Sir William Beveridge, Sir Richard Acland, the Archbishop of Canterbury and Phyllis Bottome herself; Part Two is called 'Voices of America' and has sections of speeches by Franklin D. Roosevelt, Henry A. Wallace, Cordell Hull, John. G. Winant, Sumner Wells, Milo Perkins, Paul H. Appleby, Herbert Agar and Pearl S. Buck.

Austria's Contribution Towards Our New Order (London, Austrian Youth Association, 1944)

Austria, A Beautiful Country (London, Austrian Youth Association, 1944)

Not in Our Stars (London, Faber & Faber, 1955)

Biography

Stella Benson (San Francisco, Grabhorn Press, 1934)

From the Life (London, Faber & Faber, 1944; Freeport, NY, Books for Libraries Press, 1971); includes essays on Alfred Adler, Max Beerbohm, Ivor Novello, Sara Delano Roosevelt, Ezra Pound, Margaret McDonald Bottome)

Alfred Adler, Apostle of Freedom (London, Faber & Faber, 1939); as *Alfred Adler: A Biography* (New York, Putnam, 1939); republished as *Alfred Adler: A Portrait from Life* (New York, Vanguard Press, 1957)

Autobiography

Search for a Soul: Fragment of an Autobiography (London, Faber & Faber, 1947; New York, Reynal & Hitchcock, 1948)

The Challenge (London, Faber & Faber, 1953; New York, Harcourt Brace, 1954)

The Goal (London, Faber & Faber, 1962; New York, Vanguard Press, 1962)

Uncollected periodical articles, short stories and letters

'The Invasion', *The Tatler*, 25 November 1927

'Would you have children again?', *The Boston Herald*, 8 April 1934

'Woman – In Reverse', *New York Herald Tribune*, 15 April 1934

'Alfred Adler', *Time and Tide*, 5 June 1937

'Choice of Evils', *Evening Standard*, 27 July 1937

'How to Keep a Heart', *Modern Woman*, September 1937

'Austrian Refugees', *Time and Tide*, 2 April 1938

'Helping the Refugees: A Plea for British Action', *Daily Telegraph and Morning Post*, 12 July 1938

'Idols: Ancient and Modern', *New English Weekly*, 28 November 1938

'Marriage Today', *Evening Public Ledger* (Philadelphia), 18 October 1938

'I Accuse', *New Republic*, 28 December 1938

'Speaking as one who should know. A novelist talks about the screen version of her book ', *New York Times*, 16 June 1940

'Broken Bottles', reprinted from *Free Austria*, 1941

'What Democracy Means to Me', *Home*, 14 March 1942

'Serpent Doves', *The Spectator*, 15 October 1943
'The Birch and the Child', *The Spectator*, 28 January 1944
'Women after Two Wars', *Independent Woman,* 23 February 1944
'The Responsibilities of the Artist', *Penwith Broadsheet*, 2, Summer 1951
Letter to *The Times*, 14 December 1951
'A New Delilah', *Housewife*, 3 March 1953
Letter to *The Times*, 8 April 1953
'Marriage is for Two', unattributed magazine article, April 1953 (Manuscripts by and Relating to Phyllis Bottome, Vertical File G1, Harry Ransom Humanities Research Center, University of Texas at Austin)
Letter to the editor of the *News Chronicle*, 27 January 1955
Letter to the editor of the *St Ives Times*, 29 October 1958
Letter to the editor of *The Spectator*, 29 January 1960

FILMOGRAPHY

Film adaptations of Phyllis Bottome's books

Private Worlds, US (Paramount, 1935), bw; producer: Walter Wanger; director: Gregory La Cava; screenplay: Lynn Starling; cast: Claudette Colbert, Charles Boyer, Joan Bennett, Helen Vinson, Joel McCrea

The Mortal Storm US (Loew's/MGM, 1940), bw; producers: Sydney Franklin and Victor Saville; director: Frank Borzage; screenplay: Claudine West, George Froeschel, Hans Rameau; Cast: Margaret Sullavan, James Stewart, Robert Young, Bonita Granville, Irene Rich, William T. Orr, Maria Ouspenskaya, Gene Reynolds, Russell Hicks, William Edmunds, Esther Dale, Dan Dailey, Granville Bates

Danger Signal US (Warner, 1945), bw; producer: William Jacobs; director: Robert Florey; screenplay: C. Graham Baker; cast: Faye Emerson, Zachary Scott, Richard Erdman, Rosemary DeCamp, Bruce Bennett, Mona Freeman, John Ridgely, Mary Servoss, Joyce Compton, Virginia Sale

Heart of a Child UK (Rank, 1948), bw; producer: Sydney Box; director: Clive Donner; screenplay: Leigh Vance; cast: Jean Anderson, Donald Pleasance, Richard Williams, Maureen Pryor, Norman Macowan, John Glyn-Jones, Willoughby Goddard, Andrew Keir, John Boxer, Carla Challoner, Raymond Adamson, Charles Gray, Philip Locke, Lee Montague, Tina Robson

SECONDARY SOURCES

Books

Alfred Adler, *What Life Should Mean to You*, edited by Alan Porter (George Allen & Unwin Ltd, 1932)

Alfred Adler, *Superiority and Social Interest*, edited by Heinz L. Ansbacher and Rowena R. Ansbacher (Routledge & Kegan Paul, 1965)

Noel Annan, *Changing Enemies: The Defeat and Regeneration of Germany* (HarperCollins, 1996)

Kenton Bamford, *Distorted Images: British National Identity and Film in the 1920s* (I. B. Tauris, 1999)

Nicola Beauman, *A Very Great Profession: The Woman's Novel 1914–1939* (London, Virago, 1983)

John Belton, *The Hollywood Professionals*, Volume Three (Tantivy Press, 1974)

Sven Berlin, *The Coat of Many Colours* (Redcliffe Press, 1994)

Jennifer Birkett, *Margaret Storm Jameson: A Life* (Oxford University Press, 2009)

Clive Bloom, *Bestsellers: Popular Fiction Since 1900* (Palgrave Macmillan, 2002)

Rosa Maria Bracco, *Merchants of Hope: British Middlebrow Writers and the First World War 1919–1939* (Berg, 1993)

Rosa Maria Bracco, *Betwixt and Between: Middlebrow Fiction and English Society in the Twenties and Thirties* (University of Melbourne, 1990)

H. W. Brands, *Traitor to His Class: The Privileged Life and Radical Presidency of Franklin Delano Roosevelt* (Doubleday, 2008)

Piers Brendon, *The Decline and Fall of the British Empire 1781–1997* (Jonathan Cape, 2007)
Vera Brittain, *Testament of Experience* (London, Virago 1979)
Mary Cadogan and Patricia Craig, *Women and Children First* (Gollancz, 1978)
Agnes Cardinal, Dorothy Goldman and Judith Hattaway, *Women's Writing on the First World War* (Oxford University Press, 2002)
Humphrey Carpenter, *A Serious Character: The Life of Ezra Pound* (Houghton Mifflin, 1988)
Helen Carr, *The Verse Revolutionaries: Ezra Pound, H. D. and the Imagists* (Jonathan Cape, 2009)
Charles Carrington, *Soldier from the Wars Returning* (Hutchinson, 1965)
Susan L. Carruthers, *The Media at War: Communication and Conflict in the Twentieth Century* (Palgrave Macmillan, 2000)
David Cecil, *Max* (Constable, 1964)
John Chancellor, *Wagner* (Little, Brown & Co., 1978)
James Chapman, *The British at War: Cinema, State and Propaganda, 1939–1945* (I. B. Tauris, 1998)
Sarah Jane Checkland, *Ben Nicholson, The Vicious Circles of His Life and Art* (John Murray, 2000)
Ian Colvin, *Vansittart in Office* (Victor Gollancz, 1965)
Anne Conover, *Olga Rudge and Ezra Pound* (Yale University Press, 2001)
Nicholas John Cull, *Selling War: The British Propaganda Campaign Against American 'Neutrality' in World War II* (Oxford University Press, 1995)
Alex Danchev, *9Alchemist at War: The Life of Basil Liddell Hart* (Weidenfeld & Nicolson, 1998)
George Dangerfield, *The Strange Death of Liberal England* (Serif, 1997)
Darnley, Earl of (ed.), *Frank Lascelles: 'Our Modern Orpheus'* (Oxford University Press, 1932)
Jean Davidson, *Lewis Davidson: Man of Vision and Action* (William Culross & Son, 1992)
Cecil Davies, *The Plays of Ernst Toller: A Revaluation* (Harwood Academic Publishers, 1996)
Elmer Davis, *Not to Mention the War* (New York, 1939)

Bernard F. Dick, *The Star-Spangled Screen: The American World War Two Film* (University Press of Kentucky, 1996)

Thomas Doherty, *Projections of War: Hollywood, American Culture and World War Two* (Columbia University Press, 1993)

Thomas Dormandy, *The White Death: A History of Tuberculosis* (Hambledon, 1999)

Rudolf Dreikurs, *Fundamentals of Adlerian Psychology* (Alfred Adler Institute of Chicago, 1989)

Felix Driver and David Gilbert, *Imperial Cities* (Manchester University Press, 1999)

Claire Duchen and Irene Bandhauer-Schoffmann (eds), *When the War Was Over* (Leicester University Press, 2000)

Louis Dudek, *Some Letters of Ezra Pound* (Montreal, DC Books, 1974)

Hervé Dumont, *Frank Borzage: The Life and Films of a Hollywood Romantic*, translated by Jonathan Kaplansky (McFarland & Co., 2006)

Daniel Mark Epstein, *What Lips My Lips Have Kissed: The Loves and Love Poems of Edna St Vincent Millay* (Henry Holt, 2001)

David Faber, *Munich: The 1938 Appeasement Crisis* (Simon & Schuster, 2009)

Sally Festing, *Barbara Hepworth: A Life of Forms* (Viking, 1995)

Fergus Fleming, *Amaryllis Fleming* (Sinclair-Stevenson, 1993)

Hugh Foot, *A Start in Freedom* (Hodder & Stoughton, 1964)

Margaret Forster, *Daphne du Maurier* (Chatto & Windus, 1993)

Brian Foss, *War Paint: Art, War, State and Identity in Britain 1939–1945* (Yale University Press, 2007)

Margaret Gardiner, *A Scatter of Memories* (Free Association Books, 1988)

Martin Gilbert, *The Roots of Appeasement* (Signet, 1966)

Martin Gilbert, *The Righteous: The Unsung Heroes of the Holocaust* (Doubleday, 2002)

Martin Gilbert, *Kristallnacht: Prelude to Disaster* (HarperCollins, 2006)

Robert Gildea, *Marianne in Chains: Daily Life in the Heart of France During the German Occupation* (Macmillan, 2003)

Mary Ann Gillies, *The Professional Literary Agent in Britain 1880–1920* (University of Toronto Press, 2007)

Leigh Gilmore, *Autobiographics: A Feminist Theory of Women's Self-Representation* (Cornell University Press, 1994)
W. E. Glassman, *Approaches to Psychology* (Open University Press, 2001)
Dorothy Goldman (ed.), *Women and World War I: The Written Response* (Macmillan, 1993)
Douglas Gomery, *The Hollywood Studio System: A History* (bfi publishing, 2005)
Helen Graham, *The Spanish Civil War* (Oxford University Press, 2005)
Mark N. Grant, *The Rise and Fall of the Broadway Musical* (Northeastern University Press, 2004)
Margaret Haig (Viscountess Rhondda), *This Was My World* (Macmillan, 1933)
Frank Halliday, *Indifferent Honest* (Gerald Duckworth & Co., 1960)
John Halperin, *Eminent Georgians* (Macmillan, 1998)
Karen Burroughs Hannsberry, *Femme Noir: Bad Girls of Film* (McFarland & Co, 1998)
Lynne Hapgood and Nancy L. Preston, *Outside Modernism* (Macmillan, 2000)
James Harding, *Ivor Novello: A Biography* (Welsh Academic Press, 1997)
Leon Harris, *Upton Sinclair: American Rebel* (Thomas Y. Crowell, 1975)
Jenny Hartley, *Millions Like Us: British Women's Fiction of the Second World War* (Virago, 1997)
Ruth Henig, *The Origins of the First World War* (Routledge, 2000)
David Heymann, *Ezra Pound: The Last Rower: A Political Profile* (Faber & Faber, 1976)
Pam Hirsch, *Barbara Leigh Smith Bodichon: Feminist, Artist and Rebel* (Chatto & Windus, 1998)
Pam Hirsch, *Teacher Training at Cambridge: The Initiatives of Oscar Browning and Elizabeth Hughes* (Woburn Press, 2004)
J. Hoberman and Jeffrey Shandler, *Entertaining America: Jews, Movies and Broadcasting* (Princeton University Press, 2003)
M. Paul Holsinger and Mary Anne Schofield, *Visions of War* (Bowling Green, 1992)
Hazel Holt, *A Lot to Ask: A Life of Barbara Pym* (Macmillan, 1990)

Nicola Humble, *The Feminine Middlebrow Novel, 1920s to 1950s: Class, Domesticity and Bohemianism* (Oxford University Press, 2001)

James M. Hutchinson, *The Rise of Sinclair Lewis 1920–1932* (Pennsylvania State University, 1996)

Maroula Joannou (ed.), *Women Writers of the 1930s: Gender, Politics and History* (Edinburgh University Press, 1999)

Maroula Joannou, *'Ladies, Please Don't Smash These Windows': Women's Writing, Feminist Consciousness and Social Change 1918–1938* (Berg, 1995)

Margaretta Jolly (ed.), *Encyclopedia of Life Writing: Autobiographical and Biographical Forms* (Fitzroy Dearborn, 2001)

Sandra Kemp, Charlotte Mitchell and David Trotter (eds), *The Oxford Companion to Edwardian Fiction* (Oxford University Press, 1997)

Angela Kershaw and Angela Kimyoungur (eds), *Women in Europe Between the Wars: Politics, Culture and Society* (Ashgate, 2007)

Victor Klemperer, *I Shall Bear Witness: The Diaries of Victor Klemperer 1933–1941*, abridged and translated from the German by Martin Chalmers (Phoenix, 1998)

Elizabeth Knowles (ed.), *Terry Frost* (Scolar Press, 1994)

Maik Kopleck, *Munich 1933–1945*, translated by Adelheid Korpp (Links, 2006)

Clayton R. Koppes and Gregory D. Black, *Hollywood Goes to War: How Politics, Profits and Propaganda Shaped World War Two Movies* (University of California Press, 1990)

Peter Kurth, *American Cassandra: The Life of Dorothy Thompson* (Little, Brown & Co., 1990)

Phyllis Lassner, *British Women Writers of World War II: Battlegrounds of Their Own* (Palgrave Macmillan, 1998)

Phyllis Lassner, *Colonial Strangers: Women Writing the End of the British Empire* (Rutgers University Press, 2004)

Emily Wortis Leider, *California's Daughter: Gertrude Atherton and Her Times* (Stanford University Press, 1991)

Jeremy Lewis, *The Life and Times of Allen Lane* (Penguin, 2006)

Ted Lever and Nigel Jeyes, *Memories of Wartime St Ives* (A St Ives Trust Archive Study Centre Publication, 2005)

Alison Light, *Forever England: Femininity, Literature and Conservatism Between the Wars* (Routledge, 1991)

Louise London, *Whitehall and the Jews 1933–1948: British Immigration Policy and the Holocaust* (Cambridge University Press, 2000)

Mary S. Lovell, *The Mitford Girls* (Abacus, 2001)

Andrew Lownie, *John Buchan: The Presbyterian Cavalier* (Pimlico, 2002)

Andrew Lycett, *Ian Fleming* (Phoenix, 2002)

Geoffrey Macnab, *Searching for Stars: Rethinking British Cinema* (Cassell, 2000)

W. MacQueen-Pope, *Ivor: The Story of an Achievement* (Hutchinson, 1954)

Philip Mairet, *A. R. Orage: A Memoir* (University Books, 1966)

George Makari, *Revolution in Mind: The Creation of Psychoanalysis* (HarperCollins, 2008)

Michael Marrus, *The Unwanted: European Refugees in the Twentieth Century* (Oxford University Press, 1985)

Billie Melman (ed.), *Borderlines: Gender and Identities in War and Peace 1870–1930* (Routledge, 1998)

Nancy Milford, *Savage Beauty: The Life of Edna St Vincent Millay* (Random House, 2002)

Roy Moseley, *Evergreen: Victor Saville in His Own Words* (Southern Illinois Library, 2000)

H. V. Nelles, *The Art of Nation-Building: Pageantry and Spectacle at Quebec's Tercentenary* (University of Toronto Press, 2000)

Peter Noble, *Ivor Novello: Man of the Theatre* (Falcon Press, 1951)

Ursula E. Oberst and Alan E. Stewart, *Adlerian Psychotherapy: An Advanced Approach to Individual Psychology* (Brunner-Routledge, 2003)

Hertha Orgler, *Alfred Adler: The Man and His Work: Triumph Over the Inferiority Complex* (Vision, 1946)

Sharon Ouditt, *Fighting Forces: Writing Women, Identity and Ideology in the First World War* (Routledge, 1994)

Inderjeet Parmar, *Special Interests: The State and the Anglo-American Alliance 1939–1945* (Frank Cass, 1995)

Graham Payn and Sheridan Morley (eds), *The Noël Coward Diaries* (Macmillan, 1982)

John Pearson, *The Life of Ian Fleming* (Jonathan Cape, 1966)
Clive Ponting, *Churchill* (London, Sinclair-Stevenson, 1994)
Clive Ponting, *The Pimlico History of the Twentieth Century* (Pimlico, 1999)
Roy Porter, *The Greatest Benefit to Mankind: A Medical History of Humanity from Antiquity to the Present* (HarperCollins, 1997)
Sir Richard Douglas Powell, *On the Principal Varieties of Pulmonary Tuberculosis with Practical Comments* (1872)
Suzanne Raitt, *May Sinclair: A Modern Victorian* (Oxford University Press, 2000)
Christopher Robbins, *The Test of Courage: A Biography of Michel Thomas* (Century, 1999)
David Ross, *Richard Hillary: The Definitive Biography of a Battle of Britain Fighter Pilot and Author of 'The Last Enemy'* (Grub Street, 2003)
Marion K. Sanders, *Dorothy Thompson: A Legend in Her Time* (Houghton Mifflin, 1973)
Martha Schad, *Hitler's Spy Princess: The Extraordinary Life of Stephanie von Hohenlohe*, translated and annotated by Angus McGeoch (Sutton Publishing, 2004)
Karen Schneider, *Loving Arms* (University Press of Kentucky, 1997)
Michael Seth-Smith, *The Cresta Run* (Foulsham, 1976)
Andrew Sharf, *The British Press and Jews under Nazi Rule* (Oxford University Press, 1964)
Pamela Shatzkes, *Holocaust and Rescue: Impotent or Indifferent? Anglo-Jewry 1938–1945* (Palgrave Macmillan, 2002)
Colin Shindler, *Hollywood Goes to War: Films and American Society 1939–1952* (Routledge & Kegan Paul, 1979)
Upton Sinclair, *The Autobiography of Upton Sinclair* (W. H. Allen, 1963)
Peter Singer, *Pushing Time Away: My Grandfather and the Tragedy of Jewish Vienna* (Granta, 2003)
Daniel Snowman, *The Hitler Emigrés: The Cultural Impact on Britain of Refugees from Nazism* (Chatto & Windus, 2002)
Stephen Spender, *The Thirties and After* (Macmillan, 1978)
Manes Sperber, *The Unheeded Warning 1918–1933*, translated from the German by Harry Zohn (Holmes & Meir, 1991)

Peter Stansky, *The First Day of the Blitz* (Yale University Press, 2007)

Isaac Stern, *My First 79 Years*, written with Chaim Potok (Alfred A. Knopf, 1999)

Judy Suh, *Fascism and Anti-Fascism in Twentieth-Century British Fiction* (Palgrave Macmillan, 2009)

Frank J. Sulloway, *Born to Rebel: Birth Order, Family Dynamics and Creative Lives* (Pantheon Books, 2007)

John Sutherland, *Bestsellers: A Very Short Introduction* (Oxford University Press, 2007)

John Sutherland, *Stephen Spender: The Authorized Biography* (Penguin, 2005)

Julia Swindells (ed.) *The Uses of Autobiography* (Taylor and Francis, 1995)

A. J .P. Taylor, *The Origins of the Second World War* (Penguin, 1971)

David Thomson, *The New Biographical Dictionary of Film* (Little, Brown & Co., 2002)

David Thomson, *Have You Seen? A Personal Introduction to 1,000 Films* (Allen Lane, 2008)

Ian Thomson, *The Dead Yard: Tales of Modern Jamaica* (Faber, 2009)

Jane Tompkins, *Sensational Designs* (Oxford University Press, 1985)

Freda Troup, *In Face of Fear: Michael Scott's Challenge to South Africa* (Faber & Faber, 1950)

Freda Troup, *South Africa: An Historical Introduction* (Butler and Tanner, 1972)

John Trumpbour, *Selling Hollywood to the World: US and European Struggles for Mastery of the Global Film Industry, 1920–1950* (Cambridge University Press, 2002)

Claire M. Tylee, *The Great War and Women's Consciousness: Images of Militarism and Womanhood in Women's Writings, 1914–1964* (University of Iowa Press, 1991)

R. Vaughan, *Chalk and Cheese, a Co-Educational School* (John Miles, 1934)

Peter Viereck, *Metapolitcs: From Wagner and the German Romantics to Hitler* (Transaction Publishers, 2007)

Selman A. Waksman, *The Conquest of Tuberculosis* (Robert Hale, 1964)

George Weidenfeld, *Remembering My Good Friends: An Autobiography* (HarperCollins, 1995)

Andrew Wheatcroft, *The Habsburgs: Embodying Empire* (Penguin, 1996)
Peter Wilby, *Eden* (Haus Publishing, 2006)
Michael Williams, *Ivor Novello: Screen Idol* (bfi publishing, 2003)
Richard Winston, *Thomas Mann: The Making of an Artist, 1875–1911, from his Childhood to the Writing of 'Death in Venice'* (Constable, 1982)
Michael David Zellman (ed.), *300 Years of American Art* (Wellfleet Press, 1987)

Articles and essays

E. W. Adams, 'Ethel Ruth Gwatkin, 1875–1952', *Newnham College Roll Letter* (1953)
Alfred Adler, 'Individual Psychology', in *Journal of Abnormal Psychology*, volume xxii, 1927/8
M. G. Ash, 'Psychology and Politics in Interwar Vienna: The Vienna Psychological Institute, 1922–1942', in *Psychology in Twentieth-Century Thought and Society*, edited by M. G. Ash and W. R. Woodward (Cambridge University Press, 1980)
Barbara Brothers, 'British Women Write the Story of the Nazis: A Conspiracy of Silence', in *Rediscovering Forgotten Radicals: British Women Writers, 1889–1939* (University of North Carolina Press, 1993)
Katy Deepwell, entry on Eileen Agar in *Dictionary of Women Artists*, volume 1, edited by Delia Gaze (Fitzroy Dearborn, 1997)
Rudolf Dreikurs, 'Democratic and Autocratic Child Rearing', in *The Children's Culture Reader*, edited by Henry Jenkins (New York University Press, 1998)
Alice Gardner, 'In Memoriam: Three Distinguished Friends of Newnham College', *Newnham College Roll Letter* (1917)
Henry Louis Gates Junior, 'A Liberalism of Heart and Spine', *New York Times* (27 March 1944)
Pam Hirsch, 'Charlotte Brontë and George Sand: The Influence of Female Romanticism', in *Brontë Society Transactions* (1996); 'Women and Jews in *Daniel Deronda*', in *The George Eliot Review* (1994); 'Apostle of Freedom: Alfred Adler and his British Disciples', in Special Issue 'Insiders and Outsiders', *History of Education Journal*, volume 34, number 5, September 2005; 'Phyllis Bottome', in *Encyclopedia of British Women's Writing, 1900–1950*,

edited by Faye Hammill, Esme Miskimmin, Ashlie Sponenberg (Palgrave Macmillan, 2006)

Marilyn Hoder-Salmon, 'Phyllis Bottome', in *Late-Victorian and Edwardian British Novelists*, Volume 197 of *Dictionary of Literary Biography*, edited by George M. Johnson (Bruccoli Clark Layman, 1998)

Marilyn Hoder-Salmon and Phyllis Lassner, Introductory Essay to Phyllis Bottome, *Old Wine* (Northwestern University Press, 1998)

Marilyn Hoder-Salmon and Phyllis Lassner, Introductory Essay to Phyllis Bottome, *The Mortal Storm* (Northwestern University Press, 1998)

M. Jahoda, 'The Migration of Psychoanalysis: Its Impact on American Psychology', in D. Fleming and B. Bailyn (eds), *The Intellectual Migration: Europe and America 1930–1960* (Harvard University Press, 1969)

Phyllis Lassner, 'A Cry for Life: Storm Jameson, Stevie Smith, and the Fate of Europe's Jews', in M. Paul Holsinger and Mary Anne Schofield (eds), *Visions of War: World War Two in Popular Literature and Culture* (Bowling Green, 1992) ; ' "Objects to Possess or Discard": the Representation of Jews and Women by British Women Novelists of the 1920s', in *Borderlines: Genders and Identities in War and Peace 1870–1930*, edited by Billie Melman (Routledge, 1998) ; 'A Bridge Too Close: Narrative Wars to End Fascism and Imperialism', in *Journal of Narrative Theory*, vol. 31 (Summer 2001); ' "On the Point of a Journey": Storm Jameson, Phyllis Bottome, and the Novel of Women's Political Psychology', in *And In Our Time: Vision, Revision, and British Writing of the 1930s*, edited by Antony Shuttleworth (Bucknell University Press, 2003)

P. F. Lazarfedl, 'An Episode in the History of Social Research: A Memoir', in D. Fleming and B. Bailyn (eds.), *The Intellectual Migration: Europe and America, 1930–1960* (Harvard University Press, 1969)

François Lebeau, 'Hollywood revisité: Sur *The Mortal Storm* de Frank Borzage', *Images*, no. 10, September 1981

Hermione Lee, 'Father & Son, Philip and Edmond Gosse', in Hermione Lee, *Body Parts: Essays on Life-Writing* (Chatto & Windus, 2005)

Robert K. Lightning, ' "We have secrets": Borzage, Romance and the Bourgeois State', in *Cineaction*, June 1988, pp. 64–77

John Morrison, entry on Wilhemina Barns-Graham in *Dictionary of Women Artists*, volume 1, edited by Delia Gaze (Fitzroy Dearborn, 1997)

Sally Parry, 'Learning to Fight the Nazis: The Education of Upton Sinclair's Lanny Budd', in M. Paul Holsinger and Mary Anne Schofield (eds), *Visions of War: World War Two in Popular Literature and Culture* (Bowling Green, 1992)

Stephen Petrina, 'Luella Cole, Sidney Pressey, and Educational Psychoanalysis, 1921–1923', in *History of Education Quarterly*, vol. 44, no. 4, Winter 2004

Deborah S. Ryan, 'Staging the Imperial City: The Pageant of London, 1911', in *Imperial Cities*, edited by Felix Driver and David Gilbert (Manchester University Press, 1999)

Deborah S. Ryan, 'The Man Who Staged the Empire: Remembering Frank Lascelles in Sibford Gower, 1875–2000', in *Material Memories: Design and Evocation*, edited by Marius Kwint, Christopher Breward and Jeremy Aynsley (Berg, 1999)

Virginia Woolf, 'Middlebrow', in *The Death of the Moth and Other Essays* (Hogarth Press, 1942)

Online Sources

Oxford Dictionary of National Biography at oxforddnb.com

Paul Addison, 'Churchill, Sir Winston Leonard Spencer (1874–1965), prime minister'

Alan Bishop, 'Brittain (married name Catlin), Vera Mary (1893–1970)'

Alan Bowness, 'Hepworth, Dame (Jocelyn) Barbara (1903–1975)'

Sophie Bowness, 'Nicholson, Benhamin Lauder (Ben) (1894–1982), artist'

R. W. Burns, 'Baird, John Logie (1888–1946), television engineer'

Katharine Chubbuck, 'Frederick Locker-Lampson (1821–1895)'

Howard Coster, '(Helen) Violet Bonham Carter (1887–1969)'

Howard Coster, 'Hart, Sir Basil Henry Liddell (1895–1970), military thinker and historian'

Cherry Drummond, 'Drummond, Victoria Alexandrina (1894–1978), marine engineer'

David Finkelstein, 'Pinker, James Brand (1863–1922), literary agent'

Maryna Fraser, 'Beit, Sir Otto John, first baronet (1865–1930)'

Margaret Garlake, 'Lanyon, (George) Peter (1918–1964)'

N. John Hall, 'Beerbohm, Sir Henry Maximilian (Max) (1872–1956), caricaturist and writer'

Philip Hoare, 'Noël Pierce Coward (1899–1973), playwright and composer'

Raymond Holden, 'Rainer (Ivy) Priaulx (1903–1986)'

Lena M. Jeger, 'Foot, Hugh Mackintosh, Baron Caradon (1907–1990), colonial administrator and diplomatist'

Lionel Kelly, 'Pound, Ezra Loomis (1885–1972), poet'

Robert Lusty, 'Swinnerton, Frank Arthur (1884–1982), writer and publisher's reader'

Andrew Lycett, 'Fleming, Ian Lancaster (1908–1964), writer'

Ruddock Mackay and H. C. G. Matthew, 'Balfour, Arthur James, 1st Earl of Balfour (1848–1930)'

H. C. G. Matthew, 'Buchan, John, 1st Baron Tweedsmuir (1875–1940)'

Mark Pottle, 'Carter, (Helen) Violet Bonham, Baroness Asquith of Yarnbury (1887–1969)'

Judith Priestman, 'Jameson, Margaret Ethel (Storm) (1891–1986), novelist'

Rev. Denis Richards, 'Hillary, Richard Hope (1919–1943)'

H. D. Rolleston, revised by Anita McConnell, 'Powell, Sir Richard Douglas, 1st baronet (1842–1925)'

Max Saunders, 'Mary Amelia St Clair Sinclair (May) (1863–1946)'

Beverley E. Schneller, 'Bottome (married name Forbes Dennis), Phyllis (1882–1963)'

Rev. Rivers Scott, 'Dennis, Nigel Forbes (1912–1989), writer'

Peter R. H. Slee, 'Gwatkin, Henry Melvill (1844–1916), historian and theologian'

John Smelson, 'Novello, Ivor (real name David Ivor Davies) (1893–1951)'
Duncan Sutherland, 'Murray, Katharine Marjory Stewart, Duchess of Atholl (1874–1960)'
Paul Usherwood, 'Butler (née Thompson), Elizabeth Sotherden, Lady Butler (1846–1933), military painter'
Benedicta Ward, 'Sampson, Margaret Phoebe (name in religion Mary Clare) (1906–1988), Anglican nun'
Philip Ziegler, 'Cooper, (Alfred) Duff, 1st Viscount Norwich (1890–1954)'
Caroline Zilboorg, 'Orage, Alfred Richard (1873–1934), journal editor and advocate of social credit'

Other Online sources

British Library Times Digital Archive
Andrea Crawford, 'A Woman Out of Time' http://www.nextbook.org/cultural/feautre.html?id=286

Index